NEGOTIATION

The Irwin Series in Management and The Behavioral Sciences
L. L. Cummings and E. Kirby Warren   *Consulting Editors*

NEGOTIATION

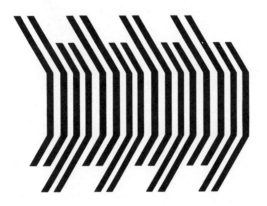

Roy J. Lewicki
The Ohio State University

Joseph A. Litterer
The University of Massachusetts

1985

IRWIN
Homewood, Illinois 60430

ISBN 0-256-02633-5

Library of Congress Catalog Card No. 84–62531

Printed in the United States of America

3 4 5 6 7 8 9 K 2 1 0 9 8 7 6

To our children: Karen, Susan, Aaron and two Davids: who probably taught us more about negotiation than we ever wanted to know.

Preface

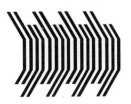

This book has been a long time in the making. Since Roy Lewicki developed a course on bargaining and negotiation for business students, he had envisioned this book. The objective of this book is to integrate the theoretical work from social psychology, the literature on collective bargaining from the field of labor relations, and the "how to do it" writings of popular works on negotiation, and apply them to managerial negotiation. Joe Litterer joined Roy Lewicki as a coauthor in 1979. Since then, the literature in these areas has grown rapidly, as has the interest in managerial negotiation. Negotiation is a skill needed for effective management. Courses in this subject have been introduced at a number of leading business schools. Research articles and even entire journals are now devoted to this subject, and to the related subjects of power and conflict management. Finally, a large number of well-known and popular books have been written for managers and the general public. In short, negotiating skills for managers is a field that has "come into its own."

We hope you enjoy this book. A great deal of time and effort has gone into covering the subject as definitively as possible, and making the examples as clear as possible. Since the field of negotiation is closely related to other fields such as persuasion and attitude change, power, conflict management, and justice in organizations, we have used some of that literature to enhance the understanding of negotiation. We hope you find this treatment useful and relevant.

The authors believe that the most important learning about the negotiation process comes from skill, training, and practice, not just reading a book. Thus, we encourage our readers to *practice* negotiation as well as read about it. One vehicle for doing this is through the accompanying volume to this text, *Negotiation: Readings, Exercises, Cases,* also published by Richard D. Irwin. We also encourage all students of negotiation to "keep a diary" of their negotiations, commenting to themselves on the things they did well and did poorly. As you will learn in this book, negotiation can be reasonably simple and straightforward, or an extremely complicated social process. Only through experimentation and practice can negotiators really learn to be more sophisticated at their craft.

We owe our thanks to a number of people who have helped get this book from idea to reality:

- Toby Bethea, for helping us get the idea crystallized and contracted with Richard D. Irwin;

- Secretaries Betty Jo Stevens, Tom Booth, Linda Simerson, and Becky Gregory for endless patience on drafts of the manuscript;

- Max Bazerman, Larry Churchill, Blair Sheppard, and other colleagues who have been helpful on various chapter drafts;

- Our intellectual mentors, particularly Mort Deutsch, for their inspiration to take a serious interest in this field;

- Finally, our wives, Debbie and Marie, who have put up with long telephone calls, lost weekends spent writing, and the endless chattering of home computers crunching out drafts. We know they're as glad as we are to see this work completed.

R. J. L.
J. A. L.

Contents

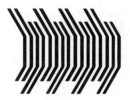

1

The Nature of Negotiation

When we began this book, we were often asked by others what we were writing. "A book on bargaining?" "What type of bargaining?" "Labor-management relations?" "Do you mean negotiating a business deal?" or some similar question. Our answer was that the book was going to approach bargaining as a basic, generic human activity—a process that is often used in labor-management relations, in business deals like mergers and sales, in international affairs, but also in many different everyday activities. The negotiations that take place to free hostages, to keep peace between nations, or to end a strike dramatize the need for bargaining and its capabilities as a dispute management process. While the stakes are not usually as dramatic, we all negotiate; sometimes on major things like a job, at other times on relatively minor issues, such as who will do the dishes. The structure and processes of negotiation are fundamentally the same at the personal level as they are at the diplomatic and corporate level.

The basic premise of this book is that we all negotiate about many different things in many different situations, and that knowledge about and skill in negotiating is essential to anyone who has to work with and through other people to accomplish his objectives. We may fail to negotiate at times when it is appropriate to do so, perhaps because we do not recognize that we are in a bargaining situation. By choosing options other than negotiation, we may fail to handle our problems as well as we might like to. We may recognize the need for bargaining, but do poorly at the process because we misunderstand it and do not know the methods for negotiating. The objectives of this book are to teach our readers how to recognize situations that call for bargaining, what the process of bargaining involves, and how to analyze, plan, and carry out a successful negotiation.

Before going further, note that we use the words bargaining and negotiation interchangeably. Sometimes the terms are used as if the words mean different things, e.g., that bargaining is more like the haggling that goes on at a flea market, while negotiation is the more formal, civilized process that occurs at disarmament talks. At times we thought we saw a distinction between the two, but the distinctions evaporated on closer examination. Perhaps there is a difference; we cannot make a useful one for this book, and hence, use the terms interchangeably.

To better understand what this book is about, let us consider a hypothetical, but not unrealistic, situation:

> Over breakfast, Joe Carter's wife again raised the question of where to go for their summer vacation. She wanted to sign up for a tour of the Nile River being sponsored by her college graduating class. The idea of two weeks on a guided tour with a lot of other people was not what Joe wanted. He needed to get away from people, crowds, and schedules, and wanted to charter a sailboat and cruise the Maine coast. They had not argued (yet), but it was clear that they had a real problem here. Some of their friends handled problems like this by taking separate vacations. With both of them working full time, though, the one thing he and Debbie did agree on is that they would take their vacation together.
>
> As Joe drove to work, he thought about the problem. What bothered Carter most was that there seemed to be no way to handle the conflict. With some conflicts, they could compromise; but given what each wanted this time, there seemed no way to compromise. At other times they would flip a coin; while that might work for choosing a restaurant, this time it would be committing them to a big block of time that was scarce and precious to both of them. Flipping a coin might be more likely to make one of them feel like a loser and the other feel guilty than to help either one feel really satisfied.
>
> Walking through the parking lot, Joe met the purchasing manager, Ed Laine. Ed reminded Joe that they had to settle a problem that the engineers in Joe's department were creating with the purchasing managers by contacting vendors directly. Joe knew that purchasing wanted all contacts with a vendor to go through them; but he also knew that his engineers badly needed technical information for design purposes, and waiting for the information to come through the purchasing agent slowed things considerably. Ed Laine was not unaware of this side of the issue; and Joe thought the two of them would probably be able to find some way to handle this if they could find some time to work things out. They were both aware that higher management expected them (and all other managers) to settle differences among themselves; failing to keep a problem from "getting upstairs" was looked upon as evidence of not being a competent manager. Shortly after getting back to his desk, Joe received a telephone call from an automobile salesman

with whom he had been talking about a new car. The salesman asked what Joe's wife, Debbie, had said about the car. At their last meeting, Joe had said he wasn't quite sure that his wife would go along with the car they were talking about because of the price. Actually, Debbie's only interest in a car was that it started reliably and that it would be easy to load and unload when doing shopping. Joe was pleased with the latest offer the salesman had made, but thought he might still get a few more concessions out of him; he introduced Debbie's concerns in order to put more pressure on the salesman to lower the price.

Most of Joe's afternoon was taken up by the annual budget meeting. Joe hated these meetings. The people from finance came in and arbitrarily cut everyone's figures, and then they had to argue endlessly to try to get some reasonable numbers put back. Joe had learned to work with a lot of people, some of whom he did not like at all, but these people from finance were the most arrogant, arbitrary, pig-headed "bean-counters" imaginable. He could not understand why the top brass did not see how much harm they were doing to the company. Joe considered himself a reasonable guy; but he recognized that the way these people acted made him feel like he didn't want to give them an inch. He was prepared to draw the line and fight it out as long as it took.

In the evening, Joe attended a meeting of the town Conservation Commission, which, among other things, was charged with protecting the town's wetlands and nature preserves, but in a way that would also take into account the economic needs of the town. This evening's case involved a request by a small new electronics firm to change the course of a stream in order to accommodate a new plant they wanted to construct. The new plant was badly needed to replace several others that had closed, putting a sizeable number of people out of work and reducing the town's tax revenues. The building plan, however, would change the direction of a stream and dry up some of the wetlands. The initial plan proposed by the company had some serious difficulties with it; and Joe had been appointed by the Commission to see if an acceptable solution could be developed. Eventually a siteplan had been worked out that would have considerably more benefits than draw-backs. But now Joe was having difficulties with some members of the Commission who were ardent conservationists and argued against *any* change in the stream bed; in addition, some members of the town's board of selectmen, who basically wanted to keep the town unchanged, had joined the conservationists in the fight.

At 11:30 P.M. that evening, Joe finally got home. As he sat on the patio and listened to the crickets, he thought about his day and realized why he felt so tired.

CHARACTERISTICS OF A NEGOTIATION OR BARGAINING SITUATION

A day in the life of Joe Carter brings out the variety of situations that can be handled by negotiation. Any of us might encounter one or more of these situations over the course of a few days or weeks. We identify them as "negotiation situations" because they have fundamentally the same characteristics as peace negotiations between countries at war, labor negotiations between management and union, or a hostage crisis between police and a radical political group.

We bargain when:

1. There is a conflict of interest between two or more parties; that is, what one wants is not necessarily what the other one wants.

2. There is no fixed or established set of rules or procedures for resolving the conflict, or the parties prefer to work outside of a set of rules and procedures to invent their own solution to the conflict.

3. The parties, at least for the moment, prefer to search for agreement rather than to openly fight, to have one side capitulate, to permanently break off contact, or to take their dispute to a higher authority to resolve it.

Let us look more closely at these distinguishing features.

CONFLICT

Conflict occurs when people have separate but conflicting interests. They both want to occupy the same piece of real estate; one wants the other to do something the other does not want to do, i.e., pay more for (or receive less for) the piece of real estate. One party can always break off contact and eliminate conflict, but that will usually mean giving up whatever the party wanted that caused the conflict. Hence, as long as the parties' desire for the goal is greater than their need to break off the relationship, their search for a way to resolve the conflict will give them what they want.

Fight or Use of Force

A classic line in gangster novels or movies connected with resolving conflict is, "I made him an offer he couldn't refuse." Wars, strikes, lockouts, boycotts, sabotage, social isolation, violence, and physical abuse are means we may use to force the other party to give us what we want. The aim of such tactics is to end conflict by resolving it in our favor. There are lots of situations, however, in which the parties do not want to settle conflict in this way. In addition, conflict tactics more frequently lead to retaliation and escalation rather than to reduction.

Giving in and Breaking off

Some people, when faced with a conflict, decide it's not worth the stress and strain to argue, and choose to accept what the other person offers. If we are generally nonassertive, this may be the most common way we respond to a dispute. This may be a reasonable thing to do at times. But if we do it with any degree of regularity, giving in just because it is easier, we may find ourselves getting angry for getting a bad deal and for being a "wimp" or "marshmallow." Negotiation is a key element in the process of taking care of ourselves and our needs, often under difficult circumstances. While we occasionally have to give in to another's needs, and frequently must understand that we can't get everything we originally wanted, nevertheless we must learn to negotiate to get our needs satisfied.

Breaking off negotiations is another key component of the process. Breaking off can occur for several reasons. It may occur as a result of the negotiator's frustration and anger at the other's behavior. If the other party is belligerent or uncooperative, we may walk away in disgust. Breaking off may occur because we invented a better way to resolve our conflict—one that satisfied our needs by "going it alone," or working with someone else. Finally, breaking off may occur as a tactic—a threat that if the other party doesn't meet our needs, we will leave him or her in a lurch. Any of these options may occur separately, or they may all occur together. We will say more about this option in later chapters.

Conventions

When the Carters had a conflict about what restaurant to visit, they usually flipped a coin. It was a traditional way for them to solve this sort of conflict. People who work or live together often develop a number of conventions or traditions. Unions and managements that have worked together for a long time often alternate each year as to who will choose the site for their negotiations. In some areas of international affairs, it has become a convention that negotiations will be conducted in some neutral city like Geneva or Vienna. A widely used convention in selling merchandise in the United States is the "fixed price." On a vast number of items, prices are established by the seller, and the buyer simply takes the price or moves on. It is not a bad system, since if the buyer is really concerned about price, there are usually other suppliers who are offering different prices. The haggling and argument that accompanies even the most ordinary purchase in many other parts of the world does not exist here. American shoppers go to the supermarket and pay the posted price for a dozen oranges; in other parts of the world, shoppers might banter over the price of those same oranges for 10 minutes. Another convention for settling conflicts over prices and the demand for an item is the auction. The conflicting parties inspect an item, i.e., an antique desk or an old clock, and then bid for the item in an open or a "sealed bid" auction. The item goes to the highest bidder. If the parties have more items for sale than there are buyers, a "reverse auction" can take place,

---

FIGURE 1-1

"I have $162.50 round trip over here,
Do I hear $150?"

From *The Wall Street Journal*, with permission of Cartoon Features Syndicate.

by which the sellers drive the price down to rock-bottom level. The deregulation of prices for air travel in the 1980s frequently produced auctionlike settings in airports around the country (see Figure 1-1).

Rules, Laws, Reason

At other times, conflicts are settled by some procedure or rules. Income taxes are computed by rules based upon some system of rationality, namely that taxes will be proportional to income. Real estate taxes are developed through rules based upon the principle that taxes will be proportional to market value. Conflicts, like which restaurant we will go to, or who will choose, may not be resolved by a convention such as flipping a coin, but by reason such as choosing a restaurant that can handle one party's dietary needs, or one which will be closest to a particular theater.

Third Party Settlements

Many conflicts are settled by appealing to a higher or external authority. Fighting children go to a parent to resolve their difficulty. Employees appeal to their boss. Labor and management go to arbitration. Businessmen and their organizations often go to court, but are increasingly turning to mediation, arbitration, and other extra-legal third parties to handle their disputes because of the cost of litigation and delay in getting a settlement.

Negotiation becomes necessary when parties in conflict do not have these rule-oriented conventions or techniques available to them, but also because neither wants to break off contact. Negotiation is a search for a settlement, an ongoing search for a way to resolve a dispute. Negotiation is looser, much less structured, much less predictable. It means that parties are left far more to their own resources and devices in dealing with another party in a difficult (conflict) relationship.

The search for a settlement may be direct—through offers and counter offers until a settlement is reached—or indirect, as when parties search for a principle, rule, or respected third party to find a solution. But in either event, negotiation becomes necessary when there is no immediate means at hand to resolve conflict. Little wonder that most of us feel uncertain and uncomfortable about the process, and perhaps are inclined to avoid it.

WHAT ARE THE KEY ASPECTS OF NEGOTIATION?

The Joe Carter scenario brings out the many aspects of negotiation, topics that will be covered in this book. A few of the most important ones are introduced here.

Interdependence

The conflict element highlights the dramatic aspects of negotiation, and brings out the differing and often incompatible goals the parties have. What the drama may obscure is that the parties are interdependent. Their goals are locked together. A seller cannot exist without a buyer. Joe Carter can't have a vacation with his wife unless they find a place they both want to go. To need to work with the other party, and yet not be able to find some way to agree with him/her, creates tension and stress.

Altered Perceptions

During intense conflict, when parties may feel trapped and frustrated as a result of their interdependence, the other party may come to be seen as "the enemy." "Enemies" are frequently stereotyped as persons of questionable character and deficient personality, as happened to Joe when he had to negotiate with the finance people during budget meetings. Dealing with people in this way obviously has its drawbacks. While they may sometimes behave consistent with our image of them, i.e., as dishonest, deceptive, ruthless, or just concerned with goals very different from our own, our perceptions may also cloud even the simplest business dealings. Not only may we limit our ability to work with these people when the job requires it, but our perceptions may help us create far more conflict than is actually there.

Concealment and Openness

In negotiating with the automobile salesman, Joe was satisfied with the salesman's latest offer, but was trying to get a little better deal. In order to do that, he didn't tell the salesman how good he found the present offer to be. In many negotiations, the parties conceal their real goals and feelings in order to enhance their opportunity for the best deal possible. When both parties do this, and know each other is doing it, effective communication and accurate understanding become difficult. Misunderstandings arise, and the parties come to feel that the other party is deceptive and dishonest. This is the reality of much negotiation, particularly in its more competitive forms. In other situations, for example, with his wife, Joe was being very open, for it was to his advantage for his wife to try to fully understand his needs and objectives.

This point leads us to state two primary dilemmas that occur in negotiation (Kelley, 1966). Every negotiator must decide how open and honest to be about personal preferences and needs, and how much to trust the other party. The dilemma of honesty and openness suggests that if a negotiator is completely open and honest about what he wants, or will settle for, he may not do as well as if he bluffs or fights harder for a better settlement. On the other hand, if he is deceptive and dishonest about what he really wants, or will settle for, the parties could never come to an agreement that would be workable. Most negotiators resolve this dilemma by being very careful and guarded at the beginning of negotiation, and revealing more of their true needs as they can come to trust the other side. Similarly, the dilemma of trust suggests that a negotiator has an equal problem in knowing how much to trust his opponent's words and deeds. If he believes everything his opponent says, there is a possibility that his opponent is lying or bluffing, and our negotiator could give away too much. On the other hand, if the negotiator believes nothing his opponent says, once again the parties could never come to agreement. Most negotiators resolve this dilemma by probing their opponent's statements for truthfulness, and for evidence that they will be true to their word.

Different Negotiating Situations

The reason Joe conceals his needs and objectives in one situation and is open about them in another is not necessarily because he likes one person and dislikes the other, but because the two situations are structured differently. In one situation—buying the car—Joe's goals are in conflict with the salesman's. Joe wants to buy a car at the lowest possible price while the salesman wants to sell it at the highest possible price. In order to achieve his goal, Joe needs to pursue a strategy to minimize the price he achieves. Since the salesman is trying to sell it at the highest price possible, Joe also needs to be wary of any "tricks" or tactics that the salesman might use to sell the car. This form of negotiation is frequently called *distributive* or *win-lose* bargaining. When Joe is with his wife, on the other hand, the two of them have some primary goals in common—to maintain their marital relationship and agree on where to spend their vacation. This kind of problem requires a different kind of negotiation, frequently called *integrative* or *win-win* bargaining. Each of these forms of negotiation will be described in detail in later chapters. Failure to accurately recognize which type of negotiation is necessary in a particular situation can lead to the wrong approach and to failure. The outcome of any negotiation, as we shall point out repeatedly, is dependent on both the nature of the conflict problem and the type of strategy used to solve that problem.

Creativity and the Bargaining Mix

From the diversity and range of interests that the parties bring to the negotiation, come rich and valuable opportunities to reach a successful, even a creative settlement. In any negotiation, there is the possibility of a settlement that gives each party something they want, without significant cost or loss to the other. The discovery of these options breaks the win-lose deadlock that may have initially existed, and opens new opportunities for the parties to mutually accomplish their objectives. Joe and his fellow community members on the Conservation Commission spent significant time searching for a creative solution to the stream location problem. Was there some way to give the new plant the land they wanted without significantly damaging the stream bed and the wetlands? Out of complex issues such as these can come truly creative solutions; but discovery of these solutions requires that bargainers work in an environment where they feel cooperative, unthreatened, and dedicated to finding the best possible solution rather than to satisfying only one party's needs.

Subjective Utilities

When Joe was discussing vacations with his wife, the stumbling block was what vacation meant to each of them. She wanted new, exotic parts of the world with people she could talk with; he wanted a lack of structure, in comfortable surroundings without a lot of people to deal with. There is no way of objectively defining what is a "good vacation." The markers are personal, based upon values, needs, feelings, experiences. They are not objective, but subjective. *Subjective utilities* are the things which have value—or utility—to us based on their personal rather than objective worth. Perhaps the most serious trap for a negotiator is to innocently assume that there is always an objective way of determining what the "proper" outcome or "best" solution should be. What we believe to be a desirable outcome is *not* necessarily what the other person believes is a desired outcome. Parties to a negotiation may want quite different things; the things one wants may be irrelevant to the other. The parties may also believe that each can do very little to make the other feel successful and happy. In fact, they may be able to help one another much more than they realize.

The subjective nature of bargaining makes it difficult to know in advance, or even during negotiation, what a particular outcome will mean to the other party. It also means that what is "valued" by one or both sides is defined more subjectively than objectively. Hence, there is always the possibility of raising questions after a negotiation, like, "Did I pay too much?", "Could I have gotten it for less than I paid?" These may not be valid questions. If we are satisfied with what we got for what we paid, we got a "good deal." If we are not satisfied, we got a "bad deal." Since bargainers are very seldom in exactly comparable situations (issues being negotiated, opponent's strategy, etc.) that permit objective comparisons of "how well they did," bargainers often must look for subjective factors to justify feeling good (or bad) about their settlements. This process of subjective evaluation is as important as the actual negotiation itself. It will be affected by what kind of a settlement is actually achieved, and how well (or poorly) the negotiations were conducted.

Representative Role and Managing Constituencies

At the end of his work day, Carter worked on the Conservation Commission and encountered still another aspect of negotiation. He was representing the Commission, and also the town, in negotiation with a company that wanted to build a new plant. He and the representatives of the company reached an agreement, but then he had the task of bringing the rest of the Commission members and the members of the Board of Selectmen into agreement.

In negotiations, we are often representing others' interest as well as our own. This complicates the process enormously. Not only do we have to reach agreement with the other party, but we also have to persuade our *constituency*—those we represent—to agree to a negotiated outcome in which they did not directly participate. Managing this relationship successfully is often as difficult as the actual negotiations with our opponent.

The Role and Impact of a Negotiator's Personality

Joe recognized that when dealing with the people from the finance department, something in them and the situation triggered a hard stubbornness in him. Some part of Joe's personality was being affected by others, and was having an impact on the negotiation process. Because he recognized what was happening, Joe was able to resist emotional over-reaction. Our personalities are bound to enter into how we negotiate, and, for that matter, the personalities of the other parties will affect how they negotiate. This situation brings out Joe's stubbornness; the same situation might make others feel helpless, unassertive or passive. If either party ignores this interpersonal chemistry without understanding how and why it happens, they and the negotiating process are likely to suffer.

Influence of Observers

Negotiations seldom occur in isolation. Sometimes we are indifferent to the observers, but often we care about their reaction; sometimes, we care very much. Carter and the purchasing director both knew that higher management would be observing how they handled their situation and also knew that if they made the wrong impression, they would suffer serious consequences. How impactful an observer will be clearly depends upon the situation, the kind of power and influence the observer has, and the values and sensitivity of each party. Hence, while it is a difficult factor to accurately predict, it is one that should be included in one's understanding and planning for negotiations.

Personal Relations between Parties

In the different negotiations he handles during the day, Joe Carter has a variety of different relationships with his "adversaries": a close loving relationship with his wife; a friendly, but distant relationship with the purchasing manager; and a hostile relationship with the people from finance. We might expect that he would be able to negotiate better with his wife than with the finance people or the purchasing manager. Interestingly, however, being close or friendly with the other party may not lead to the best outcome.

With parties with whom we are relatively distant, e.g., Joe's relationship with the purchasing manager or with finance, we may be willing to say what we think, or take a position and stick with it, because we are not dependent on the relationship. We feel no emotional investment in the other person, and hence, feel like we could walk away from the relationship at any time if conflict got too intense. In close personal relationships, on the other hand, we may be hesitant to create conflict or say what is on our mind for fear of damaging the personal relationship that we value. Therefore, deep or close emotional involvement with the other party may make negotiated outcomes less, rather than more satisfactory for the parties, since the dispute may either damage the relationship or keep the parties from expressing their true feelings.

The Exchange of Proposals

Once parties have established that they have a common interest in negotiating, the next step is to get the process underway. The principal vehicle for carrying out negotiations is the exchange of offers and counter offers. For example, in a buy-sell situation, something like the following could occur:

> *Buyer:* "I'll give you $1,000 for your thingblat."
>
> *Seller:* "I'm sure you would but unfortunately, I cannot sell it for less than $2,000."

After this initial salvo, the next round is equally predictable. There are usually some fulminations by the seller about the excellent condition of his thingblat and its general usefulness, and by the buyer about the somewhat doubtful condition of the thingblat that others have been selling for prices far below $2,000. After both parties have worked up a mild sweat about their position, the buyer says,

> *Buyer:* OK, we've wasted enough time on this. It's more than this thingblat is worth, but I'll give you $1,200 for it.
>
> *Seller:* Look, that's not even close to its worth. I have some people coming over on Monday who almost bought this thingblat sight unseen over the phone. However, since you are a regular customer and a nice guy, I want to get this settled, and I'll let you have it for $1,800.

At this point, another round begins. The seller states that business is really tough and she may sell the business and move to Florida. The buyer mentions that he has talked to several other suppliers about new models of thingblats about to hit the streets. Finally, the buyer says,

> *Buyer:* Look, we'll split the difference between $1,200 and $1,800; $1,450 and its yours. But that's my final offer! Not a cent more!
>
> *Seller:* $1,500 and its done!
>
> *Buyer:* Sold! Shake!

The heart of negotiation is the exchange of offers and proposals. In "good faith" negotiations, an offer is made, and either accepted or returned with a counter-offer. To reject an offer and not make a counter-proposal may well lead the other party to angrily breaking off negotiations. There is an unstated assumption in negotiation that the parties will show their commitment to the process of finding a solution by making concessions to the other party's offer, and *not* simply by rejecting them out of hand. To do so is often seen as bad faith bargaining.

Some years ago, General Electric decided that the process of negotiation was very wasteful of management's time, and fraught with lots of uncertainty about what the result would be. As a result, they decided to change their approach. They would carefully calculate what the company could pay its employees, and then announce these figures to union representatives when the contract was to be renewed. Wages were not to be negotiated, since the figures the company would give would be fair, but all the company could afford to pay. The union's response was bitter outrage and protest. The key point was not the amount of the wage rates proposed, but the refusal of the company to negotiate, to open up the wage determination process to the exchange of ideas, input, and influence by the unions. The result of this attempt to use "rationality" to reduce hostility and bickering—called Boulwarism, after the name of the chief G.E. negotiator—produced years of bitter strife. Today, the term *Boulwarism* is used to mean "bad faith" or no-concession bargaining (Kochan, 1980).

The reality is that since negotiation involves a process of exchanging offers and counter-offers and of making concessions, the party who announces exactly what they want at the beginning of negotiation is at a disadvantage. He/she will be expected to make concessions from that declaration, which may take the party below the point that he/she wanted to go in negotiation. On the other hand, the failure to make concessions conveys images of bad faith, hardline bargaining and "unwillingness to play the game" (of negotiation). Either way, the party comes out more of a "loser" than if he/she started with an inflated position and made concessions. This may be true in spite of the "fairness" and "reasonableness" of the request itself.

Hopefully, through the process of offer and counter-offer a point is reached on which both parties will agree. There is more involved in this dialogue than a series of proposed settlements. A great deal of information is being conveyed, and there are many efforts to alter the other party's understanding of where their opponent stands, to alter the opponent's ideas of what they want or what they believe is possible to attain. To be successful, a negotiator needs to be able to understand the events that are taking place during the exchange of offers, to know how to use them to advantage, and to keep the other party from using them to the negotiator's disadvantage. With all of these events taking place in a short period of time, the process is very complex, making knowledge and preparation vital for success.

Information Exchange and a Common Definition of the Situation

In addition to the process of offer and counter-offer, the exchange of information permits a "common definition" of the situation to emerge. For example, suppose I want to sell a used bicycle for $100; you say it is only worth $50. I tell you how much I paid for it, what good condition it is in, what the attractive features are, and why it is worth $100. The other party may point out that it is 5-years-old, emphasize the paint chips and rust spots, comment that the tires are worn and really should be replaced. Finally, the other party may also tell me that he can't afford to spend $100. After 20 minutes of discussion about the bicycle, we have exchanged extensive information about the original cost and age of the bicycle, its depreciation and current condition, the benefits and drawbacks of this particular style and model, the buyer's financial situation, and my need to raise cash. We eventually arrive at a realistic picture of the current condition of the bicycle, and the ability of the buyer to pay, etc. This information need *not* be 100% true—bluffs (overstatements, exaggerations), omissions, and distortions of information occur all the time. I may claim I paid $200 for the bicycle, when I only paid $150; I may not reveal that the rear brake falls apart easily and really needs to be replaced. The other party may not tell me that she can pay $100, but simply doesn't want to spend that much. Nevertheless, the information exchanged, and the "common definition" of the situation that emerges, serves as a rationale for each side to modify its position, and to eventually accept a settlement. Both of us arrive at a price we feel satisfied with; those feelings of satisfaction are derived in part from the price itself, and in part because we have "justified" the price to ourselves as a result of the negotiation process. Thus, information exchange in negotiation serves as the primary medium for justifying our own and the other's position, and eventually for making concessions.

Winners and Losers

In negotiation, we are attempting to arrive at a settlement that maximizes our outcome. During the process, we frequently become concerned only with our ends and dismiss or denegrate the goals and needs of the other party. This is most likely to happen when we define our goal in negotiation as "winning." Although it is *not* necessarily the case, most of us believe that for there to be winners, there must also be losers. Through pressure, deception, or sheer aggressiveness, we may push people to the point where they see themselves as likely to lose, as likely to come out of the negotiation worse off rather than better off. Such situations usually create problems. Opponents will retaliate and fight back, often losing sight of their original goal. Losers will be reluctant to remain committed to a settlement that they feel was made to their disadvantage. They are likely to try many ways to get out of the contract, and even if they don't, it may be very difficult to force them to comply. Even if they do stick with the settlement, they may feel bitter about its disadvantages to them and will be unlikely to want to work with the other party again. This may not be a disadvantage if we don't want to do business with them again, but most of the negotiating we do is with people or groups with whom we are likely to meet or work in the future. Further, negotiators get reputations; a person commonly believed to be a hard trader, or suspected of being a dishonest one, will tend to be avoided, or treated with suspicion. Perhaps the cardinal rules of successful negotiators are to:

1. Remember their reputation, and work to maintain that reputation through their negotiating behavior.
2. Remember that most negotiation occurs in relationships which will be maintained over a long period of time.
3. Remember that the settlements which are most satisfactory and durable are the ones that address the needs of both parties.

Tangibles and Intangibles

The deeper we probe into the Joe Carter example, the clearer it becomes that negotiation is as much a "psychological game" as it is a rational decision-making process. The parties confront alternative means for reducing conflict; the alternative eventually chosen is likely to be closely related to how comfortable they feel in conflict, not necessarily what is the "best" alternative. Conflict will affect the ways that they perceive their opponent, the assumptions they make about him/her, and the attitudes and expectations they form about how their opponent will behave. If there is a long-standing relationship between the parties, that relationship will also dramatically affect their current behavior. The parties must decide whether or not to trust their opponent, and whether to fully disclose their "bottom line" or bluff and try to get more. The parties may be performing in front of their constituencies or other observers, and are likely to be evaluated based on how well they perform. Finally, each party must decide at the end of negotiation whether they "won" or "lost," whether or not they accomplished their goals, or whether or not they are satisfied. All of these psychological factors—winning or losing, trusting or mistrusting, conflicting or avoiding, liking or disliking an opponent, looking good or looking foolish—are as central to negotiation as the actual substance of the negotiation problem (resources to be divided, price to be paid, solution to be agreed to). We call these elements *intangibles*. Intangibles are the psychological factors that affect our behavior in negotiation—how we perceive the process, how we are seen and evaluated by others, how we feel about the negotiation process and the outcomes we obtain. Some common intangibles include winning and losing; looking good and looking foolish; preserving a relationship with an "opponent" or getting what is wanted at any price; and establishing, maintaining, or changing a reputation (e.g., fair, honest, tough, no-nonsense, kind, etc.).

In contrast, we call the substantive elements of a negotiation the *tangibles*. Tangibles are those things which are on our formal agenda: the price or rate to be paid, the "terms" and "conditions" of the deal, the wording of an agreement, the language of the contract. In Joe Carter's day, he negotiated over the location of his vacation with his family, the procedure to be used by his engineers in contacting vendors, the amount of his budget, and the building plan for the new company at the Conservation Commission meeting. Each of these topics had a number of elements and sub-issues; and each of the respective parties to each conflict had preferences and priorities for what it wanted. Negotiation over the tangibles is the process of resolving conflicts over these differing preferences and priorities.

There are several very important aspects to understanding what tangibles and intangibles are at stake in any negotiation. Tangibles are often as important to us as intangibles. Whether we "win" a negotiation may be as important as our actual share of the tangibles; whether we "look tough" to our constituency may be as important as the deal we get. Therefore, as negotiators we need to understand ourselves—and our opponents—psychologically, and be able to state what psychological factors are at stake in an upcoming negotiation. We need to be able to answer the question, "what do I want out of this negotiation *emotionally* (how do I want to feel at the end) as well as *tangibly?*" Finally, we need to understand that there are many times when the intangibles of negotiation will dominate the tangibles, and that negotiations are likely to deadlock, stalemate or break off if the intangibles are not recognized. Thus, many strikes occur *not* because the parties' positions were incompatible, since closer inspection of the tangibles often reveal that the parties were only cents/hours apart. Instead, the strike occurred because neither side was willing to make one more concession and feel like a "loser," or look weak to its constituency, or compromise on an "issue of principle," or break a precedent. A negotiator's psychological needs are often as important—if not more so—as the tangibles; and failure to understand or satisfy these needs is at the root of many unsuccessful negotiations.

OVERVIEW

Each chapter in this book relates to the introductory "Joe Carter" scenario, which has in it all of the critical elements addressed during negotiations.

In Chapter 1, The Nature of Negotiation, we examined negotiating as a basic social process used to resolve conflict. It is a process that is used when there are no rules, traditions, "rational methods" or higher authorities available to resolve conflict (or when the parties choose not to use these mechanisms in favor of a negotiation procedure). By choosing to negotiate, the parties prefer to avoid fighting a win-lose battle or breaking off the relationship. Using the example of "A Day in the Life of Joe Carter," we showed that negotiation processes occur in a variety of different contexts in our work and personal lives. We also showed that there are a number of different ways to approach Joe Carter's negotiations, and that negotiation is a highly complex social activity. The remainder of this book will be devoted to exploring various aspects of that complexity.

In Chapter 2, we explore a critical aspect of negotiation—interdependence. Each party in a negotiation is interested in achieving personal goals and meeting personal needs. As a result, negotiators tend to think of themselves as autonomously pursuing a goal, and that the other party is simply "in the way," i.e., somehow blocking the achievement of that goal. In fact, the entire process of negotiation is founded on the premise that the parties are interdependent, that is, one party cannot get what he/she wants without taking the other party into account. When parties are interdependent in a relationship, each one is dependent on the other for attaining his goals, either because those goals or the means for achieving those goals are linked. This interdependence is what gives negotiation its complexity, and creates much of its drama and tension. Chapter 2 deals with the difference between dependent, independent, and interdependent human relationships. It also explains the different forms of interdependence, and how they are likely to affect the negotiation process. One valuable approach to understanding and diagnosing interdependent relationships is game theory. In Chapter 2, game theory is explained, then used to illustrate the complex dynamics of interdependent relationships.

Once the negotiating parties understand the nature of their interdependence, they can begin to plan for negotiation. Chapter 3 explains why preparation is the most important step in negotiation. Planning requires that the negotiator be able to formulate his/her own goals and aspirations. It also requires "homework" and research: putting together the information and arguments to support and defend the desired goals. Planning requires a thorough understanding of the negotiation process. Finally, planning requires a knowledge of one's adversary; understanding his/her goals, taking them into account; and considering how to best bring about changes in their outlook, perceptions, and expectations. The chapter ends with a series of overview questions that negotiators may use in planning for any negotiation.

As was pointed out in the discussion of Joe Carter's day, there are two major kinds of negotiating. One occurred when he was negotiating for the car; we defined this as distributive, or win-lose bargaining. The other occurred when he and his wife were negotiating over their vacation plans; we define this as a problem suitable for integrative, or win-win negotiation. Chapter 4 describes and evaluates the basic strategies and tactics common to competitive, win-lose, distributive bargaining. We will describe the structure of a competitive bargaining relationship, and how that structure can be used to develop fundamental strategy. We will also review the tactics that are most commonly associated with distributive strageties, and evaluate the consequences of using them.

Chapter 5 describes and evaluates the basic strategy and tactics common to cooperative, win-win, integrative bargaining. The process of integrative bargaining is significantly different from distributive bargaining. While distributive bargaining is characterized by mistrust, suspicion and strategies designed to "beat" the opponent, integrative bargaining is characterized by trust, openness and strategies designed to achieve the best possible solution for all parties involved. Integrative bargaining is a process very much like group problem solving; the strategy and tactics necessary to successfully accomplish this process are reviewed in detail.

After highlighting the fundamental difference between distributive and integrative bargaining, Chapter 6 identifies those elements that are common to both types of strategies, and must be taken into account when planning any negotiation process. These elements include:

- Evaluating the tangibles and intangibles at stake.
- Understanding the motivational orientation of the negotiating parties.
- Understanding how "rationality" (reasonableness) is defined in the negotiating context, and how rational (or irrational) behavior is handled.
- Understanding how "fairness" is defined in the negotiating context, and how fair (or unfair) judgments are made.
- Understanding the importance of selecting a site (location) for negotiations.
- Understanding the role of time and deadlines in negotiations.

Having considered the basic differences between two major strategic approaches to negotiation, as well as elements common to all negotiating strategies, we next consider several major sub-processes that are characteristic of all negotiation. Chapters 7–11 evaluate five major sub-processes that are part of the negotiation process, or can dramatically influence a negotiation outcome. These factors are: the communication process between the parties, the nature of the persuasion process used to influence the other party, the social environment in which negotiation occurs, the amount and type of power used by negotiators, and the impact of a negotiator's personality on negotiation outcomes. Chapter 7 specifically examines the communication process. Using a basic model of communication, we break negotiation into its key communication elements, and show how each may lead to successful or unsuccessful negotiating outcomes.

Successful persuasion is an important key to effective negotiation. While the parties may spend a great deal of time in assembling information to support their viewpoint, structuring and presenting effective, persuasive arguments are also important. Chapter 8 reviews the important research from the fields of attitude and opinion change, and shows how that research may be used to use persuasive tactics in the most effective manner.

Thus far, this book approaches negotiations as though it were a dialogue between two individuals, each of whom was attempting to achieve his/her own objectives. In fact, a great deal of negotiation occurs when the negotiators are representing someone else's interests. A lawyer negotiates for his client; a manager negotiates a deal for her company that must be approved by the board of directors; a labor leader negotiates for his union rank and file. When parties are representing the interests of others, and accountable to those others, a whole new dimension of complexity is added to negotiation. Chapter 9 examines the impact on a negotiator's behavior of having a "constituency" (a group to whom a negotiator is accountable for his performance). The chapter also explores the role played by "audiences" to negotiation, e.g. observers, third parties, the press and television, and shows how they affect the behavior of the negotiator and fundamentally change the nature of negotiation dynamics.

In Chapter 10, we take a closer look at the nature of power in negotiation. The chapter describes the various ways that negotiators can use power, and describes the events that usually occur when one negotiator has significantly more power than the other.

We have described negotiation thus far as a process occurring between two relatively rational, strategic, goal-oriented people. We have also consistently implied that with planning and practice, anyone can negotiate effectively. One question that experienced negotiators consistently ask is whether some individuals are better negotiators because of their personality. Chapter 11 reviews the wealth of research on this question, and proposes several ways that a negotiator's personality is indeed likely to affect his/her success in negotiation.

In discussing the negotiation process, we consistently point out the many ways that it is prone to failure. While the parties may be searching for an integrative agreement, the process may break down along the way. The "intangibles" may drive out the tangibles. Anger and defensiveness may escalate. Emotionality may lead to breakdowns in communication. The parties may use tactics that offend the other. The social structure (i.e., constituencies and audiences) may make it difficult to achieve agreement. These are only some of the contributing factors. The purpose of Chapter 12 is to show how negotiations can get back on track. Two major sets of procedures are suggested: those that negotiators can invoke themselves to restore bargaining to a more productive sequence, and those procedures that can be used by a third party to bring negotiators back together. Collectively, these procedures highlight a wide variety of different approaches that can be used to restore negotiators to a more successful course.

Negotiation is a process in which the parties engage in all manner of tactics to persuade the other. Information is concealed; the parties may be prone to bluff or to lie; "spying" on the other may be a desirable way to learn about his strategy; negotiators may decide that it is worth doing something unethical or illegal in order to achieve their goal. All of these tactics fall within a category of behavior that many would classify as "unethical." Very little attention has been given to ethical and unethical behavior in negotiation. The purpose of Chapter 13 is to explore the dimensions of ethical behavior in negotiation and to determine what types of conduct are generally viewed as unethical. This final chapter will also describe the factors which lead individuals to make decisions that involve ethical criteria, and to suggest a model of the manner in which ethics-related decisions are actually made.

2

Interdependence

In negotiation, both parties have a need for the other. A buyer cannot buy unless someone else sells and vice versa; each is dependent upon the other. We call this situation one of mutual dependency or *interdependence*. Interdependent relations are complex and have their own special challenge. When independent of another person we can, if we choose, have a relatively detached, indifferent, uninvolved outlook. When dependent on another, we are faced with a situation where we have to accept and accommodate the demands of another. For example, if totally dependent on an employer for a job, the party will have to do the job as instructed or quit. But when we are interdependent, we have an opportunity to influence the other party, and have many more options open to us. Handling those options is difficult, for the interdependent relationship is a complex one. In this chapter, we shall explain and clarify some of the key aspects of interdependent relationships.

CHARACTERISTICS OF INTERPERSONAL RELATIONSHIPS

To better understand aspects of interdependence, we will use the analytical concepts developed by Thibaut and Kelley (1959). In a relationship, we have some idea of what kinds of outcomes to expect, and we assess the desirability of these outcomes against some standard. If we are buying a house, there is a limit above which we will not (or cannot) pay; if we are accepting a job, there is a limit in salary below which we will not work. These points beyond which we will not go are a standard against which we can compare an offered price. In a broader context, we can assess an entire negotiating relationship with the other party: how we feel about negotiation in general, about negotiating with this person, and what we feel to be an acceptable price or resistance point. Thibaut and Kelley call this standard the Comparison Level (CL); it is the standard against which a person "evaluates the attractiveness of a relationship or how satisfactory it is" (Thibaut and Kelley, p. 21). A relationship or anticipated outcome (O) that is above the CL is desirable; one below the CL is unattractive or unsatisfactory. The greater the distance between O and CL, the greater the attractiveness or unattractiveness of the relationship. In the job example, if we have determined that our minimally acceptable salary is $20,000 per year, this becomes our comparison level for jobs. Anticipated salaries above $20,000 will be viewed as more attractive, while salaries below $20,000 will be viewed as unattractive and probably rejected.

When a relationship is unattractive we may think of leaving, but that depends upon our options. We may not like being out of a job, but if we are relatively unskilled, we may find it difficult to get another job. If we have many skills, we may know of several jobs to which we can easily move. Another standard by which we judge outcomes, then, is the lowest level of outcomes, experienced or anticipated, a person will accept in light of the alternatives available. This is called the comparison level for alternatives (CLalt). People leave relationships when outcomes fall below this comparison level for alternatives (CLalt). It is assumed that the more a person's actual outcome exceeds the CLalt, the more dependent upon the relationship she or he is. Thus, for example, let us assume that a job seeker took a job at $21,000 per year. Six months later her boss announced that because of major cutbacks in the business, her job had been eliminated; she could accept another job in the company at $18,000 or she would have to be laid off. While $18,000 is considerably below the $20,000 limit our job seeker had set six months earlier, the prospects for being unemployed and seeking a new job (the CLalt) may appear to be much worse than the $18,000 job opportunity. The more dependent the job seeker is on the job, the more she will stay with a salary that is below the CL but above the CLalt.

Let us use these three concepts—comparison level (CL), comparison level for alternatives (CLalt) and anticipated outcome (O)—to clarify some aspects of interdependent relations. We shall continue the example of the job seeker here, using $20,000 as the CL, not working at all or having another job opportunity as the CLalt, and the actual salary as the O. First consider the situation where a person's O exceeds both the CLalt and the CL, respectively (Figure 2–1a). When the actual outcome exceeds the CL, this is an attractive, satisfactory relationship. However, since there are alternative relations to which the person can go (CLalt) which would also have outcomes in excess of the CL, the individual is not very dependent upon the

FIGURE 2-1

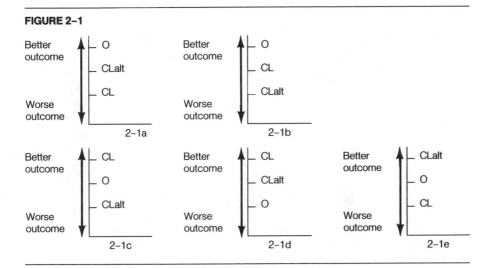

relationship. In this situation, assume that a person earning $22,000 a year was offered $21,000 a year to work elsewhere. Since $21,000 is also above the CL, the individual may feel that there are several good jobs around that pay well, and hence feel less dependent on the current job as the "only option available."

A second condition would be when a person's CL is below O but above CLalt (Figure 2–1b). Again the relationship is satisfactory, but the individual's dependence upon the relationship has *increased*. Thus, a person working for $22,000 needing $20,000 to live, and knowing that other jobs are going at $17,000, will stay in the job and feel dependent on it as the best source of income.

Third, there is the situation where a person's CL exceeds the O which in turn exceeds the CLalt (Figure 2–1c). This is clearly an unattractive, unsatisfactory relationship, but one in which the outcome still exceeds the next most attractive possibility, and hence the individual is dependent upon the relationship and can be expected to stay, albeit unsatisfied. If our job seeker needs $20,000 minimum, has her salary cut to $18,000, and has a choice between that and unemployment, she is likely to stay on in the $18,000 job but be unsatisfied. A fourth situation is where the CL and CLalt both exceed O (Figure 2–1d) in which the individual is both not satisfied and not dependent and thus will leave. If our job seeker is offered a clerk's job at $10,000 a year, and has the choice between that and unemployment, she may well decide that the job or salary is so inadequate that she would rather be unemployed, and hence quit. In our final situation, CLalt exceeds the outcome, which in turn exceeds the CL (Figure 2–1e). This is the bittersweet situation where an individual is satisfied with the relationship, but will leave because of better opportunity. If there are other attractive jobs on the market for $24,000–$26,000, the person is likely to see these as more attractive than the current salary of $22,000, and be tempted to move. A sixth possibility, in which the CLalt and CL both exceed the O is conceptually possible; but since it would be both unsatisfying and lacking either dependency or desirable alternatives, it would not exist long if it ever came into being. Thus, according to this theory, it would be hard to imagine a person staying in a job at $18,000 when his CL is $20,000 and other jobs are readily available at better than $20,000 (assuming salary is the only basis for staying).

This mode of analysis permits us to draw a distinction between attractiveness and satisfaction on one hand, and dependency on the other. A person can dislike a relationship and stay, or like a relationship and leave. In clarifying our own situation and in understanding the situation of the other party, these distinctions are important. In negotiation, the other party may dislike dealing with us, but since we have "the best deal in town," he/she will hang in and negotiate with us. Alternately, the other party may like us, but nonetheless break off negotiations because of more attractive possibilities elsewhere.

COOPERATION AND COMPETITION

The interconnectedness (interdependence) of people's goals is the basis for much social interaction. Can it help us to estimate what type of social action will occur? The answer is frequently "yes." By determining something about the way people's goals are interdependent, we can make some estimates of what type of behavior is most likely to emerge. When the goals of two or more people are interconnected so that only one can achieve the goal—such as winning a gold medal in a race, and therefore making the others losers of the race—we have a competitive situation. Deutsch (1962, 1973) defined this as *contrient interdependence*, a situation in which "individuals are so linked together that there is a negative correlation between their goal attainments" (1962, p. 276). To the degree that one person achieves his/her goal, the other's goal attainment is blocked. In contrast, when parties' goals are linked so that one person's goal achievement helps or facilitates others to achieve their goals (a positive correlation between their goal attainments), we have a situation of *promotive interdependence*. Deutsch's research has shown that situations of promotive interdependence are usually characterized by trusting relations among the parties, a successful division of labor with regard to the tasks to be performed, and successful efforts at mutually influencing one another. In contrast, situations of contrient interdependence are characterized by large amounts of mistrust and suspicion, significant efforts to block the other's goal attainment rather than help it, and the use of coercive power and force in order to exercise influence. Needless to say, therefore, the nature of the interdependence will have a major impact on the nature of the relationship and the way negotiations are conducted.

INTERDEPENDENCE

Interdependent relationships, those in which people are mutually dependent, are complex. Each party knows that they can influence the other's outcomes and that their outcomes can, in turn, be influenced by the other (Raven and Rubin, 1973; Goffman, 1969). Let us explore the salary case in more depth. Person (P) is seeking a job and being interviewed by an employer (E). Their discussion has revealed that P would like to have the job that is available, and E sees P as a desirable employee for the position. They are now attempting to establish P's salary. The job description announces the salary as "competitive." P has identified a salary below which she will not work ($20,000), but suspects that she may be able to get considerably more. The company with which P is interviewing has a reputation for running "hard and lean," and she suspects that means that they will pay no more than necessary. For this reason, P has decided *not* to state her bottom salary, since she suspects that it would be immediately accepted. Moreover, she knows that it would be difficult to get the level raised if it should turn out that the $20,000 was considerably below what E could pay. P has thought of stating her "ideal" salary—$28,000—but suspects that E will view her as either presumptuous or rude for asking that much. The interview would probably end with E viewing her negatively and making it harder for her to get the best possible salary.

Without going further, let us look at what is happening. P is making a decision based on the anticipated reactions of E to her actions. P recognizes that her actions will affect E. P also recognizes that the way E acts in the future toward her will be influenced by the way P's actions affect E. As a result, P is assessing the indirect impact of her behavior on herself. Further she also knows that E is alert to all this, and will look upon any statement by P as reflecting a preliminary position on salary, rather than a final one. To counter this expected view, P will probably try to find some way to state a salary that seems as accurate as possible, for example, by referring to salaries she knows others with similar qualifications have gotten in other companies. P is choosing among behavioral options with a thought not only to how they will affect E, but also how they will then lead E to act toward P. Further, P knows that E believes this and acts on the basis of this belief.

Behavior in an interdependent relationship is calculated behavior—calculated on the premise that the more information one has about the other person, the better will be the calculations. There is the possibility, however, that too much knowledge only confuses (Raven and Rubin, p. 158). For example, let us suppose that P knows that E needs to get a project underway and needs to fill this position promptly. E has just had a performance review with his boss, during which his superior claimed that he was not controlling costs—particularly labor cost. In addition, other people working for E are complaining that they need additional talents in the organization, such as those possessed by P, but that they also resent new personnel being brought in at salaries higher than what they are receiving. Does all this help P in determining her actions, or only confuse things? In fact, given all these complexities, E may not have reached a decision about what salary should be paid other than a maximum figure above which he will not go. This is the classic negotiating situation. Both parties have their outer limits of an acceptable settlement (how high or low they can afford to go), but within that range, neither has determined what "the" exact salary will be or must be. It is a solution to be worked toward. The parties have to engage in an exchange of information and an effort at problem solving. They must work toward a solution that takes into account each person's requirements and, hopefully, optimizes the outcomes for both (Nash, 1950; Sen, 1970).

Examine two points made in the last sentence. First, problem solving is essentially a process of specifying the elements of a desired outcome, examining the components available to produce an outcome, and searching for a way of fitting them together. A person can approach problem solving in negotiation from his/her own perspective and attempt to solve the problem by considering *only* the components that affect his/her own desired outcome. When approaching the situation as a joint problem solving effort, however, the desired outcomes of the other party must be taken into account. Our job seeker cannot determine her own salary without input from the employer about his preferences and limits (Pruitt, 1981). One difficulty is that the other party may not be open about what his real desired outcome is, or may not be clear in his own mind about what he actually wants. Hence, a necessary step in negotiation is to clarify and share information about what both parties really want as outcomes.

As negotiations evolve, some knowledge of the combined set of desired outcomes becomes known (be they stated as "positions" or real). If there is not a good fit among the elements so that they naturally coincide, negotiation continues as a series of proposals. These proposals usually suggest alterations in the other party's position, and perhaps contain alterations in the proposer's own position. When one party accepts an alteration in its position, a concession has been made (Pruitt, 1981). Concessions restrict the range of options within which a solution or agreement will be reached; when a party makes a concession, the bargaining range is confined closer to one or both sides' limits or resistance point. Our job seeker would like to get a starting salary of $28,000, but scales her request down to $25,000, thereby eliminating all of the possible salary options above $25,000. People may recognize that concessions are necessary for a settlement, but will obviously be reluctant to be the one who makes all or most of them. For our job seeker to make further concessions below $25,000, she probably will want to see some willingness on the part of the company to increase its offer or add other attractive benefits to its salary package. They may know they cannot get all they want, but they want to get as much of the settlement range as they can consistent with the other party's getting as much as it can in an interdependent relationship. To reach that optimal point by giving information and making concessions requires trust and a feeling that one is being treated fairly.

Two efforts in negotiation help to create trust and feelings of being treated fairly; one is based on perception of outcomes, while the other is based on the process. The former attempts to change a party's estimation of the perceived importance or value of something. If P, in the illustration above, is convinced by E that the relatively low salary for the job is relatively unimportant given the high bonuses people in the firm typically earn, then she can feel comfortable in making a concession on this point. In contrast, efforts based on the negotiating process help to convey images of equity, fairness, and reciprocity in proposals and concessions. When one party makes several proposals which are rejected by the other party, and the other party makes no alternate proposal, the first party often feels that it is being abused and improperly treated and may break off negotiations. When one party makes a concession, he or she will be much more comfortable and trusting if the other party responds by making a concession. This pattern of give and take is not just a characteristic of negotiation, it is essential to joint problem solving in an interdependent relationship. Parties' satisfaction with a negotiation is as much determined by the process through which an agreement is reached as with the actual outcome obtained. To eliminate or even deliberately attempt to reduce this give and take, as has been attempted in some labor-management negotiating strategies (Raiffa, 1982; Selekman, Fuller, Kennedy, and Baitsell, 1964), is to short-circuit the process, eliminating both the basis for trust and any possibility of joint decision making. Even if the position taken by the party executing such a strategy is that joint outcomes are maximized, the other party will dislike the process by which these outcomes are reached.

Negotiators must recognize that negotiation is a process of joint problem solving working toward a maximum joint return. This process is critical to successful interdependent relationships and requires trust and security for each party; this trust can be developed by adhering to certain perceptual and processual routines which contribute to feelings of satisfaction and success.

EXCHANGE THEORIES

In our discussion of the reciprocal interactions between interdependent parties, we identified three broad areas of importance: the reinforcement or learning that takes place, the way the process is perceived by the parties, and the outcomes of the interactions. Each one is now discussed in further detail.

Exchange and Learning

Any bargaining interaction is more than an exchange of information and ideas; it is a host of interpersonal experiences as well. The other party may say, "that last suggestion of yours was very helpful," which most of us would take as a compliment. Or, they may snarl, "is that all?", leaving us feeling somewhat abused. They may resist being available at the time when we can be available for a negotiation session, or they can extend themselves to accommodate our needs; these events will also impact on our feelings. They can respond to our concession with a concession of their own, or hold fast and ask us to concede again. There are even times when concessions or accommodations to the other party are neither rewarded nor punished, but just ignored. Throughout the process, we receive many rewards and benefits and incur costs and punishments. Most people like situations in which they get rewarded, and find ways to increase those rewards or the number of rewarding situations they are in. Similarly, most people seek to minimize punishment or minimize the number of punishing situations they are in. These rewards and punishments shape our behavior in negotiation, in that people "learn" what is appropriate, what works, and how to maximize rewarding environments. Thus, learning occurs in most bargaining exchanges (Blau, 1964; Homans, 1961; Skinner, 1953).

Exchange and Comparison

Behind the issue of trust are the beliefs about fairness—what is right, just, proper. We do not trust others or "the system" when we feel we will not get, or have not gotten a fair deal. But what is "fair?" Let us consider a number of ways to look at this question (Sampson, 1969; Morgan and Sawyer, 1967).

Not too long ago it was thought acceptable (fair and proper) for men to receive more pay than women for the same work. It was also acceptable, during a mixed sex discussion at work, for females to be referred to as "girls" while males were referred to as "men." There was a rationale for the difference in wages. Society expected men to become heads of households, to support a wife and children, while women were expected to get married and become fulltime housewives and mothers. If women worked, they were presumably single with no dependents, living with their parents, or soon to be married. At work, they were presumed to be young (therefore "girls") while the male work force was expected to be employed for much of their lives, were older and therefore were "men." Wages, ascribed social positions, and terms of identification were not equal, but given the prevailing social views, the difference was seen as equitable. These views have changed sharply in recent years. Both in public opinion and in the law, it is now viewed that people— regardless of sex, race, or age—should be paid the same; references to women as "girls" are less common and likely to be received coolly when they do occur.

At issue is the difference between equity and equality. While there is a general social movement toward equality on many issues, different norms of equity (fairness) prevail in many areas. Great differences in salaries are accepted. Some people make $10,000 a year and others over $100,000. People accept being interrupted by their superiors and resent being interrupted by their subordinates. People who feel they have a humble position in society may accept more aggressive behavior from a bank officer while negotiating a loan than someone who feels more equal to the banker. In negotiation, parties frequently differ on the standard they are using without making their expectations clear. For example, if one side expects that rewards will be distributed equitably—to each what he/she "deserves"—while the other side expects equality, the other will view equity arguments as unfair treatment. We can also create feelings of being unfairly treated if we treat others equally when they want equity. If the other has had a "string of bad luck" and "needs a break," he/she may resent us or feel unfairly treated if we propose an equal settlement. An interesting paradox also arises when people get more than they feel is equitable, when they in fact believe that they deserve equal treatment to others (Adams, 1965). Most of us have occasionally felt guilty when we have received more than we felt we deserved.

In all of this discussion, the key issue is that people will feel more trusting and will believe there is "justice" when they believe they are fairly treated. (See Chapter 6 for a fuller treatment of how fairness is commonly viewed in negotiation.) Initially, however, each side has its own view of what is fair and how "fairness" is defined. Somehow, they must surface these views and share them with their opponent so that they can be incorporated into the negotiating process.

Exchange and Outcomes

We now return to the heart of negotiation: the final outcome that results from the agreement. What did the negotiator get for what was invested? We "invested" x number of dollars and "got out" an automobile with some attractive options. What we "put in" is variously described as costs, time, disadvantages, money, and perhaps some "side arrangements" like leaving an extra tire with the car we traded. What we "got out" is frequently described as services, rewards, objects (like an automobile), benefits, and advantages. If the amount we get out equals what we put in, then we have a fair trade. If the amount we get out exceeds what we put in, then we have a good deal. If what we got out greatly exceeds what we put in, then we got a very good deal.

A problem arises, however, when we make detailed comparisons between input and output. How do we compare money or time invested, annoyances incurred while buying a new auto, a hug from our spouse, or the pride of showing off the new car? For some, showing off a new car to friends and neighbors may be a great source of satisfaction and help make a good deal. To others, this is of no importance and does not contribute to the outcome.

These are "subjective" factors. They vary widely from person to person and we cannot assume we know another's outcome preferences. They can be changed through the process of negotiation, and attempting to do so is one of the major tasks of negotiation.

When we think of outcomes as reward-cost or benefit-contribution ratios, we can also determine the value of an outcome (derived by subtracting costs from rewards). Most negotiators calculate the values of an array of negotiation outcomes, and compare these outcomes to their opponents'. When they do, two things stand out. First, in any agreement reached, the outcomes of the two parties are very unlikely to be equal. Second, because there is an array of possible agreements, there is also a wide array of different combinations. The differences between the parties will shift direction and change in magnitude. In some combinations, both will get less (or more) than in others. Lastly, the particular agreement reached (and therefore the outcomes arrived at) will be the result of the actions that both parties take. This is more conveniently demonstrated by using a matrix. Along each axis, each party's possible actions or positions are arrayed (Figure 2–2). The intersection of each side's various positions in the matrix represent various possible points of agreement; therein, the outcome values for each party are indicated. Those for P (person) are below the diagonal line in each box; those for O (other person) above the diagonal line (Thibaut and Kelley, 1959).

How do we assess what P and O should choose? Let us assume, for the moment, that P and O are going to make only *one* choice, and that each is out to maximize his outcomes on that selection. Let us first look at the options from each person's perspective. Of the four possible actions for P, P_1 is the most desirable because it has an outcome value of 8, provided of course that O chooses action O_4. From O's perspective, O_2 is the best choice because it also has an outcome value of 8, provided that P chooses O_2. Note, however, that

FIGURE 2–2

	O_1	O_2	O_3	O_4
P_1	2 \ 4	3 \ 2	5 \ 5	8 \ 1
P_2	2 \ 4	2 \ 8	3 \ 4	7 \ 2
P_3	3 \ 6	5 \ 1	4 \ 3	3 \ 7
P_4	2 \ 2	5 \ 2	6 \ 6	5 \ 1

the "best payoff" choices for both sides don't converge on a single cell. If P picks P_1 first, O is likely to respond *not* with O_4, but with a choice that maximizes his payoff given what P has chosen (in this case, O_3, giving each player 5 points). Conversely, if O picks O_2 first in order to get 8, P is likely to respond *not* with P_2, but with a choice that maximizes his payoff given what O has chosen (in this case, P_3 or P_4, which gives P 5 points and O 1 or 2 points). There are a variety of other decision rules which the parties could use to try to maximize their individual outcomes (7 or 8 points) or to achieve the best joint gain—6 points each at P_4, O_3. The issue is how are the parties to get from their initial positions to the best joint outcome?

Things would be simpler if both parties knew each other's outcomes for all combinations of actions, but they typically do not. Each knows his own outcomes, but is usually ignorant of the other's outcomes. Initially, the parties usually know only their own payoffs, represented by two matrices, one for P (Figure 2–2a) and one for O (Figure 2–2b). Reaching an agreement involves the exchange of enough information for both parties to know what is acceptable to the other party. This is where negotiation takes place. We can envision a discussion that might begin as follows:

> **P:** I'll pick P_1 if you'll pick O_4.
>
> **O:** No way. However, I will pick O_2 if you'll pick P_2.
>
> **P:** No good. I'll tell you what, I'll pick P_2 if you pick O_4.
>
> **O:** Well that is some improvement, but you still have a long way to go. Since you really want O_4, I'll agree to it if you pick P_3.

What is happening is that both parties are going after their best possible outcome and finding that the other party will not agree. If they had full knowledge of the outcomes for the other party as well as for themselves, they could, of course, immediately move to the best position for both of them. Since they only have information about their own preferences and outcomes, they begin an exchange of proposals and counterproposals which, even

---

FIGURE 2–2a and 2–2b

Outcomes As Seen by P

	O_1	O_2	O_3	O_4
P_1	2	3	5	8
P_2	2	2	3	7
P_3	3	5	4	3
P_4	2	5	6	5

Figure 2–2a

Outcomes As Seen by O

	O_1	O_2	O_3	O_4
P_1	4	2	5	1
P_2	4	8	4	2
P_3	6	1	3	7
P_4	2	2	6	1

Figure 2–2b

though they may be met with rejection, yield information about what the other will and will not accept. This indirect form of communication, however, can lead to misinterpretation, as O's last statement shows. However, if the parties are alert, later exchanges will usually show what is inaccurate.

Continuing the discussion between P and O,

> **P:** That does not do anything for me. We've got to settle this. I'll do P_4 if you'll deliver O_3
>
> **O:** Done!

This dialogue is abstract, making it difficult to understand how these interdependent choices operate in real-life decision making. Take another example from a manufacturing operation. A shipment has been returned by a customer to a factory for poor quality. New material has been sent to the customer, but the cost of the scrapped material has to be assigned to the department responsible for the poor work. In this case, it is not clear which of two departments is responsible for the poor work, and in fact the problem might have been created by faulty materials supplied by a vendor. Needless to say, neither of the managers of the departments involved wants the cost of scrapped material assigned to her unit. The plant manager has been upset by the matter and has told the two managers to straighten the matter out between themselves.

Each manager sees four basic options open to herself:

1. A manager can stonewall the issue, insist that her unit is not responsible, and not accept the costs of the rejected items. If the other manager gives in and accepts the costs, the manager who "stonewalled" not only avoided a drain on her department's budget but also gained a reputation as someone who cannot be pushed around, a perception which may help her in many future conflicts. However, the other manager may not accept responsibility for the rejected material. This could lead both of them to stonewalling. Lengthy arguments could ensue and both managers could appear rigid and belligerent to the plant manager who has said the two managers should settle this.

2. A manager could go to the plant manager and ask her to assign the costs. There is a loss of image or "face" to the managers in asking the plant manager to settle their conflict for them, but it would avoid a long and bitter discussion which would keep them from other pressing issues.

3. There is some reason to believe that the problem may lie in some materials supplied by a vendor. A third option is to press a claim on the supplier for the cost of the returned material. Unfortunately, it is not clear that the vendor's liability can be documented, and even if it could be, it would take considerable time to resolve.

4. A manager could accept responsibility for the poor material. This avoids a long, bitter argument, but is costly both in money and in reputation.

FIGURE 2–3

		Department Manager A			
		Stonewall D_1	Go to Boss D_2	Document Suppliers' Fault D_3	Accept Blame D_4
Department Manager B					
Stonewall	B_1	−15 / −10	−20 / −10	5 / −5	10 / 20
Go to Boss	B_2	0 / −15	−5 / −5	0 / −8	0 / −10
Document Suppliers' Fault	B_3	−5 / 0	−10 / −10	0 / 5	−10 / −15
Accept Blame	B_4	−10 / 10	−15 / −5	−10 / −10	0 / −5

The range of possible outcomes for the two managers, B and D, is shown in Figure 2–3. Most outcomes are undesirable for both parties and there are no joint outcomes which are positive for both, making it likely that the final agreed-upon outcome will be unfavorable to both. Sad to say, the real world is sometimes like that, forcing us to make the best choice among undesirable outcomes. Another thing we note is that the second course of action, of going to the boss, is not something that either would like to do, but it is more distasteful to Party D than B. In fact, if we look further we note that, for the most part, B is relatively neutral about going to the boss *except* if D also goes to the boss. As with positive outcomes, the degree of *distastefulness* for a person also varies with what the other party does.

These variations are greatly influenced by differences in individual values. B hopes that she can develop a relationship with the boss, and get a better break from her than she (B) can get by dealing with D on her own, provided that B can deal one-on-one with the boss. If D is there also, B fears that D will dominate the situation and make her look bad. D, on the other hand, is concerned with how she looks in the eyes of other managers and wants to be seen as forceful, and as one who cannot be pushed around. Hence, she is reluctant to accept blame, although if both parties accepted blame jointly, she feels the damage to her image would be relatively slight. She also does not want to be seen as one who runs to the boss for help. Hence, we can see that we need to be careful in interpreting what a refusal to accept blame by the other party means. D does not want to accept blame for the rejected material but would value doing that far more negatively if B were stonewalling than if B were also accepting blame. If we look at D_3— documenting the supplier's faulty work to justify getting the supplier to pay the costs—we see that D is *not* too eager because of the work involved, unless B will join the project and share in the labor.

Matrices are very useful for overviewing the possible outcomes of bargaining situations. However, they have limitations. For one thing, it is often hard to determine the exact payoffs or outcomes to be obtained for each combination of choices. It is not too difficult to do so when the payoffs are dollars and cents. However, as the above illustration shows, many outcome values are subjective, resting upon a person's personality or emotional judgment. Outcome values can change, even during negotiations. In fact, considerable effort may be expended to change them. Hence, D may link stonewalling by B with B's reputation in the boss's eyes, which B wants to preserve and protect in an effort to make the outcomes under any circumstance more negative in B's eyes. A second limitation is the number of actions (strategies) the matrix can handle. Three or four sets of actions for each actor make a fairly complex matrix. However, actual negotiations may lead to an even larger combination of possible outcomes, making the matrix exceedingly complex.

UNDERSTANDING NEGOTIATION THROUGH THE STUDY OF GAMES

Because interdependent relationships are complex, they are difficult to study. Ideally, we would study the structure and processes of interdependent relationships during actual negotiations. Sometimes we do. More commonly we study such relationships through simulations in laboratory settings. In proceeding this way, we obviously lose some of the richness of real experiences. On the other hand, by limiting our focus and controlling as many variables as possible, we can systematically probe what does take place. One of the principal ways to study interdependent relationships in a controlled setting is through games.

When social scientists talk of studying "games" they mean something different from what *games* commonly means. They mean they are studying behavior in an artificial, or make-believe sense, rather than in real life. They might use terms like "experiment" or "simulation." Games are artificial, simplified and reconstructed models of reality. Like all games, they have players and rules. Mathematicians and economists usually construct and study games to determine what players should do, based on certain principles and rules of "rational" economic behavior. In contrast, behavioral scientists study games to determine what people *actually* do in these situations—behavior which may be at considerable variance with the rational predictions. Thus in the study of interdependent behavior, games usually means a particular *type* of simulation. These games are structured to lead the parties to behave cooperatively or competitively. Therefore, there are numerous similarities and parallels between games and the situations we have been discussing as examples of interdependence, particularly that form of interdependent behavior called *negotiating*. In a game, what one person does influences the possible outcomes of the other party; this, in turn, will influence how the other party acts toward the first. In tennis, I hit the ball to make points, but I also consider where I place the ball to influence how the opponent will return it to me. A tennis game has limits of time, ball placement, etc. In negotiations, the limits might be price, or abusive behavior, or length of the negotiation. There are rules in games, and parties win by achieving their goal within those rules. There are also rules in negotiation—often unstated—such as responding to a concession from the other party with one of their own, or making the best case for their side, without actually lying. Finally, the term "game" or "gaming" has been used in a variety of ways. Games used to study negotiations fall into four categories: "game theory" games, distribution games, economic exchange games, and role-playing games. Behavioral scientists have learned a great deal about negotiation through the study of games; this knowledge can significantly help them understand the complexity of negotiation, if we keep in mind the limitations imposed by studying negotiation in this way.

"Game Theory" Games

The term "game theory" comes from the approach taken by the following form of analysis: two parties, each of whom have conflicting interests, can take action independently in choosing one of two alternatives. The outcomes or payoffs for both parties are displayed in a matrix, and represent the possible combinations of their individual choices. Two types of games have received most attention: zero-sum games (in which one party wins and the other necessarily loses) and mixed-motive or nonzero-sum games (in which the interests and outcomes of the parties are both in conflict and congruent, so that it is possible for one to win, both to win, or neither to win). Since most negotiations involve situations with mixed-motives, the nonzero-sum game has been widely used in research.

The first and probably most popular form of mixed-motive game is the "Prisoner's Dilemma," described by Luce and Raiffa (1957):

> Two suspects are taken into custody and separated. The district attorney is certain that they are guilty of a specific crime, but he does not have adequate evidence to convict them at a trial. He points out to each prisoner that each has two alternatives: to confess to the crime, or not to confess. If they both do not confess, then the district attorney states he will book them on some minor trumped-up charge such as petty larceny or illegal possession of a weapon, and they both will receive minor punishment. If they both confess they will be prosecuted, but he will recommend less than the most severe sentence; but if one confesses and the other does not, then the confessor will receive lenient treatment for turning state's evidence whereas the latter will get "the book" slapped at him. In terms of years in a penitentiary, the strategic problem might reduce to that shown in Figure 2–4.
>
> Admittedly a gloomy picture for either prisoner. The best they can hope for is three months in jail; and if things do not go well, they may spend ten years reflecting on the rewards of a life of crime (p. 95).

What are they to do? Let us begin with the assumption that the prisoners are

FIGURE 2–4

Prisoner A	Prisoner B	
	Not Confess	Confess
Not Confess	1 year each	10 years for Prisoner A 3 months for Prisoner B
Confess	3 months for Prisoner A 10 years for Prisoner B	8 years each

kept in separate cells and cannot talk to each other. Let us further assume that they will not be able to take revenge on each other after they are released.

For Prisoner A, the best alternative is to confess and hope that Prisoner B does not. However, Prisoner A probably assumes, correctly, that the other prisoner has the same information, and thinks the same way. There is a strong likelihood that Prisoner B looks at things the same way and will also confess. Then they both get eight years in jail. Prisoner A could note that if both do not confess they will each get a one-year sentence. Not the best for either as individuals, but it is the most favorable joint outcome. In fact, when either party takes a "not confess" position, he or she takes a position most favorable to the other party since the payouts for the other will be either one year or three months. A position that has considerable advantage to the other party is called a *cooperative* position, while a confess position, which may result in the other party receiving a ten-year sentence, is called *competitive*. Given this analysis, Prisoner A may conclude that Prisoner B will notice that the best joint position is for them both to "not confess" and take that position. If Prisoner A is not too *imaginative*, he or she may act at this point. But if he or she has some imagination (and perhaps a tinge of paranoia), there may be a further thought. "Suppose Prisoner B suspects I will think this way and is selfish and confesses, getting a three-month sentence while I get ten years?" All sorts of questions follow. "How imaginative is Prisoner B? How trustworthy? How trustworthy does Prisoner B think I am?"

These and other issues are raised by this simulation. The underlying issues of trust, honesty, cooperation, and competition are consistently raised in actual negotiations. How people respond to these issues depends in part on how they see the situation. If the parties see their interests as different, conflicting or divergent, they are likely to see evidence of dishonesty and deception in the actions of the other, and act as if the other party was not trustworthy. They may follow a line of thinking somewhat like this: "I don't trust him (or her). If he says A, he probably really intends B, but since he may be smarter than I think he is, he may anticipate that I will see through his lies and hence manipulate me, so I had better . . . " This line of thinking can go through several more iterations, getting the person so confused that he is not sure what he is doing. If the parties see their interests as the same (convergent), they are more likely to accept what the other says, especially if the first statements made seem reliable or are supported by later ones.

Let us look at some of the major factors that influence cooperation among people playing the Prisoners' Dilemma game:

1. *How parties see their goals and interests*. One way to affect the amount of cooperation displayed in the Prisoners' Dilemma game is to shape the players' motivation in the game. For simplicity, let us assume that we can shape this motivation through the kind of instructions we give the players. When participants are told that they are in a competitive situation and are to play the game to get a better score (i.e., shorter sentence) than their opponent, they almost always end up in the situation where they both confess and both get an eight-year sentence. When participants are told that they are in a cooperative situation where they are to work together (against the District Attorney), they generally both settle on the "not confess" position. When they were told to do the best they can for themselves, an individualistic position with no reference to beating or helping the other party, the outcomes are less heavily weighted toward the "confess-confess" position (Deutsch, 1958; Scodel, Minas, Ratoosh, and Lipetz, 1959).

2. *Length of interaction*. If the basic Prisoners' Dilemma game is played once, players choose an action and the game is over. Negotiation, however, frequently takes place through interaction over a longer period of time. To make gaming interaction more like real negotiations, game situations have been varied in a number of ways so that the parties win (or lose) points rather than acquiring prison terms. This permits repeated decisions or rounds of decisions, which, in turn, permits parties to be affected by and respond to each other's choices. A simple illustration of this is a game between two parties, A and B, who can take either of two actions, Low and High. Their payouts for each combination of choices are shown in Figure 2–5, and their pattern of choices for 11 rounds is shown in Figure 2–6.

   In this situation, parties typically develop a pattern of becoming more cooperative (i.e., choosing actions that will get the greatest joint return). That seems understandable since they quickly learn that the other party can cause them harm if they do not cooperate. What is surprising is that after a time, one of the parties is frequently tempted to take an action that maximizes his return even though it costs the other dearly, as when B chooses Low on round six (Figure 2–6). Further, having done it once, B is likely to continue the competitive behavior, perhaps on the belief that A will look upon this as a mistake and not change his previously established pattern, and hence continue to let

---

FIGURE 2–5

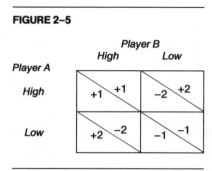

himself be exploited. Actually A responds quickly by taking a Low action; things frequently stabilize at Low-Low with both parties losing one point on each of the following rounds. Occasionally, pairs get out of this joint-loss situation when one of them takes a heroic action, choosing High and holding that position for two or more rounds. By this action, he hopes to indicate to the other party that he is willing to accept a loss in order to get them both to a winning position. Hopefully, the other party will respond; once cooperative choices are restored, they tend to be continued.

3. *Other party's strategy*. Another possible response to the heroic action by a party in choosing High for several rounds is that the other party will see this as naive or stupid and choose Low in order to exploit the situation. It is therefore sensible for the first party to set a limit to how long he or she is going to be the hero. In general, the most rewarding strategy is for one party to mirror choices the other party makes, as A did in round seven by mirroring B's Low choice on round six (Meeker and Shure, 1969). This,

---

FIGURE 2–6

	A			B	
Round	Choice	Payout		Choice	Payout
1	High	−2		Low	+2
2	Low	−1		Low	−1
3	High	+1		High	+1
4	High	+1		High	+1
5	High	+1		High	+1
6	High	−2		Low	+2
7	Low	−1		Low	−1
8	Low	−1		Low	−1
9	High	−2		Low	+2
10	Low	−1		Low	−1
11	Low	−1		Low	−1

---

as we have seen, can lead to a cooperative but sub-optimal joint solution. To break out of that cycle requires heroic action by one party, but that action should be guided by what is learned about the other party's strategy.

4. *Overt communication*. In the previous illustration, the parties are communicating through their actions. If communication is also spoken or written, it can help the parties get people more quickly into a cooperative position. Hence, after round 6, if A had said, "If you continue to choose Low, I also will choose Low, but if you switch to High, I will do the same," B would most likely have chosen to cooperate. This illustration contains both a promise and a threat. It has been found that communications containing promises are more effective than those containing threats (Tedeschi, Bonoma, and Brown, 1971).

5. *Personality characteristics of each decision maker*. Sometimes the strategy chosen reflects rational processes; at other times it reflects an individual's personality. Some people are strongly inclined to compete and others to cooperate. Some are basically suspicious and distrustful, likely to think others are the same, and hence act accordingly (Loomis, 1959; Deutsch, 1960). Dogmatic people—those who are impatient with ambiguity and delay—make fewer concessions, take longer to reach an agreement and make fewer agreements than less dogmatic people (Druckman, 1967). In general, however, the evidence of what influence personality has on bargaining is not clear since the results of one study often contradict others (Hermann and Kogan, 1977; Terhune, 1970). See Chapter 11 for a complete review.

How realistic is the situation constructed by the Prisoner's Dilemma game? Consider the problem of small businessmen—barbers, for example. Like most business people, they want to maximize their income and therefore need to be open for business when customers want service. However, barbers are also human and would like to work five rather than six or possibly even seven days a week. Fortunately for them, most states prohibit businesses to be open on Sunday. Saturday is likely to be a very busy day, while Monday is frequently a very slow day. A barber can easily reason that the few customers that want a haircut on Monday can easily wait until later in the week. The rub is that if one barber closes on Monday and others do not, the barber who closes may lose his customers to someone open on Mondays. Hence for barbers to get Monday off, all the barbers in the area need to cooperate. On the other hand, if all the barbers but one close, that one could have a very large volume on Monday. Hence, this situation has the same mixed motive structure as the PD game.

Another illustration of this process is provided by the advertising problem confronting Goodyear and Sears several years ago in their promotion of radial tires. Radial tires are mostly bought by men, and Goodyear decided

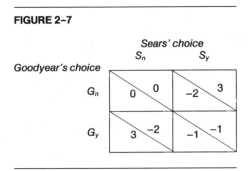

FIGURE 2–7

that the best way to reach the male audience was to advertise during football games. For several years, only Goodyear advertised during the games; then Sears also began advertising during the Monday night NFL games. After two years during which both companies advertised heavily, Goodyear dropped out (Marecki, 1974).

How can we account for the behavior of these companies? Using a Prisoners' Dilemma form of analysis, we can get some insight into the relationship between the two companies and the reasons why one was almost sure to drop out. Each year both Sears and Goodyear had to decide whether or not to advertise (Y=yes; N=no) with the NFL games. Some hypothetical payoffs reflecting income changes and costs are shown in Figure 2–7. If there is more than one advertiser in a short period like a game, brand recognition gets lost, although the overall demand for radial tires is increased. If each company adopts the strategy that gives it the greatest advantage—(G_y, S_n)—they both end up losing. In fact, when everything is considered they are both better off if neither advertises—(G_n S_n). Given that the law would stand in the way of Goodyear and Sears talking directly about a settlement, they would move toward an arrangement through a series of moves, as in the classic Prisoner's Dilemma game.

Distribution Games

In this second type of game, players are given some pot of points or money to distribute between themselves through negotiation. The objective is to get as much as possible above a minimum necessary level, or to share. They "win" not on the absolute amount of money or points, but how far the settlement is above their minimum level. The players do not know each other's minimum levels. This simulation requires the players to interact in order to reach an agreement. Pressure on players can be created by setting a deadline for reaching agreement, or by subtracting an amount from each party's profit for every minute (or some other unit of time) that passes (Kelley, Beckman, and Fisher, 1967; Fischer, 1970). Research shows that under pressure, parties become more interested in reaching *any* agreement than in the details of the agreement itself. One consequence is that the parties spend less time exchanging information about each other's minimum level, and hence reduce the information available to determine their maximum joint return. Richer and more complex than the Prisoner's Dilemma game, distribution games permit an exchange of offers even though there is a limited range of what can be offered (Morley and Stephenson, 1977).

For example, suppose the U.S. Army announces that it wishes to purchase 500,000 new sets of boots for soldiers. Two major shoe manufacturing companies are eager to get a share of the business. Each knows it cannot handle the entire order itself, but wants to get at least 40 percent of the business (200,000 pairs) and could handle approximately 75 percent of the order (375,000 pairs). If the two companies had lots of time to spare, they probably could exchange a great deal of information to determine what share each company should get in order to maximize cost effectiveness, minimize waste, and maximize efficiency and profits. However, if they have little or no time, they are likely to simply get as much of the business as they can, and hence operate in ways that will be less than efficient or effective.

Games of Economic Exchange

Games of economic exchange (Rapoport, 1963; Seigel and Fouraker, 1960; Kelley and Schenitzki, 1972) are more realistic in that they involve "buyers" and "sellers" who work to reach an agreement on price and quantity under conditions where their individual profits vary with the prices and quantities agreed on. (See Figure 2–3.) The profit table of each negotiator is unknown to the other party. The structure of the two profit tables creates conditions of both competition and cooperation. In addition, the profit tables are constructed so that there are usually several possible price-quantity arrangements that give one player the same profit, but disadvantage the other player. In some games, there is a joint maximum return (as in Figure 2–3) while in others there is not a joint maximum return.

For example, suppose a purchaser (a manufacturing company) is buying 55-gallon drums of chemicals from a supplier. The chemical decays rapidly, and so the purchaser can't buy a large amount and store it in his warehouse; instead, he has to determine (as closely as possible) how much he is going to use in a given month. If he buys too much, it decays and goes bad; if he buys too little, he runs out and his manufacturing process stops. Similarly, the chemical company makes the most money when the chemical is made in certain size batches; if too little is made, the process is very costly, while if too much is made, it is wasteful of energy. Hence, in order to "optimize," both buyer and seller must try to coordinate the amount purchased and manufactured. This kind of problem would be a game of economic exchange.

Role-Playing Games

In the games discussed earlier, we were employing different payoff structures and different communication structures. Participants acted as they chose, given the situation with which they were faced. In role-playing games, however, participants enact a particular role in the game such as a union negotiator, a manager negotiating with another manager, or a job seeker. To make the role more realistic, there are usually several issues in the bargaining mix, each one with a number of possible outcome points. Hence a union-management negotiation will probably involve not only wages and hours but also working conditions, cost of living increases, contract length, and other issues. Often the "game" is structured so there are a number of settlement points on each of these issues, each of which has different payouts for opposing parties.

As a research tool, the problem with role-playing games is that participants are not acting as themselves, but as a person in a role. Hence, performance, in part, is influenced by participants' "acting ability" and ability to understand how an experienced person in that role would perform (Etizioni, 1969; Nicholson, 1970). As a training tool, the fact that participants have to take a perspective and argue that point of view can be very helpful. Participants are forced to ask, "What would I want if I were in this position; what would I be after? How would the arguments and proposals of the other party look?" Both managers and union officials may role play a labor negotiation in which they take the position of the other party. Managers playing the role of a union negotiator who has to be reelected by his constituency may see things from the union negotiator's perspective for the first time. Similarly, a union official who is role playing a manager, may see that some of the arguments the union was planning to use, while convincing to union members, are largely irrelevant to managers; and that the union's position ignores issues that management is really concerned about.

SUMMARY

One point stressed in this chapter and the preceeding one is that negotiation is a complex process. We have at least two basic levels of issues to take into account. One is the structure of the situation. A person in negotiation has outcomes he would like to attain. Perhaps we can get what we really want, but perhaps we will have to settle for something less. While we may adjust what we will accept, there are limits beyond which we will not go. The limits, however, are not always obvious. Some take almost the form of absolutes, i.e., "I will not kill. I will not steal." Others are more relative, i.e., "What are my alternatives given this situation?" In negotiation, a party (either an individual or a group) needs to prioritize the outcomes they desire and the actions (strategies) they can employ to get them.

The outcomes of one party are linked to those of the other party by the structure of the bargaining relationship. How outcomes are linked will have a fundamental influence on how negotiations will proceed. To choose among possible outcomes requires that each party has a way of sorting them out and determining what actions or strategies will get the best outcome.

The second set of elements that needs to be considered is the effort a party may take to change the structural elements of the negotiation, i.e., the outcomes or actions available or preferences that the parties have. Here, again, we need to consider two sets of issues. The first involves what economists call preference functions, or what we will identify as the subjective nature of preferred outcomes and the meanings we attach to them. Is an offered price on a house a good one? There is no absolute answer. It depends upon how much we like a house, how much money we have, how committed we are to buying a house for less than our brother did, and a host of other considerations. In this chapter, we recognized that individual personalities, values, social relationships, immediate needs, etc., influence negotiations by actively shaping their outcome preferences. To negotiate, we need to know what the other party is really after, and what his outcome preferences are. To do that effectively, we need data about outcomes, and information about the negotiator's personality, values, social environment, etc.

The second set of forces that affect outcomes are ways in which parties in negotiation attempt to change each other's goals, perceptions, or subjective evaluations. This involves processes of communication, persuasion, and power in interpersonal relations. These processes occur in a context, the dominant characteristic of which is interdependence. Being interdependent, parties act knowing that they will impact on the other and that the way in which they impact on the other will eventually affect themselves. Hence, people engage in anticipatory decision making. Given the interdependence, and the different (often conflicting) goals of negotiators, trust and distrust can become a significant factor in shaping both the nature of the interaction and the negotiation process.

All of these elements are background components to a negotiation. In the context of the background, negotiation is the process of getting two people

FIGURE 2–8

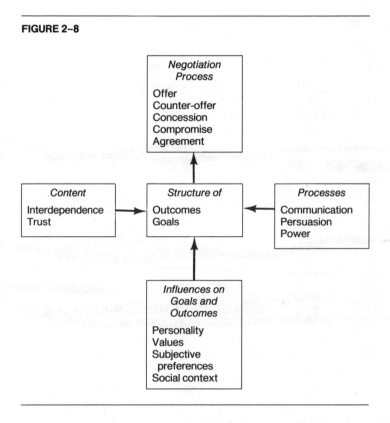

from the point where they have a problem or conflict to the point where they have a solution or agreement. Negotiation is a process of offer and counter-offer, of concession and compromise through which the parties reach a point that both understand is the best (for them) that can be achieved. While this process is the heart of negotiation, it cannot be understood and cannot be successfully carried out without a knowledge of how these other factors affect the process (Figure 2–8). The remainder of this book will be devoted to describing the likely impact of each of these factors.

3

Planning and Preparation

In this chapter, we address the collection of activities that a negotiator must attend to before actually sitting down to bargain. We believe effective planning and preparation to be the most critical elements in achieving negotiation objectives. With effective planning and goal setting, most negotiators can achieve their objectives; without it, results occur more by chance than by what the negotiator does.

To plan effectively, a negotiator must be able to anticipate the major events that will occur during negotiation, and prepare in advance for them. First, the negotiator must know what he/she wants (*goals*). Second, since there are usually several goals, they will have to be put into some order of preference (*priority*). Third, if there is more than one issue, combine them into various groupings (*packages*) that can be presented and discussed with the other party. If there are more than a few items to be discussed, prepare an *agenda* and some *administrative plan* for carrying out the negotiations: time allocated to discuss various issues, when to take breaks, etc. How the negotiator proceeds depends not only on personal goals and needs but also on the opponent's goals and needs. Hence, the negotiator will also want information about the opponent. If the negotiator is the representative of others, he will need information about his constituency and what they want.

In order to plan effectively, a negotiator must:

1. *Understand the nature of the conflict*. Conflicts, like the people who have them, vary in size and seriousness, in their characteristics, and in the

parties included. Sometimes, all of these aspects of a conflict are obvious. Sometimes, they are not; and, sometimes, what appears to be a serious conflict is not one at all. We will begin by clarifying ways to understand and diagnose the conflict that has created the need to negotiate.

2. *Specify our goals and objectives.* This includes stating all the goals that are to be achieved in the negotiation, determining their priority, and evaluating the possible trade-offs among them. Goals may also include intangibles, such as maintaining a certain precedent or getting an agreement that is satisfactory to both sides.

3. *Clarify how to manage the negotiation process* with the opponent in order to attain goals. This stage involves understanding the conflict, the possible areas of cooperation, ways to establish trust, and the issues to be negotiated. To plan for the negotiation process, negotiators must:

    a. *Identify the issues to negotiate.* Issues are those matters of substance that will be discussed with the opponent. Some issues are simple, such as the price to be paid for a used car. Other issues are more complex, such as the vast array of economic data used to justify a union's wage demands. Some issues are subtle, such as the precise wording of a clause in an agreement—a matter on which both parties are in essential agreement, but which could easily erupt into conflict if care is not taken. For example, both union and management may understand the need for, and agree to, a clause that permits reductions in the workforce in a plant; however, given the sensitivity of the matter, conflict could easily arise if the parties do not agree how it will be accomplished.

    b. *Prioritize the issues.* Which ones are more or less important, more or less critical to achieve at this time?

    c. *Develop a desirable package among the important issues, or better yet develop several alternative packages.* To discuss each issue separately may lead to sub-optimal results; we may confuse our opponent on what is really important to us, or we may miss attractive opportunities for solutions because we failed to really understand how the issues fit together.

    d. *Establish an agenda.* Write a procedure for discussing those issues which are important, and the order in which they will be discussed. This is the first step in carrying out any strategy for negotiating with the other party.

4. *Understand the opponent.* We must get information on the opponent's goals—what is most important to them. There are also two other pieces of background information that will be of great importance:

    a. *The opponent's current resources and needs.* A full diagnosis of the opponent might include their financial condition, immediate and pressing problems, and information on the opponent's operating environment (social, political, business or personal). Thus if we are buying a car, it would help to know if the dealer is overstocked, if it is close to the end of his fiscal year, if he has a quota to meet and is pressed to make a few last quick sales. In negotiating a labor contract, management might want to know if the union leadership is in a weak political position with the rank and file. Conversely, the union might want to know whether the local management is under severe pressure to not experience any interruption of production. Such information provides insight into the other side's unstated goals, and helps to clarify how they will interpret our behavior.

b. *The history of the opponent's bargaining behavior.* How people have acted in the past is usually a good indicator of how they are likely to behave in the future. Therefore, a careful assessment of the opponent's negotiating history gives us valuable information on how to prepare for them.

These are the topics that should receive primary attention in planning for negotiation, and they are the ones we will address in this chapter. First, let us briefly discuss the importance of planning, and the different types of planning that need to occur.

THE IMPORTANCE OF PLANNING

Preparation and planning are the most important parts of negotiation. On the surface, the drama and theatrics of face-to-face confrontation can easily create the impression that success lies in persuasiveness, eloquence, clever maneuvers, and occasional histrionics. While these tactics make the process interesting (and at times even entertaining), the foundations for success are the preparation and planning that take place prior to actual negotiation.

Regrettably, systematic planning is not something that most of us do willingly. Managers, for example, are much more inclined to take action than to spend time reflecting about conditions and planning (Mintzberg, 1973). Admittedly, time constraints and work pressures make it difficult for managers to feel they have the time to do adequate planning. For many of us, (textbook authors included), planning is a little boring and tedious, and therefore, easily put off in favor of "getting into the action" quickly. In addition to devoting insufficient time to planning, negotiators frequently fail because of several weaknesses in their planning process:

1. Negotiators fail to set clear objectives. Hence, when something has to give, or the other party makes a proposal that rearranges the elements in a settlement, they are not in a position to evaluate the new possibilities quickly and accurately. As a result, they may agree to something which

they later find is *not* to their advantage, or, since they are confused, they may become defensive and delay the process, causing the other party to lose patience.

2. If a negotiator has not done his homework, he may not be able to formulate convincing arguments, to understand the strengths and weaknesses of his position, or to recognize weaknesses in the opponent's arguments.

3. If a negotiator fails to consider the opponent's needs, or how the opponent has bargained in the past, a negotiator is unable to estimate what the other party really wants. He will not know his opponent's strategy and tactics, or where he needs to hold firm and where he can bend.

4. A negotiator cannot depend upon simply being quick and clever during the give and take of negotiation. When the opponent plans to win by stalling and delaying, holding to a position in order to wear the opponent down, other approaches are necessary. Being glib and eloquent in presenting one's position is not helpful when the other party assails our position as illegal or as economic nonsense.

TYPES OF PLANNING

In negotiation, three types of planning are helpful: strategic, tactical, and administrative.

The objective of *strategic planning* is to define long-range goals, and to position oneself in order to achieve these long-range goals. In corporations, the function of strategic planning is to optimize the organization's future position on a designated set of specified objectives. In negotiation, strategic planning is devoted to defining a "future" state or set of objectives that the parties would like to attain, as well as the process to be pursued to secure those objectives. For example, in a labor negotiation, management will want to define what its goals are for wage compensation, job security, etc. in the next three-year contract (or even over the next ten years), and develop a plan for achieving those goals. In negotiating a land sale for a shopping plaza, the buyer will want to define what he wants to pay, what the terms will be, and whether he wants to be in a position to acquire land for future expansion. He also will want to determine the primary strategy for achieving that goal.

Tactical planning is the process of developing short-range tactics and plans to achieve long-range objectives. Hence, in the previous labor negotiation, the management may decide that part of their goal is to avoid strikes. They decide to propose in the first session that should future negotiations not be completed by the contract expiration date, the current contract will automatically be extended until a new one is reached. This step is a tactical part of a long-range strategic goal of eliminating strikes (and reducing the ways the union could put pressure on management during negotiations). In the real estate negotiation, the buyer may ask for a "right of first refusal" on adjacent land, as part of his long-range strategic objective to expand if the shopping center is successful.

Administrative planning is the process by which both manpower and information are marshalled to make the negotiation proceed smoothly. Administrative planning includes organizing the negotiating team; i.e., designating the functions team members will perform, how jobs will be coordinated, how information will be disseminated, when the team will caucus or recess, etc. It also involves planning how to get information about the other party's goals, needs, and negotiating history.

These three categories of planning, while easy to separate in the abstract, tend to overlap in practice. Nonetheless, the categories are useful to remind us that good planning needs to consider both long-run (strategic) and short-run (tactical) objectives and plans. They also remind us that the processes of setting and attaining objectives also needs to be planned. If we only plan tactically (for the short run), we can win in the short run but ultimately lose because our final goal is not clear. Similarly, if we keep our eye exclusively on the "big picture" (our goals), we may trip and fall over obstacles right in front of us and never achieve these goals. We not only need to determine where we want to go and how we want to get there (strategic and tactical planning) but we also need to consider the means (administrative planning) by which we make the journey. Good administrative planning helps us accomplish what we set out to do, and we can achieve our goals because we have also organized ourselves to insure success.

In this chapter, we give primary attention to the data-gathering aspects of strategic and tactical planning, with specific attention to the nature of the conflict that has led the parties to negotiation. In Chapters 4, 5, and 6, we explore in depth the strategy and tactics of cooperative and competitive negotiations. In Chapters 7 through 11, we describe the major components of the processes by which negotiation is carried out. Finally, in Chapter 12, we return to the structure of the conflict itself and examine ways to change the nature of the conflict to facilitate more successful negotiations.

UNDERSTANDING THE NATURE OF THE PARTIES' CONFLICT

Outcomes As a Source of Conflict

In Chapter 2, we discussed the ways that different kinds of interdependence can lead to conflict. When the parties are *contriently interdependent* (win/lose or zero-sum) in their orientation, their goals are mutually exclusive. Party A knows that if she achieves her goal, Party B will not be able to achieve his. In contrast, when goals are *promotively interdependent* (win/win or nonzero-sum), Party A can achieve her goal only if Party B achieves his. And a final point to consider, if the parties are independent—one party's goal is totally separate from the other's—little or no conflict is likely to occur.

In actuality, these distinctions are seldom so clear and simple. For example, parties can be contriently interdependent, and one party's success can impede the other but not necessarily preclude the other's success, i.e., the goals are not entirely tied. Similarly, when parties are promotively interdependent, both parties can "win," but one can win much more than the other, or one can contribute more to the joint effort than the other. These differences are far from being a subtle distinction; when conflict arises over interdependence, these are the central issues over which negotiation occurs.

Consider the case where Jones (J) and Leominster (L) decide to open a real estate business together (J&L Properties). Both have previously worked independently for five years as real estate brokers. Each is going to put $10,000 into the business to get it started. Both will work full time in the business; however, J will get 60 per cent of the profits and L 40 percent. The rationale for this distribution is that J has lived in the area for some years and has developed contacts and visibility that will be useful in generating new business, while L is new to the community.

In this case, J and L are promotively interdependent; their outcomes, however, are not equal. It can be argued that the unequal distribution of outcomes is justified by the unequal inputs; namely, J contributes contacts and a known name in the community, while L cannot offer this. Two aspects of this situation can create conflict. First, is J's extra contribution worth the 20 percent difference in outcomes? The answer to that question is not so clear and simple. If J's contacts and visibility bring in a lot of business when the new firm opens it's doors, his contribution is certainly valuable. However, if L gets established in the community over the next 2 years and is able to bring in as much business as J, should J's contribution still be valued as significantly different? Therefore, the second conflictful aspect of this situation is the time perspective within which the interdependence is viewed. As we might expect, J will argue for a "short-term" viewpoint (favoring his current knowledge) and L will argue for a long-term viewpoint (favoring changes to be expected in the future). We can expect conflict until these different time perspectives are recognized and addressed.

Means of Obtaining Outcomes As a Source of Conflict

Conflict can arise not only over the substantive issues, such as who will invest in or collect from the relationship, but also over means: how the relationship will be conducted or how the output will be produced. In the J&L Properties example, Leominster may want to extensively advertise property available to be sold and announce properties that have been sold. In contrast, Jones may feel that advertising completed sales will not be well received in the community, and that advertisements of available properties should be few and modest. If their negotiations address not only how outcomes will be distributed but also the means by which the joint return is to be produced, the procedures themselves will become a source of conflict. In fact, conflict over means can frequently be more bitter and difficult to handle than conflicts over outcomes and contributions (Festinger, Hoffman and Lawrence, 1954).

Negotiating Procedures As a Source of Conflict

Finally, conflict can develop during negotiations from the procedures the parties will use to resolve their dispute. L may insist that the negotiations be done in a long continuous session, while J may feel that he operates better when he works in short, frequent meetings. J may also have some concerns about L's management style, growing from some rumors about L's behavior in his last business deal. Hence, there are issues of trust between the parties, and differences over how to proceed in negotiation. The issues of conflict here are *not* substantive (distribution of outcomes and/or contributions, or the means to convert one into the other), but procedural, i.e., concerned with the process of negotiation and factors which influence that process.

Tangible and Intangible Factors As a Source of Conflict

Thus far, we have been describing the "tangible" sources of conflict—the issues at stake (percent of profit a person will receive), and the way these issues will be resolved (i.e., whether negotiations will be conducted in one session or several sessions). But as we indicated in Chapter 1, intangibles must also be addressed in the bargaining process. Intangible factors may play a major role in the negotiations. Some people approach negotiation as a competitive exercise; regardless of the tangible objectives, they are going to "win." Winning may mean getting exactly what they initially asked for, not giving any concessions to the other party, beating the opponent, or doing as well or better than someone else in a similar negotiation. In buying a car, some people are determined to get a fixed amount on their trade-in; others are determined to buy the car for a better price than their brother (friend, cousin) paid. Other people are so uncomfortable with bargaining that their major psychological objective is to "get it over with" as soon as possible. Still others may feel they are in an "underdog" or low status position and there-fore push for a very favorable outcome to prove they are "equal" to their opponent. All of these goals are very important to negotiators; in many cases, bargainers are willing to make major sacrifices on other issues and priorities to achieve psychological goals.

The intangible goals in negotiation are the set of psychological objectives held by the negotiator. Intangibles are likely to be present in most negotia-tions, and we need to be alert to their existence and impact. There can be intangibles associated with outcomes (e.g., winning, getting a "good" settlement) and negotiation procedure (e.g., a "fair" and "reasonable" process). While intangibles actively influence the course of negotiations, they are seldom stated openly on the agenda. This failure to clearly define intangibles and their priorities can create several major problems. First, negotiating parties are frequently unaware of the intangibles that govern their opponent's behavior; therefore, they often have difficulty finding out "what is really important" to their opponent, or in understanding why an opponent values certain goals and outcomes. Second, negotiators may in fact be unaware of the relative importance of intangibles in relation to their own negotiating objectives. The process of preparation for negotiation must include an inventory of intangible goals as well as tangibles, so that intangible objectives are achieved. Finally, a negotiator who does not understand the impact of his own intangibles will not understand the psychological process that determines whether or not he is "satisfied" with a deal. Intangibles work as perceptual "filters" through which we view and evaluate the tangibles. For example, if "winning" is important, then we should define in our own mind what group of outcomes we will treat as "winning," and what group of outcomes will be treated as "not winning." (Note that "not winning" may or may not be equivalent to "losing"; other categories may also exist like "settling fairly," "doing o.k.," etc.). Since intangibles color, shape, and even distort our feelings of satisfaction and dissatisfaction with deals, it becomes very important to understand *which* intangibles are affecting us (and our opponents), and how much influence they have over our feelings of satisfaction and accomplishment. A simple cost/benefit analysis will not do the trick, either in determining our own satisfaction or the satisfaction of others. We must try to understand how we (and the opponent) will view and evaluate that package of economic outcomes.

Intangible issues can rarely be negotiated directly (Gallo, 1966). Even if a negotiator says, "my major goal is to win," our first question to him is usually, "what do you mean?"—i.e, "what kind of outcomes would you define as 'winning?'" It is thus helpful to recast intangible issues into more concrete terms. For many intangibles, we use symbols as a measure. For example, suppose that "equality" (equal power and status with an opponent) is the most important intangible for a negotiator. It is impossible to demonstrate status per se; instead, we define status equality (or differences) in terms of certain symbols that we all accept as evidence of equal or unequal status. Thus equal status may be built into negotiations by insuring that each party has equal control over where the negotiations will occur, has equal influence over the agenda of issues to be discussed, is allowed equal access to information sources, etc. Even "symbolic" elements such as the shape of the negotiation table can affect a party's feeling of equality, and hence satisfaction with the negotiation process (see Chapter 6 for a fuller treatment of the role played by spatial arrangements in negotiation).

When status and power are unequal, their role as an intangible is to dramatically affect satisfaction with negotiation procedure and outcomes; perceived satisfaction will be significantly different if one is in the high or low status position. The low status party is usually more concerned with equality. Thus nations newly emerging from colonial status, newly formed unions, minority groups moving into the mainstream of society, young people dealing with elders, or newly hired managers dealing with established peers may be particularly concerned that the *symbolic* possession of equal status is clearly established and demonstrated. Hence, they may be particularly concerned, as the Vietnamese were in the Paris peace talks, with the shape of the negotiating table, the use of names and titles, and explicit influence over the agenda of issues. At the same time, the high status party may view his opponent's demands for these things as trivial, extreme or unfair, since he either does not want to give up the advantages that may be afforded by his high status or he sees that status difference as irrelevant to the negotiation (Deutsch and Krauss, 1962). In such situations, the high status party may view the other's demands as time-wasting and nonsensical, and actively try to block them, or engage in "demonstrative non-deference" (Harsanyi, 1966), i.e., a refusal to acknowledge the other's bid for equality and refuse to treat him as a legitimate negotiating partner.

Frequently the ultimate result is that, while parties may achieve the psychological intangibles, they do so at the expense of protracted conflict and undesirable or hollow settlements on tangibles. This is not to say that intangibles are not worth fighting for. Issues of principle, avoiding bad precedents, maintaining a reputation, wanting to win, and wanting to look strong or avoid looking weak have been the major intangible factors in great and even heroic conflicts between individuals, organizations, and nations. However, these same intangible factors have contributed to costly strikes, painful divorces, and bloody, senseless wars, *even when both parties recognized* that it was not in their best interest to fight for intangibles at all costs. The point is *not* that intangibles are not worth trading against tangible returns; it is that each party needs to recognize the intangible elements, at least on their own side, and be willing to "trade off" tangible and intangible items to insure a satisfactory settlement.

The History of the Parties' Relationship As a Source of Conflict

There are times when individuals meet once, negotiate, reach a settlement, and then go their own ways, never to meet again. We all have had this experience, as when we buy a used desk at a yard sale or a clock at a country auction. But a great deal of our negotiating is in the context of a continuing relationship with people we know—friends, parents and children, business associates. The way that these negotiations evolved in the past, and the deals that were made (or not made) will greatly affect the way we approach the current negotiations. Moreover, in many cases, we are negotiating on behalf of some well-established group or organization, and while *we* may be new to the situation, the group or organization may have been in existence for a long time. As a result, negotiators may "inherit" (with or without their knowledge) the reputations and legacy of their predecessors. If I walk into an automobile dealership and negotiate with a salesperson I have not met before, I am a first-time experience for him (and he for me); he has to assess me and how the negotiation may proceed based on what he learns directly from me. However, if I have dealt with this agency in the past and have had a good relationship, that salesperson benefits from my past experience since I will be expecting this negotiation to be as successful as the previous ones. More precisely, I look at that salesperson as a representative of the dealership, and *assume* that we both will take this reputation into account; thus the history of my relationship with the firm becomes relevant. Needless to say, the same is true of two organizations negotiating through representatives. The negotiators may be strangers to each other, but will expect themselves and the other to act within the history of the relationship between their organizations, whether that relationship has been good or bad. In a labor relationship, there is usually a long and complex history of events between the union and management group that shapes current expectations about negotiations. In the purchasing and acquisition of materials, a relationship between supplier and customer has developed and been maintained over a long period of time in order to insure that materials consistently meet requirements of price, quality, delivery, etc. In financial matters, firms develop long-term relationships with banks, both because loans are long-term contracts and because lending money is risky and people are more inclined to take risks with those they know and trust. Finally, units within larger organizations build long-term relations. Joint exchanges occur regularly between sales and manufacturing, between marketing and engineering, and between R&D and accounting. These exchanges continually identify, clarify, and resolve disputes and disagreements, and usually occur by each unit sending its representative to a meeting or "negotiation."

The history of the relationship between the parties "sets the tone" for current relations. An upcoming negotiation between union and management cannot help but be influenced by how both groups view their past negotiations. If one side sees the other as having "won" or gained unfair advantage in previous negotiations, the "loser" is going to be wary at least, and perhaps angry and out for revenge. Even if the last negotiation was amicable, but the relations since then have been plagued with grievances, complaints, wildcat strikes, and slowdowns, the upcoming negotiations are likely to be tense, cautious, and mistrustful. Particularly when the past relationships have been strained, the situation can be very frustrating for a new representative and lead to a destructive conflict cycle. If representatives of the other organization feel their group was treated unfairly in the past, they are very likely to accuse the current representative of being dishonest, untrustworthy, deceitful, or worse. Even if they do not directly accuse the new negotiator of such things, they are likely to act as if they were true by acting suspiciously, demanding "hard proof," and being unfriendly. Regrettably, such accusations, even if conveyed by attitude and expression rather than by words, tend to become self-fulfilling prophecies. The accuser has a tendency to notice only those aspects of the other's behavior which confirm his/her suspicions. The accused may feel that, since he/she has already been tried and found guilty, he/she might as well act accordingly. Even if the accused does not act that way, it is hard not to "take these things personally" and to become angry or defensive.

It is very valuable to know in advance that the other party may be entering negotiations with a particular set of historical experiences; this permits us to anticipate how the other might view and interpret events, and to psychologically and factually prepare ourselves. At this point, a negotiator can also make an explicit choice to *maintain* or *change* the climate for the upcoming negotiations. A desire to maintain the current climate—tense and mistrustful or cooperative and pleasant—will lead to a conscious and explicit selection of strategy and tactics that will maintain the relationship in its current state. Conversely, a decision to change the relationship will be reflected in a different set of strategic and tactical choices. Those wishing to *change* the relationship will probably be more aware of their strategy and explicit in setting their objectives, since they will first have to assess whether change is feasible and likely. Unfortunately, one cannot just demand that the other party behave more cooperatively or be more trustworthy. The choice of strategy and tactics that will produce the desired change must be explicit and a conscious one. (We review a variety of tactics in Chapter 12.) Conversely, the desire to maintain present relations is usually *not* explicitly identified and, therefore, may *not* be adequately reflected in the strategies and tactics chosen, which may *not* yield the desired results. Negotiators can, in effect, become careless in their management of satisfactory long-term relationships, and, in doing so, endanger them by neglect.

GOAL SETTING—DECIDING WHAT IS WANTED

When entering a bargaining relationship, we all have some idea of what we would like the outcome to be. We often say, "I'd be happy . . . " and then state something we would really like to have, e.g. " . . . if I could buy this car at a price so that the loan payment wouldn't use up all of my paycheck." Not bad as a wish, but not too good as a goal for negotiation. First, therefore, goals are not wishes, especially in negotiation. Second, our goal is linked to the other's goal; the linking relationship between the two parties' goals defines an *issue* to be settled. My goal is to get the car cheaply, the dealer's goal is to sell it at the highest price, and thus the "issue" is the price I will pay for the car. Third, there are boundaries, or limits to what our goals can be. If what we want exceeds these limits, i.e., what the other party is capable of or willing to give, we must either change our goals or leave the negotiating situation. We have to define targets that are attainable. Fourth, goals have to be concrete or specific, and preferably measurable. The less concrete and measurable they are, the harder it is to communicate to the other party what we want, understand what he/she wants, and to determine whether a particular outcome satisfies his/her goals. To want "a price on a car so that the loan payment does not use all of the paycheck" is not very clear. Are we talking about every week's paycheck, or only one check a month? All of a paycheck, or about 50 percent, or perhaps even 25 percent? We can't negotiate well by talking about portions of paychecks. Instead we have to determine how much money we can comfortably take from our paychecks at present interest rates, add to that what we have available for a down payment, and be able to talk in terms of what we actually will pay every week or month. Even this figure is not totally clear. Is this number the largest amount we think we can possibly pay? Is it the amount we could pay with little or no inconvenience? Or is it the amount we arrived at after recalling that one shouldn't pay more than a stated amount (say 15 percent) of one's salary for automobiles? Which of these criteria should we use? The answer is that all three are probably important, for different reasons, and defining them is essential to effective planning.

THE BASIC STRUCTURE OF A BARGAINING RELATIONSHIP

As we said earlier, when entering a negotiation, we usually have some idea of what we would like the outcome to be—"I would be happy if . . . ." In bargaining terminology, we call this the *target point*; it is the point at which a negotiator says he/she would be satisfied with the deal (Walton and McKersie, 1965). Target points are the settlements that negotiators "aim for" in negotiation; in the terminology we introduced in Chapter 2, they are the point where the CL and O converge.

We also know that the other party wants a different outcome—a higher price, or to pay a lower price. As a result, we recognize that we are not going to be able to get our preferred outcome. How much higher (beyond our goal) will we go on the price we pay for a car? If we are selling our house, how much lower (beyond our goal) will we go on the price we accept for our house? What is the point beyond which we will *not* go—beyond which there is no further point in negotiating because "we can't pay more?" This is our *resistance point*. Resistance points are often set quickly and impulsively, but they very quickly become real. *Establishing a resistance point is one of the*

FIGURE 3–1a
Example of a Positive Settlement Range

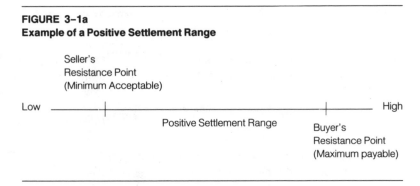

Seller's
Resistance Point
(Minimum Acceptable)

Low ————————|————————————————————————————|———— High

Positive Settlement Range

Buyer's
Resistance Point
(Maximum payable)

most important elements in planning for negotiation. Without a resistance point, negotiators can get caught up in the rush and confusion of a negotiation. As a result, they can be swept past "the point where they would not ordinarily go." All of us have been caught up in the excitement of a "going out of business" sale, an auction, or the tension involved in spending lots of money on a high priced item. Later, we regret having paid too much, or lament that we panicked and accepted too little. The clearer we are in advance about our resistance point, the less likely we are to get "caught up in the excitement" or persuaded to pay a price that we regret later (Richardson, 1977).

Settlement Range

The target and the resistance points define a range of acceptable outcomes for a negotiation. The target point defines success; the resistance

FIGURE 3–1b
Example of a Negative Settlement Range

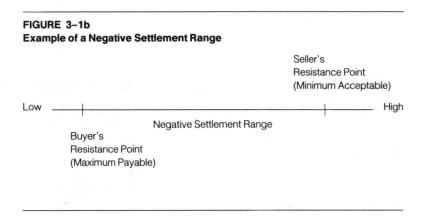

Seller's
Resistance Point
(Minimum Acceptable)

Low ————|————————————————————————————|———— High

Negative Settlement Range

Buyer's
Resistance Point
(Maximum Payable)

point defines minimum acceptability. The area between these points is defined as the settlement range. It is within this range that a negotiator expects to have most of his/her discussion with the other party.

A positive settlement range exists when the seller's resistance point is below the buyer's resistance point, for example, when the lowest wage a union will accept is below the highest wage an employer is willing to pay (see Figure 3–1a). A negative settlement range exists when the seller's resistance point is higher than the resistance point of the buyer; in this situation, no agreement is possible (Figure 3–1b).

Negotiation is the process of establishing an agreement somewhere between the two resistance points within a positive settlement range. Each party can be expected to try to reach a settlement as close to the *other* party's resistance point as possible. This objective is obvious, but not always easy to accomplish. First, each party willingly discloses his target point, but both parties will work hard to conceal their resistance point. Second, each usually attempts to convince the other party that his resistance point is close to, if not identical to, his target point. If party A knows B's resistance point, the logical strategy is for A to insist that B's resistance point is also A's own resistance point. By doing this, he thereby hopes to attain the largest part of the settlement range for himself. Finally, while neither party may want the other to know his resistance point, either is at a considerable advantage if he can convince the opponent that his resistance point is very close to his target point—closer than it really is. Consequently, along with tactics designed to conceal the actual resistance point, parties often deliberately create the illusion that they have very little room for movement from their target to their resistance point.

This is a major paradox for most negotiators to unravel. If both parties are successful in convincing the other that their resistance points are close to their target points, a negative settlement range may appear to exist. At the same time, since each side probably knows that the other party is probably trying to conceal his own real resistance point, both parties may be blinded to the fact that a real negative bargaining range exists. As we shall point out, negotiators can engage in a variety of tactics to determine whether their positions are compatible or not, and whether room exists for a mutually acceptable agreement.

In summary, a key part of the planning process is to be able to specifically define an objective (target point) and a "bottom line" (resistance point). These two points will define the feasible settlement range, and allow a negotiator to determine whether any particular offer or proposed settlement falls inside or outside of that range. Points must be set for each issue at stake in negotiation. The process of negotiation will concentrate on determining the parameters and limits of one's own settlement range and the opponent's settlement range on each issue, to explore areas of possible overlap and hence mutual agreement.

DEFINING THE ISSUES

The next step in negotiation planning is to define the issues to be deliberated. Our analysis of the conflict situation will usually help to identify the issues at stake. From what has been previously said, we know that there is usually one major issue (e.g., price, rate, central problem), and several minor issues in any negotiation. Hence, in buying a house, we would immediately recognize that the central issues would be price, date of sale, and availability. We might quickly identify other issues, such as appliances to be included, and (if it has an oil burner) amount of oil left in the tank. During the purchase process, our lawyer, banker or real estate agent might hand us a list of other things to consider: taxes to pay, "escrow" amounts for undiscovered problems, or a written statement that the house must be "broom clean" before we move into it. Note that it does not take long to generate a fairly detailed list. In addition, our list was helped by receiving advice from those people (lawyers, agents, etc.) who have negotiated similar deals. In any negotiation, a complete list of the issues at stake is best derived from:

- An analysis of the conflict problem.
- Our own past experience in similar conflicts.
- Gathering information through research (e.g., reading a book on "how to buy a house") and consultation with experts.
- Studying precedents and legal frameworks (e.g., laws and bank regulations regarding real estate purchases).
- Brainstorming on what might be an "ideal" settlement for us.
- Defining the intangible goals which are most important for us.

Before considering ways to manage our list of issues, a word of caution is necessary. First, note that we have intentionally included intangible issues on the list. As we pointed out earlier, since parties often treat intangibles as highly important goals in negotiation, it is therefore important for us to be explicit about them in our planning process. As we shall see when we discuss the processes of packaging and tradeoffs among issues, intangibles will have a major influence at this stage. Second, note that we used a simple, traditional example here—the purchase of a house. Many negotiations that occur which fall outside of traditional contracts and agreements, and in these situations, the definition of the issues may be much more complex and elusive. For example, suppose a manager gets signals from his boss that his performance is not up to par; yet every time he tries to confront his boss to discuss the problem and get a realistic performance appraisal, his boss won't talk directly about the problem (which raises the manager's anxiety even further). While the conflict in this situation is evident, the "issues" are elusive and complex. Such situations will require careful thought and planning by the manager to get his boss to directly confront and discuss the problem.

Collecting Issues and Defining the Agenda

The next step in planning is to assemble all of the issues we have defined. We will call this list of issues the *negotiating agenda*, and the combination agendas from each side in the negotiation will be called the *bargaining mix*. In generating an extensive list of issues, we may wonder if we are piling our plate too high and endangering the negotiation by being too greedy, asking for too much. This is a sensible consideration. However, presuming that all the issues are real, it often turns out that a longer list of issues makes success more, rather than less, likely. Suppose, for example, that the other party feels she cannot sell the house below a certain price—perhaps she is buying another house and needs to get her price on this one. However, she is willing to "throw in" the dollar value of the oil in the fuel tank, clean and repaint the house, and leave some attractive and expensive drapes. Having these additional items thrown in, we may feel that the earlier price, which was too high, is now acceptable. Larger bargaining mixes give us more possible components and arrangements for settlement, thus increasing the likelihood that a particular package will meet our needs and, therefore, increasing the likelihood of a successful settlement (Rubin and Brown, 1975). At the same time, larger bargaining mixes usually lengthen negotiations, since there are more possible combinations of issues to be considered. However, the length and complexity of a negotiation results from the difficulty of defining the issues, the complexity of the issues, or the incompatability of positions that people take on issues, more often simply the number of issues on the agenda.

Once issues are assembled on an agenda, the next step for the negotiator is to prioritize them. By assigning priorities to issues, the negotiator must do the following two things:

- Determine which of the issues are "primary"—most important—vs. those lower in importance. In our house example, the buyer may determine that the price is the most important issue, while closing date is secondary.

- Determine whether the issues are connected (linked together) or separate. If they are separate, they can be easily added or subtracted; if connected, then settlement on one will be related to settlement on the others. In some cases, the "connectedness" of issues is somewhat arbitrary; e.g., if all of the issues in a house sale can be translated into dollar value (the cost of drapes, oil in the tank, appliances, etc.), then everything can be seen as connected. The negotiator must decide whether issues are truly connected—e.g., that the price he will pay for the house is dependent on what the bank will loan him—as opposed to simply being connected in his own mind for the sake of achieving a good settlement.

CONSULTING WITH OTHERS

Having determined the relative primacy and importance of the issues, and having evaluated whether the issues are separate or linked together, negotiators at this stage frequently consult with others, particularly if they represent some group or organization. This may seem premature to new negotiators, but interestingly enough, considerable negotiation may occur before the formal deliberations with the opponent actually begin. A negotiator cannot determine the issues on an agenda by herself or himself. Consultation (and often negotiation) with two other groups is required—the constituency and the opponent. If a negotiator is bargaining on behalf of others (a company, union, department, club, family, etc.), they must be consulted to ensure inclusion of their concerns and understanding of their priorities. In the house buying illustration, let us assume the husband is doing the negotiating. If he fails to consider his wife's concerns about the condition in which the house is left, or his children's concern that the move not be timed during the school year, he will have a serious problem. A negotiator who is representing a constituency is accountable to that constituency; he must include their wishes in his proposals and either obtain those wishes for them through negotiation or be able to explain why their desires were not met. When negotiating for a large constituency, e.g., an entire company or union or a community, the process of consulting with the constituency can be elaborate and exhaustive. Richardson (1977) describes management's preparation for labor negotiations as consulting with both "internal sources"—talking to supervisors, rank and file members, and noting patterns of conflict or grievances during the term of the current agreement—and "external sources," e.g., monitoring agreements by other similar groups in the community, industry, etc. Many times the negotiator also recognizes that the constituency's "wish list" is unrealistic and unobtainable; negotiators will then be required to negotiate with their constituency over what goes on the agenda. (We explore this problem in Chapter 9.)

Consultation with "the opponent" prior to negotiation is all too frequently neglected. A bargainer may draw up a firm list of issues and establish priorities well before meeting with the opponent. This can be a valuable process because it forces the bargainer to think through his or her position. But there is also potential risk in this process: the bargainer may define new issues to bring to the table that his opponent is unprepared to discuss, or may define priorities that are grossly unrealistic to achieve. Negotiators do not welcome "off the wall" surprises or being embarrassed by being unprepared to discuss an issue. Moreover, most experienced negotiators will ask for a recess to get information and prepare themselves on the new issue, thus creating needless delays. The opponent may even refuse to include the new item on the agenda because they haven't had time to prepare or fear they cannot discuss it adequately. If they try to discuss the new items without preparation, they will be at a disadvantage. If they include the new items, they will have to consider what this new issue means for the goals they already had planned to achieve, thereby rearranging priorities and trade-offs. If the opponent has a constituency and they have already been consulted, the opponent may not want to go back to reopen consultations. For this reason, professional negotiators—labor negotiators, diplomats, etc.—often exchange (and negotiate) lists of issues (demands) to reach agreement about what will be discussed (the agenda) during future negotiations. The lists and the agenda should include intangible as well as tangible items, although some intangible items may not be revealed. If a party wants to get "the best possible price," and that means something equivalent to or better than the market price, it may be useful to state this clearly so that the opponent knows the market price is an issue. If "the best possible price" means the lowest price in the industry, so that the bargainer can feel he is making the best deal in the industry, this intangible goal is better kept secret.

KNOWING OUR LIMITS

What happens if the other party in a negotiation refuses to accept some proposed items for the agenda, or he states issues in such a way that they are far below our resistance point? The proposer can reassess these issues and decide how important they really are. Can they be dropped? Can they be postponed and taken up at a later negotiation? If the answer is "no," then the other has to consider whether he wants to alter his own position. The decision may well be, "no negotiation." Is that bad? Not necessarily. We can look at this situation as the first test of the question, "Is a negotiated agreement feasible?" The answer here is, "no." To avoid starting down a path that could only lead to failure is not all bad. At this point, the parties are opting for alternatives to a negotiated settlement—i.e., continuation of the status quo, finding another buyer or seller or finding a third party to bring them together—rather than trying to work out an agreement which neither party will like. At this point, it is clear that one party feels that inclusion or exclusion of the specific issue at stake is important enough to abort negotiations, and that is important information for both to consider.

DEVELOPING SUPPORTING
ARGUMENTS—RESEARCH

In negotiation, we are trying to convince the other party that our position is correct and that their position is not. The single most powerful aspect of actual negotiations is to be able to clearly argue a case and to marshall ample supporting facts and arguments. The second most powerful aspect is to be able to refute the opponent's argument with counter arguments. We will consider more about how to structure ideas into arguments and how to present them in Chapters 7 and 8. For now, we are concerned with the research necessary to assemble facts and arguments about the issues on the agenda.

Because of the breadth and diversity of issues that can be included in negotiations, it is not possible to be specific about the wide variety of different procedures that can be used to assemble information. There are, however, some good general guides that can be used on any issue. A negotiator can ask:

1. What are the "facts" that support my point of view?

2. Who may I consult or talk with who can help me elaborate or clarify "the facts?" What records, files, or data sources exist that support my arguments?

3. Have others negotiated these issues under similar circumstances? Can I consult those negotiators to determine what major arguments were used there, which ones were powerful, and which ones were weak? If the settlement was favorable to my viewpoint, what can I learn from that?

4. What is the other person's point of view likely to be? What arguments is he likely to make? How can I refute his arguments, expose flaws in his logic, undermine his confidence in his position?

5. How can I develop and present the "facts" so they are most convincing? What visual aids, pictures, charts, graphs, etc. can be helpful or make the best case?

PRIORITIZING—DEFINING THE RELATIVE IMPORTANCE OF ISSUES

The third step in negotiation planning is to determine the relative importance of issues. Being clear which issues are most important and which are least important not only speeds up the negotiating process but leads to more satisfactory settlements. Once negotiation begins, parties can easily be swept up in the onrush of information, arguments, offers, counter-offers, trade-offs, and concessions. For those who are not sure in advance of what they want, it is easy to lose perspective and to agree to suboptimal settlements, or to get hung up on points that are relatively unimportant. When a negotiator is not clear on priorities, then he will be more likely to accept those points aggressively argued by his opponent. After all, if the other party thinks they are important, maybe they are.

Priorities can be set a number of ways. One simple way is for the negotiator to rank order them: "What is most important?", "What is second most important?", "What is least important?" An even simpler process is to group issues into categories of "high," "medium," or "low" importance. When the negotiator represents a constituency, it is important to involve that group in setting priorities. They may be asked to rank or categorize issues themselves before discussion. However, other methods are also possible. The number of times various issues are mentioned in meetings, reports, or preparation sessions often reveals what is really on people's minds. Attitudes of people in key leadership positions may be attended to more than those of other members. There are other methods, such as the "nominal group technique" (Delbecq, Van de Ven, and Gustafson, 1975) in which group's preferences can be ordered without the individuals actually coming together face-to-face.

Setting priorities on the intangible issues is also very important. Because they are intangible, they are harder to discuss and rank order; yet their subjective nature may also mean that they are high priority items, factors that will be actively used to determine whether the party is getting a "fair" or "acceptable" deal. It is easy for such issues to get pushed aside in favor of matters that people can "sink their teeth into," like price. Yet more than one negotiator has received a rude shock when his/her constituency has rejected a settlement, largely because the proposed settlement ignored the intangibles or left them unsatisfied in the final agreement.

MANAGING THE GOAL SETTING PROCESS

Where to Start—Optimistic, Realistic, or Pessimistic?

Earlier in this chapter, we stated that negotiators need to set a target point (the point where a negotiator would like to achieve a settlement) and a resistance point (the least acceptable settlement point, or the point below which a negotiator is likely to reject a deal). To this we would add a third point: the best deal a negotiator could possibly hope to assume. We will call this the *optimistic settlement point*, and it is often the same as the negotiator's *asking price* or *opening bid*. The target point will be synonymous with what a negotiator realistically expects to achieve, and the resistance point will be the most pessimistic (but acceptable settlement) that is achievable. In goal setting, the question arises, where should planning start: at the most optimistic point, the likely target point, or the most pessimistic resistance point?

From a technical perspective, it really does not matter where one starts. From a personal perspective, however, it may be another matter. Bargainers who know that they tend to be too optimistic about what can be achieved may want to start with a "wish list," and then systematically moderate these demands by defining what is more realistic and what is minimally acceptable. Conversely, those who know themselves to be pessimistic about negotiated outcomes may want to start with identifying the minimum and then widen the range by defining what is realistic and then brainstorming about what might be optimistically possible. Finally, bargainers who know themselves to be "realistic" may want to start with a definition of "realistic" objectives and then push to the upper and lower boundaries. Hence, the important point to remember about goal setting is that the negotiator ought to start where he/she feels most comfortable, or where research and preparation has clearly dictated certain starting points, target points or bottom lines. Start with what is easy and most comfortable, and then deliberately and systematically move into the area which you might be inclined to avoid or think about carelessly. The second advantage to this process is that by defining one point and then determining the other two, the negotiator will be better prepared to frame offers and evaluate counter-offers.

Goal Setting Forces "Positive Thinking" about Objectives

In approaching negotiation, one becomes aware of the other party—how they will behave, what they will demand, and how the bargainer feels about dealing with them. However, many negotiators devote too much attention to the other party; they spend too much time trying to figure out what the other side is going to want, how to meet those demands, etc. If a negotiator totally focuses his attention on his opponent, and not on himself, he may plan his entire strategy as a reaction to the other's anticipated conduct. Reactive strategies are likely to make negotiators feel threatened and defensive, and make them less flexible and less creative in their negotiating behavior. In contrast, one's own goals create an alternative view for the bargainer. By defining realistic, optimistic, and pessimistic goals for oneself, negotiators become more aware of the range of possible outcomes. This permits them to be more flexible in what they will accept, and creates better conditions for arriving at a mutually satisfactory outcome. Active goal setting can thus create a positive climate for negotiation.

Goal Setting Usually Requires Anticipation of "Packaging"

Since most negotiators have a mix of bargaining objectives, they must consider the best way to achieve satisfaction on these multiple issues. Should they be negotiated one at a time? Should we try to get the best settlement on each issue separately? For reasons we shall explore in later chapters, negotiators are much more likely to "package" multiple issues together than to try to maximize goals on single issues. Negotiators propose settlements that will help us achieve realistic or optimistic targets on issues that are important to us. We balance these by settling at the more pessimistic point on things less important to us. Hence, in the real estate transaction mentioned earlier, the seller may propose a firm but high price because he needs the cash now; however, he may be willing to paint and clean the place for the buyer because he can do that with his own labor. If the buyer feels that adding a few thousand more dollars to the mortgage will not affect his monthly payment too much, (compared to being able to move into the house with a minimum of hassle), they are likely to have an agreement.

When evaluating a bargaining mix with a number of different issues, most people find that exploring different ways to combine goals into a package is a great help in evaluating outcomes. Different packages will have different outcomes for a negotiator, and each of these has to be evaluated. Some negotiators evaluate "packages" the same way we advocated evaluating individual issues; namely, define optimistic, realistic, and pessimistic packages to permit better planning of the negotiation, and to be in a better position to evaluate the other party's proposals (Rubin and Brown, 1975).

Goal Setting Requires an Understanding of Trade-offs and Throwaways

Our discussion of packaging surfaces another possible problem. What do we do if the other party proposes a package that puts issues A, B, and C in our optimistic range, item D in the realistic range, E at the pessimistic point, and does not even mention item F, which is part of our bargaining mix? Is item F a "throwaway" item that we can ignore? If it is not a throwaway item, is it relatively unimportant and worth giving up in order to lock-in agreement on A, B, and C in the optimal range? Suppose the other party had given us two proposed packages, the one described above and a second one which placed items A and E in the optimistic range, items B and F in the realistic range, and C at the pessimistic point. Would the first or the second package be more attractive?

To evaluate these questions, a negotiator needs to have some idea of what each item in a bargaining mix is worth in terms of the other items or issues. The bargainer needs some way of establishing trade-offs. This is sometimes not an easy thing to do, since different items or issues will be of different value to the bargainer and will often be measured in different terms. For example, in negotiating a lease for a retail store, the bargaining mix usually contains such items as the monthly rent, the duration of the lease, options to renew the lease, cancellation penalties, restrictions on signs and decorations, and others. For a renter, differences in the monthly rent of $25 or $50 may be relatively unimportant, while permission to put up a particular sign may be deemed vital. Hence, the renter would be willing to trade off larger rent for a larger sign. In addition, some issues in the mix may be intangibles, and can only be assessed subjectively; how do we compare or equate the value of a $25/month increase in rent to the value of "getting a fair deal on this lease"?

Even though a common dimension may be lacking for comparing issues in the bargaining mix, or for comparing tangibles with intangibles, many negotiators have found it convenient to place all items on some common dimension. The premise is that, even if the fit is not too good, any guide is better than none. Translating every issue into dollars is one way to facilitate these comparisons. Thus, in the store rental situation, the renter might estimate what the large sign will mean in attracting more customers and, hence, more revenue and then compare that with the larger rent. In labor relations, most issues included in the bargaining mix are converted into dollar equivalents for easier comparison and evaluation of alternative packages. However, not everything is easy to convert into money terms. For example, in a retail store lease, what is the value to either party of a sub-lease provision? Either party may have strong and clear feelings about the desirability of such a provision, but probably will not have much idea of what it is worth in economic terms. Negotiators who want an alternative scale for comparing items and issues have used a point or "utility scale." Instead of assigning dollar values to items, bargainers assign "utility points" to each item to indicate its relative importance to them. If the lessee feels that the success of his/her new store is uncertain, (they might go out of business and have to sub-lease the store for the remainder of the lease term), he may give the sublease change a value of 50 points. If he feels very sure that it will be a long-term success, he may give the clause a value of 5 points. Needless to say, such points are only meaningful to the party (and constituency) establishing them, and only as long as the points reflect the basic values and goals of the negotiator in that situation. As long as they do, such scales are a useful tool for planning and assessing offers and counter-offers.

ANALYZING THE OTHER PARTY

In the first two stages of the planning process—understanding the conflict and setting one's own goals—we made repeated references to the other party and the negotiator's past history with them. Gathering information about the other party is a critical step in preparing for negotiation. What information do we need about the other party to effectively prepare?

Who Is the Opponent and What Are His/Her Characteristics?

A negotiator will learn much about the other party at the negotiating table. However, as much information as possible should be gathered in advance through research and homework. That data which is most relevant will depend on the negotiation and who the opponent is. The other party's business history might be studied. An analysis of the opponent's previous negotiations, successful and otherwise, will provide useful clues. Financial data might be obtained through channels such as Dun and Bradstreet, financial statements, newspapers, files, company biographies, stock reports, and public records of legal judgments. Sometimes, much can be learned simply by visiting with an opponent, or talking to his/her friends and peers and asking questions. Another way to learn is to ask questions of people who have done business with the opponent (Calero and Oskam, 1983).

Obviously, the magnitude of the issues and the length of the relationship with the other party will influence the depth to which we probe to get information. While it does take some time and effort to get information, the results are usually more than worth the investment. It is all too easy to neglect this step, which is unfortunate considering how much valuable information can be gathered through a few simple phone calls or a visit.

What Are the Opponent's Reputation and Style?

As noted earlier, the other party's past negotiating behavior is a good indication of how they will behave in the future. Hence, even if a bargainer has had no previous experience with the other person, talking to those who have dealt with him/her in the past can be very valuable.

However, there is also a potential danger in drawing conclusions from this information. Assuming that the other party will act in the future the way they have been described as acting in the past is just that—an assumption. People can and do act differently in different circumstances at different times. While their past behavior is a reasonable starting point to make assumptions, people *do* change over time.

As Chester Karrass (1974) notes:

> Assumptions are potential hurdles that can move us in the wrong direction . . . . The reality of negotiation is that we must and should make assumptions about the opposing party . . . . The important thing to remember is that your assumptions are just that. They are no better than poorly educated guesses at best. Don't fall in love with your assumptions. Check them out; they are neither right nor wrong until proven so (p. 11).

Our impression of an opponent's reputation may be based upon:

- How the opponent's predecessors have negotiated with us in the past,
- How the opponent has negotiated with us in the past, either in the same or in different contexts, and
- How the opponent has negotiated with others in the past.

These different bases for our assumptions have different degrees of relevance and, therefore, different degrees of reliability for predicting future behavior. We can use the information to prepare, to alert ourselves about what *might* happen; but we should also act with caution, and actively look for new information that *confirms* or *denies* the validity of our assumption. There is always the danger that invalid assumptions will lead a negotiator into unfortunate "self-fulfilling prophecies." A negotiator who assumes the other party is going to be demanding and aggressive may decide that "the best defense is a good offense" and open with aggressive demands and belligerent behavior. The other party may take this all in stride; but he or she may also decide that they have to reply in kind, even though they initially intended to be cooperative. Of course, when the other party does fight back, the first negotiator finds his/her initial assumptions confirmed. If this initial misunderstanding is all that occurs, the problem may be recognized and corrected before it escalates. However, particularly when negotiations occur in longstanding relationships, our expectations can trigger an escalating cycle of competitive mistrust and hostility. These cycles are common in relationships between nations and between labor and management groups (see Lewicki and Alderfer, 1973).

What Are the Opponent's Objectives?

People are often surprised at others' descriptions and perceptions of our initial interests and objectives. They often think stereotypically about the other party's interests and goals; they use their own goals and values as a guide and assume that others are like themselves and want similar things. A manager who is always after a bigger paycheck is usually surprised that some of his workers are more interested in a challenging job than they are in maximizing their salary.

How do we size up our opponent's goals? While we may speculate about another's goals and objectives, most of us do not systematically gather information. One of the best ways to get this information is from the other party directly. Because information about the other party's goals are so important to strategy formulation of both parties, professional negotiators will often exchange information about goals or initial proposals days or even weeks before negotiations begin. (We will discuss this process further in Chapters 4 and 5.)

What Are the Opponent's Needs?

Perhaps more important than knowing the opponent's objectives is knowing the opponent's needs. There are a variety of ways to define "needs"; one well-known approach is based upon the work of Maslow (1954) and his hierarchical categories of needs. Each of these categories and some specific examples are listed below:

1.	Physiological (homeostatic) needs	Biological drives and urges— hunger, sex, thirst, chemical balance
2.	Safety and security needs	Self-protection, self-preservation, job and personal security
3.	Love and belonging needs	Affection from others, belonging, friendship
4.	Esteem needs	Freedom and independence, pride, competence, positive self-regard
5.	Needs for self-actualization	Personal growth maximizing one's human potential, creativity
6.	Needs to know and understand	Mastery, know the unknown
7.	Aesthetic needs	Appreciation of beauty, order balance, aesthetic values

More recently, Nierenberg (1973) has suggested that the Maslow typology can also be used to describe the differing needs of negotiators. Nierenberg's approach helps us recognize that needs are often the driving forces that underlie a negotiator's "position" on issues. Moreover, understanding an opponent's needs may help us predict the intangibles which will be most important to him. Thus, a negotiator motivated by security will be searching for an agreement that guarantees safety, protection, assurances; one motivated by esteem probably seeks recognition or a positive public image. Learning about the opponent's needs will help us to predict what is most likely to satisfy him or her.

Research on the opponent may also help to reveal something about his or her motives. If the opponent has a strong need for achievement, (evidenced by setting and accomplishing goals through his/her own efforts) then he or she is likely to respond to goal and target setting to meet these objectives. If the other party has a high need for affiliation, he or she is likely to want to develop and maintain supportive relationships with others (e.g., the opponent or the constituency), and not do anything to endanger it. If the other party has a high need for power, he or she is likely to want to control the situation, the other bargainer, and the negotiated outcomes. High-power needs can lead to conflict in negotiations, particularly when the other negotiator has similar high-power needs (McClelland, 1975). We shall discuss these needs and their impact further in Chapters 10 and 11.

In summary, when preparing for negotiations, we can get several levels of information about the other party: the "surface" level that describes their desired outcomes, the subsurface level of their self-image, feelings of self-worth, and social position and the deeper level that reveals basic patterns of motivation. All can be helpful in preparing for and carrying out a plan for negotiation.

What Authority Does the Other Party Have To Make Decisions?

When negotiators represent others, their power to make agreements may be limited; in fact, their ability to carry out negotiations may be restricted in many ways. Sometimes negotiators are told by their constituency that they cannot make any agreements; often they can only pass on proposals from the constituency, or collect information and take it back to their superiors.

There are many reasons for limiting a negotiator's authority. He cannot be "won over" by a persuasive opponent and commit his constituency to something that is not wanted. He cannot give out sensitive information carelessly. While these limitations may actually be helpful to a negotiator, they can also be frustrating. The opponent will often ask, "Why should I talk with this person, if he/she cannot make a decision and may not even be well informed about what the other side wants?" Negotiation under these circumstances can seem an exercise in futility. When a negotiator always has to "check things out" with those he or she represents, the other party may refuse to continue until "someone who has the power to answer questions and make decisions" is brought to the table. Negotiating teams, therefore, should think seriously about whether they send a negotiator to the table who has limited authority. While that person will not be able to make unauthorized decisions, their limited authority may frustrate an opponent and create an unproductive tension in the negotiating relationship. (See Chapter 9.)

SUMMARY

As we have stressed repeatedly in this chapter, we believe planning to be the most important activity in negotiation. A negotiator who has carefully planned has made efforts to do the following:

- Understand the nature of the present conflict situation.
- Clarify the goals and objectives that he would like to achieve.
- Understand the key issues at stake in the negotiation, and be able to specify which ones are important to him, what he would like to achieve, and what will be minimally acceptable.
- Understand the fundamental predictability of the negotiation process, so that he can strategically plan how to achieve his goals and objectives.
- Understand his opponent, and how his opponent's personality, history and negotiating style is likely to affect his own strategy.

If a negotiator is able to consider and evaluate each of these factors, we believe that he/she has a significant competitive advantage over his opponent and a clear sense of direction on how to proceed. This sense of direction and the confidence derived from it will be the singlemost important factor in affecting negotiating outcomes.

In order to assist negotiators in preparing for their upcoming negotiations, we have devoted the remainder of this summary to a questionnaire-format outline of key planning points. We encourage the reader to make copies of this form and use them in your own negotiation planning process.

PLANNING GUIDE FOR NEGOTIATIONS

The Conflict Relationship

1. What kind of a conflict situation is this going to be (i.e., does it appear possible for all parties to achieve their goals)?

2. What has been the nature of my relationship with my opponent in the past, and how will that affect the current negotiations?

Goals

3. What are my TANGIBLE goals in the negotiation?

4. What are my INTANGIBLE goals in the negotiation?

5. Which TANGIBLE goals are most important?

6. Which INTANGIBLE goals are most important?

7. What is the relative importance of the intangibles to the tangibles?

8. Given what I know about the opponent, what are the major tangible and intangible issues likely to be?

Issues

9. Given my goals, assumptions and information about the opponent, what would be the best deal I could expect from this negotiation?

10. What would be a "fair and reasonable" deal?

11. What would be a minimally acceptable deal?

12. What will be the major issues at stake in this negotiation?

13. Do I have all the information I need on each of these issues? If not, where can I get it?

14. Which issues have higher priority for me? Which have lower priority?

15. Which issues are linked together and therefore easy to package?

Analysis of Opponent

16. What are my opponent's major characteristics?

17. What are my opponent's reputation and style?

18. Is there anything I need to learn about my opponent or (his) position to make this negotiation successful?

Competitive Advantages

19. What are the strongest points in my arguments? What advantages do I have going for me?

20. What are the strongest points in my opponent's arguments? What will be the advantages he has going for him?

21. What is the weakest point in my position?

22. What is the weakest point in his position?

23. At this point, do I want to modify my goals or objectives in any way?

The Negotiating Process

24. What kind of a strategy do I want to use in this negotiation? (Primarily, what kind of tone or climate do I want to set?)

25. What do I have to get the other negotiator to do to make this strategy work?

26. If my strategy or plan does not work, what is my fall-back option?

27. What are the most important items for me in setting the agenda with my opponent, e.g., time limits, how and which items are discussed (such as procedural rules)?

CHECK BACK OVER THIS QUESTIONNAIRE TO REVIEW YOUR ASSESSMENT. THEN, . . . GOOD NEGOTIATING!

4

Strategy and Tactics of Distributive Bargaining

One of the authors of this book (whom we'll call L) recently purchased a house after deciding 18 months earlier to move closer to his place of work. Following the decision to move, he put his house on the market and started to look for a new one. Fourteen months later he had neither sold his house nor found another that he wanted to buy. Then he received the first offer to buy his house and, after a brief negotiation, settled on the price that he wanted. Because he had not yet found a house to buy, he postponed the closing of the sale for six months to get additional time to look. The buyer (A) had not been happy to wait that long because of the inconvenience and the difficulty of getting banks to agree to an interest rate for so long in advance. The price and other things had to be adjusted so buyer A would accept this postponement, and it was clear that the buyer would be very happy if the date could be moved closer.

At that time, there were relatively few houses on the market in the area L wanted, and none of them was satisfactory. He jokingly said that unless something new came on the market, he would be sleeping in a tent on the town common when the leaves turned in the fall. Two months later a house came on the market that met his requirements. The seller's (B) asking price was $145,000, which was $10,000 above what L hoped to pay but about $5,000 below what he would be willing to pay. L was conscious that the more he paid for the house, the less money would be available for making some very desirable alterations, buying draperies and some new pieces of furniture, and hiring a moving company. There were attractive drapes already

75

in B's house. She was moving to a new house; and if she could not use the drapes in the new house, they might be purchased or included with the house. The same might be true for some rugs, hall tables, and other items. L also learned that B's new home was supposed to be finished soon, about the time L was to close the sale of his present house.

THE DISTRIBUTIVE BARGAINING SITUATION

This illustration offers the basic elements of a distributive bargaining situation. Although there are a number of definitions of distributive bargaining it is perhaps most useful to define it as competitive, or win-lose, bargaining. In a distributive bargaining situation, the goals of one party and the attainment of those goals are in fundamental and direct conflict with the goals of the other party. Resources are fixed and limited, and each party wants to maximize his/her share of the resources. As a result, each party will resort to a set of strategies and tactics in order to maximize his/her share of the outcomes that are obtained. Whether or not one or both parties achieve their objectives will depend upon the strategy and tactics they employ (Walton and McKersie, 1965). Thus the situation is one of interdependence as described in Chapter 2.

To understand how the distributive bargaining process works, limit the opening example to the discussion of the house price. Several prices were mentioned: (1) the asking price, (2) the price L would like to pay for a new house, and (3) the price above which he would not spend to buy the house. These prices represent key points in the analysis of any distributive bargaining situation. L's preferred price is the *target point*. A target point is the point at which a negotiator would like to conclude negotiations—his/her optimal goal. The price beyond which L will not go is the *resistance point*. A resistance point is a negotiator's bottom line—the most one will pay, the smallest amount one will settle for and so on. Finally, the *asking price* is the price set by the seller; L might decide to counter this price with his *initial offer*—the first number he will quote to the seller. Using the house purchase as an example, we can treat the whole range of possible prices as a continuum and represent the various points along that dimension as shown in Figure 4–1.

How does L decide on his initial offer? There are many ways to answer this question, some of which were discussed in Chapter 3; but, fundamentally, L must understand something about the process of negotiation. If he opened at his target point and then had to make any concessions, he would be moving away from this price with the first concession to a price closer to his resistance point. Hence, he will likely start at a price even lower than his target point to have some room for "negotiation." At the same time, the starting point cannot be too far from the target point. If the buyer made the first offer too low, the seller might break off negotiations believing the buyer

FIGURE 4–1
The Buyer's View of the House Negotiation

	L's target point		Seller's asking price	L's resistance point
$130,000	$135,000	$140,000	$145,000	$150,000

to be unreasonable or foolish. Although judgments about first offers can often be quite complex and can have a dramatic impact on the course of negotiation, let us stay with the simple case for the moment and assume that L decided to offer $133,000 as a "reasonable" bid—less than his target point and well below his resistance point. In the meantime remember that, although this illustration concerns price, all other issues or agenda items for negotiation also have starting, target, and resistance points.

Both parties to a negotiation have starting, target, and resistance points. Starting points are usually in the opening statements each makes (i.e., the seller's listing price and the buyer's first offer). The target point is usually learned or inferred as negotiations get under way. People usually give up the margin between their target and starting points as they make concessions. The target point is something they would like to have, and moving lower than this point is usually more difficult. The resistance point, the point beyond which a person will not go or the point at which one will break off negotiations, is not known to the other party and is usually kept secret. One party may not learn the other's resistance point even after the end of a successful negotiation and will only learn it in unsuccessful negotiations when the other party breaks off negotiation.

Two parties usually have their starting and resistance points arranged in reverse order, with the resistance point being a high price for the buyer and a low price for the seller (Figure 4–1). Continuing the illustration, L would have been willing to pay up to $150,000 for the house the seller had listed for $145,000. L can speculate that the seller may be willing to accept something less than $145,000 and probably would think $143,000 a desirable (target) figure. What L does not know, but would dearly like to know, is the *lowest* figure that the seller will accept. Is it $140,000? $135,000? Let us assume it is $130,000. The seller, on the other hand, initially knows nothing of L's position but soon learns L's starting point when he offers $133,000. The seller may suspect that L's target point is not too far away (we know it was $135,000) but has no idea of L's resistance point ($150,000). This information—what is known by L or *inferred* about the seller's position—is represented in Figure 4–2.

FIGURE 4–2
The Buyer's View of the House Negotiation (Extended)

Seller's inferred resistance point	L's initial offer	L's target point	Seller's inferred target	Seller's asking price	L's resistance point
$130,000		$135,000	$140,000	$145,000	$150,000

Note: L's initial offer was $133,000.

Settlement Range

Of particular importance for us is the spread between the resistance points, called the bargaining or settlement range. In this range, the actual bargaining takes place, for anything *outside* these points will be summarily rejected by one or the other of the negotiators. When the buyer's resistance is above the seller's—he is minimally willing to pay more than she is minimally willing to sell for, as is true in the house example—there is a *positive* bargaining range. When the reverse is true—the seller's resistance point is above the buyer's, and the buyer simply won't pay more than the seller will minimally accept—there is *negative* bargaining range. In the house example, if the seller would minimally accept $145,000 and the buyer could maximally afford $140,000, then a negative bargaining range exists. Negotiations that begin with a negative bargaining range are likely to stalemate. They can only be resolved if one or both parties are persuaded to change their resistance points, or someone else forces a solution upon them that neither one likes. However, since negotiators don't begin their deliberations by talking about their resistance points (they're talking initial offers and demands instead), it is often hard to know whether a positive settlement range exists until the negotiators get into the process. Only after protracted negotiations have exhausted both parties may they realize that there was no overlap in their resistance points; at that point, they will have to decide whether to end negotiations or reevaluate their resistance points, a process to be described in more detail later on.

Settlement Point

Negotiation is fundamentally the process of reaching a settlement within the bargaining range. The objective of both parties is to capture as much of the bargaining range as possible—that is, to get the settlement as close to the other party's resistance point as possible.

Both parties know that they are most certainly going to have to settle for something less than they would prefer, and it is almost certain that they hope the agreement will be somewhat better than their resistance point. These factors make it necessary for both parties to believe that the settlement point, although less desirable than they would prefer, is the best that they can get. Having each party believe that the settlement point is the best he/she can get is essential, both to have each agree on the point and to have each support and maintain the agreement after the negotiations. Parties who do not think they got the best that was possible or who believe that they "lost" all too frequently will try to get out of the agreement later or find some other ways to later recoup what they feel they missed. If L thinks he got the short end of the deal, he can make life miserable and expensive for the seller by claiming hidden damages—fixtures that were supposed to come with the house were removed by the seller, and so on. As we will point out, therefore, one of the factors that will affect satisfaction with a deal and willingness to live with the consequences is whether the parties can "get even" in the future or whether they will ever see one another again.

Bargaining Mix

In this illustration, as in almost all negotiations, there are many points or issues about which agreement is necessary: price, closing (sale) date, renovations to the house, and other items that could remain in the house (such as drapes and appliances). This package of issues for negotiation is called the *bargaining mix*. Each item in the mix can have its own starting, target, and resistance points. Some items are of obvious importance to both parties; others are of importance to only one party. Needless to say, as was pointed out in the planning chapter, it is important for negotiators to know what is important to them and to the other party.

In this example another issue that was important to both parties was the closing date on the sale—the date when the ownership of the house would actually be transferred. L learned when the seller's new house was going to be completed and anticipated that the seller would want to transfer ownership of the old house to L shortly after that point. L then requested a closing date very close to when seller B would probably want to close; thus the deal looked very attractive to the seller. As it turned out, L's closing date on his own house—his own target point—was close to this new date as well, thus making the deal attractive for both L and seller B.

FUNDAMENTAL STRATEGIES

How does the definition of these points affect a negotiator's strategy? With these points in mind, the buyer has four fundamental strategies available in a distributive bargaining situation:

1. To push for a settlement close to the seller's (as yet unknown) resistance point, thereby getting for the buyer the largest part of the settlement range by attempting to influence what solutions the seller thinks is possible. The buyer might do this by making very extreme offers and small concessions.

2. To get the seller to change her resistance point by influencing the seller's *subjective utilities,* thereby increasing the bargaining range and opening more favorable settlements to the buyer.

3. If a negative settlement range exists, to get the seller to change her resistance point, to create a positive range, or to modify one's own resistance point to create that overlap.

4. To get the other party to think that this settlement is the best that is possible—*not* that it is all one can get or that one is incapable of getting more or that the other side is winning by getting more. The distinction between a party believing that an agreement is the best possible and these other positions may *appear* subtle and semantic, but is of major importance from an emotional perspective, which is so important in getting people to agree.

In all of these strategies, the buyer is attempting to influence the seller's perceptions of what is possible through two means: (1) the exchange of information and persuasion and (2) positions and actions taken during the negotiation process itself. We will now look at each of these approaches.

DISCOVERING AND DETERMINING THE OTHER PERSON'S RESISTANCE POINT

Information is the life force of negotiation. The more one party can learn about the other's subjective utilities, resistance point, feelings of confidence, motivation, and so on, the more capable one will be in striking a favorable agreement. At the same time, there is some information about oneself that one does not want the other to have. One's real resistance point, some of the subjective utilities, confidential information about weak strategic position or emotionally depressed moods, and so on are obviously best concealed. Alternatively, there is some information one wants the other to have. Some of it is factual and correct; some of it contrived in order to lead the other to believe things that are favorable to oneself. Since each side wants to get some information and to conceal other information and knows that the other also wants to conceal and get information, communication can become complex. Information is often conveyed in a code that evolves during negotiation. People answer questions with other questions or less-than-complete answers; yet, for either side to influence the other's perceptions, they must establish some points effectively and convincingly.

INFLUENCES ON THE OTHER'S RESISTANCE POINT

Central to planning strategy and tactics for distributive bargaining is the location of the resistance point and relationship of the resistance points of the parties. The resistance point is established by the utility one expects from a particular outcome, which in turn is the product of the worth and costs of an outcome. Thus L sets a resistance point on the amount of money he would pay for a house based on the amount of money he could afford, the estimated market value or worth of the house, and how other factors in his bargaining mix might be resolved (closing date, curtains, etc.). A resistance point will also be influenced by the cost an individual attaches to delay or difficulty in negotiation or in having negotiation aborted. If L, who had set his resistance point at $150,000, were faced with the choice of paying $151,000 or living on the town common for a month, he might well have reevaluated his resistance point. Hence, in attempting to influence the other person's resistance point, one must deal with the following:

1.   The utility the other attaches to a particular outcome.

2.   The costs the other attaches to delay or difficulty in negotiations.

3.   The cost the other attaches to having the negotiations aborted.

A significant factor in shaping the other person's understanding of what is possible—and therefore his or her subjective utilities—is the other's understanding of one's situation. Therefore, in influencing the other's viewpoint, one must also deal with the other party's understanding of:

4.   One's utilities for a particular outcome.

5.   The costs one attaches to delay or difficulty in negotiation.

6.   One's cost of having the negotiations aborted.

To simplify how these elements affect the process of actually planning strategy and tactics, we will make four major propositions (refer to Walton and McKersie, 1965, pp. 59–82, for a more extensive treatment of this subject):

1.   The other party's resistance point will vary directly with her/his estimate of the cost of delay or aborting negotiations to the first party. Seeing that one *needs* a settlement quickly or is incapable of deferring a settlement, the other person has the possibility of pressing for a more advantageous outcome. Therefore, expectations will rise and he/she will set a more demanding resistance point. The more one can convince the other that the cost of delay or aborting negotiations are low for oneself, the more modest will be the other's resistance point.

2.   The other's resistance point will vary inversely with the cost to him/her of delay or aborting. The more needy the person is of a settlement, the

more modest he/she will be in setting a resistance point. Therefore, the more that one can do to convince the other that delay or aborting negotiations will be costly to that party, the more likely the other is to establish a modest resistance point. In contrast, the more viable the other's options to not settle—a BATNA, or Best Alternative to a Negotiated Agreement (Fisher and Ury, 1981)—the more that person can hold tough with a high resistance point. If negotiations are unsuccessful, then the other can move to a viable option or backup. In the earlier example, if L had known of a house to rent in the event that the deal with seller B fell through, he would not have needed to buy a house as quickly and would have been able to hold out for a price that was closer to his original target.

3. A resistance point will vary directly with the utilities that the other attaches to the outcome. Therefore, the resistance point becomes lower or more modest as the person reduces the subjective utility for that outcome. If one can convince the other party that a present negotiating position will not have the desired outcome or that the present position is not as attractive because other positions are even more attractive, then the other's resistance point will be lowered or made more modest.

4. The other's resistance point varies inversely with the perceived utility the first party attaches to an outcome. Knowing that a position is important to the opposition, one will expect resistance to giving up on that issue, and therefore less possibility of a favorable settlement in that area. As a result, expectations will be lowered to a more modest resistance point. Hence, the more one can convince the other that one values a particular outcome, the more pressure is put on the other to set a more modest resistance point.

TACTICAL TASKS

From the above assessment, four tactical tasks emerge for a negotiator:

1. Assessing the other's outcome utilities and costs of terminating negotiations.

2. Managing the other's impression of one's outcome utilities.

3. Modifying the other's perception of her/his own utilities.

4. Manipulating the actual costs of delaying or aborting negotiations.

Each of these tasks will now be described.

Assessing the Other's Outcome Utilities and Costs of Terminating Negotiations

An obvious first step is for a negotiator to get information about the other party's utilities and resistance point. Many specific things can be done in this area, but two general routes are open. One is to get more information indirectly about the background or underlying factors of an issue; the other is to get information directly from the other party about his/her utilities and resistance points.

Indirect Assessment.   As pointed out earlier, the process by which an individual sets a resistance point may be based on many factors. How do we decide, for example, how much rent or mortgage payment we can afford each month? Or how do we decide what a house is minimally or maximally worth? Certainly, there are lots of ways to go about doing this, and a great deal of information is used to set these points. The process of indirect assessment is aimed at determining what information an individual probably used to make judgments and how this information was used. For example, in labor negotiations, management can infer whether or not a union is willing to strike by how hard a union will bargain. Management decides whether or not the company can afford a strike based on size of inventories held, size of a union's strike funds, market conditions for the company's product, and the percentage of workers who are members of the union. In a real estate negotiation, how long a piece of property has been on the market, how many other potential buyers actually exist, how soon a buyer needs a place for business or living, and the financial health of the seller will be important factors. An automobile buyer might view the number of new cars in inventory on the dealer's lot, refer to newspaper articles on how automobile sales are going, or consult reference guides to find exactly what a dealer pays to acquire and prepare a new automobile.

There are a variety of sources of such information. Direct observation, readily available documents and publications, and surveys of organization members' feelings on various issues are some sources.

It is important to note, however, that these are *indirect* indicators. What these factors would mean for one person could be different for another. A large inventory of automobiles may make a dealer willing to reduce the price of an auto. However, the dealer may expect the market to change soon, may have just started a big advertising campaign that the buyer does not know about, or may see no real need to reduce prices at that time and instead intend to wait for a market upturn. Thus indirect measures are valuable as a starting point in that they may reflect a reality the other person will have to face eventually; but they are only one source of data on which to make a judgment.

Direct Assessment.   One does not usually expect *accurate* and precise information about utilities, resistance points, and exceptions from the other party. Sometimes, however, the other will give accurate information. When up to the absolute limit and requiring a settlement, the other is likely to take pains to tell the facts quite clearly. Management that believes a wage settlement above a certain point would drive the company out of business may choose to state quite directly what its absolute limit is and go to considerable lengths to explain the background factors in order to be convincing. Similarly, a house buyer may tell the seller what his/her absolute maximum price is and support this by an explanation of income and other expenses. In these instances, of course, the party revealing the information must believe that the settlement being proposed is within the settlement range.

Most of the time of course the other party is not so forthcoming and the methods chosen to get direct information are more involved. In international diplomacy various means are used to gather information illicitly. Messages are intercepted and codes broken. In labor negotiations, companies have been known to bug the meeting rooms of the union, and unions have had members collect papers from executives' wastebaskets. In real estate negotiations, sellers have entertained perspective buyers with abundant alcoholic beverages in the hope that tongues will be loosened and information will be revealed. Other approaches involve provoking the other party to an angry outburst or putting negotiators under pressure to cause them to make a slip and reveal valuable information. One party may simulate exasperation and angrily stalk out of negotiations in the hope that the other, in an effort to avoid a break, will reveal what is really wanted.

Managing the Other's Impressions of One's Outcome Utilities and Perceived Possibilities

One attempts to get information about the other party and vice versa. An obvious tactical task, therefore, is to keep the other from getting *accurate* information about one's position while simultaneously guiding the other party to form a preferred impression of one's position. One's tasks, then, are to screen actual positions and to misrepresent them as he/she would *like* the other to believe.

Screening Activities.   Generally speaking, screening activities are more important at the beginning of negotiation, and misrepresentation is useful later on. This sequence gives more time to concentrate on gathering from the other party information useful in establishing one's own resistance point and determining the best way to feed misleading information about one's own position. The simplest way to screen a position is simply to say and do as little as possible. Silence is golden in answering questions; instead, words should be spent in asking them. This reticence reduces the likelihood of slips or the presentation of clues in a dialogue that can be used by the other to draw conclusions. A look of disappointment, fidgeting with boredom, or probing with interest all can give clues about the importance of points under discussion. Concealment is the most general of screening activities.

Another approach, possible when group negotiations are carried on through a representative, is "calculated incompetence." Here, the actual negotiator is not given all the information by the represented party, making it obviously impossible for information to be leaked in any way. Instead, the negotiator is sent with the task of gathering facts and bringing them back to the group. This strategy can make negotiations more complex and tedious, and it often causes the other party to protest vigorously at the inability of a negotiator to be informed fully enough to make agreements. Lawyers, real estate agents, and investigators are frequently used by others to perform this role. Representatives may also be limited, or limit themselves, in their ability to make decisions. For example, a man buying a car may *claim* that he must consult his wife, or vice versa, before a final conclusion is reached.

When negotiation is carried on by a team—as is common in diplomacy, labor management, and many business negotiations—the inadvertent revealing of information can also be reduced by having all communication channeled through a team spokesperson. In addition to reducing the number of people who can actively reveal information, this frees the other members of the negotiating team to listen to and observe carefully what the other party is saying in order to detect as many clues and pieces of information about the other party's position as is possible.

Still another approach is to present a great many items for negotiation, only a few of which are truly important to the presenter. In this way, the other party has to gather so much information about so many different items that actually detecting which items are the really important ones becomes difficult and unlikely. This tactic is frequently called the "snow job" or "kitchen sink" in that so many demands are raised that the negotiator's real priorities are disguised (Karrass, 1974).

Direct Action to Alter Impressions.   A negotiator can take a number of actions to present facts that will enhance his/her position or the interpretations that will be drawn from the data. One of the most obvious methods is *selective presentation,* in which negotiators reveal facts that support their case or that will lead the other side to form impressions of one's resistance point or possibilities that are more favorable to the presenter than those that actually exist. Another approach is explaining or interpreting known facts to present a logical argument that shows the costs or risks to oneself were the other party's proposals implemented. An alternate is to say, "If you were in my shoes, here is the way these facts would look in light of the proposal you have presented."

These arguments are most convincing when the facts used have been acquired through a third source, since they are not seen as facts biased by a party's preferred outcome. However, even with facts that you provide, these interpretations can be helpful in managing the impression the other has of your side's preferences and priorities. It is not even necessary for the other to agree that this is the way things would look, were she/he in your position. Nor must the other agree that the facts lead to only the conclusion you have presented. As long as the other understands the possibility that you see things that way, her/his thinking will be influenced.

The *emotional reaction* given to facts, proposals, and possible outcomes and conclusions provides the other information as to what is important and significant. Disappointment or enthusiasm suggests something important is at hand, and boredom or indifference suggest triviality or unimportance. A loud, angry outburst or an eager response suggests the topic is very important and, in addition, gives it a prominence that can make it appear very significant.

The length of time and amount of detail used in presenting a point or position can also convey importance. Checking on the details the other side has presented about an item, or insisting on clarification and verification, all convey a particular impression.

Taking direct action to alter another's impression raises a number of hazards. It is one thing to select certain facts to present and to accurately emphasize or de-emphasize their importance, but it is a different matter to directly lie and fabricate. One is expected and understood; the other, even in hard-core negotiations, is resented and often angrily attacked. Between the two extremes, however, what is said and done as skillful puffery by one may be dishonest distortion to the other. (These issues are discussed in detail in the last chapter of this book.) Other problems can arise when trivial items are introduced or minor ones magnified in importance. The purpose is to conceal the truly important and to direct the other's attention away from the significant. The danger is that the other person may become aware of this maneuver and, with great fanfare, concede on the minor points, thereby gaining the right to demand equally generous concessions on the central points and thus to defeat the maneuverer at his/her own game.

Modifying the Others' Perceptions of His/Her Own Outcome Utilities and Possibilities

Altering the other's impressions of his/her own objectives may make the outcomes less attractive and/or make the cost of obtaining them appear higher. One also tries to make demands and positions appear more attractive or less unattractive to the other party.

Several approaches may be used. One approach is *interpreting for the other party* what the outcomes of that side's proposal will really be. This can be done by explaining logically how an undesirable outcome would result if the other really did get what was asked for. It may involve pointing out something that has been overlooked. For example, in union/management negotiations, management may point out that a union request for a six-hour day would, on one hand, not increase the number of employees, since it would not be worthwhile to hire people for two hours a day to make up the two hours taken from the standard eight-hour day. On the other hand, if the company were to keep production at the present level, it would be necessary to use present employees on overtime, thereby increasing the total labor cost and, subsequently, the price of the product. This rise would reduce demand for the product and, ultimately, the number of hours worked or the number of workers. Similarly, a union might point out that if the company were to win on some desired issue, the union membership would be likely to reject the agreement and also reject the present union leadership—perhaps bringing in a different union that would be much harder to deal with.

Another approach to modifying other's perceptions is through the concealment of information. Management may not reveal to the union that certain technological changes are going to lead to some jobs being eliminated, thereby reducing the likelihood that the union will introduce top security issues. A seller of real estate may not tell a perspective buyer that in three years a proposed highway will isolate property being sold from attractive portions of the city.

PRESENTATION

The above are arguments or facts that one wants to present to modify the other's perceptions. The next question is, "How can these be presented most effectively?" One way is to present things in a way that others can verify for themselves. Can the facts be substantiated independently of one's interpretation? When using this approach, there is always the danger of appearing to be patronizing and of the other party rejecting points in order not to appear inferior. Therefore, tone and tact at this point are crucial. Negotiators must also decide whether they *want* the other to verify the facts or just think them possible. If the facts have been shaded or distorted in some way, it might be better to leave the impression that although the facts are verifiable, to do so would require a lot of time and effort.

When a negotiation is conducted between representatives and the line of argument and interpretation presented by one party is somewhat sophisticated, it may be necessary to locate individuals in the other organization who can better assess what is being said. Company negotiators may go to higher union officials who may have more experience and information to draw upon and who, therefore, may be better able to understand management's argument. Diplomats may contact others in host governments besides those in the diplomatic corps in order to be able to present their points effectively to someone who understands. Another variation on this approach is for the negotiators to make their presentations to those who will be least disturbed by or alert to the proposed costs. Hence, union representatives may find a more receptive audience to their proposals on seniority provisions among the management team who come from the personnel department than from those who come from the production units, and they may find the opposite reaction when proposing the easing of discipline and firing procedures.

Manipulating the Actual Costs of Delay or Termination of Negotiation

As noted previously, negotiators have deadlines. A contract will expire. Agreement has to be reached before a large meeting is going to occur. Someone has to catch a plane. Therefore, extending negotiations beyond a deadline can be costly, particularly to the person who has the deadline, since that person has to either extend the deadline or go home emptyhanded. Therefore, manipulating a deadline or failing to agree by a particular deadline can be a powerful tool in the hands of the person who does not face deadline pressure. A second observation is that, in some ways, the ultimate weapon in negotiation is to threaten to terminate negotiations, denying both parties the possibility of a settlement. This pressure will usually be felt more acutely by one side than by the other and presents a potent weapon. To counter actual or threatened use of either of these approaches, negotiators can take steps to increase the cost to the other party of using them or reduce the cost to themselves should the settlement be delayed (Cohen, 1980).

Disruptive Action. One way to encourage agreement is to increase the collateral cost of continuing or breaking negotiations. In one instance, a group of unionized food service workers negotiating with a restaurant rounded up supporters, had them enter the restaurant just prior to lunch, and had each person order a cup of coffee and drink it leisurely. When regular customers came to lunch, they found every seat occupied (Jacobs, 1951). In other instances, people dissatisfied with automobiles they have purchased have had their cars painted with large, bright yellow lemons and then drove them around town in an effort to pressure the dealer to make a settlement. Public picketing of a business, boycotting, and locking negotiators in a room until they reach agreement are all forms of disruptive action that increase the costs on negotiators for not settling and, hence, bring them back to the bargaining table.

Ally with Outsiders. A common feature of threatened strikes, particularly in the public sector, is for management to appeal to the courts for an injunction. In many business transactions, a private party may profess that, if negotiations with a merchant are unsuccessful, they will go to the Better Business Bureau and protest the merchant's actions. Individuals who are protesting the practices and policies of businesses or government agencies form task forces, coalitions, and protest organizations in order to bring greater pressure on the target. Schools of business administration, for example, often enhance their negotiation with higher management on budget matters by citing requirements of accreditation organizations to substantiate their budget requests.

Scheduling of Negotiations.   Negotiation schedules can often put one party at considerable disadvantage. Businesspeople going overseas to negotiate with customers or suppliers often find negotiations are scheduled to begin immediately after their arrival, when they are still suffering from the fatigue of travel and jet lag. In contrast, the automobile dealer will probably negotiate somewhat differently with the customer a half hour before quitting time than at the beginning of the work day. Contract negotiations scheduled with union representatives after they have worked all day will not be the same as those scheduled at a time when they could have been fresh and alert.

The opportunities to increase or alter the cost of delay or termination of negotiation vary widely from field to field. There are numerous opportunities in labor/management negotiations to increase the cost of strikes and make appeals to third parties. There are far fewer opportunities for an individual negotiating a home purchase to create costly delays. Nonetheless, the tactics of increasing these costs in what might be called the "hard knuckles" aspect of negotiations are important both to enhance one's own position and to protect oneself from the other party's actions.

POSITIONS TAKEN DURING NEGOTIATION

Another powerful way of influencing negotiations is through the position one takes. At the beginning of negotiations, each party takes a position. These positions usually change in response to information from the other party, or they change the other party's position. Change in position is usually accompanied by new information concerning intentions, utilities, and final settlement point. Such change also provides an opportunity for the other side to communicate new information that may influence the opposition and perhaps change its own position.

Opening Proposal

When negotiations begin, the negotiator is faced with a perplexing problem. What is the opening offer to be? Will the offer be seen as too high by the other and contemptuously rejected? An offer seen as modest by the other party could perhaps have been higher, either to leave more room for maneuver or to achieve a higher eventual settlement. Should the opening offer be somewhat closer to the resistance point, suggesting a more cooperative stance? These questions become less perplexing the more the negotiator knows about the other party and his or her limits. However, that knowledge only limits the range of the problem; it does not eliminate the problem. The fundamental question is whether the opening offer should be more toward the extreme or more toward the low end. Studies indicate that negotiators who make an extreme original offer believe they get a more satisfactory settlement than do those who make low or modest opening offers (Hinton, Hamner, and Pohlen, 1974; Chertkoff and Conley, 1967; Komorita and Brenner, 1968). There are at least two reasons for the advantage that accrues to taking an extreme opening position. First, it gives more room for movement in negotiation and therefore allows more time during which one can learn of the other's priorities and influence the other. Second, an extreme opening has the possibility of creating in the other party's mind the impression that there is a long way to go before a reasonable settlement is achieved, and that more concessions than originally intended may have to be made to bridge the difference between the two opening positions. The disadvantages of an extreme initial offer are (1) that it may be summarily rejected by the other side and (2) that it communicates an attitude of "toughness" that may be destructive to long-term relationships. Negotiators who make extreme initial offers should also have viable options or BATNAs that they employ if the opposing negotiator refuses to deal with them.

Opening Stance

A second decision to be made at the outset of negotiation is the stance or attitude to adopt. Is one going to be competitive—fighting to get the best on every point—or reasonable—willing to make concessions and compromises? Some negotiators take a belligerent stand, attacking the position, offer, and even the character of the other. In response, the other party may mirror the initial stance, meeting belligerence with belligerence. Some negotiators adopt a position of reasonableness and understanding, seeming to say, "Let's be reasonable people who can solve this problem to our mutual satisfaction." Even if the attitude is not mirrored, the other's response is most likely to be constrained by one's opening stance. The other party may not directly counter a belligerent stance but, at the same time, is rather unlikely to respond with hopeful reasonableness.

In order to communicate the most effective message, a negotiator should try to send a consistent message through both attitude and initial offer. A reasonable bargaining position is usually coupled with a friendly attitude, and an extreme bargaining position is usually coupled with a tougher, more competitive attitude. Opponents will find conflicting messages most confusing to interpret and to answer.

Initial Concessions

An opening offer is usually met with a counter-offer, and these two offers define the bargaining range. Sometimes, an opponent will not counter-offer but will simply state that the first offer (or set of demands) was unacceptable and ask the opener to come back with "a more reasonable set of proposals." In any event, after the first round of offers, the next question is, "What movement or concessions are to be made?" One can choose to make none, hold firm, and insist on the original position, or one can make some concessions. If concessions are to be made, the next question is how large they are to be. For now, it is sufficient to observe that the initial concession conveys a message, frequently a symbolic one, to the other about how one is going to proceed.

Opening offers, opening stances, and initial concessions are elements at the beginning of negotiations that parties can use to communicate how they intend to negotiate. An extreme original offer, a determined opening stance, and/or a very small opening concession signal a position of firmness; a more moderate opening offer, a reasonable, cooperative opening stance, and a more generous initial concession communicate a basic stance of flexibility. By taking a firm position, one attempts to preempt for oneself most of the bargaining or settlement range in order to maximize the final outcome or to preserve maximum maneuvering room for later in the negotiations. Firmness also creates a climate in which the other side may decide that concessions are so meager that it is worthwhile to settle rather than to drag things out. Hence, firmness is a way of quickly shortening negotiations. There is a possibility of course that firmness will be reciprocated by the other. One or both parties may become either intransigent or disgusted and withdraw completely.

There are several reasons for adopting a flexible position. First, by taking different stances along the way, one can learn from responses to these stances what the other side's utilities and perceived possibilities are. One may want to establish a cooperative rather than a combative relationship, hoping to get more concessions. Last, flexibility keeps the negotiations going; the more flexible one seems, the more the other party will believe that a settlement is possible.

Role of Concessions

Concessions are central to negotiation. Without them, in fact, negotiations would not exist. If one side is not prepared to make concessions, either the other must capitulate or negotiations will deadlock.

People enter negotiations expecting concessions. One's original position may be good for both sides and might have been the final settlement if the parties started negotiation from different points. Even so, the other party will usually resent a take-it-or-leave-it position and may refuse to accept an offer it might have accepted had the very same offer emerged as a result of concession making. This has been illustrated many times in labor relations. Management leaders have often "objectively" analyzed upcoming contract talks and made their initial offer at the point that their final offer was going to be (i.e., set their opening offer, target point, and resistance point as the same). They have then insisted there were no concessions to be made because the initial offer was fair and reasonable based on management's analysis. These positions were bitterly fought by unions and continued to be bitterly resented years after the companies abandoned this bargaining strategy. (Selekman, Selekman, and Fuller, 1958; Northrop, 1964). Conversely, there is ample data that parties feel better about a settlement when there has been a progression of concessions (Baranowski and Summers, 1972; Crumbaugh and Evans, 1967; Deutsch, 1958; Gruder and Duslak, 1973). This data seems to support the point made by Rubin and Brown (1975) that "a bargainer wants to believe he is capable of shaping the other's behavior, of causing the other to choose as he (the other) does" (pp. 277–278). When making concessions, one is communicating that the other party is someone to whom one will make adjustments.

Since concession indicates an acknowledgment and a movement toward the other party's position, it implies a recognition of that position and its legitimacy. Status and position are as much at stake as the substantive issues themselves. Concession making also exposes the giver to some danger. If the other party does not reciprocate, the giver may appear to be weaker by having given something up and gotten nothing in return. Hence, not reciprocating a concession sends a powerful message about firmness and leaves the giver open to feeling his or her esteem has been damaged or reputation diminished.

A reciprocated concession cannot be on just any topic or just any amount. If the giver has made a major concession on a significant point, it is expected that the return offer will be on the same item or one of similar weight and somewhat comparable magnitude. To make an additional concession when none has been given (or when what was given was inadequate) can imply weakness and can squander valuable maneuvering room. When receiving an inadequate concession, a negotiator may state what is expected first before offering further concessions. "That is not sufficient; you will have to go up X before I consider offering any further concessions."

To encourage further concessions from the other side, negotiators link their concessions to a prior concession made by the other. They may say, "Since you have given up on X, I am willing to concede on Y." More powerful concession making may be wrapped in a package, sometimes described as "log rolling." For example, "If you will give A and B, I will give C and D." Packaging of concessions also leads to better outcomes for a negotiator than making concessions singly on individual issues (Froman and Cohen, 1970).

Pattern in Concession Making

The pattern of concessions a negotiator makes contains valuable information that is not always easily interpreted. When successive concessions get smaller, the most obvious message is that the concession giver's position is getting firmer and that his or her resistance point is being reached. This generalization needs to be tempered, however, by pointing out that a small concession late in negotiations may also indicate that there is little room left to maneuver. Especially when the initial offer is extreme, the negotiator has considerable room available for packaging new offers, making it relatively easy to give fairly substantial concessions. When negotiation has moved closer to a negotiator's hoped-for settlement point, to give a concession the same size as the initial one may take a negotiator past his or her resistance point. Suppose a negotiator makes a first offer $100 below the other's target price; an initial concession of $10 would reduce his maneuvering room by 10 percent. When negotiations get to within $10 of the other's target price, a concession of $1 gives up 10 percent of the remaining maneuvering room. A negotiator cannot communicate such mechanical ratios in giving or interpreting concessions, but this example illustrates how the receiver can construe the meaning of concession size and place in the negotiating sequence.

Final Offer

Eventually a negotiator wants to convey the message that there is no further room for movement—that the present offer is final. A negotiator will probably make such statements as these: "This is all I can do." "This is as far as I can go." Sometimes, however, it is clear that no simple statement will suffice; an alternate is to use concessions to convey the point. A negotiator might simply let the absence of any further concessions convey the message in spite of invitations and urging from the other party. The second party may at first not recognize that the last was the final offer and might volunteer a further concession to get the other to respond. Finding that no further concession results, the second party may feel betrayed and see the pattern of concession–counterconcession as being violated. The resulting bitterness may further complicate negotiations.

One way negotiators may convey the message, "This is the last offer," is by making the last concession substantial. This conveys the message that one is throwing in the remainder of one's negotiating range. The final offer has to be large enough to be dramatic, yet not so large that it can create the suspicion that the negotiator has been holding back and that there is more to be had on other points in the bargaining mix (Walton and McKersie, 1965).

COMMITMENT

A key concept in creating a bargaining position is that of commitment. One definition of *commitment* is "taking of a bargaining position with some explicit or implicit pledge regarding the future course of action" (Walton and McKersie, 1965, p. 82). An example would be a union official who, during negotiation, says to management, "If we do not get the salary increase asked for, I will resign from the union." Such an act identifies a position the negotiator insists on achieving and the threat of some future action if that position is not conceded. The purpose of a commitment is to remove ambiguity about the actor's intended course of action. By making a commitment, a negotiator signals the intention to take this course of action, make this decision, pursue this objective and says, "If you pursue your goals as well, we are likely to come into direct conflict; and either one of us will win or neither of us will achieve his/her goals." A commitment is often interpreted by the other as a threat—if the other doesn't comply or give in, some set of negative consequences will occur. Some commitments can be threats, but others are simple statements of intended action that leave the responsibility for avoiding mutual disaster in the hands of the opponent. A nation that publicly states it is going to invade another country and that war can only be averted if no other nation tries to stop the action is taking a bold and dramatic commitment position. Commitments can also involve future promises such as, "If we get this salary increase, we'll agree to have all other points arbitrated as you request."

Returning to the management-union example, there are at least two possible messages in the union official's threat to resign. One is that if the present negotiator resigns, the management will probably have to start all over with a new, and perhaps less cooperative, union negotiator. The other is based upon the premise that the union official does not want to resign but will have to resign if his/her terms are not met in order to maintain the credibility of the threat. This premise leads to the conclusion that the official will fight long and hard before taking this ultimate step of resigning and that management should expect no further concessions on this point. Thus management can decide either to go through long, difficult negotiations until the union negotiator resigns and the new party comes in or to reconsider its own position and concede.

Because of their nature, commitments are statements that usually have to be acted upon. A union official who threatens to resign, fails to get the objective, and then does not resign is hardly going to be believed in the future. In addition, a person often suffers a loss of self-esteem after not following through on a publicly made commitment. Hence, once a negotiator makes a commitment, there is strong motivation to hold to it. Since the other party most likely will understand this, a commitment, once believed, will often have a powerful effect on what the other party believes to be possible (Pruitt, 1981).

Tactical Considerations in Using Commitments

Like many tools, commitments are two edged. They may be used to gain the advantages illustrated above, but they also inextricably fix a negotiator to a particular position or point. Commitments trade off flexibility for emphasis but create difficulties if it becomes desirable to adopt a new position. For example, suppose that, after committing oneself to a course of action, additional information indicates that a different position is desirable. Later information shows an earlier estimate of the other party's resistance point to be inaccurate and that there is actually a negative negotiating range. It may be desirable, or even necessary, to shift positions after making a commitment. For these reasons, in making commitments, one should also make contingency plans that permit one to get out of a commitment if it should prove to be unsound. The contingency must, of necessity, be secret for the original commitment to be effective. For example, the union leader might have planned to retire shortly after the expected completion of negotiations. By advancing retirement, the official can thereby cancel commitment and leave his successor unencumbered. A purchaser of a house may be able to back away from a commitment by discovering the hitherto unnoticed "cracks in the plaster" in the living room or the fact that the neighborhood is unacceptable.

A party to negotiation may find commitment a useful tool but may also find it advantageous to keep the other party from becoming committed. Further, if the other party should take a committed position, it is to the first party's advantage to keep open ways for the other to get out of its commitment. The remainder of this chapter will be devoted to examining details of these tactical issues.

Establishing a Commitment

Given that strong, passionate statements—some of which are pure bluff—are made during negotiation, how does a negotiator establish that a statement is to be understood as a commitment?

A commitment statement has three properties: a high degree of finality, a high degree of specificity, and a clear statement of consequences (Walton and McKersie, 1965). A union negotiator could say, "We are going to get a cost-of-living increase, or there will be trouble." This statement is far less powerful than the same negotiator saying, "We must have a 10 percent cost-of-living increase in the next written contract, or we will go on strike when the contract terminates at midnight tomorrow." This latter statement communicates finality, how and when the cost of living increase must be granted; specifically, how much of a cost-of-living increase is expected; and a clear statement of consequences, exactly what will happen if the grant is not given. It is, therefore, far stronger than the earlier language.

Public Pronouncement.   A commitment statement increases in potency when more people know of it. The union leader's statement about resigning, if given at the bargaining table, will have a differing impact than one made at a meeting of a few union members. Some parties in negotiations have placed ads in newspapers or other publications stating what they want and what they will or will not agree to. In each of these situations, the larger the audience, the less likely the commitment is to be changed.

Linking with an Outside Base.   Another way to strengthen a commitment is to link up with an ally. Unions may bring in other unions to join them in threatening a strike. Employees who are dissatisfied with management form a "committee" to express these concerns. A variation of this process is to create conditions that make it more difficult for the negotiator creating the commitment to move from a position. For example, by encouraging dedicated colonists to settle onto the West Bank in Jerusalem, the Israeli government has made it more difficult to concede this land to Egypt or Jordan, a point they wanted to reinforce all along.

Increase the Prominence of Demands.   Many things can be done to increase the prominence of commitment statements. If most offers and concessions have been made orally, then writing out a commitment statement draws attention to it. If prior statements have been written, then using a different-sized typeface or a different-colored paper will draw attention to them. Repetition is one of the most powerful ways of making a statement prominent. Using multiple means to convey a commitment hammers a point home. For example, tell the other party of a commitment; then hand them a written statement; then read the statement to them.

Reinforce the Threat or Promise.   When making a threat, there is the danger of going too far—stating a point so strongly that one looks weak and/or foolish rather than threatening. Statements like, "If I don't get this point, I'll see that you don't stay in business another day!" are more likely to be greeted with annoyance and to be dismissed than to evoke concern and compliance. Long, detailed statements—ones that are highly exaggerated—undermine credibility. In contrast, simple, direct statements of demands, conditions, and consequences are most effective.

There are things that can be done to reinforce the implicit or explicit threat in a commitment. One is to review similar circumstances and what the consequences were; another is to make obvious preparations to carry out the threat. Facing the prospect of a strike, companies build up their inventories, move cots and food into factories; unions build strike funds and give advice to their members on how to make out with less income should there be a strike. Another route is to create and fulfill minor threats in advance, thereby increasing one's credibility that major threats will be fulfilled. For example, a negotiator could say, "If the progress of these negotiations does not speed up, I am going to take a five-day weekend," and then do just that.

Keeping the Other Party from Getting Committed

All the advantages of a committed position work against a negotiator when the opponent becomes committed. Therefore, a general strategy is to try to keep the other party from getting committed. People often take committed positions when they become angry or feel pushed; these commitments are often unplanned and can work to both parties' disadvantage. Consequently, there is a need for negotiators to pay careful attention to their opponent's level of irritation, anger, and impatience.

Good, sound, deliberate commitments take time to establish, for the reasons covered above. Hence, one way to prevent the other party from establishing a committed position is to deny them the opportunity to take this time. In a real estate deal with an option about to run out, a negotiator may use up the time simply by being unavailable or requiring extensive checking of deeds and boundaries, thereby denying time to the opponent to make a case. Another approach to keep the other negotiator from getting into a committed position is to ignore or downplay the threat by not acknowledging the other's commitment or even by making a joke about it. A negotiator might say, "You don't really mean that" or "I know you can't be serious about really going through with that" or simply move negotiations along as though the commitment were never heard and understood. If the negotiator can pretend that the other party's statement was not heard or was not understood to be significant, the statement can be ignored at a later point without incurring the consequences that would have occurred had it been taken seriously. Although the other side can still carry out the threat, the belief that it *must* be carried out (that control of the situation has been given up) may be reduced.

There are also times that it is to a negotiator's advantage for the other party to become committed. When the other party takes a position on an issue relatively early in a negotiation, it may be very much to a negotiator's advantage to pin down that position so it will not be changed as the negotiation on other issues progresses. A negotiator may handle this situation in two ways: by pointing out the significance of a commitment when it is made or by taking notes and keeping track of the other's statements when it is to the negotiator's advantage to do so. An employee might be very upset about the way a particular problem was handled but may say that he/she will never get upset enough about it to resign. The manager might focus on this point when the statement is made or refer to it later when the employee is very upset. Both actions are designed to keep the employee on the job in spite of the employee's anger.

Finding Ways to Abandon a Committed Position

Most of the time a negotiator wants to get the other party out of a committed position, and many times that party may want to get out of his/her own committed position. How can this be done? One method has already been noted: A negotiator, when establishing a committed position, will also plan a private way out, if necessary, by finding new data or by wording the commitment so that the condition by which it applied may be expected to change. Sometimes, information provided by the other party during negotiations can permit a negotiator to say, "Given what I've learned from you during this discussion, I see I am going to have to rethink my earlier position." The same could be done for the other party. A negotiator, wanting to make it possible for an opponent to move from a committed position, and yet not lose credibility, might say, "Given what I've told you about the facts of the situation (or given this new information), maybe I can help you see that your earlier position no longer holds." Needless to say, the last thing a negotiator wants to do is to embarrass the other party or make judgmental statements about their shift in position; rather, the other party should be given every opportunity to retreat with dignity.

A second way to abandon a commitment is to silently let the matter die. After some lapse of time, a negotiator can make a new proposal in an area where the other party has taken a committed position but without ever alluding to the earlier commitment. A variation on this process is to make a tentative step in a direction previously excluded by the other's commitment. If the other party, in response to either of these moves, indicates through silence or verbal comment a willingness to let things move in that direction, further steps should be taken.

A third route to take is to restate the commitment in more general terms. Another party that wants to move and is alert will detect this shift and make a proposal, changing some of the details to be more in line with her/his needs, while ostensibly still living with the "general principles" as previously stated.

Last, if the other party backs off from a committed position, it is usually important to help reduce any possible damage to the other party. One strategy to use in this instance is publicly to attribute the other's move to some noble or higher outside cause. A union official can back off from a position because of "concern for public welfare"; so can a management negotiator. Diplomats can withdraw from a committed position because of their "deep concern for peace and humankind." A party can back off from a point during a real estate transaction to "support the economic well-being of the community."

A committed position is a powerful tool in negotiation; it is also a rigid tool. As such, it must be used with care; and as with any other tool, we must be as alert to ways of denying it to our opponent as we are to ways we can use it for ourselves. Unfortunately, far more commitments are made as a result of anger and the desire to stop making concessions than are made as a result of clearly thought-out tactical planning. In either case, the essential property of a committed position is the arrangement of the consequences of an action so that some point is no longer an item of discussion or can only be negotiated at grave risk to one or both parties; that is, the events are inevitable unless stopped at grave risk to both sides and their relationship. The committed position has to be believable, and what has to be believed is that nothing can be done to change the conditions—if X happens, Y is inevitable. Convincing the other party that its fate is sealed on the matter at hand is demanding, requiring preparation, time, and skill. Consequently, getting out of a committed position is not easy but is made simpler by planning a secret means of escape at the time the commitment is being established. Many of the steps a negotiator can use to get out of a commitment can also be used to help the other party out of a committed position or, even better, to keep the opposition from establishing one in the first place.

SUMMARY

In this chapter we examined the basic structure of a competitive or distributive bargaining situation and some of the basic strategies and tactics used in distributive bargaining. The basic structure consists of setting one's own opening target and resistance points. The other party's starting points are soon learned, and target points also become known directly or through inference. Resistance points, the point beyond which a party will not go, are usually unknown until late in negotiation and are often jealously concealed by the other party. All points are of interest, but the resistance points are of the greatest interest. The spread between the parties' resistance points defines the bargaining range. If positive, it defines the area of negotiation, with each party working to get as much of the bargaining range for itself as possible. If negative, successful negotiation is impossible.

It is rare that a negotiation includes only one item; more typically, there is a set of items referred to as a bargaining mix. Each item in a bargaining mix can have starting, target, and resistance points.

Examination of the structure of distribute bargaining reveals many options for a negotiator to achieve a successful resolution, most of which fall within two broad efforts: to influence the other party's belief in what is possible and to learn as much as possible about the other party's position, particularly in regard to resistance points. The negotiator's basic strategy is to manipulate the final settlement as close to the other party's resistance point as possible. The tactics used to achieve this goal involve getting information about the opposition and its positions; convincing members of the other party to change their minds about their ability to achieve their own goals; and promoting one's own objectives as desirable, necessary, or even inevitable.

Distributive bargaining is basically a conflict situation, wherein parties seek their own advantage—in part through concealing information, attempting to mislead, or using manipulative actions. All of these tactics can easily escalate interaction from calm discussion to bitter hostility. Yet, negotiation is the attempt to resolve a conflict without force, without fighting. Further, to be successful, both parties to the negotiation must feel at the end that the outcome was the best that they could achieve and that it is worth accepting and supporting. It is a process that requires skill but, even more important, it requires understanding and adequate planning.

5

Strategy and Tactics of Integrative Bargaining

Periodically, we read of tragic fires in restaurants, night clubs, or theaters that kill large numbers of people. Often there is panic; in the rush to escape, exits are blocked, trapping many and causing unnecessary deaths. People seem to act as if their lives depended upon being first out of the building. In contrast, most of us are taught from our earliest school days that there is ample time for everyone to leave a burning building safely if people move out in an orderly fashion. As children, we were urged to have a shared concern to get everyone out of the building, to collaborate rather than to compete. The need for orderly, cooperative behavior comes not from ideals, but from reality.

The same principles are true for negotiation. In bargaining, there need not be winners and losers; everyone can be a winner. Rather than assume that all conflicts are win-lose events, negotiators can learn that win-win solutions are possible. These assumptions will lead them to search for the win-win options, and usually to find them. This win-win approach to negotiation is called *integrative bargaining*.

THE STRUCTURE OF INTEGRATIVE BARGAINING SITUATIONS

In distributive bargaining, the goals of the parties are initially irreconcilable—or at least they appear that way to the parties. Central to the conflict is the belief that there is a limited, controlled amount of key resources available—a "fixed pie" situation. Both parties may want to be the winner; both may want more than half of what is available. For example, both management (on behalf of the stockholders) and labor (on behalf of the rank-and-file) believe that they deserve the larger share of the company's profits. Both may want to win on the same dimension, such as the financial package or control of certain policy decisions. In these situations, their goals are mutually exclusive, and hence lead to conflict.

In contrast, in integrative bargaining, the goals of the parties are not mutually exclusive. If one side pursues his goals, it does not necessarily preclude the other from achieving his goals. One party's gain is not necessarily at the other party's expense. The fundamental structure of an integrative bargaining situation is that it is possible for both sides to achieve their objectives (Walton and McKersie, 1965). While the conflict may initially appear to be win-lose to the parties—and may create the same kind of competitive "panic" we described in the fire example—discussion and mutual exploration will usually suggest win-win alternatives. The strategy by which these alternatives are discovered is the focus of this chapter.

WHY INTEGRATIVE BARGAINING IS DIFFICULT TO ACHIEVE

Integrative bargaining is the process of identifying a common, shared, or joint goal and developing a process to achieve it. It is meant to be a collaborative process in which the parties define their "common problem" and pursue strategies to solve it. Unfortunately, negotiators do not always perceive situations as having integrative potential. People frequently view conflict-laden situations (such as the fire) with a fundamentally more distrustful, win-lose attitude than is necessary or desirable. The approach that individuals take toward conflict and negotiation is essential to understanding the differences between distributive and integrative bargaining. We first describe a basic model of conflict management, and then use this model to emphasize the differences between the integrative and distributive bargaining processes.

Individual Styles of Managing Conflict

Five fundamentally different perspectives or orientations that individuals can take toward conflict have been identified: contending (competing), accommodating (yielding), compromising (splitting the difference), collaborating (problem solving), and avoiding (inaction) (Blake and Mouton, 1964; Thomas, 1976; Pruitt, 1983).

Contending. When we try to convince another party to accept a position that favors only our own interests, we are *contending* or competing. This is the process we discussed in Chapter 4 on distributive bargaining, and is also called "positional bargaining" (Fisher and Ury, 1981). Successful contending requires persuasion, manipulation, concealment of true position, and the use of threats and pressure tactics.

Accommodating.   In contrast to contending, an accommodating strategy tries to help the other party meet his/her objectives. Instead of focusing on our own needs, we focus on the other's needs. The first priority is to assure that the other party is fully satisfied; anything we derive for ourselves comes only after the other's goals are fully met. Negotiators may accommodate for several reasons: to end the negotiations, to leave the other completely satisfied now so that we may ask for something from them later, or because the issues are significantly more important to the other party than to us.

Compromising.   When negotiators compromise, they split the difference. Neither side wins, nor loses. Instead, each side agrees to some division of the issue so that each gets something out of the solution—but not everything. Parties agree to compromise when they view the issue in fixed-sum terms, and settle their differences by each getting a piece of the pie. As we will constantly stress, compromise is a mechanism for satisficing—making sure that each party gets something—but not optimizing, so that both parties can achieve all of their objectives.

Collaborating.   When negotiators collaborate, they work together to maximize their joint outcome. Good collaboration is closely akin to good group problem-solving. The parties understand that they share a problem, and define their problem in terms of shared goals and interests. Each party states his needs, and the parties work together to invent options that will meet these needs in an optimal manner.

Avoiding.   Finally, negotiating parties may approach conflict and decide to avoid it. If a negotiator neither pushes for his own objectives nor shows concern for the other's objectives, he is avoiding the conflict. Avoiding is akin to withdrawal from the conflict situation. The consequence is that the other person can do what he wants, or—if he/she is dependent on the other for some action—that this withdrawal will frustrate an opponent. Avoiding is an approach that may be used when a negotiator fears conflict, when the issues are seen as too insignificant to bargain over, or when he/she wants to stall or delay a negotiation. The consequences are that the opponent and the conflict may "go away," or that they may be put off to a future time.

The Dual Concerns Model

These five separate approaches to conflict can be organized into a single framework or model (see Figure 5-1) (Blake and Mouton, 1964; Filley, 1975; Thomas, 1976; Gladwin and Walter, 1980; Rahim, 1983). The model pro-

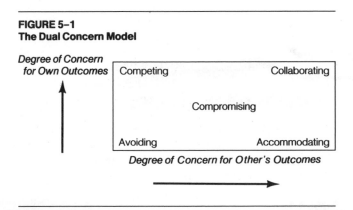

FIGURE 5-1
The Dual Concern Model

poses two dimensions that account for differences among the five styles: one dimension describes the degree of concern an individual shows for obtaining his own outcomes, and the other dimension describes the degree of concern the individual shows for the other party's outcomes. These two dimensions give us a simpler and more precise way of understanding the approach a negotiator may take to conflict.

Dimension I: Concern For Own Outcome. The more important an outcome is to a negotiator, the more likely he/she will be to assume a style that will lead to achieving that outcome. Concessions will be made slowly, and in small steps. Thus, the stronger the concern a negotiator shows for his own outcome, the more he will either try to obtain the outcome on his own (competitive behavior) or work with others to obtain that outcome (collaborative behavior). In contrast, when an individual doesn't care very much about the outcome, he/she is more likely to maintain an accommodating stance (let the other side benefit) or an avoiding stance (the conflict and/or the stakes are not worth an investment of time or energy) (Longley and Pruitt, 1980; Fry, Firestone, and Williams, 1979). When negotiators are acting as representatives of some group or constituency, these dynamics are enhanced. Representatives are more resistant to yielding than individuals negotiating on their own behalf (Benton and Druckman, 1973), even more so when they are distrusted by their constituents (Wall, 1977), are strongly accountable to their constituents (Klimoski and Ash, 1974), or are lower in status than their constituents (Kogan, Lamm, and Trammsdorf, 1972).

Dimension II: Concerns for Other's Outcome. Negotiators can also be concerned about the other party attaining his outcomes. Concern may be shown for at least two reasons: (1) personal (we have a stake in the other's welfare) and (2) strategic (we can not obtain our own ends without considering what the other wants) (Pruitt, 1983). Personal reasons include liking the other person, having to live with them after negotiations so that their unhappiness makes life unpleasant for us, or deriving satisfaction from the other party's success. Strategic reasons may involve not pushing past the other party's resistance point, trying to keep them in the negotiation, or attempting to reduce some of their distrust. The two reasons have different implications. When the reasons are strategic, a negotiator recognizes that he is dependent on the other party and wants to shape the other party's perceptions and behavior in order to affect his own goals. We will discuss the variety of approaches used in these situations in Chapters 6–10. In contrast, when the reasons are personal, the negotiator's behavior may contribute to feelings of appreciation or reciprocal accommodation by the opponent, but no significant impact on outcomes is likely to be noticed.

Applications of the Dual Concerns Model

The dual concerns model can help us understand several aspects of the negotiation process. First, it can provide a convenient set of terms for describing different negotiation styles, based upon the amount of concern shown by a negotiator for his own and/or the other's outcomes. Second, we may also represent behavior in this model by drawing a diagonal line from the upper left to lower right corners of the model (from the contending to the accommodating styles). This line represents the fundamental way that individuals view the distributive bargaining process. In most distributive bargaining situations, either the negotiator wins (contending), loses (accommodating or letting the other side win), or they compromise and each side gains something. In contrast, if we draw a diagonal line from the lower left to the upper right corner (from avoiding to the collaborating style), this represents the possibilities of the integrative bargaining process. Parties can both neglect the conflict, both settle for something less than the maximum (compromise) or both try to optimize their outcomes through problem solving. The choice of these options has been confirmed by several research studies (e.g., Pruitt, 1983). When negotiators were confronted with strong concerns for both their own outcomes and their opponent's outcomes, there was a high frequency of information sharing and joint efforts at problem solving. When parties had a high concern for their own outcome but low concern for their opponent's, the result was arguments, use of threats, contentious behavior, and moderately low joint outcomes. Finally, when each party was very concerned about the other's outcomes but not about his own, the lowest joint outcomes were produced, suggesting yielding behavior by both parties. A second study explored the effect of accountability on the approach taken. When negotiators felt highly accountable to their constituencies, competitive behavior increased and low joint outcomes resulted. However, when negotiators felt accountable to their constituencies and to their opponents (because they would have to work with them in the future), highly cooperative behavior and high joint outcomes resulted.

In conclusion, these studies show that a collaborative, problem-solving approach to conflict is more likely to occur when parties reduce their level of aspiration for high outcomes, in order to give themselves more leeway to develop mutually acceptable solutions. Thus, the greater the pressure on negotiators to achieve mutually beneficial solutions to the bargaining problem, the more likely problem-solving behavior is to occur.

Additional Factors That Make Integrative Bargaining Difficult

We have stated that the primary reason negotiators do not pursue integrative agreements is that they fail to perceive a situation as having integrative potential, and are primarily motivated to achieve outcomes that only satisfy their own needs. Three additional factors contribute to this difficulty: the history of the relationship between the parties, the tendency toward black/white thinking, and the "mixed motive" nature of most bargaining situations.

1. The history of the relationship between the parties. The more competitive and conflict-laden their past relationship, the more negotiators are likely to approach the current negotiation with a defensive, win-lose attitude. Parties are unlikely to trust their opponents, or to believe that a cooperative gesture is not some ruse or set-up for future exploitation. Since their opponent has never shown any genuine interest in cooperation in the past, why should the present be any different? Even if the parties have no past history with one another, the *expectation* of a competitive opponent is sufficient to create defensiveness. While these perceptions are often loaded with self-serving rationalizations, that is, negotiators expect competition from their opponent in order to justify their own strategies, the perceptions nevertheless deter them from initiating an integrative negotiation process.

2. A belief that an issue can only be resolved distributively, that is, has a bias toward "either-or" or "black-white" thinking. For example, unions and management have historically clashed over the introduction of new technology that replaces men with machines. Labor usually upholds "job security," believing that the new machines will eliminate workers, while management takes the position that the new machines will increase efficiency, quality, and profit, and that it is management's right to make decisions regarding these issues. On the surface, the two positions seem irreconcilable: either the workers make the decisions to keep employees at the expense of machines, or management makes the decisions about

how to introduce new technology. However, analysis of actual cases reveals that labor and management have devised a number of ways to solve the problem to both sides' satisfaction—retraining and realloca- tion of employees, reducing employees through attrition rather than layoff, etc.

3. The "mixed-motive" nature of most bargaining situations. Pure integra- tive bargaining situations are rare. Most situations are "mixed motive," containing some elements that require distributive negotiation pro- cesses, and others that require integrative. For example, when people become partners in a business, the common goal of profit-making pro- vides a basis for their collaboration. However, how to allocate the profits becomes a different matter, and is much more likely to create conflict. In this example, the parties must recognize that the integrative element is more important, that is, there must be a business before there can be profits to divide. Nevertheless, their competitiveness over profit distri- bution may make it hard for them to stay in business at all. As a general rule, conflict and competitiveness "drive out" cooperation and trust, making it more difficult for the parties to find common ground.

In summary, one of the most fundamental problems in integrative negotiation is that negotiating parties fail to recognize (or search for) the integrative potential in a negotiating problem. The primary cause of this failure is the negotiator's approach to conflict, motivated by his desire to satisfy his own concerns without regard to the other's concerns. Negotiators may also be led to this assumption: (1) when they are accountable to someone else for their performance, (2) when the parties have had a conflictive history, and (3) when the issues are too complex to disentangle and inter- preted more easily in simple win/lose terms. As a result, negotiators fail to invest the time and energy to truly explore and search for integrative options.

THE FUNDAMENTAL PROCESSES
OF INTEGRATIVE NEGOTIATION

If past history, biased perceptions and the truly distributive aspects of negotiation make integrative agreements more difficult, it is somewhat remarkable that integrative agreements occur at all. But they do occur, largely because negotiators work hard to overcome the inhibiting factors and search for common agreement. In order for integrative agreements to occur, both negotiating parties must be able to engage in the following critical processes:

1. Attempt to understand the other negotiator's real needs and objectives. As we noted earlier, negotiators differ in their values and preferences. What one side needs and wants may or may not be what the other side needs and wants. If one is to help another satisfy his needs, he/she

must first understand them. Hence the parties must engage in a dialogue in which preferences and priorities are openly shared, rather than disguised and manipulated.

2. **Create a free flow of information.** For this open dialogue to occur, negotiators must be willing to reveal their true objectives, to listen to the other negotiator carefully, and to accept a joint solution that incorporates both sides' needs. In short, negotiators must create the conditions for a free and open discussion of all related issues and concerns. Again, this is significantly different from a distributive bargaining situation, in which the parties distrust one another, conceal and manipulate their true priorities, and attempt to learn about the other's needs to use that information to their competitive advantage.

3. **Emphasize the commonalities between the parties, and minimize the differences.** For a free flow of information to occur, negotiators need a different outlook or "frame of reference." Individual goals need to be viewed as part of a collaborative effort to achieve a larger goal. Sometimes the larger goal is clear and obvious, for example, victory at the polls, changing an unprofitable firm into a profitable one, winning a war. At other times, the larger goal is not so clear, nor is it as easy to keep in sight. For example, one of the authors worked as a consultant to a company that was closing down a major plant, and, at the same time, opening several others in different parts of the country. The company was perfectly willing to transfer employees to new plants and let them take their seniority with them. The union agreed to this arrangement. However, conflict developed because some employees could leave immediately while others were needed to gradually close and dismantle the old plant. If workers acquired seniority in the new plant when they arrived, those who stayed would have less plant seniority (as compared to company seniority) than those who went earlier. The union wanted everyone to go at the same time to avoid this inequity. Management was adamant that this was unworkable. In the argument that resulted, both parties lost sight of their larger goal—to transfer all employees who wanted to move to the new plant with their seniority intact. Only by constantly stressing this larger goal were the parties able to maintain a focus on commonalities that eventually led to a solution. Their solution was to permit transferred workers to select in advance the jobs they moved into, and to have their seniority "pegged" to those jobs when the choice was made, not when the physical move actually occurred.

4. **Search for solutions that meet the goals and objectives of both sides.** Finally, successful integrative bargaining requires that the negotiators search for solutions that meet both sides' objectives and needs. When the parties have traditionally held a combative, competitive orientation toward each other, they are more prone to be concerned only with their

own objectives. Their concern with the other's is twofold: to make sure that what the other obtains does not take away from one's own accomplishments; or to keep the other from obtaining his objectives because of a strong desire to win and even defeat the opponent. In contrast, successful integrative bargaining requires each negotiator to define and pursue goals that will meet and satisfy the needs of both sides. Outcomes are measured by the degree to which they meet both negotiators' goals. They are *not* measured by determining whether one party is "doing better" than the other. If the objective of one party is to get more than the other, integrative bargaining is difficult at best; if both strive for this objective, integrative bargaining is impossible.

In summary, successful integrative bargaining requires a fundamentally different negotiation process. Negotiators must attempt to probe below the surface of their opponent's "position" to discover underlying needs. They must create a free and open flow of information, and use their desire to satisfy both sides as the perspective from which to structure their dialogue. If negotiators do not have this perspective—if they approach the problem and their opponent in win-lose terms—integrative bargaining cannot occur.

CONDITIONS NECESSARY FOR SUCCESSFUL PROBLEM-SOLVING BEHAVIOR AND INTEGRATIVE BARGAINING

In addition to being predisposed to find a mutually acceptable joint solution, several other factors contribute to a predisposition toward problem solving. These factors are also the preconditions that are necessary to accomplish the integrative bargaining process (Pruitt, 1981, 1983; Filley, 1975). They are as follows:

Some Common Objective or Goal

When the parties believe that they are likely to benefit more from working together than by competing or working separately, the situation offers greater potential for successful integrative bargaining. Three types of goals may facilitate the development of integrative agreements:

- A common goal, by which all parties share the result equally, each one benefiting in a way that would not be possible if they did not work together. A town government and an industrial manufacturing plant may debate one another over the amount of taxes owed by the plant, but are more likely to work together if the common goal is to keep the plant open and employ half the town's workforce.

- A shared goal, by which the parties work toward a common end but benefit differently. For example, partners can work together in a business but not divide the profits equally. One may get a larger share of the profit because he contributed more experience or capital investment. Inherent in the idea of a shared goal is that parties will work together to achieve some output that will be shared. The same result can also come from cost cutting, by which the parties can earn the same outcome as before by working together, but with less effort, expense, or risk. This is often described as an "expandable" pie as contrasted to the "fixed pie" (Chapter 4).

• A joint goal. Individuals may personally have different goals but agree to combine them in a collective effort. For example, people joining a political campaign can have different goals; one wants to satisfy a personal ambition to hold public office, a second wants to "serve her community," and a third wants to benefit from policies that will be implemented under the new administration. All will unite around the joint goal of helping the new administration get elected.

The key element of an integrative bargaining situation is the belief that all sides can benefit. Whether each side attains the same outcome, or they achieve different outcomes, all sides must believe that they will be better off by working in cooperation than by competing or working independently.

Faith in One's Own Problem-Solving Ability

Parties who believe they can work together usually are able to do so. Those who do not share this belief in themselves are less willing to invest the time and energy in the potential payoffs of a collaborative relationship, and more likely to assume a contending or accommodating approach to conflict.

The Motivation and Commitment to Work Together

In order for integrative bargaining to succeed, the parties must be motivated to collaborate rather than to compete. They need to be committed to a goal which benefits both of them rather than pursue their own ends. Finally, they must be willing to adopt interpersonal styles that are more congenial than combative, more open and trusting than evasive and defensive, more flexible (but firm) rather than stubborn (but yielding). Needs have to be made explicit; similarities have to be identified, and differences recognized and accepted. Uncertainties have to be tolerated and inconsistencies unraveled.

It might seem that in order for successful integrative bargaining to occur, each party should be as interested in the objectives and problems of the other as each is in his own, i.e., to assume responsibility for the other's needs and outcomes as well as for his own. This is an incorrect interpretation; in fact, such a position is more likely to be dysfunctional. Parties who are deeply committed to each other and each other's welfare often do not work out the best solution (Kelley and Schenitzki, 1972; Fry, Firestone, and Williams, 1979). There are several reasons for this. First, as close as the parties may feel to one another, they still may not fully understand one another's needs, objectives, and concerns, and thus fall into the trap of not meeting the other's objectives while thinking they are (Rubin and Brown, 1975). Further, parties strongly committed to each other are likely to yield more than they would otherwise; the result being that they may arrive at a joint outcome that is less satisfactory than if they had remained firm in pursuing their own objectives. Parties in negotiation maximize their outcomes when they assume a healthy, active self-interest toward achieving their own outcomes, yet also recognize that they are in a collaborative problem solving relationship (Kelley and Schenitzki, 1972).

Motivation and commitment to problem solving can be enhanced in several ways:

- The parties can come to believe that they share a common fate, i.e., "if we do not hang together, we will surely hang separately."

- The parties can demonstrate to one another that there is more to be gained by working together (to increase the payoffs or reduce the costs) than by working separately.

- The parties can emphasize that they may have to work together after the negotiations are over—or recognize that they may be able to work together and continue to benefit from the relationship they have created.

In spite of these efforts, competitive and contentious behavior may persist. In Chapter 12, we will elaborate upon these approaches, as well as others that may be used to enhance the parties' predisposition toward cooperation and problem solving.

Trust

While there is no guarantee that trust will lead to collaboration, there is plenty of evidence to suggest that mistrust inhibits collaboration. People who are interdependent but who do not trust each other will act defensively. Defensiveness usually means that they will not accept information at face value, but instead look for hidden, deceptive meanings. When people are defensive, they withdraw, hold back information, and communicate less than complete information. Defensive people also attack their opponent's statements and position, seeking to defeat their position rather than to work together. Either of these responses is likely to make the negotiator hesitant, cautious, and distrustful (Gibb, 1961).

Generating trust is a complex, uncertain process; it depends in part on what the parties do to one another, and also on the personal characteristics of the parties. When people trust one another, they are more likely to communicate accurately their needs, positions, and the facts of the situation. In contrast, when people do not trust one another, they are more likely to engage in positional bargaining, use threats, and commit themselves to tough positions (Kimmel, Pruitt, Magenau, Konar-Goldband, and Carnevale, 1980). As with defensiveness, this behavior is likely to be reciprocated and to lead to unproductive negotiations. For trust to develop effectively, each negotiator must believe that both he and the other choose to behave in a cooperative manner; moreover, each must believe that this behavior is a signal of the other's honesty, openness, and a similar mutual commitment to a joint solution.

Trust in itself is not sufficient to create good problem solving; it must be linked to several other behaviors on the part of both negotiators. The first is a firm commitment to one's own position. If a negotiator is trustworthy but very willing to yield his own position to the other in negotiations, the other will be likely to take advantage of this yielding. While trust may exist, the willingness to yield leads his opponent to take a tough, firm position. In contrast, if the other party is firm in his commitment to his position, it is clear that the negotiator must work hard to find alternatives that will meet both parties' needs. Thus, good problem solving is likely to come from a combination of trust and firmness (Michener, Vaske, Schleifer, Plazewski, and Chapman, 1975; Wall, 1977). The second key behavior is support in the solution-exploration process. A person brainstorming about ways to solve a problem will respond differently if met with ridicule or silence than if met with interest and respect. A person who finds his/her ideas accepted and developed by someone will be encouraged to continue.

A number of key factors contribute to the development of trust between negotiators. First, we are more likely to trust someone whom we perceive as similar to us, or holding a positive attitude toward us. Second, we often trust people who are dependent upon us, since we are in a position to help or hurt them (and they frequently can do the same to us) (Solomon, 1960). Third, we are more likely to trust people who initiate cooperative, trusting behavior. Acting in a cooperative, trusting manner serves as an invitation to others, especially if the invitation is repeated despite initially contentious behavior from the opponent (Bonoma, Horai, Lindskold, Gahagan, and Tedeschi, 1969; Gahagan, Long, and Horai, 1969; Gruder and Duslak, 1973; Heller, 1967; Kleinke and Pohlan, 1971). Finally, we are more likely to trust negotiators who make concessions. The more the other's behavior communicates that they are holding firm in their fundamental commitment to their own needs, but at the same time working toward a joint solution, the more we are likely to find their conduct trustworthy, in the spirit of the best joint agreement (Rubin and Brown, 1975).

Given that trust has to be built during the negotiation, opening moves are crucial. The more cooperative, open, and nonthreatening the opening statements and actions of a party are, the more trust and cooperation is engendered in the other party (Crumbaugh and Evans, 1967; Michelini, 1971; Oskamp, 1970; Sermat and Gregovich, 1966). Once a cooperative position is established, it is more likely to persist. If cooperative behavior can be established at the very beginning, there is a tendency for parties to "lock in" to this cycle and make it continue (Pilisuk and Skolnick, 1978). Finally, these opening moves not only set the tone for the negotiation, but also the momentum. The longer the cycle of trust and cooperation continues, the easier it is to restore should the cycle break down (Komorita and Mechling, 1967; Sermat, 1967; Swinth, 1967b).

Clear and Accurate Communication

The next precondition for high quality integrative negotiation is clear and accurate communication. First, negotiators must state their needs in specific, concrete terms. Generalities and ambiguities should be avoided. Second, the communication must be understood by the other party. At a minimum, they must understand the meaning we attach to our statement; hopefully, they also attach the same meaning to the facts we do. Ambiguities and breakdowns in communication can frequently be picked up by others at the negotiating table. If someone on a bargaining team makes a confusing statement, others can try to clarify it. When one person on the other side does not grasp a difficult point, someone else from the same side will often be able to find the words or illustrations to bring out the meaning.

The more variety used in the communication channels, the better. Conversations over coffee breaks, separate meetings between chief negotiators outside the formal sessions, etc. all serve to channel communication through several negotiators and at different time periods, to insure that the message is accurately sent and understood. In addition, the more informal the communication channels, the better. Formal procedures for communication are useful during conflict, when there are strong negative feelings, when one or more parties is inclined to dominate. Under these circumstances, negotiators should follow a procedure that gives everyone a chance to speak; stick to the agenda so that everyone can be heard and their contributions can be noted. Other ways to insure effective communication processes in negotiation are covered extensively in Chapter 8.

A Belief in the Validity of the Other's Position

Finally, in distributive bargaining, negotiators invest time and energy in inflating and justifying the value of their own positions; they also may devote significant energy to debunking and demeaning the value and importance of the other's position. In contrast, integrative bargaining requires negotiators to accept the other's attitudes, information, and desires as accurate and valid. If the other's views are challenged or questioned, they may become angry and defensive, and hence unproductive in the problem solving process. The purpose of integrative bargaining is not to question or challenge the other's viewpoint, but to incorporate it into the definition of the problem, and to attend to it as the parties search for mutually acceptable alternatives. In addition, these views are to be given equal value to one's own position and viewpoint.

Summary

We identified six major factors that are fundamental preconditions for successful integrative bargaining to occur: establishment of some form of shared or common goal, faith in one's own ability to solve problems, the motivation and commitment to work together, trust in the opposing negotiator, the ability to accurately exchange information in spite of conflict conditions, and a belief in the validity and importance of the other's position. If the parties are not able to successfully meet all of these preconditions, they will need to make efforts to resolve these problems as the integrative bargaining process evolves. We will now turn to a fuller examination of the key strategies and stages in the integrative bargaining process.

STRATEGIES OF INTEGRATIVE BARGAINING

There are three major steps in the integrative bargaining process: problem identification, generating alternative solutions to the problem, and choosing a specific solution from among those alternatives. Our description will draw heavily from the writings of several authors who have studied the integrative process in great detail (Walton and McKersie, 1965; Filley, 1975; Pruitt, 1981, 1983). While these authors have frequently described the process in more than three steps, the fundamental process is the same.

Problem Identification

The problem identification step is often the most difficult one; this is even more true when several parties are involved. Consider the following example:

> In a large electronics plant, there was considerable difficulty with one of the subassemblies used in the final assembly department. Various pins and fittings that held the assembly in place were getting bent and distorted. When this happened to a unit, it would be laid aside as a reject. At the end of the month, these rejects would be returned to be reworked. The material to be reworked often arrived at the subassembly department at a time when they were under pressure to meet end of the month schedules; in addition, they were often low on parts. As a result, the rework often had to be done in

a rush and on overtime. The extra cost of overtime and expediting the rush work presented an additional problem, since it did not fit into the standard cost allocation system. The manager of the subassembly department did not want the costs allocated to his overhead charge. The manager of the final assembly department insisted that he should not pay the additional cost since his unit did not cause the problem; he argued that subassembly should bear the cost since it was their poor work that caused the problem. The subassembly department manager countered back that the parts were in good condition when they left his area and that it was the poor workmanship in the final assembly area that created the damage. The immediate costs were relatively small. What really concerned both parties was setting a long term precedent for paying the costs.

Eventually, an integrative solution was reached. During any given month, the subassembly department had a number of short slack time periods. Arrangements were made to regularly return damaged subassemblies in small batches, allowing them to be worked on during the slack periods. It also became clear that many people in the final assembly did not fully understand the parts they were handling, and may have contributed to some of the damage. Arrangements were made for some of these people to be temporarily transferred to the subassembly department during slack periods to learn more about that department, and to pick up some of the rush orders in that department.

This example helps us to identify a number of key aspects of the problem identification process (see Filley, 1975 and Shea, 1983 for fuller treatments of these points):

1. Define the problem in a way that is mutually acceptable to both sides. Ideally, parties enter the integrative bargaining process with little or no preconceptions about the solution, and with a totally open mind about the other negotiator's needs. As a problem is jointly defined, it should accurately reflect both parties' needs and priorities. Regrettably, this is not what we usually encounter. An understandable and widely held fear about integrative bargaining is that during the problem identification process, the other party is manipulating information and discussion so that the problem is stated to the other's advantage. In order for positive problem solving to occur, both parties must be committed to stating the problem in "neutral" terms. The problem statement must be mutually acceptable to both sides, and not stated so that it favors the preferences or priorities of one side over the other. The parties may be required to work the problem statement over several times until each side agrees upon its wording.

2. Keep the problem statement clean and simple. The major focus of an integrative agreement is to solve the primary problem. Secondary issues and concerns should be raised only if they are inextricably bound up with the primary problem. Discipline is required to identify the less important

issues and keep them out of the picture. This approach is in stark contrast to the distributive bargaining process, in which the parties are encouraged to "beef up" their position by bringing in a large number of secondary issues and concerns, in order to be able to trade these items off during the hard bargaining phase. If there are several issues on the table in an integrative negotiation, the parties may want to clearly identify the linkages between the issues and decide whether they will be approached as separate problems (which may be packaged together later) or redefined as one larger problem.

3. State the problem as a goal and identify the obstacles to attaining this goal. The problem should be defined as a *specific* end purpose to be achieved, or a goal to be attained, rather than as a solution. Moreover, problem definition should then proceed to specify what obstacles must be overcome for the goal to be attained. For example, in the previous example, the problem might be defined as "minimizing the number of rejects." This is not as clear and explicit as "cutting the number of rejects in half." Moreover, while this is a noble statement of a goal, greater progress may be made toward its solution if the parties can specify what they need to know about how the product is made, how defects occur, what must be done to repair defects, etc.

4. Depersonalize the problem. As we have pointed out earlier, when parties are engaged in conflict, they become evaluative and judgmental. Their own actions, strategies, and preferences are viewed in a positive light, and the other's actions, strategies, and preferences are generally viewed in a negative light. As a result, when negotiators attempt the integrative bargaining process, their evaluative judgments of the value or worth of the opponent's preferences can get in the way of clear and dispassionate thinking, simply because the other happens to own those preferences. Viewing the situation as, "your point of view is wrong and mine is right" inhibits the integrative bargaining process because we cannot attack the problem without attacking the person who "owns" the problem. In contrast, by depersonalizing the definition of the problem, i.e., "there is a difference of viewpoints on this problem," both sides can approach this difference as a problem "out there," rather than as one they personally own.

5. Separate the problem definition from the search for solutions. Finally, we will repeat the maxim that is stressed in every discussion of the problem solving process: don't jump to solutions until the problem is fully defined. In distributive bargaining, negotiators are encouraged to state the problem in terms of their preferred solution, and to "negotiate down" from this most desired alternative. In contrast, the integrative bargaining process cannot work unless negotiators avoid a premature jump to solutions (which probably favors one side or the other) and until

they have fully defined the problem and examined all of the possible alternative solutions.

Generating Alternative Solutions

The search for alternatives is the creative phase of integrative negotiations. Once the parties have agreed on a common definition of the problem, the next phase is for them to generate a variety of possible alternative solutions. The objective is to create a list of options or possible solutions that solve the problem; selecting from among those options will be the task of the final phase.

A number of techniques have been suggested to help negotiators generate alternative solutions. These approaches fall into two general categories. The first category includes those approaches that take the problem "as given," and simply attempts to create a long list of alternative options. In contrast, the second approach works to redefine, recast, or reframe the problem so as to create win-win alternatives out of what earlier appeared to be a win-lose problem.

Group Approaches To Generating Alternative Solutions

1. *Nominal groups.* In the nominal group technique, negotiators must start with the problem as defined; each one then individually prepares a written list of possible solutions. They are encouraged to list as many solutions as they can. Individuals then meet in small groups and read their solutions aloud, while a recorder writes them on flip charts or a blackboard. Particularly in a large group, this approach can generate a great number of possible options in a short period of time. These solutions can then be examined by all those working on the problem, and efforts begun to "weed them out" and seek preferred options.

2. *Surveys.* The disadvantage of nominal groups is that they usually do not solicit the ideas of those who are not present at the negotiation. In addition, the nominal group technique can be a time-consuming procedure. A second approach is simply to distribute a written questionnaire to a large group of people, stating the problem and asking them to list all of the possible solutions they can imagine. This process can be conducted in a very short period of time; however, the liability is that the parties cannot benefit from seeing and hearing the other people's ideas, as this occurs in the nominal group discussion stage.

3. *Brainstorming.* Individuals are asked to work in small groups, generating as many possible solutions to the problem as they can. Someone records the solutions as they are identified. Parties are urged to be spontaneous

and even impractical, and not to "censor" any idea because they think it is unworkable, too expensive, etc. Moreover, parties are required *not* to discuss or evaluate any solution as it is proposed, since discussion and evaluation will criticize ideas and stop the free flow of new ideas. The success of the brainstorming approach depends upon the free flow of ideas and the intellectual stimulation that should occur as these ideas are tossed around. Therefore, successful brainstorming and group discussion/generation of alternatives requires that the following rules be observed:

a. Avoid judging or evaluating solutions. As we stated earlier, criticism inhibits creative thinking. In addition, some of the most creative solutions come from ideas that initially seemed "wild" and impractical. Parties should impose a clear rule that no idea will be evaluated or ruled out until the group is finished generating options.

b. "Separate the people from the problem." Fisher and Ury (1981) and several other authors (e.g., Walton and McKersie, 1965; Filley, 1975) have noted that group discussion and brainstorming processes are often constrained because the parties attach "ownership" to certain preferred solutions and alternatives. Since competitive negotiators assume an offensive posture toward the other negotiator, they are unlikely to see the merits of a suggested alternative that appears to favor their opponent's position or was suggested by their opponent. In order for effective problem solving to occur, negotiators must concentrate on attacking the problem, and treat all possible solutions as equally viable, regardless of who initiated them. For example, if the parties try to depersonalize the suggestions by collectively listing them on a blackboard or flip charts, then they will be less likely to be able to identify who originated any particular idea, and in a better position to pick the solution which best solves the problem.

c. Be exhaustive in the brainstorming process. Many times, the best ideas come to us after a meeting is over, or after a problem is solved. Sometimes, this may also happen because the parties did not "stay with it" long enough. Research has shown that when brainstormers work at the process for a long period of time, the best ideas are most likely to surface during the later part of the activity. As Shea (1983) notes:

"Generating a large number of superior ideas apparently increases the probability of developing superior ideas. Ideas, when expressed, tend to trigger other ideas. And since ideas can be built one upon the other, those that develop later in a session are often superior to those without refinement or elaboration. What difference does it make if a lot of impractical ideas are recorded? They can be evaluated and dismissed rapidly in the next step of the win-win process. The important thing is to ensure that few, if any, usable ideas are lost." (p. 57)

d. Ask outsiders. Often people who know nothing about the past history of the conflict, or even about the issues, can suggest options and possibilities that haven't been considered. Outsiders can provide additional input to the list of alternatives, or can help to orchestrate the process and keep the parties on track.

Generating Viable Solutions: Moving from Positions to Needs

Nominal groups, surveys, and brainstorming groups are three different ways negotiators can involve others in the process of generating alternative solutions. The success of these approaches relies on the principle that groups of people are frequently better problem solvers than single individuals, particularly because groups provide a wider number of perspectives on the problem, and hence can invent more alternative ways to solve it. However, as we noted, groups must observe the rules and "constraints" as we have just identified, or the group process will quickly degenerate into a win-lose competition.

Two negotiators working by themselves can also use these techniques, with the same precautions that we have imposed on groups. However, there is a second approach that has also been identified for generating alternatives. This approach states that rather than simply attempting to brainstorm alternative solutions, the parties should specifically attempt to define their underlying needs, and develop alternatives that will successfully meet those needs. Research by Pruitt and his colleagues (1981; 1983; Pruitt and Lewis, 1981; Pruitt and Carnevale, 1982) has led them to identify five different methods for achieving integrative agreements. Each of these approaches successfully refocuses the issues under dispute, but also requires progressively more information about the other side's true needs. Each will be illustrated by an example concerning a husband and wife and their attempts to decide where to spend their two-week vacation. The husband wants to go to the mountains, and the wife to the seashore.

Expanding the Pie.   Many conflicts begin with a shortage of resources. It is not possible for both sides to satisfy their interests because there is a limit to the amount of available resources, and the parties cannot both obtain their objectives under the current allocation. Suppose the married couple could persuade their employers to give them four weeks for their vacation; this would be an example of expanding the pie. Expanding the pie requires no information about the other party other than his or her interests, and is a simple way to solve resource shortage problems. In addition, the approach assumes that simply enlarging the resources will solve the problem. Thus, four weeks would be a very satisfactory solution if the husband and wife both liked the mountains and the beach but preferred one or the other. However, expanding the pie would not be a satisfactory solution if their conflict were based on other grounds, i.e., the husband couldn't stand the beach, or the wife wouldn't go to the mountains under any conditions.

Nonspecific Compensation.   A second way for the conflict to be resolved is that one person obtains his objectives, while the other person is "paid off" for accommodating the other's interests. This is called nonspecific compensation. In the vacation example, the wife could tell the husband that if he agrees to go to the seashore, she will buy him a new videorecorder. For nonspecific compensation to work, the person doing the compensating needs to know what is valuable to the person, and how seriously the other is inconvenienced (i.e., how much compensation is needed to restore a feeling of equity). Several different kinds of "offers" might need to be tested in order to find out how much compensation it will take to satisfy the other. This discovery process can turn into a secondary negotiation itself, as the husband may choose to set very high "demands" as the price for going along to the beach.

Logrolling.   Successful logrolling requires that the parties establish (or find) more than one issue in conflict; the parties then agree to "trade off" these issues so that one party achieves his top priority on the first issue, while the other person achieves her top priority on the second issue. Each party gets what is most important. Thus, suppose that the husband and wife not only disagree about where to take their vacation, but also about the kind of accommodations. The husband prefers inexpensive housekeeping cabins while the wife prefers a luxury hotel. If the wife decides that the quality of accommodations is a more important issue than location, they may be able to agree that a luxury hotel in the mountains would meet both their needs. In some ways, logrolling is a variation of nonspecific compensation; the parties "compensate" each other in exchange for attaining their most important priority issue. It is also a process that is frequently done by trial and error, as the parties experiment with various "packages" of options that will satisfy both the other person and themselves. The parties must establish which issues are at stake, and which issues are of high and low priority to themselves and to the other. Even if it appears initially that there is only one issue at stake, the parties will frequently find secondary issues that allow the logrolling process to begin.

Cost Cutting.   By cost cutting, one party achieves his/her objectives and the other's costs are reduced by going along. In the vacation example, suppose that the husband really likes a quiet and peaceful vacation, and dislikes the beach because of the crowds, while the wife really likes the beach because of all the activity. If peace and quiet is what the husband really wants, then he may be willing to go to the beach if the wife assures him that they will stay in an inexpensive place at the beach that is also located far away from the other resorts. Unlike nonspecific compensation, where the compensated party simply receives "something" for going along, cost cutting tactics are specifically designed to minimize the other party's costs and suffering. The technique is a more sophisticated form of integrative negotiation because it requires knowledge of more than the other party's preferences—e.g., their interests, what really matters to them, how their needs can be more specifically met.

Bridging.   Finally, by bridging, the parties are able to invent new options that meet each side's needs. Thus, if the husband reveals that what he really wants to be able to do on his vacation is hunt and fish, while the wife wants to swim, go shopping, and enjoy the nightlife, they may be able to discover a resort area that will satisfy all of these desires. Successful bridging requires a fundamental reformulation of the problem such that the parties are no longer squabbling over their "positions"; instead, they are disclosing sufficient information in order to discover their interests and needs, and then inventing options that will satisfy both parties' needs. Bridging solutions do not always remedy all concerns; the wife may not get the salt sea air at the resort, and the husband may spend more money than he wanted to. But both have agreed that taking their vacation together is more desirable than taking it separately (i.e., they have committed themselves to interdependence) and have worked to invent a solution that meets their most important needs. If negotiators fundamentally commit themselves to a win-win negotiation, bridging solutions are likely to be highly satisfactory to both sides.

Summary.   The approaches to problem solving that we have discussed— nominal groups, brainstorming, inventing options, etc.—may lend the impression that if bargainers simply invent enough different options, they will "luck" into a solution to solve their problem. While this sometimes happens, the best options and bridging solutions are usually attained by virtue of hard work and pursuit of several related processes: information exchange, focusing on interests rather than positions, and firm flexibility (Fisher and Ury, 1981; Pruitt, 1983). Information exchange will allow the parties to maximize the amount of information commonly available. Focusing on interests will allow the parties to move beyond opening positions and demands to determine what the parties really want, what needs truly need to be satisfied. Finally, firm flexibility means that the parties must be firm with regard to the ends they want to achieve (i.e., interests), while remaining flexible on the means by which they are achieved. Firm flexibility recognizes that negotiators have one or two fundamental interests or principles which must be achieved, while there may be a wide variety of positions, possible solutions or secondary issues that get drawn into the negotiations. Thus, while there are many viable alternative solutions that will satisfy a negotiator, some are more important because they directly address the "bottom line" or most important priorities. Negotiators need to be able to signal to the other where they are firm, and where they are willing to be flexible. Pruitt (1983) and Fisher and Ury (1981) suggest several tactics that may be used to communicate firm flexibility to an opponent:

1. Use contentious (competitive) tactics to defend and establish basic interests, rather than using them to demand a particular "position" or solution to the dispute. State what you want clearly.

2. At the same time, send signals of flexibility and concern about your willingness to address the other party's interests. Openly express concern for the other's welfare, and "acknowledge their interests as part of the problem" (Fisher and Ury, p. 55). Thus, you communicate that you have your own interests at stake but are willing to try to address the other's as well.

3. Indicate a willingness to change your proposals if a way can be found to bridge the two parties' interests.

4. Demonstrate a problem solving capacity. For example, use "experts" on a negotiating team or bring them in as consultants based on their experitise at inventing new ideas.

5. Maintain open communication channels. Do not eliminate opportunities to communicate and work together, if only to continually demonstrate that you are willing to work together with the other.

6. Reaffirm what is most important to you through the use of "deterrent" statements—i.e., "I need to attain this; this is a must; this cannot be touched or changed." These statements communicate to the other that a particular interest is fundamental to your position, but does not necessarily mean that the other can't satisfy their interests as well.

7. Reexamine any aspects of your interests which are clearly unacceptable to the other party, and determine if they are still essential to your fundamental position. It is rare that negotiators will find that they truly disagree on basic interests.

8. Separate and isolate contentious tactics from problem solving behavior so that neither undermines the other. This may be accomplished by clearly specifying a "shift in gears" in the negotiation process, by separating the two processes with a break or recess, or, in team negotiations, by having one party act contentiously and then having a second negotiator offer to engage in problem solving. This last approach is called a "good guy/bad guy" or "black hat/white hat" act and is also frequently

used as a purely distributive negotiating tactic. In this situation, however, the desire is to separate the competitive from the collaborative elements of the process by changing the individuals who represent those positions.

Evaluation and Selection of Alternatives

The final stage in the integrative bargaining process is to evaluate the options generated during the previous phase, and to select the best alternatives to implement them. When the problem is a reasonably simple one, the evaluation and selection steps may be effectively combined into a single step. When confronted with complex problems or a large number of alternative options, however, the evaluation stage may take considerably longer. Negotiators will need to determine criteria for judging the options, and then rank order or weigh each option as it matches the criteria. Finally, the parties will be required to engage in some form of a consensus decision process, by which they debate the relative merits of each side's preferred options and come to agreement on the best options. The following guidelines should be used in evaluating options and reaching a consensus decision (Walton and McKersie, 1965; Filley, 1975; Shea, 1983).

1. Narrow the range of solution options. Examine the list of options generated and focus on the options that are strongly supported by any negotiator. This approach is more positive than allowing people to focus on negative, unacceptable criteria. Solutions not strongly advocated by at least one negotiator would be eliminated.

2. Evaluate solutions on the basis of quality and acceptability. Solutions should be judged on two major criteria: how good they are, and how acceptable will they be to those who have to implement them. These are the same two dimensions that research has revealed to be critical to the effective use of participative decision making in organizations (Vroom and Yetton, 1973). The quality dimensions will be evaluated by determining what is best, what is most rational, what is most logical. To the degree that parties can support their arguments with statements of hard fact, logical deduction and appeals to rational criteria, these arguments will be more compelling in obtaining the support of others. "Appeal to objective standards" for making decisions, suggest Fisher and Ury (1981). The acceptance dimension will be judged based on what is fair and equitable to all concerned. These criteria may be different from what is most rational or judged to be the "best" solution. When a specific solution must meet the criteria of both quality and acceptability (fairness), those evaluating the solution options may have to be prepared to make tradeoffs between the two to insure that both criteria are met.

3. If the decision making process is expected to be controversial, agree to the criteria in advance of evaluating options. This process is often followed when groups have to narrow the choice down to a single

alternative, i.e., to pick a candidate for a new job, or to select the option that is "most likely to succeed." If the parties first debate their criteria and determine which ones are most important, they will be able to decide on criteria independent of the consideration of any particular candidate or option. Then, when the individual candidates or options are considered, they will pick the best one based on their criteria, not on the individual preferences of one side or the other. If the parties agree, they may revise their criteria later to improve their choice, but this should only be done by the agreement of all negotiators. In fact, it is not a bad idea to periodically check criteria and determine whether each negotiator places the same priority on them as before. Discussion of alternatives frequently leads negotiators to revise their preferences, as well as their estimates of the probability of success, cost of particular options, etc.

4. **Parties should not have to justify their personal preferences.** Why someone likes what he likes, or dislikes what he dislikes, is often hard to publicly justify. "Why do you like that?" "I don't know, I just do," is usually the reply. Moreover, little is gained by requiring negotiators to conjure up some justification, other than to make them angry because the simple statement of their preferences is not viewed as sufficient. For example, if the topic under negotiation is what to have for dinner, and one party states that he hates clam chowder, no amount of justification or persuasion is likely to change that person's mind. Instead, the parties would be more productive if they accepted this information and attempted to explore other options for dinner.

5. **Be alert to the influence of intangibles in selecting options.** Some options will be favored more by one side because they help that negotiator satisfy some intangible—gaining recognition, looking strong or "tough" to a constituency, feeling like they have "won," etc. The presence of particular intangibles will lead a negotiator to fight harder to attain a particular solution option, because that option satisfies both tangibles and intangibles. Help the other party identify those intangibles and make them public as part of the evaluation process; options which satisfy those intangibles are likely to be more preferred by the other, and to the degree that you can live with them, they may be important concessions to make to the other.

6. **If the problem of evaluating and judging options is large and complex, use subgroups.** Small groups may be particularly helpful when there are lots of complex options that must be considered, or when many people will be affected by the solution. Groups of 6–8 people, composed of representatives from each "faction," "side," or subgroup, will be able to work more effectively than a large group.

7. **If the parties become emotional, take time out to cool off.** Even though

the parties may have completed the hardest part of the process—generating a list of viable options—they may become upset if communication breaks down or they feel their preferences are not being acknowledged, or the other side pushes too hard for a particular option. If the parties become angry, take a break. Negotiators should make their dissatisfaction known, and the reasons for it should be openly discussed. Make sure the parties are back on an even emotional keel before attempting to return to evaluating the options. Finally, work as hard as possible to keep discussions on the specifics of the proposals, and not on the people advocating them. Keep the people advocating a point of view separate from the options for settlement, and depersonalize the discussion as much as possible.

8. Keep "decisions" tentative and conditional until all aspects of the final package proposal are put together. Even though a rather clear consensus may be emerging as to the solution option(s) that will be selected, the parties should talk about the solution in conditional terms. This tentative tone allows any side to change or revise the final package at any time. Points agreed upon in earlier discussion are not necessarily firm until the entire package is determined. Parties do not have to feel that because they "gave up" on an earlier option, that they have burned their bridges behind them; rather, nothing is final until everything is final.

9. Minimize formality and record keeping until final agreements are closed. In general, the parties do not want to lock themselves into any specific language or written agreement until they are close to a consensus. They want to make sure that they will not be held to comments made and recorded in notes, transcripts, etc. In general, the fewer the transcripts, minutes, or written records during the solution generating phase, the better. In contrast, when the parties are close to consensus, one side should attempt to write down what has been agreed to. This document may then be used as a "single text" (Fisher and Ury, 1981), passed around from party to party as often as necessary until all sides agree to the phrasing and wording of their agreement.

PRINCIPLED NEGOTIATING TACTICS

Fisher and Ury (1981), in their book *Getting to Yes*, have summarized the major principles of the integrative bargaining process, and used these principles to generate a set of "stock phrases" that capture the basic sequence of an integrative negotiation. While negotiators do not need to use the phrases verbatim, or in this specific order, the phrases capture the essence of an integrative negotiation.

Stock Phrases	*Underlying Concepts*
1. Please correct me if I'm wrong.	1. Verify the facts so that both sides agree to them.
2. We appreciate what you've done for us.	2. Separate the people from the problem. Give personal support to the other person but not to his or her position.
3. Our concern is fairness.	3. Our position is based upon principle.
4. We would like to settle this on the basis not of selfish interest and power, but principle.	4. Defend your position based on the principle, even if the opponent tries to personalize it.
5. Trust is a separate issue.	5. Same. Return to the principle of fairness.
6. Could I ask a few questions to see whether my facts are right?	6. Ask questions rather than making assertions.
7. What's the principle behind your actions?	7. Find out the principle behind the other's actions if there is one.
8. Let me see if I understand what you are saying.	8. Use "active listening"—clarify your understanding of the other's position.
9. Let me get back to you.	9. Evaluate your position outside of the negotiation. Verify facts, think it over, check with constituency.
10. Let me show you where I have difficulty following your reasoning.	10. Present your rationale before presenting a new proposal.
11. One fair solution might be.	11. Present your proposal in context of the principle (fairness).
12. If we agree, or if we disagree.	12. Present alternative outcomes in the event of agreement or no agreement.
13. We'd be happy to settle in a manner most convenient for you.	13. Let the other have some influence on the final agreement.
14. It's been a pleasure dealing with you.	14. End the negotiation on a conciliatory note, even if you don't feel conciliatory.

SUMMARY

In this chapter, we have reviewed the strategy and tactics of integrative bargaining. The fundamental structure of integrative bargaining is that the parties are able to define goals which allow both sides to achieve their objectives. Integrative bargaining is the process of defining these goals and engaging in a set of procedures that permit both sides to maximize objectives.

The chapter began with a discussion of a model of conflict management. This model allows us to describe differences in individual approaches to conflict according to the degree of concern an individual shows for attaining his own outcomes, and/or helping the other party attain his outcomes. It also shows that a collaborative, problem solving approach is best represented by a high level of concern for both sides achieving their objectives. Negotiators frequently fail at integrative bargaining because they fail to perceive the integrative potential of the negotiating problem. However, breakdowns also occur due to "distributive" assumptions about the bargaining problem, the "mixed-motive" nature of the issues, or the negotiator's previous relationship with one another.

Successful integrative bargaining requires several preconditions. First, the parties must be able to understand the other's true needs and objectives. Second, they must be able to create a free flow of information and an open exchange of ideas. Third, they should attempt to focus on their similarities, and emphasize their commonalities rather than their differences. Finally, they should engage in a search for solutions that meet the goals of both sides. This is a very different process from the one described in the previous chapter. In order for this integrative bargaining process to occur successfully, several preconditions are necessary. First, the process will be greatly facilitated by some form of common goal or objective. This goal may be one that the parties both want to achieve, one that they want to share, or one that they could not possibly attain unless they worked together. Second, they must share a motivation and commitment to work together, to make their relationship a productive one. Third, they must be able to trust one another, and to work hard to establish and maintain that trust. Fourth, there must be clear and accurate communication about what each one wants, and an effort to understand the other's needs. Finally, the parties must be willing to believe that the other's needs are valid. Rather than talk the other out of his needs, or be unwilling to acknowledge them as important, each must be willing to work for both their own needs and the other's needs to find the best joint arrangement. Given these preconditions, the integrative bargaining process is most likely to be successful.

There are three major stages in the integrative bargaining process: problem identification, generating solutions, and choosing a specific solution. For each of these stages, we proposed a number of techniques and tactics to make the process successful. In spite of all of these suggestions, it needs to be stated again that the process is not as "easy" as it seems for parties who are locked in conflict, defensiveness, and sticking to a hard line position. Only by working to create the necessary conditions for integrative bargaining can the process occur with ease and success. In Chapter 12, we shall discuss a number of ways that parties can defuse hostility, defensiveness, and the disposition toward hard line negotiating in order to create the conditions for successful integrative negotiation.

6

Key Elements in the Strategic Process

In the previous two chapters, we described the fundamental nature of distributive and integrative bargaining processes. Knowledge of both of these processes is necessary to negotiate effectively. In this chapter, several other key elements of the negotiation process are explored. These include:

- the tangibles and intangibles at stake;
- the motivational intentions of negotiators;
- the normative "rules" that negotiators use to decide what is "rational" and "fair" in negotiations;
- the physical site where negotiations take place; and
- the role of time and time limits (deadlines) in negotiation.

TANGIBLES VS. INTANGIBLES REVISITED

In Chapter 1, we stated that one of the most important elements in planning any negotiation is to diagnose the tangible and intangible elements at stake. By tangible elements, we mean the issues on the table in the formal deliberations—such as, the price of a particular commodity, the rate to be charged for services, the wording of a contractual agreement, or the budgeted amount for next year's office supplies. The tangibles are those negotiable items that will be included in the formal agreement; these are the substantive issues which consume the most time and attention in normal deliberations.

Intangibles, on the other hand, are the wide variety of "psychological" factors that heavily influence an individual's *motivation* toward negotiation, and his comfort and satisfaction with both the *process* and *outcome* of that negotiation. Motivational factors may be a predisposition to "win" (however that may be defined), to defeat an opponent, to do better than one did in a previous negotiation, to appear "tough" to a constituency, or to minimize losses. Comfort and satisfaction with the negotiation process encompasses a variety of perceptions about whether the procedure and the outcomes were fair, just, or equitable. Not only do intangibles play a strong role in determining how satisfied we felt with the tangibles, but concern for a particular intangible can become so important to a negotiator that it can dominate the process and "drive out" productive discussion of tangibles. For example, major strikes by unions may be called because the parties deadlocked over several cents an hour difference in their wage contract deliberations. The "substance" of their conflict (the relative value of several cents an hour) is minor compared to the total value of the contract at stake. However, both sides probably took a position that neither was going to make another concession, and hence the "principle" of no further concession making (a very important intangible) would be sufficient to cause the strike to occur.

Because intangibles can play such a central role in determining individual satisfaction with both the negotiation process and its outcomes, we will devote the first part of this chapter to examining several key intangibles in detail. We will first explore the role of a negotiator's motivation in negotiation, and then turn to an understanding of the ways that bargainers judge what is rational and fair in negotiation.

MOTIVATIONAL ORIENTATION OF THE PARTIES

One aspect of the process that often surprises new, less "experienced" bargainers is that all negotiators do *not* approach bargaining with the same motivations. It may initially seem that the dominant and primary motivation of most bargainers is to achieve the best deal they can. While this is often true, closer examination of individual motivations usually reveals a far more complex picture. One bargainer may want to get the best deal he can—but still be fair; a second may want to get the best deal she can—and also do better than her opponent; a third may want to get the best deal he can—but make sure that he and his opponent are good friends after negotiations are completed. A negotiator's *motivational orientation* will be defined as that group of attitudes and perceptions which predisposes a negotiator to behave in certain ways, and to expect the other to behave in certain ways. These predispositions and intentions have an extremely powerful impact on the manner in which negotiators approach bargaining.

Rubin and Brown (1975), reviewed a variety of experimental research on the role played by motivational orientation, and concluded that motivational orientation (MO) can be roughly distinguished into three general types: individualistic, cooperative, and competitive. These orientations may be briefly summarized as follows: A negotiator with an *individualistic MO* is predisposed to maximize his outcomes without regard to how the other bargainer fares. He is not interested in how the other party does, i.e., whether the other wins or loses, in relative or absolute terms; he is only concerned about maximizing his own individual outcome.

A negotiator with a *cooperative MO* is predisposed to want to work with the other negotiator toward maximizing their joint outcome. Each party is concerned with the other's welfare; whether the other wins or loses is as important as whether the negotiator achieves his/her own outcomes. The negotiator wants to win as much as he can, but in addition, he wants the other negotiator to win as much as she can.

A negotiator with a *competitive MO* is predisposed to want to do better than his opponent. The party is concerned with his opponent's welfare and outcomes to determine how well he himself is doing; the primary motivation is to win as much as possible, *and* do better than the other.

Rubin and Brown's review of earlier research lends great credibility to the importance of motivational orientation for several major reasons. First, motivational orientation has a clear and strong impact on a negotiator's perceptions, predispositions, and expectations *prior to* actual negotiation. Negotiators with a cooperative motivational orientation approach negotiation desirous of working out a collaborative joint agreement with the opponent; they expect the other to behave cooperatively and reciprocate their offer. In contrast. bargainers with a competitive motivational orientation want to do better than their opponent, and hence approach negotiation with an eye to developing and using tactics which will accomplish that objective. As a result, they are also likely to be more suspicious and mistrustful of their opponent's intentions, and expect similar behavior from their opponent. Negotiators with an individualistic motivational orientation simply want to maximize their outcomes. As a result, they may be more likely to "size up" the situation and their opponent early in the negotiating dialogue, to determine what strategy will lead to optimal results. Individualistically motivated bargainers may therefore be more likely to depend on reading "cues" from their opponent, or from the issues at stake to determine how to behave.

In addition to shaping attitude and expectations, motivational orientation also affects the way bargainers actually behave. Those with a cooperative MO behave more cooperatively toward their opponent, while those with a competitive MO behave more competitively. Rubin and Brown also report that in most cases, the cooperative MOs also achieve greater actual gains from the negotiation than those with an individualistic or competitive MO. However, this result may be a consequence of the ways many experimental bargaining research situations were constructed, (for example, that the payoffs in the experimental games often favored the cooperative alternatives as the most economically rewarding one). Therefore, we don't know whether cooperative MO negotiators do better because of their style, or because of the structure of the negotiating problem given to research subjects.

While experimental laboratory research has investigated three primary forms of motivational orientation, in reality, there are many other motivations that can be identified. One bargainer may want to look good to an audience who will evaluate his performance; a second may want to gain revenge for a previous embarrassment. A third may want to establish a reputation for integrity or credibility; while a fourth may wish to set a precedent for future deliberations. All of these intangible (but important) motivators will shape, modify or constrain the way a bargainer will define objectives, and the strategy he/she will select to pursue those objectives. The more a negotiator can clearly understand his/her own motivation in a negotiation, as well as that of his/her opponent, the better that negotiator will be able to design and implement a strategy, or predict the other's strategic response.

Variations in the motivation orientation of negotiators may be traced to four key sources and contributing factors.

Individual Personality, Attitudes and Predispositions.   Predispositions toward cooperative, individualistic, or competitive behavior may be the result of deeply rooted historical experiences and differences in an individual's personality. These differences in experience and personality shape and condition individual attitudes and expectations. As a result, when approaching any situation of interdependence, individual differences in personality and background will predispose bargainers toward a cooperative, competitive or individualistic style. Many of the specific personality dimensions that predispose individuals toward more cooperative or competitive behavior are discussed in Chapter 11.

Specific Situation Factors.   In many of the experimental research studies that investigated the effects of motivational orientation, research subjects were directed by the experimenter to behave in a cooperative, individualistic, or competitive manner. What are the analogies to this in real-world negotiations? There are at least *two* kinds of situational factors that might orient a bargainer toward adopting a particular MO: specific directions and instructions given by his/her constituency (or some audience who will evaluate and judge the negotiator), and cues picked up in the preliminary stages of a negotiation that reveal how the opponent intends to behave. The impact of audiences and constituencies on a bargainer's behavior will be explored extensively in Chapter 9. Preliminary cues from the opposing negotiator include a variety of things: a willingness or unwillingness to communicate, gestures of friendliness or hostility, or the opponent's reputation for being cooperative or competitive. Bargainers who are unsure of what their opponent will do (but want that information in order to define their own strategy) will "have all of their antenna out" to scan the other's behavior in the first few minutes of contact. Negotiators should, therefore, carefully plan what kinds of signals they want to send, and also take care that they accurately read the other's intentions from these early signals.

Reward Structure. A third way that motivational orientation may vary is simply by altering the specific economic reward derived from cooperative, competitive or individualistic behavior. If it is significantly more profitable for the parties to cooperate, most will cooperate; if it is significantly more profitable for the parties to compete, they will try to compete—even if such competition leads to mutual frustration and stalemate. In most negotiation situations—both simulated and real—"rational behavior" is frequently equated with maximizing one's own outcomes, i.e., rationality is defined as economic rationality. As a result, if individuals are behaving rationally in an economic situation, we can expect that they will calculate the costs and benefits of alternative behavioral strategies and select the one that maximizes the rewards.

Apparent Reward Structure. We have identified this fourth category—apparent reward structure—as a separate category from "real" reward structure because *perceived* differences in the distribution of rewards often are as important as actual differences. Negotiators often do not perform as close an analysis of the reward structure as we might want. As a result, many negotiators can be easily tempted toward competitive or cooperative behavior simply by the way information about reward structure is presented to them. For example, Rubin and Brown reviewed 25 bargaining studies, each of which had systematically varied the perceived "size" of a conflict—that is, the perceived rewards associated with cooperation (or competition) relative to the perceived costs. "Larger" conflicts were ones where the rewards for competition were greater relative to the rewards for cooperation. Twenty-one of these 25 studies found that the larger the *perceived* conflict, the more negotiators were predisposed toward competitive behavior. A second element of "apparent" reward structure may be the short-run vs. long-run rewards and cost associated with competitive and cooperative strategies. Negotiators are frequently short-sighted, and hence choose in favor of the apparent benefits obtained from short-run competition—a "hit and run" strategy—rather than systematically determining the rewards that could be derived from investing time to develop a long-term collaborative relationship. If the relationship with an opponent is, of necessity, going to be long-term—long-term purchasing agreement, a labor contract, or a treaty—the parties would do well to recognize the harmful long-term consequences that come from self-serving, short-run strategies.

Taken as a group, these four factors—negotiator personality and attitudes, situational pressures, "real" reward structure and "apparent" reward structure—contribute a great deal to understanding what motivates bargainers, and how that motivation will affect their expectations, intentions, and strategies. As we stated earlier, the more a negotiator can learn about what major factors are contributing to his/her own motivations, and those of the opponent, the more decisively he/she can plan a strategy and predict his/her opponent's behavior.

INTANGIBLES AND NORMATIVE RULES IN NEGOTIATION—RATIONALITY AND FAIRNESS

In the previous section, we argued that one major intangible element in negotiating strategy is the motivational orientation of the negotiating parties. While this motivation may be a direct result of the nature of actual rewards to be derived from cooperative or competitive behavior, motivation may also be highly influenced by perceived rewards, personality factors, and expectations shaped by their constituencies or by the other bargainer's behavior. A second major way that intangible factors affect negotiators is by shaping their perception of the social rules, or norms, that govern the bargaining process. It is not unreasonable to assert that most negotiators expect their deliberations to be based on a *rational* dialogue between the parties, and that both parties will behave rationally in the negotiation process. In addition, most negotiators expect that the negotiation process—and the outcomes—will be *fair* and *just*. Differences over these three key expectations—rationality, fairness, and justice—are at the root of many fundamental misunderstandings and breakdowns in negotiation. Perceptions of what is rational, fair, and just will differ significantly among cooperative vs. competitive parties. These differing perceptions and expectations of what behavior is "proper" or "improper" will greatly affect the strategy and tactics selected by a negotiator, and/or the reaction to strategy and tactics employed by an opponent. We shall now consider each of these three rules separately.

RATIONALITY

Rational behavior in negotiation is usually defined as economic rationality. Economists traditionally presume that people are capable of determining which outcomes are more valuable or worthwhile than others, and motivated to maximize "value" or "utility." Rational behavior is defined as behavior which is consistently directed toward maximizing this utility (Rapoport, 1966; Schelling, 1960). Since the substance of bargaining is focused on the division of tangible resources (price, quantity, rate, delivery time, quality level, etc.), most negotiators expect that the bargaining process will be a rational exchange of offers and counter-offers. By "rational," we mean again that the parties expect that the other will direct his/her behavior toward those outcomes which maximize their payoffs. Deviations from this expected behavior, for whatever reasons, are frequently classified as "irrational."

Let us use an example to illustrate the definition of rational and irrational conduct. Seigel and Fouraker (1960) conducted a series of experiments in which two parties exchanged bids in a simulation of a "bilateral monopoly," for example, one seller and one buyer in a simple economic market. Both buyer and seller were given a chart which represented a range of prices of a commodity on one side of the table, and a range of quantities of the commodity on the other side. Within the table were represented the profit to each person for every combination of price and quantity sold. (See Figure 1 for a simplified example of their tables.) The parties sat in separate rooms and traded bids back and forth by means of written messages. The Seller always began by quoting the price for the commodity; the Buyer then responded by quoting the number of units he/she wanted to purchase. Each party then recorded his/her profits by reading the intersection of the particular price/quantity amount in the table.

If you study Figure 6–1, it is clear that the Seller makes more money if he quotes a higher price; however, the Buyer makes more money if he purchases a greater amount at a lower price. The Seller will thus quote prices which are toward the $10 end of the scale. Since the Seller always quotes price first, the Buyer's most *rational* strategy (in economic terms) would be to maximize his own payoff given whatever price the Seller quotes. Thus, even if the Seller is quoting a very high price ($10), and clearly making significantly more money than the Buyer (e.g., in the range of $2,940–$4,380 for the Seller, compared to $540–$1,020 for the Buyer), the Buyer should pick that option which maximized his payoff given what the Seller has quoted. Thus, suppose that the Seller quotes a price of $10 per unit. To maximize his payoff, the Buyer should purchase nine units; the Seller would make $3,190 and the Buyer would make $1,030. If the Seller quoted a price of $7 per unit, then the Buyer would maximize his profit by purchasing 12 units; the Seller would make $3,100 and the Buyer would make $1,660.

When we play this game with students in our classes, it becomes readily clear that many Buyers engage in behavior which can only be called "irrational," (i.e., behavior which does not economically maximize their outcome on each transaction). In response to high bids by the Seller, Buyers sometimes quote a quantity to punish the other (they deny the Seller maximum profit); they sometimes even bid zero (thus denying any profit to both of them). Why would they do this? What motivates behavior to obtain no profit at the expense of gaining some profit? The Buyers have several explanations. They are upset that the Seller always goes first. They want to somehow communicate to the Seller that they would prefer prices which would allow the Buyer to earn greater profits. Is this behavior "rational?" By the pure standards of economic rationality, no. But by the "intangible"

FIGURE 6-1
Bilateral Monopoly Negotiations[a]

	Price		Buyer, Quantity Purchased in Thousand Units								
			8	9	10	11	12	13	14	15	16
Seller,	$ 3	B	$2140	$2290	$2420	$2530	$2620	$2690	$2740	$2770	$2780
Dollars/Unit		S	1820	1930	2020	2090	2140	2170	2180	2170	2140
	$ 4	B	1980	2110	2220	2310	2380	2430	2460	2470	2460
		S	1980	2110	2220	2310	2380	2430	2460	2470	2460
	$ 5	B	1820	1930	2020	2090	2140	2170	2180	2170	2140
		S	2140	2290	2420	2530	2620	2690	2740	2770	2780
	$ 6	B	1660	1750	1820	1870	1900	1910	1900	1870	1820
		S	2300	2470	2620	2750	2860	2950	3020	3070	3100
	$ 7	B	1500	1570	1620	1650	1660	1650	1620	1570	1500
		S	2460	2650	2820	2970	3100	3210	3300	3370	3420
	$ 8	B	1340	1390	1420	1430	1420	1390	1340	1270	1180
		S	2620	2830	3020	3190	3340	3470	3580	3670	3740
	$ 9	B	1180	1210	1220	1210	1180	1130	1060	970	860
		S	2780	3010	3220	3410	3580	3730	3860	3970	4060
	$10	B	1020	1030	1020	990	940	870	780	670	540
		S	2940	3190	3420	3630	3820	3990	4140	4270	4380

[a]Table entries are dollar profits for buyer and seller, based on price and quantity negotiated.

standards of what is perceived to be fair and just, or by their view of the long-run vs. short-run objectives, their strategies become quite credible and persuasive.

For the purposes of our discussion, "irrational" behavior will be described as behavior which is interpreted as: (a) not conforming to the strict principle of economic outcome maximization, and/or (b) unpredictable. With regard to the first definition, we have used the example of the Seigel and Fouraker bargaining situation to show that a negotiator's "efforts" may be oriented toward intangible factors as well as economic outcomes. This is particularly true when negotiators are motivated to save face and look good to an audience or constituency, or get revenge or retribution from their opponent, or keep their opponent from succeeding, or behave consistent with some "principle" (e.g., integrity, reputation) rather than maximize economic outcomes. They will be more likely to ignore economic rationality in favor of some form of socially-defined rationality and consistency.

The second definition of irrationality applies when a negotiator's behavior is unpredictable and/or inconsistent. "Unpredictability" covers a wide variety of behaviors, since what is unpredictable is very much related to what a negotiator expects the opponent to do, and whether these expectations are met or not. Since expectations are shaped by both past experience and the basic definition of a negotiation situation (Chapter 1), a wide variety of behaviors may be classified as "irrational" ("unpredictable"). Some of the most common examples include:

- Refusing to make any concessions at all.
- Making concessions in "the wrong direction," i.e., solidifying a position and making more extreme demands.
- High degrees of emotionality, and making decisions based on volatile emotional moods.
- Eliminating one's ability to control one's own behavior, i.e., allowing fate, chance, or luck to determine the outcomes both parties achieve.

The last two examples—emotionality, and the willingness to abandon control over outcomes—are very powerful negotiating tactics that often occur in competitive, distributive negotiations. By suggesting that he will make his decisions largely on the basis of his emotional mood, a negotiator communicates that he is personally "out of control." Decisions are no longer being made on rational, predictable grounds. In addition, the negotiator's emotional conduct may embarrass others, particularly in public; this embarrassment may motivate others to let the negotiator have his way. A child who throws a temper tantrum in front of his mother in a department store may get the toy he wanted, "just to keep him quiet." Similarly, a manager who "throws a fit" and storms out of a negotiation may get his way, because others around the table "didn't know that he felt that strongly about the issue." Cohen (1980), in his popular book on negotiations, uses the example of Soviet leader Nikita Khrushchev pounding his shoe on the table during a meeting of the United Nations—behavior highly inappropriate to this decorous social gathering, but effective in getting the attention he wanted.

Eliminating one's ability to control future outcomes is the second form of irrationality. Schelling (1960), in his pioneering essay on negotiations, has termed this the "rationality of irrationality," or brinksmanship. A bargainer pursuing this alternative is usually engaged in a competitive, distributive negotiation with his opponent. At some point, the negotiator sets his course for maximizing his own gain at the expense of the opponent, and then throws away his ability to waiver from that course. If destruction is to be avoided, therefore, it is totally in the hands of the opponent. Analogies to this situation might be found in the game of "chicken" that teenagers play with automobiles. Two cars speed toward one another on a deserted road; the first one who veers away is the "chicken." If one driver suddenly throws the steering wheel out the window, he is communicating to his opponent that he can no longer control his car—thereby saying to his opponent, in effect, "either you veer away and become the chicken, or we are going to crash." Deutsch and Lewicki (1970) demonstrated that giving one bargainer the capacity to behave in such a manner definitely increased the bargainer's willingness to use the mechanism, and increased his negotiating advantage. In contrast, when both parties had the mechanism, both tended to use it, and the parties engaged in a significantly greater amount of mutually disastrous conflicts.

The reputation for irrationality may thus be a very powerful negotiating tactic. On the one hand, this reputation creates in others' minds an image of unpredictability as a negotiator; many people will choose to acquiesce to this negotiator's desires rather than to directly confront and test whether the reputation is deserved. (A negotiator with this reputation may have to occasionally *act* irrationally—throw a temper tantrum, or make decisions impulsively—in order to maintain the reputation.) Others will choose to confront the irrationality and be willing to live with the consequences— either winning the confrontation, or provoking the mutual destruction that was feared. Irrationality is clearly a tactic which is more likely to be used in distributive, and competitive negotiations. Irrational behavior is *inconsistent* with the overall aims of integrative bargaining, and would be immediately condemned as "not in good faith."

FAIRNESS AND JUSTICE

To return to the discussion of the Buyer/Seller bilateral monopoly game, we pointed out that Buyers are frequently willing to act "irrationally" in order to persuade their opponent to change strategy. This behavior is frequently motivated by the Buyer's perception that he *deserves* more of the payoffs than he is receiving, and that the current allocation of payoffs isn't *fair*. Like judgments about rationality, judgments regarding the fair distribution of resources, and fair processes for resolving differences, are central to the norms that regulate negotiation.

Judgments about what is fair in negotiations are based on two kinds of evaluations: what is a fair distribution of outcomes resulting from the negotiations, and what is a fair process by which negotiations are conducted. The ways that outcomes are distributed are commonly referred to as standards of *distributive justice*; procedures by which disputes are resolved are commonly referred to as standards of *procedural justice*. Most of our attention in this chapter will be given to various aspects of distributive justice; procedural justice issues will be given more significant treatment in Chapter 12.

Deutsch (1975), Leventhal (1976), and Pruitt (1981) have identified five normative principles that govern decisions of fairness: equity, equality, responsiveness to needs, opportunities, and historical precedent. The first three are the most common, and have received the most attention in research. We will review them in some detail.

Equity

According to the principle of *equity*, people should receive rewards in proportion to what they contribute; those who contribute more should receive higher outcomes (Walster, Walster, and Berscheid, 1978). A positive "contribution" is best defined as "any action or characteristic of a receiver that (the) person believes will foster attainment of desired goals, satisfy important needs, or otherwise prove useful" (Leventhal, p. 212). Similarly, a negative contribution is any action or characteristic that has the reverse effect. By this rule, therefore, contributions may be judged on the basis of not only amount of effort and direction of action, but good looks, status, education or any other characteristic deemed relevant. A wide variety of research studies support the importance of the equity principle. Thus, those who do better in a competition are usually awarded the prizes (even when the judging is done by other competitors). A research study by Messe (1971) showed that when negotiators first invested time in an essay writing task and then negotiated for the distribution of the payment, those who invested more time almost always received greater pay. In the Buyer/Seller game, the Seller almost always argues in favor of the equity rule—that he "deserves" more payment because he has been designated to be the Seller, or because he goes first in the negotiation.

Equality

The equality rule states that parties should receive equal outcomes. The equality principle usually prevails when the parties see themselves as roughly equivalent in their actions or contributions, and/or when there is no clear basis for discriminating among their various contributions to differentially reward them. In addition, Pruitt (1981) has argued that the equality principle traditionally prevails as parties search for a *mutually prominent alternative*. In attempting to find common ground for agreement, negotiators frequently search for an alternative that "stands out," i.e., one that is unique, very simple, consistent with precedent, etc. When no other rules exist on how parties should divide a dollar, most will split it 50/50. When told to meet someone in New York whom they cannot contact, many will choose only two or three uniquely prominent places, e.g., Broadway and 42nd Street, or the New York Public Library. In the Buyer-Seller game, when the Seller argues for "equity," the Buyer will traditionally respond that the Seller's position was allocated at random, and that the Seller possesses no particular characteristic or has not done anything to "deserve" favored treatment. The Buyer usually insists on the equality rule, leading him to try to move the Seller to a 4, 15 bid (see Figure 6–1) and an equal split of the payoffs at $2,470 each.

As Pruitt has pointed out, the equality rule is extremely powerful, particularly if parties are prone to question the legitimacy of resource distributions that were previously made on the grounds of equity. For example, if one party received a larger share of the outcomes because he/she had more power, or was of higher status (e.g., the member of some privileged group, or "president"), the other party may be likely to question whether that power or status is a valid reason for distributing resources unequally. To put it simply, should the "faculty" or "alumni" get better seats in the football stadium simply because they are "faculty" or "alumni"? Many confrontations in our society between high power, establishment groups and low power, "disenfranchised" groups are based on this resource distribution question (Brown, 1983).

Applications of the equality rule are frequently questioned in the procedural aspects of a negotiation. Parties often judge the fairness of a negotiation based on the behavior of each side. Several variations of the equality rule may be applied. First, parties may question or demand the *principle of equal concessions*—a rule suggesting that negotiators generally expect one another to make an equal number of concessions from their initial starting point toward a middle ground. For example, if there is a uniquely prominent solution (e.g., an "obvious" midpoint or middle ground), parties are expected to make concessions toward it. To repeat our earlier example, if you ask two people to divide a dollar, and give them no other rationale for how to split it, they will say that it is "obvious" that it should be split 50/50. Negotiators also make judgments about "equality" based on the number of concessions made (you gave in three times, and I gave in three times), as well as the total "distance" moved from initial offer to settlement point (we started $1 apart in our bids, and therefore, we each should give in 50 cents). Second, the parties may invoke the *principle of equal sacrifice*. By this rule, "equality" is judged by how much an individual concedes *relative* to his aspirations—in other words, who makes the bigger sacrifice. Such evaluations are common when parties are conceding along scales or dimensions that are not equal. For example, suppose one party really wants to go to the beach this weekend, while the other only mildly cares about staying at home. If the first party agrees not to go to the beach, she may argue that the other "still owes her something" because she gave up a very strongly desired alternative. Concessions judged by the equal sacrifice rule will be evaluated in terms of *who makes the larger subjective sacrifice*. Finally, application of equality rules may occasionally lead the parties to invoke the *rule of equal excess*. Here, each party is "equating" the value of a joint agreement by comparing it to other viable options. Suppose that two businessmen are determining whether to enter into a joint business venture, or to remain independent. If they enter the joint venture, they must decide how to divide up the profit of the joint venture. They might use principles of equity: greater rewards go to the person who works harder, or who contributes the most money, equipment, etc. to the joint business. They might use principles of equality; i.e., everything that comes out of the joint venture should be divided 50/50. However, if they applied the equal excess rule, then they would be agreeing to divide the resources in the following way: each party should make what he could have earned independently, plus half of whatever is added by the joint agreement. Thus, Party A can earn $200 from being on his own and B can earn $100, but together they can earn $500, then they are likely to split the pot *not* at $250 each but at $300 for A and $200 for B (each person's earnings on his own plus half of the additional $200 generated by the joint venture). Komorita and Kravitz (1979) suggest that when the proper information to make this kind of decision is available to negotiators, this rule is more successful in predicting their distribution of the outcomes than either the equity or equality rules.

Principles of Needs, Opportunities, Historical Precedent

Three other principles tend to govern decisions about justice: *needs, opportunities, and historical precedent*. The *needs* rule of distributive justice suggests that a fair distribution of outcomes is based on the strength of a legitimate need. The more a party can demonstrate the need for some outcome, the more convincing a case can be made for a distribution of rewards consistent with those needs. While no studies have specifically demonstrated the operation of this norm on negotiation, it could be expected that if one negotiator could show, for example, that he "needed" some concession to satisfy a constituency and successfully conclude a deal, he/she could probably win the concession. Note that trying to demonstrate a "need" for a concession in order to remedy some past inequity in the distribution of payoffs, or to compensate for some past inequality, is merely the process of combining the needs principle with the equity or equality principle.

The *opportunities rule* (Pruitt, 1972) specifies that people should receive rewards in proportion to the use they can make of them. If one negotiator can show that if he receives a payoff, he can put it to more immediate use, double its value quicker, or generate some larger payoff for both parties, the opportunities principle would be at work. Finally, the *historical precedent* rule states that parties will look to the past, or to the first in a series of cases, to determine how outcomes will be distributed in the current negotiation. Historical precedents are extremely important in several ways:

1. As a standard for judging outcomes, the historical precedent rule views the current agreement as the "status quo," and encourages the parties to agree that neither party would ever "go below" the level of the current agreement. This is a common phenomenon in recurrent negotiations such as labor-management contracts. Labor always encourages management to understand that labor would never accept a settlement *below* the settlement now in effect. However, in the early 1980s, an economic recession forced many companies to negotiate "give-backs" from labor as

a way for some companies to survive foreign competition. It was only the pressure of massive layoffs, business shutdowns, and possible company bankruptcies that forced unions to accept this "reversed tide of progress" rather than to push for more new benefits each year.

2. As a dimension of negotiating procedure, the historical precedent rule implies that the current pattern of allocating resources should be continued because "it's always been done this way." Some parties are not prone to negotiate on an issue simply because the issue has never been negotiated before; they believe that they become vulnerable by being willing to negotiate issues that were not previously negotiable. If two partners entered into business many years ago and decided to split the profits 60/40, the party earning the greater share is likely to want to continue to distribute the profit this way, even if business conditions no longer support 60/40 as a "fair" distribution. Historical precedent may also be used as a standard when multiple negotiations are at stake. An international labor union that has upcoming contract negotiations with a number of companies may select the "weakest" company as the target for its first negotiation. It would hope that the weakest would be the easiest one from which to win a favorable settlement; it would then use the historical precedent rule to encourage all the other companies to adopt the same settlement.

Conflicts among Fairness Rules

Some of the most volatile and sensitive negotiations occur when parties strongly disagree over which distributive justice rules apply to a particular situation, and/or which ones should be used to determine the proper allocation of resources. Note that these discussions are about an *intangible*—which rules to use—but that the resolution of this intangible frequently leads directly to an easy and unchallenged resolution of the tangibles. Thus once the parties decide on whether an equality or equity rule might be used, the resource distribution question is "resolved" as the rule is applied. It is important, then, to understand how parties seek to resolve conflicts over fairness rules. Leventhal (1976) has proposed that parties determine what outcomes they feel they deserve, and then weigh the various fairness rules to determine the impact that each will have on what they think they deserve. The following factors seem to have the most impact on weights given to particular rules:

1. When *effective performance* and *effort* are valued by a party, then the *equity* rule will be weighted highly. This emphasis is consistent with the Protestant Ethic—hard work, taking responsibility, and performing well should be rewarded.

2. When the parties hold different degrees of *power, rank, or status,* the *equity* rule will be weighted highly by those parties who accept and agree

with the legitimacy of the differential power/rank/status. Thus presidents "deserve" more rewards than vice presidents.

3. When a *prominent solution* is available, the parties will gravitate toward that solution as the most viable one, and stress *equal* concessions toward that solution.

4. When *no prominent solution* is available, the parties may frequently emphasize a *midpoint* between their opening bids as a prominent solution, and stress *equal* concessions toward that solution.

5. When *friendship, harmony, and solidarity* are important to one or both sides, *equality* will be stressed as the fairest distribution of resources. Conflict prevention and minimization appear to be important criteria in maintaining long-term relationships, and equality is likely to be the least conflict-laden procedure.

6. When one negotiator *likes* another who has argued for a personal need, or when a negotiator *feels responsible* for the outcomes and welfare of another person, they are likely to be responsive to *needs* as a basis for fairness. In addition, negotiators are likely to be more responsive to *needs* when they are "in a good mood" and feel better about themselves. Thus, the higher the self-confidence and esteem of a negotiator, the more the other's appeals to have needs satisfied will be acknowledged.

7. When *precedents* exist, one or both parties will be more prone to follow *historical precedent* unless there is some clearly competing rule. Thus, an historical precedent for the status quo, or for a way of making decisions, will prevail unless otherwise challenged.

8. When the process of judging among a variety of competing rules is *too cognitively complex* for the parties, i.e., too complicated to understand, or too detailed in its precision—the parties will opt for an equality rule. In other words, when things get too complex to determine which rules are best, equality will prevail.

NEGOTIATION AND LOCATION—THE IMPORTANCE OF TURF AND TERRITORY

Another aspect of negotiation strategy that does not receive as much attention as it should is the physical environment in which negotiations take place. Observers of current events will note that a great deal of care is taken when diplomats pick the locations for international arms talks or peace treaties, or when unions and management decide where to negotiate or where to announce an agreement. Not only may the site itself have an impact on the negotiation process, but furniture and decor itself may also influence the process—whether their negotiations take place in a formal conference room, in a restaurant, or in a crowded airline terminal. In this section, we explore the specific impact that the site and decor may have on negotiations.

Negotiation Site—Ownership or Neutrality

The territory or "site" of a negotiation generally has the same impact that a baseball park or football stadium has on the teams; teams do better in their home ballpark. The home team generally has better facilities—their locker rooms are better, and they have access to more special equipment and luxuries than they would normally take on the road. They are able to spend the night in their own familiar homes and apartments, rather than strange hotels. They don't suffer from travel fatigue. They have their own local familiar surroundings, newspaper, and television channel. Finally, the home team has the fans on its side. Thus the feeling of psychological support and morale is greater in the home environment.

The same is true for negotiations. Many negotiators feel that they are more comfortable, and perform more effectively, when negotiating on their own "turf" than on their opposition's turf. This advantage may be relatively minor—as when two managers use one person's office or the other's to decide on how to resolve an interdepartmental dispute—or major, as is the case in some international agreements. There are several major advantages to having the negotiation on one's home turf:

1. *Control*. The party hosting the negotiation generally has the responsibility (and opportunity) for making all the local arrangements. In a relatively simple negotiation, it may be that control over the territory allows a negotiator to sit behind his own desk, to be able to get coffee when he wants it, or to schedule the time and date of the negotiation to suit his own preferences. In an elaborate international negotiation, control may extend to what hotel facilities the visitor uses, whether the visitor is "free" to travel around or is restricted in movement, what kind of food is served (and when) and even in what language the negotiation is conducted. The cultural customs and norms of the host country may also come into play. Rubin and Brown (1975) cite a newspaper report of President Nixon's historic summit talks in China in 1972. Since President Nixon solicited the trip, and very much wanted the meeting to occur, he consciously avoided taking any action which might prompt the Chinese to cancel the trip. In contrast, the Chinese might have been willing to exploit their advantage by taking actions in international affairs (while the trip was pending) that they would not otherwise take, on the expectation that "they could get away with it" and escape any United States reprisal. The more pronounced the cultural and territorial differences between the respective negotiators, the greater the home territory advantage.

2. *Assertiveness*. Negotiators bargaining on their home turf are more likely to be assertive than negotiators on unfamiliar ground. Martindale (1971) conducted a study in which students simulated a plea-bargaining situation between prosecuting and defense attorneys; the role play took place

in one of the two students' rooms. Whether playing the role of prosecution or defense, students negotiating in their own rooms spoke significantly longer than visitors, and won more settlements for their respective side. In addition, the difference in negotiation site contributed significantly more to explaining the results than a paper and pencil measure of assertiveness (the Dominance Scale of the California Personality Inventory). There may be several reasons why this occurred.

First, again, bargainers are more familiar with the surroundings. Second, the social norms of "politeness" ingrained in many of us dictate that it is rude to be assertive or dominating on someone else's turf. We are expected to be gracious guests—particularly if the host is footing the entertainment bill. Thus, being the "guest" not only implies socially proper norms of graciousness, but in fact may also involve a sense of obligation to the "host" for his/her generous hospitality. Studies of territorial behavior in both animals and humans confirm that aggressive displays are much more common by the owner of the turf than the "visitor." Third, if any sizeable physical distance is involved, those who travel may be more fatigued when they arrive. Moreover, the resident has had potentially more time to prepare for negotiations because travel time and energy were not factors. Fourth, negotiators may feel that hosting the negotiations affirms a higher level of status and prestige, i.e., that "they are coming to us" rather than us going to them. Even when the boss wants to see us, we generally go to his office, rather than he coming to ours. Finally, negotiators may be more assertive on their home turf because the perceived costs of losing are higher—that is, to lose at home may significantly undermine one's sense of self-worth as a good competitor. Moreover, one has to "live with" the "aura" of loss that may pervade the turf long after the opponent leaves, as a constant reminder of one's defeat.

The distinct awareness that one is more comfortable on his own turf, and less comfortable on his opponent's, pushes many negotiations to a *"neutral"* site. Again, this can most commonly be seen in international negotiations such as the choice of Geneva, Switzerland and Helsinki, Finland (as sites for major arms limitation and reductions talks), or the United Nations complex in New York City, a neutral territory located within the heart of a major U.S. metropolitan area. Panmunjom, the site of the peace talks for the Korean war, is also frequently cited as an example of neutrality afforded by equalized power—in this case, having both teams on their own turf simultaneously. The peace talks building, and the very negotiating table itself, straddles the 38th parallel that separates North and South Korea. When the original talks were held, and when minor border disputes and problems arise today, each side is able to enter the building from its own turf, and sit in its own territory while negotiating. Thus, equalizing territorial advantage may be symbolically the same as minimizing it through neutrality.

Other examples abound in major labor negotiations. Certain hotels take on reputations for "neutrality" so as not to allow either labor or management to feel that the other has a competitive advantage. Major championship athletic events are typically played in "neutral" stadiums and ballparks, where neither side "owns" the facilities or has a dominant share of the visiting spectators. Also, it is well known that most third parties intervening in disputes frequently bring the parties to a neutral turf, or a turf "owned" by the third party, in order to enhance the likelihood that the parties might get together. The mayor may invite leaders of management and a striking union to meet in City Hall, or the president may invite the leaders of warring factions in Congress to meet in the White House to hammer out an agreement. As "ownership" of turf has major symbolic significance for the group that owns it, neutral turf has high symbolic significance for the parties because neither side owns it; therefore neither side sees the other as having the potential psychological advantage afforded by territorial ownership.

Negotiation Setting—Formal or Informal

The second major factor in a negotiation setting that may affect outcomes is the degree of "formality" or "informality" created by the environment. Formality refers to all of the physical arrangements in the negotiation setting—furniture arrangement, type of furniture, and decor, and the general ambiance of the setting. Examples of the impact of formality or informality on meetings are presented in Figure 6–2.

Physical Arrangement. The physical arrangement of furniture seems to vary considerably as a function of the degree of cooperation or competition between the parties. Research (e.g., Sommer, 1965) has shown that parties who are cooperatively disposed toward one another seem to prefer seating arrangements that are side by side, while parties who are competitively oriented tend to prefer seating directly across from one another. While side-by-side seating may be somewhat awkward in terms of conversation, it is the preferred mode for working together on common documents and drafting common agreements. Directly opposing seating, on the other hand, allows each party to "keep an eye on the other" and "keep the opponent at arm's length"—common colloquialisms that in fact express the competitive sentiments of each party. In larger group situations, cooperative working arrangements tend to be represented by circular tables or circular arrangements of informal furniture; more competitive interactions usually occur across large, rectangular tables, with each group lined up along a side.

Physical Distance. A second difference between cooperative and competitive interaction is the sheer physical distance between the parties. More cooperative parties are comfortable in closer proximity; commonalities in attitudes, dispositions or preferences allow individuals to be physically close without discomfort. In contrast, competitive parties seek greater physical distance from one another, and/or are more likely to place "barricades" of furniture between themselves and the other person. Thus, cooperative parties may be very comfortable sitting next to one another (twelve–eighteen inches apart); competitive parties may place tables (of all sizes and shapes) or other barriers between them in order to prevent the other's encroachment on their territory. We can observe these dynamics in many situations: the physical distance between friends or competitors as they informally stand around at a cocktail party, or the width of a table between Soviet and American negotiators at the Strategic Arms Limitation Talks.

Formality and "Atmosphere."   A third difference created by the nature of furniture and decor is in the atmosphere of the negotiating environment. Cold, sterile, and formal surroundings are generally related to competitive interactions. A very large and formal wood table, formal chairs, white walls, muted colored carpets and curtains—businesslike atmosphere—tend to be the location of formal talks and deliberations. These rooms communicate a "no nonsense" tone that suggests that cold, hard businesslike transactions are to be carried out within them. In contrast, overstuffed chairs, "living room" arrangements of furniture, soft lighting, and the addition of music and artwork create a significantly more comfortable environment in which parties are more relaxed; their guard is let down, and they may be predisposed to act more cooperatively. Adding food and drink to this environment usually adds an additional positive element. Not only are food and drink pleasurable and relaxing, (it's not easy to enjoy a good meal with a competitive knot in your stomach), but they both play a significant role in almost every culture as symbols of a harmonious relationship. Banquets, cocktail parties, champagne toast, or even simple receptions are common ceremonial functions for celebrating unity (and demonstrating unity to other interested audiences). It is not surprising, therefore, that a great deal of business every day is transacted *not* in a cold office building, but over lunch or cocktails. In negotiations, therefore, it may clearly be beneficial for some parts of the deliberation to occur in a formal environment, but leave the most complex parts of the negotiation—as well as the ceremonial signing and ratification of the agreement—to more informal environments where food and drink can also play their role in softening the parties toward cooperation.

Formality and Status.   Finally, furniture and decor may be extensively used to communicate relative status—that is, how important each side is, and how much power (clout) they may have. In more formal negotiations, such as international deliberations, status may be communicated by the size of flags and nameplates, the degree of comfortableness of a chair, the height of the back of a chair, or the number of parties at the table. In more informal

FIGURE 6–2
Alternative Meeting Room Layouts

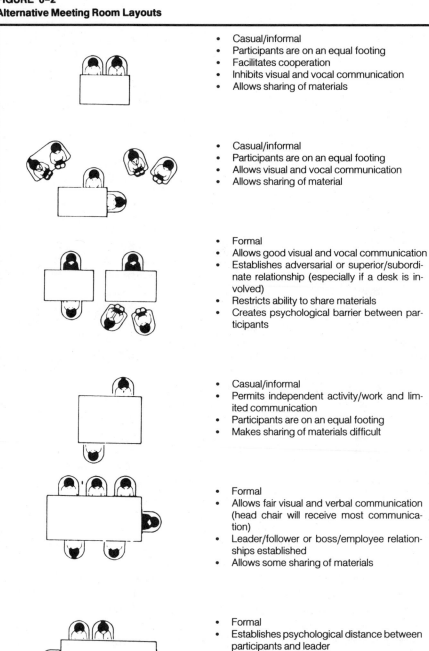

- Casual/informal
- Participants are on an equal footing
- Facilitates cooperation
- Inhibits visual and vocal communication
- Allows sharing of materials

- Casual/informal
- Participants are on an equal footing
- Allows visual and vocal communication
- Allows sharing of material

- Formal
- Allows good visual and vocal communication
- Establishes adversarial or superior/subordinate relationship (especially if a desk is involved)
- Restricts ability to share materials
- Creates psychological barrier between participants

- Casual/informal
- Permits independent activity/work and limited communication
- Participants are on an equal footing
- Makes sharing of materials difficult

- Formal
- Allows fair visual and verbal communication (head chair will receive most communication)
- Leader/follower or boss/employee relationships established
- Allows some sharing of materials

- Formal
- Establishes psychological distance between participants and leader
- Nuclear group lessens authoritative posture of leader at opposite end of table
- Establishes leader/follower, boss/subordinate or adversarial relationships
- Restricts sharing of materials

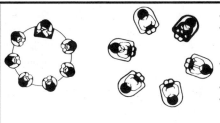

- Casual/informal
- Places leader in less influential posture as communication channels between all participants are equalized
- Excellent for opening up discussion and brainstorming
- Participants are on roughly equal footing
- Allows sharing of material

- Semiformal
- Leader's control is diminished somewhat but not compromised
- Allows fair visual and verbal communication
- Poor arrangement for speaker

- Formal
- Control by leader is lessened by seating of persons in adjacent chairs
- Allows excellent communication across the table/inhibits communication diagonally and laterally
- Poor arrangement for observers

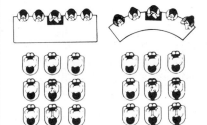

- Semiformal
- Good for panel discussions, seminars, instruction and information exchange
- Inhibits verbal and visual communication involving audience
- Fine for public hearings, debates and presentation/question and answer sessions

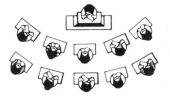

- Semiformal
- Enhances control of leader by creating an instructor-student relationship
- Facilitates lectures, briefings, speeches, demonstrations, etc.
- Inhibits group discussion

- Casual/informal
- Balances the leader's authority by creating subgroups
- Facilitates lectures, briefings, speeches, panels, and demonstrations
- Allows group discussion and work

negotiations, status is most commonly observed through office decor. In many corporations, for example, the status of a person in the organization may be measured by the size of the office, number of chairs, size of desk, desk construction (wood or metal), plushness of the desk chair, number of outside windows, or depth of pile of the rug. In addition, the office occupant may enhance his perceived status even further with framed diplomas, pictures (e.g., shaking hands with an important official), awards and trophies, etc. (Korda, 1975). The impact of all of this status-enhancing symbolism may be a subtle undermining of confidence on those who negotiate. For the "owner" of the office, the setting not only provides home-turf advantage but an additional group of symbols that enhances the occupant's perceived status and power. If the occupant chooses to seat his visitor across the desk from him (a competitive location), and on a chair lower than his own (so that there is no eye-to-eye contact, but the visitor is "looking up at" the occupant), and looking at all the status symbols carefully arranged behind the occupant, the scene is well set for a competitive negotiation that places the visitor at a significant disadvantage. In contrast, if the office occupant moves out from behind his desk, (seating himself in a "conversational grouping" of chairs), maintains level eye contact, and minimizes the number of status symbols within the office, he will help to create an environment that encourages more equal-status communication.

Formality and Symbolism.   In the previous section, we discussed the role played by furniture and decor in communicating differing degrees of status and power. Furniture may also be used to communicate *equal* status and power—as when chairs, tables, living arrangements, or even the number and size of ash trays are specifically equalized to assure that no side is seen as "bigger" or "better." Furniture itself may become a significant "intangible" in negotiation—an issue which is not directly tied to specific outcomes, but symbolically represents the relationship between the parties and may indirectly affect outcomes.

In conclusion, it is important to stress two points again. First, we are talking about a "two-way" effect of space on negotiations. The physical environment can contribute to the *tone* and *mood* of negotiations, and the anticipated mood of a negotiation can lead parties to prefer one site to another. Negotiators should be aware of the impact that a particular site will have on a negotiation (neutrality, formality, equal vs. unequal status), and consciously choose sites that create the desired mood. Second, most of the site characteristics we have just described have their strongest impact on a bargainer's *perceptions* of the environment, rather than some actual, tangible, substantive impact on the negotiations themselves. Sites are not inherently neutral—they are *perceived* as neutral; a lounge is not inherently "warm" or "cold," but rather *perceived* that way by virtue of the decor, colors, etc, that are used. Therefore, bargainers must be aware that their own perceptions of site characteristics are not the only ones that are important; others' perceptions are equally important to insure the desired end.

THE ROLE OF TIME

In preparing for a negotiation, negotiators pay a great deal of attention to information and research, strategy and "psyching out" their opponents. Yet they frequently fail to consider one of the most important determinants of negotiation settlements: time. All negotiation takes place over a time horizon. Time can have two key roles in determining a negotiation settlement. The first is the role played by time deadlines—points when negotiation must be completed. The second role is the passage of time, and the impact that time passage has on a negotiator's position and perceptions.

Deadlines and "Eleventh Hour" Dynamics.   Even the most casual observer of "public" negotiations, e.g., labor disputes, legislative budget battles, etc., is aware of the tendency for many major negotiations to drag on until the last few minutes. Labor and management, who may have started negotiations six months previously, do not reach an agreement until two hours before the contract is to expire. Negotiators of an international trade agreement may be together for several weeks, and yet not reach an agreement until an hour before one party has to leave for the airport. Why does this occur? Many of us attribute it to procrastination, e.g., we have weeks or even months to complete a class assignment and still find ourselves having to stay up until 3:00 A.M. the night before the project is due. While procrastination may help to explain some of the reasons, "eleventh hour" dynamics are also an integral part of negotiations.

In negotiations, parties begin with inflated demands and positions, and press to have those positions accepted by the other side. In theory, this process could continue *ad infinitum*, with little or no movement by either side. What causes the parties to ever modify their position and make a concession? One explanation is that one side could find the other side's facts, information, or argument more compelling. Thus, one side "gives in" by saying that the other side's arguments hold more weight than his. This may occur, but such instances probably account for a small amount of the concession-making. In *most* situations, time and the passage of time play a critical role. Over time, the parties wear each other down. The point and counterpoint of argumentation lead each side to see some validity on the other's arguments as well as his own. Second, the parties may truly desire an agreement, and want to reach one quickly in order to reap the benefits of implementing it. Third, time is costly to most of us; we can't "afford" a long negotiation because we need to be doing other things, attending to other business. The more costly time is, the more that the cost of time invested may begin to outweigh the value of the settlement. Finally, *not* settling may also be very costly. If we are unable to settle by a deadline, and have to walk away from the negotiation "empty handed," we are much more motivated to achieve that agreement. Therefore, deadlines play an extremely important role because they force us to evaluate the tangible and intangible rewards and costs of: (a) coming to an agreement, (b) not coming to an agreement, and/or (c) investing a certain amount of time in reaching that agreement.

A number of research studies and treaties have examined the impact of time pressures on negotiation (e.g., Stevens, 1963; Pruitt and Drews, 1969; Rubin and Brown, 1975). These studies have confirmed the following:

1. Time deadlines lead negotiators to soften demands. Bargainers are less likely to have high bargaining aspirations, to bluff, and more likely to make concessions under high time demands than low time demands.

2. Time deadlines increase the pressure to reach agreement. Bargainers appear to move their negotiating positions more rapidly under high time pressure.

3. Under time pressure, the softening of demands and the desire to seek agreement are less likely to be perceived as weakness. Thus, both bargainers and audiences can explain and justify concession-making on the basis of an *external* source of pressure—the time deadline—rather than pressure from the opposing negotiator. Justifying concessions in this way is likely to help negotiators maintain an image of strength and toughness while still making concessions to their opponent.

Using Deadlines Effectively. Knowing the impact that time and deadlines can have on negotiations can lead bargainers to effectively apply the following rules:

1. *When deadlines are present, the frequency of concessions is likely to rise quickly as the deadline approaches*. This process is represented in Figure 6–3. Given that negotiators open with positions that are reasonably far apart, concession-making is most likely to occur as the deadline approaches. Justification for concessions will be attributed to "time pressures" rather than to increased credibility of the other side's arguments, or weaknesses in one's own position.

2. *Deadlines are frequently negotiable*. It is common for deadlines to be set arbitrarily, or for the convenience of others. Two parties agree to try to achieve a settlement by the first of the month. A third party states that a contract, agreement, report, etc. is due by a certain date and time. Such dates are frequently set arbitrarily, or at the convenience of the third party; yet they are treated by negotiators as though they are hard, fast, and immutable. As a result, negotiation and decision making may be artifically rushed to meet the deadline. In fact, it may be wise for

FIGURE 6–3
Concession - Making Over Time

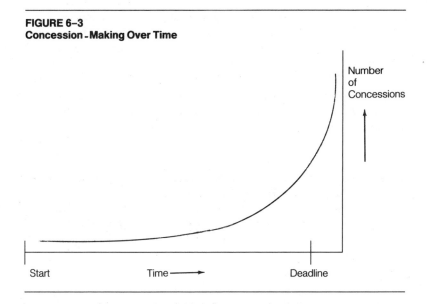

negotiators to frequently examine their deadlines and to try to renegoti-
ate the deadline if necessary.

3. *If no deadlines exist, parties may create deadlines in order to create move-*
   ment in negotiations. When no deadlines exist in negotiations, the parties
   may not feel any "pressure" to reach agreement. In the case of some
   negotiations, e.g., the Strategic Arms Limitations Talks during the 1970s
   and 80s—the magnitude, complexity, and seriousness of the issues may be
   so important that time pressures are undesirable. Both sides want the best
   possible solution that all can agree to, regardless of when it is achieved.
   However, in many other contexts, parties *are* concerned enough about an
   issue to negotiate, and want to agree, but are under no pressure to meet a
   certain deadline. In these situations, negotiators may agree to set their
   own deadlines to insure progress. Committee members may agree to have
   a rough draft of a document available by a certain date, or make a report to
   the President by a certain time, knowing that the deadline will be the
   major motivating force in getting the committee members to do their
   work. Even when an agreement is needed "urgently," a specific deadline
   will serve to insure that the work is accomplished. Similarly, in very long,
   complex negotiations with multiple issues, parties may wish to break the
   issues into smaller packages so that intermediate deadlines can be set and
   overall progress can be measured.

4. *When both sides do not share the same deadline, the party without the*
   deadline has more power. The only exception to this rule is if the party

with the deadline is willing to walk away without an agreement. Herb Cohen (1980) uses the humorous example of discovering one day that your refrigerator has failed, and going out to buy a new one. If you've got a refrigerator full of rotting food, you've either got to decide that the value of the food is worth sacrificing, or buy the first refrigerator you see. Your ability to negotiate a favorable price is severely limited. Similarly, if one party has to catch a plane, or report back to his boss, or firm up a deal by a certain date, the party without the deadline may hold out and force the time-bound party to make more concessions than would otherwise occur.

5. *Parties at a "deadline disadvantage" may overcome this disadvantage by creating positive incentives for quick agreement.* Negotiators who know that their power is lessened because of the pressure for a quick settlement need a way to make quick agreement more attractive to their opponent. In general, the best way to accomplish this objective is to offer the opponent added features and options that "disappear" if they are not quickly accepted. A car dealer may ask the prospective buyer, "what can I do to get you to buy today?" A negotiator may offer a "sale price," or an added bonus for agreeing to consummate the deal quickly. If a negotiator can assume that the other bargainer knows the advantage of stalling, i.e., waiting and putting pressure on his opponent—then he must use some positive incentive to overcome his disadvantage. While these positive incentives may appear as "unnecessary" concessions in the short run, such measures are taken to insure the viability of a prompt agreement for the long run.

Time Passage and Investment in the Negotiations

In addition to the critical function that is played by deadlines, time has a second critical role: the more time people spend on a negotiation, the more effort they invest and the less willing they are to sacrifice the agreement and walk away empty-handed. Further, as a result of devoting time and energy to negotiations and making significant progress toward an agreement, negotiators generally feel more committed to the final agreement. Conversely, they are also less willing to abandon a negotiation due to minor impediments to achieving a solution. As a result, the more time and energy a negotiator has invested in deliberations, the more susceptible he/she is to being pressed for additional concessions and sacrifices in the closing stages of a deal.

The vulnerability experienced by a negotiator in this situation is similar to other forms of entrapment—situations in which parties make a risky investment, realize the investment is potentially lost, and then are forced to determine whether to invest more resources in order to "turn it around." Bankers face this question constantly when they loan money to a small business. If the business does not succeed, the borrower may ask for more money in order to recoup the original investment. Many of us face the same dilemma when we call an airline for reservations, are placed on "hold," and don't know whether to hang up or wait for the operator to return. Those who have studied the entrapment process (Teger, 1980; Lewicki, 1980) suggest at least two clear solutions to the entrapment problem:

1. Have a clear, pre-established deadline or resistance point beyond which you will not go. If it is a deadline (even an artifical one), make it clear that negotiations must be completed before the deadline or they will be broken off. Even if this message is designed to convince yourself more than your opponent, make it strong and firm. If it is a resistance point, use that point as a way of refusing to make further concessions and sacrifices at the last minute.

2. Treat last-minute "add-ons" or concessions by the opponent as an opportunity for you to reopen and re-examine all other issues in negotiation. Again, negotiators will resist making this demand because of the additional time and effort it will take. Nevertheless, parties making last minute requests may well be exploiting your good faith and desire to settle; if you request a total reopening of the other negotiated issues, this position itself may lead the opponent to withdraw his request for any additional considerations. If not, you will be able to bargain for favorable concessions in exchange for incorporating the other's request into the larger package.

SUMMARY

In Chapters 4 and 5, we described two major approaches to negotiation: a distributive, competitive approach and a collaborative, problem solving approach. We have reviewed the fundamental assumptions of each strategy, the tactics that are most likely to accompany them, and the conditions under which each strategy is likely to be used. In this chapter, we explored elements of negotiation strategy that are common to both distributive and integrative bargaining, and ways that those elements will change, or be affected by, a cooperative or competitive approach. These elements include:

1. *Tangibles vs. intangibles at stake in the negotiation.* Intangibles are a key factor in many negotiations, and will dramatically affect how satisfied a negotiator will feel about the tangible outcome. When intangibles are not clearly "put on the table" and their value understood to both negotiators, intangibles can dominate the negotiation and lead to a highly distributive, competitive procedure.

2. *Motivational orientation of the parties.* Negotiations can be distributive or integrative based on the nature of the tangible issues at stake, i.e., whether the possible range of outcomes is fixed, and must be divided in a

win/lose manner, or whether both parties can maximize outcomes. Bargaining will also take on a distributive or integrative character based upon the motivations of the negotiators. MO thus becomes a very important "intangible" that will shape the course of negotiations. Motivational orientation will be affected by individual differences in personality, specific situational factors such as constituency pressures and audience evaluation, the economic reward available for cooperative or competitive behavior, or the amount of perceived conflict, i.e., how competitive the reward structure *appears*, rather than how competitive it actually is.

3. *The normative rules in the situation for determining what is rational and what is fair*. Rationality is usually defined in economic terms, i.e., that negotiators will always make choices so as to maximize their economic outcomes. Yet we pointed out that bargainers frequently behave in a manner which could be classified as "irrational," and that this behavior often has a broader rationality about it. Similarly, while negotiators disagree about what is "fair" in negotiation, there is no single set of standards for making such judgments. A number of different standards exist for judging the fairness of outcomes (who gets what) and procedures (how it gets divided), and standards which are applied in any given situation.

4. *How physical space is used*. The site for negotiations, and the "climate" conveyed by that site, can affect negotiating outcomes. Whether the site is seen as favoring one side, or as neutral, will be one factor. A second will be whether the furniture and decor create an air of formality or informality, and whether they enhance the status and power of one side or treat the parties equally. The more a site is viewed as neutral, and the more the decor creates informality and status-equalization, the more likely negotiations will take a cooperative direction. Conversely, the more a site favors one side, communicates formality, and enhances one side's perceived power, the more likely the site will encourage competitive behavior.

5. *Time pressures*. Finally, we pointed out that negotiations operate according to Parkinson's Law—they fill the time available. Deadlines work to encourage concessions that parties might not otherwise make if they had plenty of time left. Deadlines lead negotiators to soften demands, make concessions without appearing weak, and move toward agreement. In addition, the longer negotiators invest themselves in the negotiating process, the more committed they feel to try to get a solution. Negotiators, therefore, must decide when they want deadline pressure (on themselves, the other party, or both parties), and learn how to either create deadlines or move them in order to create the most favorable conditions for agreement.

7

Communication Processes

The following two chapters focus on the processes by which negotiators influence one another's understanding, beliefs, and outlook—and ultimately, their behavior. The topics that we will review in these chapters frequently overlap. In this chapter on communication, we will discuss the basic structure and process by which information and meaning are transmitted from one person to another. Chapter 8, on persuasion, examines the communication process more fully, with particular attention to how communication tools can be used to influence another in the desired manner. In addition, we will review the ways that we can use persuasion tactics to defend ourselves against another's influence attempts.

Communication is at the heart of the negotiating process. While planning, prework, evaluating the bargaining situation, and strategizing are all key elements to the diagnosis and understanding of negotiation, communication is the central instrumental process. Unless negotiators deal with one another strictly by trading bids and offers on slips of paper, communication processes, both verbal and nonverbal, are critical to the achievement of negotiating goals.

In this chapter, we will present a basic model of communication. We will first demonstrate the applicability of this model to the negotiating process, and then point out the critical role that perception plays in negotiation. We then evaluate ways to determine communication effectiveness, and the numerous factors that contribute to "ineffective" or diminished communication—particularly in negotiating environments. Finally, we will examine several communication techniques that can be used to improve negotiation effectiveness. In Chapter 8, we will use a communication model to examine the persuasion process in negotiation. In doing so, we shall employ the wide variety of applied theory and research that is available from social psychological studies of opinion and attitude change to understand the negotiation process.

A BASIC MODEL OF COMMUNICATION

Most analyses of communication begin with a basic model of the process itself. Probably the most commonly used model, and one that will serve our purposes well, was developed by Shannon and Weaver (1948), and is represented in Figure 7–1.

While all of the complexities of human communication can not be captured in a single model, this diagram will offer a reasonable beginning. A sender source has a message in mind. The source intends to "encode" the message into language that will be understood by the receiver. Perhaps it is a statement of the sender's preference for a particular outcome in a negotiation. The message may be encoded into verbal language—words and sentences—or it may be encoded into nonverbal expression—facial gestures, handwaving, and finger pointing. Once encoded, the message is then transmitted—sent via voice and/or facial expression, or written statement, and through face-to-face interaction, video, letter, telegram, etc.—to the receiver. The receiver's receptors—eyes and ears—pick up the transmission, and "recode" the message to give it meaning to the receiver.

In a one-way communication cycle—from sender to receiver—this would constitute a completed transmission. A source who puts his message in writing and sends it by mail to the receiver generally assumes that the message is received and understood. However, most communication— particularly in negotiation—involves continued dialogue and discussion between at least two parties. As a result, the receiver takes on a more active role in the communication process in two ways. First the receiver provides information on how the message was received, and second, the receiver becomes a "sender" himself and responds to, or builds upon, the earlier message of the sender. For the current discussion, we shall refer to both of these processes as "feedback." In the feedback process, the receiver encodes the message—through reading or listening—to assure his own understanding and comprehension of what the sender said, and what the message meant. He then ascribes "meaning" to the communication—a comprehension of the information content of the message, as well as an "interpretation" of that content. The receiver then becomes a "sender" of communication back to the original source. The encoded message may take multiple forms: questions or other communications to obtain clarification or better understanding of the earlier message; exclamations or reactions to the information

FIGURE 7-1

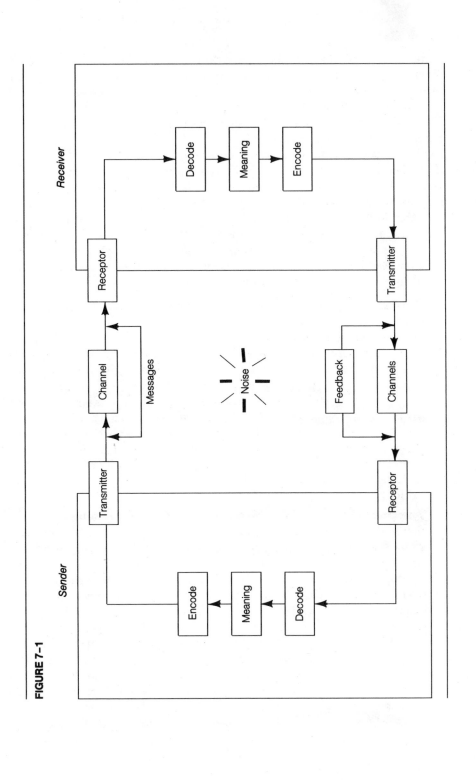

content of the message; or rebuttals to the content of the first message. All of these are encoded, transmitted through various channels, received, and decoded by the original source. The entire sequence may be as simple as a question by one employee, "Want to go for a cup of coffee?" and an affirmative headshake by the other, to complex statements and responses used by negotiators in shaping a contract.

This model of communication "works" to the degree that a wide variety of information—facts, opinions, feelings, preferences, and experiences—are completely and thoroughly shared between the parties. However, as most of us know from experience, human communication systems seldom perform with this high degree of efficiency and effectiveness. Most of the linking elements in the model are subject to external factors that distort messages and their meaning, hampering them from getting through accurately. We will first describe each element in the sequence, and then more fully explore how distortions occur in communication.

1. *Senders and receivers* each have goals and objectives—things that they want to accomplish. The sender may want to change the receiver's mind, or secure concessions toward a negotiated agreement. The receiver may not want to have his mind changed, and not want to make concessions; moreover, the receiver may have the identical objective in mind for his opponent. The more diverse the goals of the sender and receiver, or the more antagonistic they are in their relationship, the greater likelihood of distortion and error in communication. Similarly, senders and receivers differ in their individual makeup—each is likely to have a different pattern of personal values, attitudes toward certain issues and objectives, previous experiences, life history, and personality characteristics. Each of these elements contributes to a different way of viewing the world.

2. *Transmitters and receptors* are simply the equipment by which information is sent. Information can be sent verbally—by speaking or by writing—and nonverbally, by body posture, hand and facial gestures, tone of voice, etc. The choice of transmitter can affect outcomes, i.e., some messages may be better spoken, while others need to be written. Moreover, when presenting information face-to-face, congruence or incongruence between multiple transmission channels is often a problem. The old expression that "your lips tell me 'no, no' but there's 'yes, yes' in your eyes" highlights the incongruity of messages sent simultaneously by both verbal and nonverbal channels, and the possible error introduced by this duplicitous communication. On the receiver's end, poor eyesight or faulty hearing may similarly diminish the ability to accurately receive a message.

3. *Messages and channels* are the vehicles by which information is communicated. As noted by many writers on communication, human beings are

unique in their ability to use "symbolic" forms of communication—primarily the written or spoken language—to transmit information. Some messages are direct expressions of meaning—I lean over the table and grab the pencil that I want—while others are "symbolic representations"—I ask the person seated across the table, "Please pass me the pencil." The more we are prone to use symbolic communication, the more likely that symbols may not accurately communicate the meaning we intend. In the simplest example, if the person does not understand English, or if there are several pencils on the table, there is increased likelihood that the communication will be less than effective.

Channels are the vehicles by which messages are carried. If we speak directly, it is the airwaves; if we write, it is the paper and pen or typewriter; if we talk over the telephone, it is the telephone circuitry and microwaves. Both messages and channels are prone to distortion from "noise," which we will use as a broad descriptive category of various forms of interference in the communication process. Messages can be transmitted more clearly in a quiet room than in a loud, distracting hotel ballroom. The greater the sources of distraction and confusion in the communication environment, the more that "noise" will interfere with accurate and complete message transmission.

4. *Decoding, meaning, and encoding* are the processes that the individual uses to interpret the messages of others, and to formulate messages themselves. Decoding is the process of translating messages from their symbolic form into interpretations that we can understand. If the parties speak the same language, or use the same common nonverbal gestures to communicate messages, the process is reasonably simple and error-free; if they do not, decoding is prone to contribute a high degree of error. While "translators" may help to decode the other's messages, full translation may not be possible, i.e., understanding the other's meaning or tone, as well as the words—or may introduce additional error into the communications.

Meanings are the facts, ideas, feelings, reactions, or thoughts that exist within individuals, and act as a set of "filters" through which the decoded messages are interpreted. If a party has asked the other to "please pass me that pencil," and the other party has said "no," the encoded "no" back to us is likely to stimulate a variety of reactions in the search for "meaning." Did the other hear the message? Was the "no" a direct refusal to the request? Why did the other say "no"? Does he need the pencil too? Is he being obstinate and intentionally blocking me? Answers to these questions will vary depending upon a variety of other aspects of the communication sequence and the relationship between the parties, and will lead to different ascriptions of "meaning" to the word "no."

Finally, *encoding* is the process by which messages are put into symbolic form. The encoding process will be affected by varying degrees of skill in encoding, e.g., fluency in language, skill at expression in written and verbal form, etc. It will also be affected by the meaning attached to earlier communication—what we want to communicate, how we have reacted to earlier communications, etc. Senders are likely to choose to encode messages in a preferred form; this form may not be the same preferred by receivers. Two managers may need to discuss a negotiated contract; while one may prefer to "get together and discuss it over lunch," the other may prefer to have each one prepare a written draft that they can exchange and revise individually. How this contract will eventually be prepared may thus be the subject of the negotiation itself.

5. *Feedback* is the process by which the receiver "reacts" to the sender's message. Even in a one-way communication cycle, feedback is essential. It is necessary to let the sender know that the message was (a) actually received, (b) encoded, and (c) ascribed with the same meaning that the sender intended. The absence of feedback can contribute to significant distortions in communication, since senders never know whether their message is being received, much less understood. Anyone who has ever talked to a large audience may find himself directing his comments to the individual who is nonverbally shaking her head "yes," or smiling, or in some other way acknowledging that the communication is being received and even appreciated. The sender is unlikely to direct comments to a receiver who is shaking his head "no," or asleep, unless the comments are specifically designed to change the receiver's disposition.

THE ROLE OF PERCEPTION

Perception is the process by which individuals "tune in" to their environment. We stated earlier that the process of ascribing meaning to messages is likely to be strongly affected by how we answer a variety of questions about the other's current state of mind or comprehension of our earlier communications. Perceptions of the other person, of the environment we are operating in, and of our own dispositions are likely to affect how these meanings are ascribed. Moreover, these same perceptions are likely to affect the decoding process, and our ability to accurately ascertain the other's message. The manner in which perceptions are determined, and the ways that they commonly contribute to accurate or inaccurate communication, will now be examined.

Perception is a complex physical and psychological process. It is defined as "the process of screening, selecting, and interpreting stimuli so that they have meaning to the individual." (Steers, 1984, p. 98). Perception is a "sense-making" process; individuals interpret their environment so that appropriate responses may be made to it (see Figure 7–2). The body's physical receptors—eyes, ears, touch, smell, etc.—pay attention to, and pick up cues from various stimuli in the environment. Most environments are extremely

FIGURE 7–2
The Perceptual Process

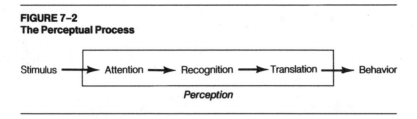

Stimulus ⟶ Attention ⟶ Recognition ⟶ Translation ⟶ Behavior

Perception

complex. To become quickly aware of this, lift your head up from this book, close your eyes, and then open them slowly. Whether it is the room you are sitting in, or the window you are looking out of, begin to make a list of all of the different stimuli that you "see"—e.g., walls, pictures, furniture, carpets, or trees, cars, building, etc. Next, for each item on the list, identify all of the different properties of each object—e.g., size, color, texture, shape, etc. The task quickly becomes unmanageable. While the individual sensors take in all of this information, the brain cannot efficiently process it all; hence perception must be selective, focusing only on some stimuli while "tuning out" others. A wide variety of factors affect this selectivity, and we shall discuss several of them later in the chapter.

Once attention and recognition have occurred, the individual then translates that recognition into reactive behavior. This part of the process is called *perceptual organization*—once stimuli have been recognized, appropriate responses need to be made. The message of a hot stove, transmitted from our fingertips to the brain, will lead us to quickly withdraw our finger before we are burned. The message of a verbal warning, "look out for the truck," transmitted from our ears to the brain, will lead us to quickly look for the truck and move out of its way. As we noted earlier, perceptual selectivity and organization are affected by two groups of influences: those which are physical properties of the stimuli themselves, and those which are characteristic of the social environment in which the perception occurs. We propose that perceptions in negotiations are affected *most* by the social-environment properties; but the physical stimulus properties can have effects as well. We will first review these physical properties, and then explore the social properties in more detail.

Physical Properties of Stimuli

The following physical properties are likely to dramatically affect perception:

1. *Size of stimuli*. Generally, the larger the object, the more attention it receives. Big signboards or posters are likely to be seen more quickly than smaller ones.

2. *Intensity of stimuli*. Intensity works much like size. In the visual media, brighter colors are better than duller ones. In the auditory senses, louder voices are attended to more than quiet ones. However, "contrast effects" also prevail. If the speaker is always loud, he will be tuned out; the calm, quiet, even voice can command attention in the middle of a loud and boisterous shouting match.

3. *Contrast*. Setting the stimuli off from their background—by color, by size, by starkness (big black letters on white paper)—creates a visible contrast.

4. *Novelty or familiarity*. Unique stimuli attract more attention than familiar ones. A manager who dresses in a suit every day will attract attention when he wears jeans to the office.

5. *Repetition*. Advertisers know that repetition of a message is critical to acceptance—it increases the likelihood that the stimuli are attended to, and makes us more alert to the stimuli. A negotiator making a persuasive case for a position should repeat the position several times, in different phrasing and approach, to insure that it is accurately received.

6. *Ordering*. Finally, when there are multiple stimuli, the order in which the stimuli are presented can be important. In general, there are two kinds of ordering: primacy—the first piece of information or stimulus in a series order is most likely to be remembered, and recency—the last piece of information or stimulus is most likely to be remembered. In making a presentation during negotiations, the speaker might rely on recency effects by presenting a variety of facts and then building up to the conclusion. In contrast, if the speaker wanted to rely on primacy effects he would begin with the conclusion and then present the facts and arguments to support it. The use of repetition and ordering as persuasive tactics in negotiation will be discussed more thoroughly in the next chapter.

SOCIAL PERCEPTION AND PERCEPTUAL DISTORTIONS

Many of the properties of stimuli that were just described are characteristics of rather simple stimuli—sounds, simple visual images of different size and shape, etc. We can see how variations in these stimuli can have limited applicability to negotiation, particularly in the positioning of arguments, the use of visual media in presentation, etc. However, the impact of perception on communication and negotiation outcomes is much more dramatic when we consider the perception of other people. People as perceptual stimuli are more complex than simple letters, sounds, or colors. They have many physical characteristics—height, weight, age, sex, race, dress, and speech patterns (how articulate they are with words, whether they speak with an accent, what tone of voice they use)—that affect our perceptions. People differ in their emotional expressiveness—how they "communicate" with facial gestures, body posture, hand movements, etc. Finally, we come to know things about people that fundamentally affect how we organize the mass of stimulus information we are receiving. A person's occupation "tells us a lot"—whether she is an accountant, attorney, or housewife; whether he is a plumber, Senator, or advertising executive. Social status has the same impact, as does information about a person's previous behavior patterns, or "reputation." A person with a reputation for being exploitative is likely to be perceived differently in negotiation from one who has a reputation for being open and honest. Many research studies have shown that *perceived similarity* between the perceiver and the target, on a variety of dimensions, is likely to lead to a favorable attitude toward the target, trust, and a cooperative relationship. Conversely, perceived dissimilarity between the perceiver and target, on a variety of dimensions, is likely to lead to an unfavorable attitude toward the target, mistrust, and a competitive relationship. (See Rubin and Brown, 1975, for at least one review of research in this area.)

Not only are people more complex as stimuli, but the social context of the perceptual event can have an impact on perception. The nature of the negotiation issues, or the previous experience of the parties, "define" the situation as a competitive or a cooperative one. Deutsch (1973), on the basis of his research, indicates that perceptions will vary as follows:

(a) A cooperative process tends to increase sensitivity to similarities and common interest, while minimizing the salience of differences. It stimulates a convergence and conformity of beliefs and values.

(b) A competitive process tends to increase sensitivity to differences and threats, while minimizing the awareness of similarities. It stimulates the sense of complete oppositeness: 'You are bad, I am good.' It seems likely that competition produces a stronger bias toward misperceiving the other's neutral or concilliatory actions as malevolently motivated than the bias induced by cooperation to see the other's actions as benevolently intended (pp. 29–30).

Therefore, the representation of the relationship between the parties as competitive or cooperative, based on the appearance of issues as zero-sum or nonzero sum in nature, or the previous history of the parties with one another, can lead the parties to judge their opposition's personal characteristics. They may also misdiagnose the degree of perceived similarity between them, and this misperception triggers assumptions about the other's behavior. These perceptions subsequently affect attitudes toward the other party, communication processes between the parties, and their strategic approach to the negotiating task.

Finally, characteristics of the perceiver himself are likely to affect his perceptions. We have already mentioned several elements. First, judging the "similarity" or "dissimilarity" of the target person is a process of comparing the target's characteristics against one's own. Hence many of the same attributes that we use to form judgments of others, e.g., age, sex, race, physical appearance, background, status, occupation, etc., are likely to be evaluated against the perceiver's own qualities. If the characteristics are "prominent", i.e., they stand out as a defining characteristic of the target person and the perceiver, these characteristics will be used to form initial judgments of similarity or dissimilarity, and then of liking or disliking.

Second, the perceiver's own needs, desires, motivations, and personal experiences are likely to create a predisposition about the target in an upcoming negotiation. These predispositions are most problematic when they lead to biases and errors in perception and subsequent communication. Five major perceptual errors are typical: stereotyping, halo effects, selective perceptions, projections, and perceptual defenses. The first two—stereotyping and halo effects—are examples of perceptual distortion by *generalization*—small amounts of perceptual information are used to draw large conclusions about individuals. The last three—selective perception, projection, and perceptual defense—are examples of perceptual distortion by the *anticipation* of encountering another whom we believe to have certain attributes and qualities.

Stereotyping is a very common perceptual process. Stereotyping occurs when attributes are assigned to people solely on the basis of their membership in a particular social or demographic group. Stereotypes are formed about a wide variety of different groups: young people and old people, males and females, Italians and Germans, union and management. In each case, stereotype formation generally happens the same way. One piece of perceptual information enables us to assign the individual to a group (e.g., young or old); then characteristics of some other group members are also assigned to this individual (e.g., "old people are conservative, therefore this old person is conservative," or "young people are disrespectful, therefore this young person is disrespectful"). There is no factual basis for the conclusion; it is based on the generalization of qualities that have been ascribed to the larger group; and the error is compounded by applying the category to this single individual. In organizations, problems of age stereotyping, sex-role stereotyping, and discrimination, have received considerable attention in recent years.

The simple process of using some criterion, even an arbitrary one, to divide people into groups allows group members to begin to define themselves as "we" and the other group as "they," and then to make evaluative comparisons and judgments between them. Direct competition for resources, or conflicting values and ideologies, will significantly enhance the stereotyping process—Soviets vs. Americans, men vs. women in the workforce, or union vs. management(Sherif, 1979). In all cases, an individual's membership in one of these groups leads those from the other group to react stereotypically. Haire (1955), for example, showed photographs, labeled "manager" and "labor leader," to groups of managers and labor leaders. The managers attributed characteristics of honesty, dependability, and interpersonal competence to the individual in the "manager" photograph, while union leaders stereotyped the same individual in the "manager" photograph with the opposite characteristics. The findings were reversed for photos of "labor leaders."

Halo effects in perception are similar to stereotypes. Rather than using a target individual's group membership as a basis for classification, halo effects occur when one attribute of an individual allows the perceiver to generalize about a wide variety of other attributes. A smiling person is judged to be more honest than a frowning or scowling person, even though there is no necessary relationship between a smile and honesty. Halo effects can be positive or negative—a good attribute can be generalized so that one sees people in a very positive light, while a negative attribute has the reverse effect. The more prominent or salient the attribute is in influencing the overall judgment of an individual, the more it will be used to "cast" further information into a perspective consistent with the initial judgment. Research shows that halo effects are most likely to occur in perception when (1) we have very little experience about a person along some dimension (and hence generalize about that person from our knowledge of him in other contexts), (2) when we know a person well, and (3) when the qualities have strong moral implications (Bruner and Tagiuri, 1954).

Halo effects are likely to be as common as stereotypes in negotiation; we are likely to form rapid impressions of new opponents based on very limited initial information, such as their appearance or initial statements. We also maintain these judgments as we get to know people better, fitting each piece of "new" information into some consistent pattern. Finally, as Bruner and Tagiuri suggest, the mere suggestion that an adversary can be viewed in moral terms—"honest" or "dishonest," "ethical" or "unethical"— is likely to affect our perception of a wide variety of other attributes.

In contrast to *perceptual generalization*, a second class of perceptual distortions is introduced by *anticipation*. Distortion by anticipation occurs in three major ways: selective perception, projection, and perceptual defense. In each case, the anticipation of perceiving and encountering a particular individual allows the perceiver to filter and distort perceptual information.

Selective perception occurs when the perceiver singles out certain information which supports or reinforces a prior belief, and filters out information which may not confirm that belief. Thus selective perception has the effect of perpetuating stereotypes or halo effects—quick judgments are formed about individuals on the basis of limited information, while any further evidence that might disconfirm the judgment is "filtered out" by attending only to the confirming information. An initial smile from the opponent, which leads the perceiver to believe that the opponent is honest, might also lead the perceiver to ignore statements by the opponent that he intends to be competitive and aggressive. The same smile, interpreted by the perceiver as a smirk, similarly leads the perceiver to ignore other information that the target wants to establish an honest and cooperative relationship. In both cases, the perceiver's own biases—predisposition to be cooperative or competitive—are likely to affect how the other's cues are selected and interpreted.

Projection occurs when an individual ascribes to others characteristics or feelings he possesses himself. Projection usually arises out of a need to protect one's own self-concept. Individuals have a strong need to see themselves as consistent and in a positive light; therefore, if negative attributes are perceived, they tend to be ascribed to others rather than to oneself. In negotiation, for example, it is extremely common for negotiators to claim that they want to be cooperative and to develop a positive relationship with the other negotiator, but that it is the opponent who is behaving uncooperatively and untrustingly. Such assertions often mask the negotiator's ability to admit to himself that he really wants to be deceptive and dishonest. American political leaders, fearful of "threats to national security," may project aggressive and militaristic motives on the Soviet Union, and then argue that these images justify our own build-up of armaments, or even justify a "pre-emptive" strike on the enemy before they have the opportunity to attack us. It is easy to see how such projection can lead to both self-fulfilling logic and highly destructive behavior.

Perpetual defense is the result of the same instinct for self-projection, and helps our perceptual apparatus defend us by "screening out," distorting, or ignoring information which is threatening or unacceptable to us. Information about ourselves or others which doesn't "fit" our self image, or the image of others, is likely to be denied, modified, distorted, or redefined to bring it into line with earlier judgments. We "refuse to believe" that a person whom we respect may have committed a serious crime. We perceive ourselves as "moral" individuals, and therefore are likely to deny that we have ever done anything wrong. We learn that a person we see as manipulative and dishonest has just contributed a great deal of money to a local charity; in order to rationalize this to ourselves, we decide that the donor must be using the contribution as a tax dodge, rather than as a true expression of benevolence and generosity.

Perceptions, Attributions, and Assumptions

There is a wide variety of factors that can affect accurate perception. Each of these elements adds a source of noise, distraction or distortion to the perceptual process. Some of the distracting elements relate to properties of the stimuli themselves: the specific facts or information being used to support and defend a position. However, the more problematic distortions in perception come from social factors that affect perceivers, and those who are being perceived. Stereotypes, halo effects, selective perceptions, and perceptual defenses bias and distort the information being received. Moreover, as much research has demonstrated, *these processes are likely to be more active and more common between groups which are competing for power and control, or for scarce resources*.

It cannot be stated strongly enough that these perceptual distortions are frequently at the heart of breakdowns in communication between conflicting individuals. Perceptual biases tend to cast one's own position and behavior in more favorable terms, and to cast the other person ("the opponent") in more negative terms. These biases will affect the expectations that one has for his opponent, and lead to assumptions about the opponent: the position he is likely to take, his willingness to cooperate or make concessions, etc. Finally, these negative assumptions are likely to influence the party to assume a competitive, defensive stance in their initial negotiations. The tragic fallacy in this process is that if his assumptions are incorrect, there may be no way for the actor to discover it! By the time he is in a position to accurately judge the predisposition of his opponent, his own competitive mood and defensive posture have been interpreted by the opponent as offensive and antagonistic. This problem is likely to be most acute between groups which have had long-standing, hostile relationships—unions and management that have been plagued by bitter strikes, Middle Eastern nations, or marital partners in divorce proceedings. In order to break this self-fulfilling perceptual spiral, individual negotiators and their constituencies must take *clearcut*, *specific*, and *public* actions to signal to their adversaries a desire for cooperative behavior. Detailed approaches for engaging in this process are discussed in Chapter 12.

BARRIERS TO EFFECTIVE COMMUNICATION

We began this chapter by presenting a model of interpersonal communication (Figure 7–1). In describing parts of that model, we have tried to show how perception plays an important role in communication, and how distortions, inaccuracies, and "noise" in the perceptual process can hamper and confound accurate communications. But there are other numerous imperfections in the communication process itself that contribute to misunderstanding and breakdowns. As we will note, many of these distortions share commonalities with the perceptual distortions we have already reviewed, or are compounded by perceptual difficulties. Several of the more common and problematic distortions follow.

Distractions

One barrier to effective communication is the presence of distractions. A professor was noted for keeping "banker's hours," coming to work sometime between 11:30 and noon and leaving between 2:30 and 3:00. When asked about his schedule one afternoon, and whether he were ducking out early for some tennis or golf, he said, "No, I'm going to go home and see if I can get some uninterrupted work done!" Ringing telephones, visitors, and distracting noises interrupt clear thought and coherent communication. All of us have been in a meeting where people are constantly coming in and leaving for one reason or another, and experienced the frustration that is created by this distracting traffic flow.

These distractions also contribute to communication *overload*, where an individual is bombarded with so much information, or so many different requests, that it is impossible to maintain a single communication sequence. Farance, Monge, and Russell (1977) report the following typical incident between an employee, George, and his manager:

> Okay, George, let's hear your problem. [phone rings, boss picks it up, promises to deliver a report, "Just as soon as I can get it done."] Uh, now where were we—oh, you're having a problem with your secretary. She's . . . [the manager's secretary brings in some papers that need immediate signature, so he scribbles his name where she indicates; secretary leaves] . . . you say she's depressed a lot lately, wants to leave . . . is she pregnant, maybe? [laughter] I tell you what, George, why don't you [phone rings again, lunch partner drops by] . . . uh, take a stab at handling it yourself . . . I've got to go now.

Finally, time pressures create a source of distraction. In the example above, the communication overload occurs in part because the manager does not have time to effectively sequence and control all of the different individuals who want access to him—his secretary, his employee, the lunch partner, the person asking for the report, etc. Under these time pressures, communication frequently gets abbreviated or even omitted entirely. Breakdowns occur because time pressure forces the sender to communicate messages that are incomplete, erroneous, or do not meet the needs of the receiver. Many of us have had the experience of waiting for two hours to see a doctor, only to have him spend two minutes with us and then prescribe a medication before we can even completely describe our symptoms. Time pressures also lead to distortion in negotiations, particularly as a deadline approaches, and complex agreements must be established in very short time periods. These conditions frequently lead to agreements that are difficult to implement or ratify, since the time pressures force the parties to reach agreement without attending to the details of wording, contingencies, etc.

Morley and Stephenson (1977) conducted an interesting series of experiments on the formality/informality of the communication channels and their impact on negotiation. These authors proposed that communication channels can be defined as "formal" to the degree that only the communicator's verbal messages passed through the channel (e.g., a telephone or a teletype), as opposed to "informal," where direct, face to face contact is permitted. The researchers proposed that *formal* communication channels minimize the amount of distracting information a negotiator receives—

facial reactions, gestures, etc. from the opponent—and hence increase the attention paid to the formal messages. As a result, formal channels should increase the negotiator's attention to the verbal exchange in negotiation, and lend strong competitive advantage to the side with the more persuasive or better negotiating case (better arguments, more facts, etc.). In contrast, more *informal* channels permit a great deal of distracting nonverbal information and communication, but also help the development of personal relationships. Under these conditions, social norms of equity and fairness will come into play, and relationships between the parties will develop which may enhance or inhibit the formal negotiations. The researchers propose, therefore, that under informal (wide open) communication channels, personal considerations will temper the effect of formal negotiating "power" (a strong case), and lead to more mutual concession making and a relatively weaker settlement for the stronger case. The authors report a number of research studies to confirm this hypothesis.

Semantic Problems

A second source of distortion in communication comes from semantics—the use of words or expressions which have a different meaning for the sender than for the receiver. Semantic problems typically occur when communicators speak in ambiguous generalities, or express vague degrees of intention. A negotiator says to his opponent, "We might be willing to make a minor concession on this issue if you were to propose something more substantive." Ambiguity fills the statement! How big is a minor concession? What would be a more substantive proposal? If the proposal were made, would it be sufficient for the concession to be given? Most negotiators, like most communicators, will not be likely to pursue clarification of these ambiguities, however. Instead, under the pressure of time, the receiver places his own interpreted meanings on the communication without ever bothering to check whether his understanding matches the intent of the communicator.

Semantic problems are also created when communicators use technical jargon—usage common to a particular field or specialization, but not known to those who are unfamiliar with the field. Often, mastering this technical jargon is akin to learning a foreign language. Most communicators are blind to the jargon of their own fields, but critical of the jargon of other fields. Businessmen criticize social scientists for using big words to describe simple phenomena, while they themselves are steeped in the jargon of accounting and finance.

Absence of Feedback

A third source of distortion in communication is contributed by the absence of feedback channels. Using the communication diagrams in Figures

7–1 and 7–2, one can see that cutting off the feedback loop does not permit the sender to know whether his message was received, or received accurately. Research on one-way vs. two-way communication highlights this problem. Two-way communication with discussion and questions of clarification takes longer, but is much more likely to be accurately received. One-way communication, in contrast, takes a shorter period of time, and is usually more "efficient," but it is more frustrating to the sender. Both teachers and students experience this problem. Teachers frequently wish that students would ask more questions, to make sure that a particular lecture is well understood; students frequently wish that the instructor would stop and ask for questions, rather than continuing on without probing at the right time. Negotiation is, by definition, a "give and take" process, one that requires two-way communication to be effective. The more "dedicated" or one-way it becomes—for example, from superior to subordinate—the more likely error and distortion will be introduced because of the absence of feedback channels.

Climate

In a well-known article on the impact of climate on negotiations, Gibb (1961) described the difference between supportive and defensive climates in communication. Defensive behavior, as defined by Gibb, is "behavior which occurs when an individual perceives threat or anticipates threat in the group" (p. 141). Defensive behavior is characterized by devoting attention to defending oneself from the other communicator—anticipating the other's reaction to his comments, protecting himself from attack by the opponent, and/or trying to impress, dominate, retaliate against, or attack the opponent. Defensive communication, like the stereotypic perceptual defensives described earlier, is self-fulfilling. The communication pattern of the defensive person tends to create similarly defensive postures and attitudes in the other, which confirms the communicator's initial "hunch" about his opponent's predisposition.

Gibb described a number of distinguishing characteristics of supportive vs. defensive climates. These are represented in Table 7–1. As is indicated by the descriptions and examples, defensive communication is plagued by evaluative language, efforts to control and dominate the other communicator, absolute "certainty" in one's own position and its rightfulness, low concern for the opponent, and "strategic" communication that disguises some ulterior, unstated set of motives. Many of these characteristics may or may not be intended by the sender, but they are definitely perceived by the receiver. Since defensive communication is much more likely to occur when the parties do not trust one another, or have dissimilar and conflicting goals and objectives, or have power differences between them, defensive communication is a common problem for negotiators. Negotiators who are competitive in the pursuit of their particular goals, may have low trust of one another's intentions or

TABLE 7–1
Characteristics of Supportive and Defensive Communications Climates

Defensive Climates	Characteristics and Example	Supportive Climate
Evaluate the receiver	Words, manner of speech, tone of voice, or other "judgmental" characteristics of communication that appear to evaluate the receiver negatively, rather than communicate neutrally.	Describe an event or ask for information "neutrally"
	Example: "Why in the world did you schedule a dentist appointment for me at 9 A.M.?""	
Control the receiver	Words or manner of speech which tries to control the receiver, rather than describe a problem.	Orient the receiver to the problem
	Example: "Go to the store and get coffee now!" vs. "Dear, we have no coffee for breakfast."	
Strategic communication	Words or speech perceived as part of a direct strategy to change the receiver's mind or behavior, rather than as spontaneous and free of deception.	Spontaneous communication
	Example: "Dear, the electric coffee maker is broken again. Don't you think it's time we got a new one?" (Received as an "intentional" message to get the spouse to buy a new one on the way home from work.)	
Emotionally neutral communication	Sender's communication indicates a lack of concern for the receiver's welfare, rather than clearcut concern.	Emotionally empathic communication
	Example: Spouses response to the previous coffee pot example: "That's nice. You ought to learn to drink tea anyway."	
Superiority-enhancing communication	Sender's communication indicates superiority and dominance over the receiver, rather than equality of power or status.	Equality-enhancing communication
	Example: "Your proposal is totally wrong and inadequate. When you come back with some kind of reasonable suggestion, I'll give it some consideration."	
Dogmatic "certainty" of communication	Sender's communication indicates that he knows all the answers, needs to be right, cannot be challenged.	Tentative "provisionalism" of communication
	Example: "There is absolutely no way that Professor X could have written this book because he is not bright enough to do it."	

strategy, may have power differences between them, and may perceive that the other is out to "change their mind" on the issues (strategic communication). Moreover, negotiation involves a certain amount of bluffing and deception that further undermines trust. As a result, communication is easily distorted. Negotiators become defensive and resistant toward the other, leading to distortions in understanding (1) how to interpret the meaning of the other's communication, (2) what they really want, and (3) whether we should make concessions of our own to give it to them. Supportive communication climates in negotiation are rare; they are more likely to occur when negotiators find themselves on the "same side" (that is, not having mutually conflicting interests), and pursuing an integrative bargaining process rather than a distributive one. In highly defensive climates, it may be impossible for supportive communications to be introduced without the aid of a third party. For example, Ravich (1969) reported on a series of research studies with married couples in crisis. In order to understand the nature of the communication difficulties between husband and wife, he asked them to play a bargaining game that required clear communication in order for both parties to succeed. By analyzing the failures of the parties to bargain effectively, largely as a result of breakdowns in their communication patterns or their defensive communication, Ravich was able to help the couples communicate more effectively and to deal better with their marital difficulties. Similar results are reported by mediators in a variety of disputes (Chapter 12).

Status and Power Differences

Differences in status and power between communicators can make the "one-way" communication problem more acute. Research tends to show that managers spend a great deal of their time "telling" their subordinates what they want to have accomplished—in other words, higher status and power tends to lead to one-way communication from manager to subordinate. In contrast, communication upward tends to be characterized by distortions that are self-serving to the subordinate—to make him look good in the superior's eye, or to keep him from looking bad. Subordinates often don't communicate with superiors "freely" on an open and honest basis. Particularly when there is low contact between boss and subordinate, subordinates will use the communication opportunities to pass along good news and leave out the "bad news," to highlight things that the subordinate has done well and hence gain the boss's approval, or to flatter or please the boss rather than to accurately report on problems and difficulties that the boss should know about.

When power differences exist between negotiators, differences in communications are likely to parallel the differences in power. Surprisingly, given the importance of communication in negotiation, relatively few studies have examined these communication patterns in detail. Many studies have shown that imbalance or asymmetry in negotiating power leads the high power party to perform significantly better than the low power party. Unfortunately, much of this research has been conducted with relatively simple experimental games that do not permit systematic study of communication patterns. However, we can infer that when power differences between negotiators exist, high power parties use power to their advantage, are more predisposed to use threats than promises, and use communication to direct the opponent toward compliance. In contrast, we might expect low power parties to use a variety of appeals in order to persuade the high power party to be more equitable, fair, and just in his use of power in the negotiation.

Communication in Negotiation—
The Analysis of Processes

One reason that communication processes in negotiation have received relatively little research attention is the high cost of studying this process. Many of the other elements that affect negotiation outcomes—power of the parties, magnitude of stakes, nature of the problem, etc.—can be approached in research through relatively simple manipulations. In contrast, studying "live" negotiation deliberations requires intensive analysis of a great wealth of free-flowing communication, and effective mechanisms for reducing this information to meaningful categories, sequences and generalizations. As a result, researchers have either reported detailed transcripts (Douglas, 1962), or have preferred to characterize the communication patterns by broad generalizations (competitive, defensive, supportive, antagonistic).

Morley and Stephenson (1977) proposed that a scheme for analyzing communication in small groups (Bales, 1950) might be modified to understand negotiation dialogue. Bales proposed a framework for analyzing dialogue from small group meetings, and assigning each statement to one of twelve categories. These categories represented two major dimensions of group activity: "task" activities, in which group members focused on the nature of the problem to be solved or job to be accomplished, and "process" activities, in which group members displayed various social-emotional reactions to one another as the activity progressed. By analyzing the patterns of communications in these categories, Bales demonstrated that communication changed as the group worked on the task, and that definite "stages" of group work, characterized by different communication patterns, could be identified by this process.

In the spirit of this research, Morley and Stephenson defined a content communication analysis mechanism, Conference Process Analysis, for assessing negotiation deliberations. The major dimensions of communication are identified as: mode, resource, and reference. The *mode* dimension indicates how information is being exchanged, for example, by offers, acceptances, rejections, or the seeking of responses from the other side. The *resource* dimension refers to the function of the information being exchanged. Four major resources are identified: structuring the negotiations (for example, procedures), focusing on outcomes (discussing settlement points, limits, positive or negative consequences), acknowledgments (praising or criticizing the other for their behavior in negotiations), and exchange of information (facts, supporting data, etc.). Finally, the *reference* dimension indicates who is being talked about in the information: the negotiator, a person on his own team or someone on the other team, the negotiator's organization, the opposing organization, or some combination of the above groups.

By applying this coding scheme to transcripts of negotiations in a complex role play, the authors were able to confirm that negotiation, like communication in problem solving groups, proceeds through distinct phases or stages. In the early stages, negotiators are engaged in behavior to state and defend their own position, (and their group's position), to the opponent. The most important elements of this stage are building a strong case and demonstrating power. At some point, negotiators move to a second phase of communication. During this phase, negotiators become less competitive and protective of their original position; they move from a more expository to "problem-oriented" mode, searching for possible solutions to the criteria or "limits" that were earlier defined. Finally, in the third stage, negotiators work to achieve a joint solution. At this point, they are trying to agree on a settlement point that will satisfy them and those they represent. As the reader can observe, the analysis of communication patterns follows the "stages" or "sequences" model of negotiation which has been proposed by many observers (Chapter 3), but not confirmed by specific content analysis of communication.

Improving Communication Effectiveness in Negotiation

Given the many ways communication can be disrupted and distorted, one can only marvel at the amount that actually gets accomplished. It is the authors' belief that failures and distortions in perception and communication are the single most dominant contributor to breakdowns and failures in negotiation. Research cannot directly confirm this assertion, since the processes of perception and communication are so intertwined with the other major factors—commitment to one's own position and objectives, the nature of the negotiating process, the use of power and power tactics, and the negotiators' personality. Nevertheless, it is the authors' experience, through the study of many simulated and actual negotiations, that parties whose goals are compatible, and whose overriding objectives are the same, may not reach agreement because of their misperceptions of the opponent, or because of breakdowns in the communication process. Research is available to support this proposition in a more limited way. For example, Deutsch and Krauss (1962) conducted a series of experiments on the impact of threat behavior in a simulated negotiation game. They first studied what impact the opportunity to threaten the opponent would have upon its use in negotiation; as might be predicted, when bargainers could threaten their opponents, the threat was used; and its use contributed to a significant decrease in each negotiator's outcome. The researchers predicted that the opportunity to communicate with the other party might improve bargaining efficiency and decrease the impact of the threat; however, they found that when communication was permitted, and even when it was required, it did not significantly affect outcomes. Parties without threat used communication to enhance their bargaining coordination, but not significantly so; parties with threat used communication to enhance the competitiveness between them. Only when the negotiators were *tutored* in how to communicate—how to make proposals that would improve their coordination in the bargaining game—did the participants use communication effectively (Krauss and Deutsch, 1966).

Since the Deutsch and Krauss experiments, a number of techniques have been suggested for improving the accuracy and efficiency of communications in negotiation. "Tutoring" communication—helping the parties learn how to communicate accurately and appropriately—is a role typically played by third parties. Their activities will be reviewed in detail in Chapter 12. However, in this chapter, we review several techniques that the parties themselves can use to insure that some of the typical perceptual and communication blocks are not confounding their ability to reach satisfactory agreement.

Questioning

One of the most common techniques for clarifying communications, and eliminating noise and distortion, is the use of questions. Nierenberg (1973) emphasized that questions are essential elements in negotiations for securing information; asking good questions enables a negotiator to secure a great deal of information about the opponent's position, supporting arguments and needs.

Nierenberg proposes that questions can be divided into two basic classifications: those that are manageable, and those that cause difficulty (Table 7–2). Manageable questions are primarily questions that cause attention (prepare the other person's thinking for further questions, for example, "How are you?"), get information ("How much will this cost?") and start thinking ("Do you have any suggestions for improving this?"). Unmanageable questions, or ones that cause difficulty, are ones that give information ("Didn't you know that we couldn't afford this?") and bring the discussion to a false conclusion ("Don't you think we've talked about this enough?"). As the reader can determine from descriptions and examples of the "unman-

TABLE 7–2
Questions in Negotiation

Manageable Questions	*Example*
1. Open-ended questions—ones that cannot be answered with a simple "yes" or "no." *Who, what, where, when* and *why* questions	1. "Why do you take that position in these deliberations?"
2. Open questions—invite the other's thinking	2. "What do you think of our proposal?"
3. Leading questions—points toward an answer to the question	3. "Don't you think our proposal is a fair and reasonable offer?"
4. Cool questions—low emotionality	4. "What is the additional rate that we will have to pay if you make the improvements on the property?"
5. Planned questions—part of an overall logical sequence of questions developed in advance	5. "After you make the improvements to the property, when can we expect to take occupancy?"
6. Treat questions—flatters the opponent at the same time it asks for information	6. "Can you provide us with some of your excellent insight on this problem?"
7. Window questions—aid you in looking into the other person's mind	7. "Can you tell us how you came to that conclusion?"
8. Directive questions—focus on a specific point	8. "How much is the rental rate per square foot with these improvements?"
9. Gauging questions—ascertains how the other person feels	9. "How do you feel about our proposal?"

Unmanageable Questions	*Example*
1. Close-out questions—forces the opponent into seeing things your way	1. "You wouldn't try to take advantage of us here, would you?"
2. Loaded questions—puts the other person on the spot regardless of his answer	2. "Do you mean to tell me that these are the only terms you will accept?"
3. Heated questions—high emotionality, triggers emotional response	3. "Don't you think we've spent enough time discussing this ridiculous proposal of yours?"
4. Impulse questions—occurs on the "spur of the moment," without planning—tends to get conversation off the track	4. "As long as we're discussing this, what do you think we ought to tell other groups who have made similar demands on us?"
5. Trick questions—appear to require a frank answer, but really are "loaded" in their meaning	5. "What are you going to do—give in to our demands, or take this to arbitration?"
6. Reflective "trick" questions—reflects the other into agreeing with your point of view	6. "Here's how I see the situation—don't you agree?"

ageable" questions, most of these questions are likely to produce defensiveness and anger in the opponent. While they may yield information, they are not likely to let the target feel comfortable or create a climate for him to provide more information in the future.

Active Listening/Reflecting

"Active listening" and "reflecting" are terms that are commonly used in the helping professions—counseling and therapy (Rogers, 1965). Counselors recognize that communications are frequently loaded with multiple meanings, and that the counselor must try to "tease out" these several meanings without making the communicator angry or defensive. One technique for gaining more information is to ask questions; however, as we pointed out in the previous section, frequent questions, particularly when the communication is emotionally charged, may contribute to defensiveness. The questioner should have the other party voluntarily elaborate on his earlier statements, rather than making the communicator feel cross-examined by multiple questions. Another method of gaining more information is by listening. There are three major forms of listening:

Passive listening is merely the reception of the message, providing no feedback to the sender about the accuracy or completeness of reception. As we pointed out in the communication model at the beginning of this chapter, listening is the key process in the reception and decoding stage of communication. Sometimes passive listening is enough in itself to keep a communicator sending information. Some people like to talk, and can't handle long silences. Negotiators who have an opponent with this characteristic may find that their best strategy is to sit and listen, and his opponent will eventually talk himself into, or out of, a position on his own.

Acknowledgment is the second form of listening, slightly more active than complete passivity. When acknowledging, the receiver occasionally nods his head, maintains eye contact, or interjects responses like "I see," "mm-hmm," "interesting," "really," "sure," "go on," etc. These responses are sufficient to keep the communicator sending messages, but the sender often misinterprets the acknowledgments as the receiver's *agreeing* with the position, rather than simply receiving the message.

Active listening is the third form of listening. When the receiver is actively listening, he restates, or paraphrases, the sender's message in his own language. Some examples (from Gordon, 1977):

> *Sender:* I don't know how I am going to untangle this messy problem.
> *Receiver:* You're really stumped on how to solve this one.

> *Sender:* Please, don't ask me about that now.
> *Receiver:* Sounds like you're awfully busy right now.

> *Sender:* I thought the meeting today accomplished nothing.
> *Receiver:* You were very disappointed with our session.

As noted by Athos and Gabarro (1978), successful reflective responding (active listening) is characterized by the following:

- a greater emphasis on *listening* than on talking.

- responding to that which is *personal* rather than abstract (personal feelings, beliefs, positions rather than abstract ideas).

- *following* the other in his exploration rather than leading him into areas we think we should be exploring (exploring his frame of reference rather than forcing ours upon him, at least until we fully understand his position).

- *clarifying* what the other has said about his own thoughts and feelings rather than close questioning, or telling him what we believe he should be thinking or feeling.

- *responding* to the other's feelings in his communication.

The active listening/reflection technique advocated by Athos and Garbarro, Gordon, and others, has generally been recommended more for counseling-oriented communications such as employee counseling and performance improvement. In negotiation, it may appear initially that active listening/reflecting is unsuitable because, unlike counseling sessions, the receiver *does* have a position of his own, and usually *does* feel strongly about the issues. By recommending active listening, we are not suggesting that the receiver should automatically adopt or agree with his opponent's position and abandon his own. Rather, we are suggesting that active listening can be a skill which encourages the opponent to talk more fully about his frame of reference—the position he is taking. In doing so, we may better understand the nature of his position, the factors and information that support it, and the ways that the opponent's position can be compromised, reconciled, or negotiated in accordance with our own preferences and priorities.

Role Reversal

The third way communication distortions may be eliminated is through role reversal. Rapoport (1964) suggests that continually arguing our own position in debate leads to a "blindness of involvement," or a self-reinforcing cycle of argumentation that prohibits us from recognizing the possible compatibilities between our own position and the opponent's. In the description of active listening, we suggested that one objective was to gain a better understanding of the other party's frame of reference, rather than to be concerned about advocating our own. Active listening, however, is still a somewhat "passive" process. Role reversal techniques allow us to understand the other's position by actively arguing his position to his satisfaction. In doing so, it is expected that the communicator will more fully *understand* his opponent's position, perhaps come to accept the validity of that position, and discover ways that both positions can be modified or changed to bring them into greater compatability.

A number of studies have examined the impact and success of the role reversal technique (Johnson, 1971; Walcott, Hopmann and King, 1977). In general, the research supports the following conclusions:

1. Role reversal is effective in producing cognitive changes (greater understanding of the opponent's position) and attitude changes (perceived similarities between the two positions).

2. When the parties' positions are fundamentally compatible with one another, role reversal is likely to produce better results (cognitive and attitudinal change); when the parties' positions are fundamentally incompatible, role reversal may sharpen the perceptions of incompatability and inhibit positive attitude change.

3. While role reversal may induce greater understanding of the opponent's position, and highlight areas of possible similarity, it is not necessarily more effective overall as a means of inducing agreement between parties.

Role reversal may be a useful tool for reducing the distortions in communication that prohibit accurate understanding of, and appreciation for, the other position in negotiation. However, such understanding may not necessarily lead to an easier resolution of the conflict, particularly when accurate communication reveals a fundamental incompatibility in the positions of the two sides. The use of role reversal will be discussed further in Chapter 12.

SUMMARY

In this chapter, a model of the communication process has been described. In assessing the components of this model, we have suggested that many of the elements are prone to error and distortion, and that human perception can often compound this distortion. Such distortions are very likely to occur when communicating parties have conflicting goals and objectives, and strong feelings of dislike or disdain for one another. Since conflicting goals, objectives, and a negative view of the other party are typical characteristics of many negotiations, it follows that perception and communication in negotiation are frequently prone to the same distortions and breakdowns that characterize other conflict settings. The most common distortions in perception include stereotypic reactions to the other party, halo effects, selective perceptions, projection and perceptual defense. These perceptual hazards are often compounded by breakdowns in communication, and five typical sources of breakdown were identified: distractions, semantic problems, the absence of adequate feedback mechanisms, defensive climates, and status/power differences between the two parties.

Because these distortions and errors in perception and communication frequently cause trouble for negotiators, restoration and maintenance of effective communication are essential for success. Several strategies can be used to assure progress. First, negotiators can insure that their perceptions are accurate. Stereotypes, halo effects, and selective perception are all potentially open to disconfirmation if the negotiator chooses to recognize the distortion and seek new information. Sometimes this exposure may occur as a result of prompting by others, and sometimes a third party is necessary to introduce new information and disconfirm previous judgments. Second, negotiators can eliminate many of the problems of miscommunication by checking and rechecking their understanding of the other's statements, as well as by monitoring the other's understanding of their own position. Systematic questioning, active listening and role reversal are effective techniques for correcting distortions and misperceptions. Finally, negotiators need to be more willing to have third parties intervene to help them overcome communication breakdowns. Particularly when emotional passions are strong and communication becomes highly distorted, third parties are needed to change the communication climate and serve as a channel for re-establishing a clear understanding of the actual similarities and differences between each party's position. More will be said about the third party's conduct in Chapter 12.

We have explored communication from the perspective of both parties, and the channels and mechanisms used by each. We shall now turn to a different approach to communication—the techniques used by one party to structure messages so as to be maximally persuasive to the other in negotiation deliberations.

8

The Persuasion Process

We have been examining the strategy and tactics a person uses to get the largest part of a negotiated settlement for himself. As a negotiator, my goals are usually to convince other persons that what I am giving them is more valuable than they realized, that I cannot give more than I have offered, and that what I have offered is reasonable. I will also try to alter the other person's beliefs about how important their own objectives are to them; and that what they are giving up is probably not as valuable as they thought. I will try to convince them that I am a likeable person, one who should be treated decently. I may also try to convince them that other people will be watching us negotiate, and will be evaluating us based on the outcome. All of these efforts are designed to influence another person's positions, perceptions, opinions, and attitudes, and will be collectively called "persuasion."

People differ widely in their ability to persuade. We sometimes think of the ability to persuade as something we are born with, something we either "have" or "don't have." While the natural persuasive abilities of people do differ, persuasion is as much a "science" as it is a native ability; thus, it is possible for everyone to learn how to improve their persuasive abilities.

There are three key elements in the process of persuasion: the sender, i.e., the person or persons who is attempting to persuade; the target, i.e., the person or persons to be persuaded; and message, i.e., the content that the sender wants the target to believe, accept, or understand. (See Figure 8–1.) Dimensions of each of these elements may be used singly, or in combination,

FIGURE 8-1

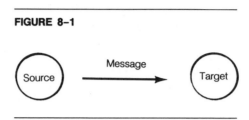

to bring about a successful persuasion effort. In this chapter, we first examine the different aspects of message structure and content, then look at the credibility of the source of the message, and finally review characteristics of the target person receiving the message.

ARCHITECTURE OF THE MESSAGE

Obviously, facts and ideas are important in changing another's opinions and perceptions. But there are many ways that facts can be selected, organized, and presented. There are three major issues to consider in structuring a message: which facts or topics are covered, how the topics and facts are arranged, and the style used to present them.

Which Topics and Facts to Cover

Attractiveness of the Offer to the Target.   One obvious thing to emphasize in negotiations is the advantage to be gained by the other party from accepting our proposal (Michener and Suchner, 1971). While this may be obvious to us as observers, it is surprising how many negotiators, even experienced ones, spend more time in explaining and defending what is attractive to *them* in their offer rather than identifying what is likely to be attractive *to the other party*. Salespersons often identify a customer's needs and requirements before they get down to the details of what a particular automobile or outboard motor can do. Labor negotiators will often have preliminary, unofficial meetings with management, at which they can discuss the upcoming deliberations and sound each other out on the things that will be really important this year. The negotiators are hardly likely to reveal the minimums they would really settle for; but they will usually give indications of major priorities and general objectives. With this information, offers can be crafted to be more appealing to the other party.

When we are on the receiving end, of a proposal, we probably do not choose to talk about the attractive features of an offer, but rather the *undesirable* features, and why the things offered are not as valuable to us as the offerer tried to make us believe (Emerson, 1962). A strategy often followed by customers in foreign bazaars or antique shops is to spend a considerable amount of time discussing something they do not want and then, after dropping that topic, to casually examine and ask about the price of the thing they do want. The idea is, of course, that the trader will grab at the chance to make a sale before this apparently unsatisfied customer walks out. The trader may also accept a low price, one close to his or her resistance point. One would suspect that even if professional traders had only a fraction of their reputed craftiness, they would have long ago figured out this trick. But then this customer is about to walk out . . . perhaps.

Fears and Threats.   Messages that contain threats—threats of strikes by unions, lockouts by management, or threats to do harm or break off negotiations—can be very useful at certain times and in certain places. Because of their dramatic nature and the emotional response they evoke, we hear more about the use of threats than about many other negotiation tactics. In fact, threats are probably used less frequently than we might expect. One reason seems to be that the target person's reaction to a threat is hard to predict. Some people respond by becoming belligerent and antagonistic themselves, some by becoming defensive, cautious, or inflexible, and others respond by actually complying with the threat. The nature of the response depends upon the personality of the target person and the situation they are in (Burgoon and Bettinghaus, 1980). A second reason is that it is hard to know how menacing the threat appears to the other party. Often our threats appear more powerful to us than to others. Third, threats put the other party in a position where he can "call our bluff," forcing us to carry out the threat. Often, to follow through with a threat may cost us more than we are willing to pay. Lastly, threats produce compliance, but not necessarily agreement. As we have pointed out, negotiating parties want to reach an arrangement they can and will live with. People can find many ways to get out of arrangements they do not "buy into."

Fear-arousing messages may be sent without issuing threats. One manager, negotiating with another manager about the flow of work between their two departments, may point out that if an agreement is not reached, the other manager will be seen by higher management as uncooperative. To be effective, this kind of message has to be accompanied by a suggested alternative action that will reduce or eliminate the feared outcome, and a reassurance that the action will work (Leventhal, 1976). For example, the manager could then propose that he will reassign some of his employees to help the other speed up the work flow if the other will provide some additional storage space, and then show how these changes will eliminate their problem.

Distractions.   One factor that makes the persuasion process complex is that people start to defend themselves against being persuaded as soon as they suspect that someone is trying to persuade them. As they listen, part of their attention is usually devoted to what is being said, but a large portion is devoted to developing counterarguments (Festinger and Maccoby, 1964; Brock, 1963). Negotiators can be more effective at persuasion if they can determine how to "turn off" others' efforts at developing counterarguments. One way to do this is to have a distraction occur at the same time we are sending our message. The distraction apparently absorbs the effort that normally would go into building counterarguments and the listener is "... left vulnerable to the message appeals" (Reardon, 1981, p. 192). For example, during an oral presentation of the economic advantages of our offer we could lay out papers with charts and graphs, hand them to the other party and help them turn from one to another as we continue our oral presentation. Presumably, the charts and graphs absorb that part of the person's attention that might normally go into formulating counterarguments. Distractions appear to work because they seem to inhibit the receiver's subvocalization (what he says to himself as he hears the message). Sometimes these subvocalizations are counterarguments, ones that occur when we are opposed to or cautious about the message; but they can be supportive arguments as well. When we really do like what is being said, such as when a hostess is trying to persuade us to take a second helping of a high calorie dessert, subvocalizations will encourage us to accept her offer. At that time, if we want to protect ourselves from her temptations, we should create distractions. If the hostess wants to be successful, she should try to eliminate any distractions (Petty, Wells, and Brock, 1976).

Something "Yesable." The advertising media discovered long ago that when people agree with one statement or proposal, even though it may be minor, they are likely to agree with a second, more significant statement or proposal from the same person or on the same topic (Freedman and Fraser, 1966; Seligman, Bush, and Kirsch, 1976). Hence, if we can get the other party to agree with us on anything, we have laid the foundation for subsequent agreement. The task is to find something to which the other party can agree and which has costs we can accept. A real estate salesperson who gets us to agree that the house we are looking at is in a nice neighborhood for our children has made the first step toward getting us to say "yes" to buying the house.

Agreements "in Principle." There are times when getting an agreement "in principle" may be a valuable step in a negotiation. For example, when there is bitter conflict between two parties who cannot seem to agree on anything, getting agreement on a general principle may be the first "yesable" statement that both parties can agree to. Hence, in the negotiations between Israel and Egypt over the Sinai, no details were settled about the fate of the Palestinians, but an agreement on the principle of Palestinian self-rule was reached. While agreement "in principle" is a desired thing to achieve when other options are blocked, agreements based on principle *only* are probably less fruitful for a clear and implementable agreement than those containing specific action proposals. Principles sound good, and most people may agree with what they advocate, but there is always uncertainty about how a principle applies to the specific situation. For example, if the parties agree that "honesty is the best policy," we are left with questions. Is honesty best all of the time? Some of the time? Most of the time? Specific, concrete statements in negotiation eliminate errors in meaning and interpretation, thereby making them easier to implement.

Normative Messages.   It is easy to assume that people are driven by simple and direct self-interest. However, there is also plenty of evidence to indicate that people are motivated to behave consistent with current religious, social, or ethical standards of behavior. These standards become part of a person's self-image, a "picture" in their mind of what they are really like. People often go to considerable lengths to act or say things consistent with their self-image. We are polite at times when we really want to tell another person to "drop dead." We are generous when we are actually financially strained and feel like being greedy (Reardon, 1981). We behave in these ways to preserve our self-image, and to convince others that we are the person we would like to be.

A powerful argument in negotiation is to show the other person that by following a course of action (our proposal), they will be acting in accordance with some higher (more noble, moral, or ethical) code of conduct. An automobile salesperson may argue that by accepting his price and buying his car you are also helping the nation by supporting American manufacturers (Fisher and Ury, 1981). At times, the simple statement, "this is the right (proper) thing to do," may carry considerable weight. People work hard to take responsibility for actions that lead to positive outcomes (Schlenker and Riess, 1979).

Message Structure

People are influenced not only by what we say, but by the way we arrange the words. Any writer or speaker faces the question of whether to present material in the most logical, rational manner or to appeal to the receiver's emotions. Should the most important information or strongest arguments be placed at the beginning, the middle, or the end of a presentation? Should counterarguments or opposing ideas be mentioned at all? There has been a considerable amount of study on the persuasive power of these different aspects of message structure. Surprisingly, many things we might expect to have an important impact, such as the structure of logic in the message, have *not* been clearly shown to be significant. Aspects of message structure that *have* been shown to be significant are discussed next.

Message Order.   In preparing a persuasive argument, we usually have one major point, piece of information, or illustration that we think is particularly important or compelling. Where should we place it in our message? At the beginning? In the middle? At the end? Research tells us one thing clearly— do *not* place the important point in the middle (Bettinghaus, 1966). Should it be at the beginning or at the end? When the topics are familiar, interesting, and/or controversial to the receiver, the important points should be made early, exposing the receiver to the *primacy effect*. The primacy effect occurs because the first item in a long list of items to be presented is the one most likely to be remembered. Thus, messages that are desirable to the receiver should be stated early, before we present something the other will not want to hear. In contrast, when the topic is uninteresting, unfamiliar, or not very important to the receiver, the most critical point should be placed at the *end* of the message to take advantage of the *recency effect*. The recency effect is the tendency for the *last* item presented to be the best remembered, and should be considered when the message we want to give is likely to be contrary to a current point of view (Rosnow and Robinson, 1967).

In summary, people remember the beginning and the end of messages better than they do the middle. In negotiation, given that we are presenting new material on a topic important to the listener, it is usually best to put our most important and persuasive material toward the end of our message. For those messages we feel the other party will like, our important point should come first. When we are not sure about the other party's interest or familarity with our arguments, we can take the safe route and make our strong point at both the beginning *and* at the end of our presentation.

One-and Two-Sided Messages.   We are trying to persuade another person because we believe he holds an opinion different from ours. Many people deal with this problem by completely ignoring arguments and opinions which might support their opponent's position. Many politicians not only do not mention their opponent's point of view, but make a policy of never mentioning their opponent's name. Until recently, for example, advertisements for a consumer product would never mention the name of competing products, or openly compare the products.

An alternate approach to ignoring the competition is to mention and describe the opposing point of view, and then show how and why it is less appropriate or desirable than the presenter's point of view. Which of these approaches is most effective? As usual, the answer is not straightforwardly simple:

1.   Two-sided messages (those that mention and then criticize the competition) seem to be more effective with better educated audiences.

2.   Two-sided messages seem to be more effective when the other party initially *disagrees* with our position.

3. Two-sided messages seem to be preferable when the other party will be exposed to arguments and points of view *different* from the one we advocate (that is, people who try to counter-persuade the other toward *their* point of view).

4. *One-sided* arguments are more effective when the other party is already in agreement with our point of view.

5. When presenting two-sided arguments, it is more effective to present our preferred argument last (Bettinghaus, 1966; Zimbardo, Ebbesen, and Maslach, 1977).

In summary, when dealing with reasonably intelligent audiences, it is a mistake to ignore the impact of counterarguments. The other party will be formulating them as we speak, and it is to our advantage to address and refute them by using two-sided messages, placing our own position last.

Mountains into Molehills: Fractioning Disputes.   Big ideas or large propositions are hard to grasp and accept, especially when they are significantly different from our own. We can help the other party understand and accept our arguments by breaking them into smaller, more understandable pieces (Fisher, 1964; Ikle, 1964). It is even better if we can show that our ultimate objective contains component parts that the other party has already accepted or agreed with. For example, a company negotiating a change in work rules with a union might have trouble getting the whole package of rule changes accepted, but could break its presentation down into separate discussions of specific rules: transfers between departments within a plant, transfers between plants, permanent changes in work classifications, temporary changes in work classifications, etc. In one case, for example, a union was very interested in interplant and interdepartmental changes in work rules to preserve job security; having already said yes (getting to a "yesable" point) to these changes, the union seemed more receptive and flexible to management's argument for other work rule changes.

Repetition.   We only have to think of typical television advertisement to realize that ad writers believe in the power of repetition to get their message through. Repeating a point is effective for the first few times. After that, additional repetition does not significantly change attitudes (McGuire, 1973).

Drawing Conclusions.   Sometimes writers or speakers will lay out a line of argument, and then state the conclusion; other times, they will let the receivers draw their own conclusion. Letting the other draw his own conclusion (but the conclusion *you* want drawn) can lead to a very effective presentation. The research shows that for the intellectually inclined, or for those who have not yet made up their mind, leaving the conclusion open is a good approach. In contrast, for people whose ideas are firm, leaving the conclusion implicit is to leave the most important part of our persuasive effort undone. In general, draw explicit conclusions for your audience (Hovland and Mandell, 1952; McGuire, 1964).

Style of Presentation

In designing our message to persuade, we need to consider topics, structure, and style. In selecting a style, we set the emotional tone and manner of our presentation. Some people are belligerent, others solicitous and accommodating. Some people make speeches, others start a dialogue. Some present detailed facts and draw specific conclusions, while others paint beautiful word pictures and use metaphors. We will now consider some of the major elements of persuasive style and their impact on successful persuasion.

Active Participation vs. Passive Responding. People learn better, and are more likely to change their attitudes and beliefs, when they are actively involved in the process of learning and understanding new material (Bettinghaus, 1966). Good teachers know this. Rather than lecture, they ask questions; learning is even more effective when teachers can get people both intellectually and physically involved. In trying to persuade a car dealer that the car we are trading in is really worth a premium price, we could present facts and ask questions, but it would be better to have him or her walk around the car with us, examine what we think are exceptional points, take the car for a drive, examine the repair records and note our frequent routine maintenance. Exerting effort leads to involvement which leads to attitude change.

Metaphor. While facts and logical conclusions are important to persuasion, metaphors can be even more potent (Bowers and Osborn, 1966; Burgoon and King, 1974). An auto salesperson can give us details about the construction of a car's carburetor and the miles per gallon of gasoline used at different speeds and rates of acceleration, but he will probably get his point across just as well by saying, "I've got the facts that show this car is not a gas guzzler." The same salesperson could show you the fine finish of a car, have you examine the underside of the body and attend to the immaculate condition of the engine, or he could say, "this car is a cream puff." An excessive use of metaphors may lead the other party to believe that we are "filled with hot air" (a metaphor itself for not having the facts to support our arguments), but when used to summarize some facts, or to establish clear visual impressions, metaphors are very valuable persuasion tools.

Intensity of Language. The intensity of the language we use has a major impact on our persuasiveness. If I say, "This is certainly the best price you will get," I speak with more intensity than if I say, "This is probably a very good price." Similarly, the statement, "I don't feel like going out tonight," is not as intense as, "You could not drag me out tonight with a team of elephants." The intensity of language can also be increased through the use of sexual or violent metaphors, swear words, or even a change in our intonation—from quiet to loud, or loud to quiet (Bowers, 1964).

We might think that more intense language would automatically be more persuasive. To the contrary, language of relatively low intensity seems to be more effective than intense language (Bowers, 1964). Evidence indicates that people react negatively to persuasive attempts using language they perceive as too intense (Burgoon and King, 1974). People under stress seem to be particularly receptive to messages using low intensity language and more inclined to reject those using high intensity language (Jones and Burgoon, 1975). To show that the impact of intensity is even more complex, research has shown that the effect of intense language depends, in part, on who uses it. In our society it is considered more acceptable for men to use intense language than women. Sources with high credibility can use more intense language than those not seen as credible (Burgoon and Stewart, 1975). Hence, clergymen can speak with more intensity about the characteristics of Heaven and Hell, and the likelihood of someone going there, than can the authors of this book. In conclusion, while there is a strong temptation to use intense language to make our point, we do better to moderate this impulse.

Violation of Target's Expectations.   In his book *All the Kings Men*, Robert Penn Warren describes a scene in which Willy Stark, the demagogic, radical candidate for Governor, is about to speak to a group of wealthy citizens to raise funds for his campaign. The citizens are not supportive of his radical proposals, nor of his violent manner of speech. When he arrives, he is conservatively dressed and greets them in a quiet, relaxed manner. In a conversational tone, he proceeds to lay out some modest proposals for social change, along with some sensible ways of financing them. His audience is at first surprised, then impressed, and finally won over. Stark is employing the technique of "expectation violation." Another example of the technique occurs when we expect one style of delivery from the speaker and then experience a totally different style. For example, if we expect that we will be subjected to intense language, (loud, volatile, provocative, etc.), we marshall up our defenses and counterarguments. When we are met with moderate, casual, reasonable language, we relax the defenses we don't think we will need any more, listen to the message relatively uncritically, and end up being persuaded (Miller and Burgoon, 1979). Great orators throughout history have used this style, frequently changing the intensity of their voice to hold the audience's attention. While this is not a stylistic tactic that everyone can use, those who have a reputation for intense language have a valuable tool at their disposal. Clearly, the process may also work in reverse—audiences who are expecting a quiet, controlled, highly rational discourse may be equally persuaded by an emotionally intense speaker because they were unprepared to defend themselves against such passionate persuasion.

CHARACTERISTICS OF SOURCES

Source Credibility

During a negotiation, the other party gives us information, opinions, and interpretations. What should we believe? From what we have learned about negotiation, there is reason for the other party to try to mislead us. At the same time, we have to accept and believe *some* of the information we are given, or else successful negotiation and agreement are impossible. We can't check every fact and statement. The more information we are willing to accept, the more persuaded we will be. Obviously, the reverse is true—the more credible we are to the other party, the more persuasive we will be.

The degree to which a person is willing to accept what another person says depends upon three things: how trustworthy the source is seen to be, how qualified the source is seen to be, and what type of person the source appears to be. Let us assume we are buying a house. The seller tells us that she has three other parties coming to look at the house in the afternoon; two of them are being transferred to this area and only have one day to locate a house. If this is true, and we like the house, it would be to our advantage to make an offer now rather than to delay our decision and possibly find that one of the afternoon visitors has bought the house. But are the seller's statements accurate? There is no doubt that the seller knows accurately whether or not there are other potential buyers coming that same day; hence there is no question that she is competent or qualified to have good information. The issue is whether or not the seller is telling the truth.

When people are determining how much to believe another person, the two most important things they take into account are, (1) is this person in a position to possess the information they claim to have, i.e., are they competent or qualified, and (2) are they reporting accurately what they know, i.e., are they personally believable or trustworthy (Berlo, Lemert, and Mertz, 1966). People also appear more or less credible because of their "presence"— the way they present themselves to others. Three components of behavior are instrumental in creating a favorable presence: composure, sociability, and extroversion (McCroskey, Jensen, and Valencia, 1980). A person who seems hesitant, confused, or uncertain when giving us information is not as convincing as a person who appears to know what he or she is talking about and is comfortable in talking about it. A friendly, open person is easier to talk to, to like, and therefore to believe than someone who is distant, abrasive, or haughty. A person with a dynamic vocal style and who is confident in his delivery is often more persuasive than one who is not. As mentioned earlier, trustworthiness and perceived expertise seem to be the more powerful characteristics, but all three play a critical role in determining our perception of another's credibility.

Origins of Source Credibility

Many things about us influence others' perceptions of our credibility. We will now discuss the primary elements that have been found to contribute to or detract from a person's credibility. By using these elements as standards, we can make some assessment of how we are perceived by others as we enter negotiations, and discover what we might do to maximize our perceived credibility.

Personal Reputation.   When a person is described as someone whom, "I wouldn't believe even if he told me it was raining while I was outside getting wet," we're probably hearing about a person with a reputation for dishonesty. This type of person is going to have an extremely difficult time in negotiations. It is not surprising that professional negotiators work very hard to protect their reputations for honesty. As we noted in earlier chapters, negotiators are expected to engage in puffery and to present things in the best possible light for their side—but not to lie or misrepresent what they are offering. They may also succeed at lying and deception in one negotiation, but it is likely that few will believe them in later negotiations. They know they must appear believable.

Frequently, we enter negotiations with strangers, people whose reputations are unknown to us. If the substance of the discussion is important to us, it is sensible for us to "check out" the other party's reputation, and for them to do so with us. We might want to help them check this out by identifying, perhaps during early discussions, other people who can vouch for our integrity.

Position Bias of a Stranger.   When meeting others they don't know, people generally tend to adopt a positive rather than a negative evaluation (Greenberg and Miller, 1966). There is a cultural norm to be open-minded when meeting new people; if we do form a first impression, we tend to err toward the positive viewpoint. While that norm is an obvious advantage to us in helping us to appear more persuasive to the other party, we should also keep in mind that the same normative expectation is probably working on us as well.

Intention to Persuade.   The statement, "First impressions are lasting impressions" has a great deal of psychological validity. In the first few minutes after meeting a stranger, how we dress, behave, and speak can be enormously important. Do we initially come across as a huckster or as a persuasive promoter for our cause? Even appearing very confident can make people feel uncomfortable and feel guarded. Similarly, if we appear very cool, poised, polished, or calculating, we can also expect to put others on their guard. In short, the more "prepared" or "rehearsed" we appear to be in our persuasive efforts, the more suspicious others may be that they are about to have their attitudes changed, and the less receptive they may be. In contrast, the ability to communicate "natural" enthusiasm, sincerity, and spontaneity takes the "edge" off persuasive communication. Many skillful negotiators and persuaders, therefore, may take on a mild-mannered or even slightly confused demeanor in order to minimize the negative impact of a hard, persuasive style.

Status Differential.   Most people are acutely (but unconsciously) aware of status and status differences. We assess status by a variety of criteria: occupation, age, sex, level of education, religion, community in which a person lives, dress, type of automobile, etc. A president of a major corporation, for example, has more status than a university professor, but less than a Justice of the Supreme Court. A person's persuasiveness is influenced by his status—not in an absolute sense, but by the difference in status between him and others. University professors will be better able to influence high school teachers than vice versa. Higher status plays several roles in increasing persuasiveness. It gives a person visibility, which allows him to get attention and be listened to. It also confers prestige on a person, lending the image that she is worth listening to or more believable (Bettinghaus, 1980). However, not everyone holds the same views on status. If I am concerned with my ability to influence another person, I need to understand what he or she views as "high" or "low" status. For example, corporate presidents are usually viewed as having higher status than union presidents, but union members might think the reverse is true.

Appearance.   It is hardly earth-shaking to observe that how we dress, speak, and behave will influence how credible we appear to others. What may *not* be as obvious is the way we should adjust our appearance to increase our credibility. Should we "dress up" and wear a tie and jacket, even if we usually wear jeans and a sport shirt? Should we adopt some of the local speech pronunciations and drop those which are native to us? In general, researchers have found that it is best to be "normal" (Bettinghaus, 1980). A Harvard-educated politician from New England who tries to spice his language with "aw, shucks" and "y'all" in the South will not appear normal; neither will a college student who drops in to buy a Porche dressed in cutoff jeans, dirty running shoes and uncombed hair.

Associates.   Whom we associate with can influence how we are perceived, influencing our perceived status and perhaps our perceived expertise. Judicious name dropping, mentioning well-known references, even arranging for introductions by people who can add to our reputation, are all useful steps. More is said about this in Chapter 10.

Expertise.   Sometimes our occupation, education or past experiences will establish our expertise and therefore the perception of our competence. At other times, there are no obvious ways for our expertise to be known; more unfortunately, there are still other times when one piece of knowledge about us diminishes the likelihood that we are seen as an expert in certain areas. Stereotypes often lead us to see women as lacking knowledge of mechanical things, or single men as being ignorant of child care. In situations where our expertise is unknown or likely to be viewed stereotypically, we need to take extra efforts to establish our position. If people don't know our expertise, we can often find some way to mention our education or experiences. "When I went to college, we were taught that . . ." When our expertise is being stereotypically denied, we may need to prove our expertise as well as refer to its source. Asking questions or drawing quick conclusions that could only be derived from in-depth, firsthand knowledge or experience are subtle but effective ways to establish credibility. In one situation, a woman manager was representing her department on a committee meeting to plan a new office building. The other committee members, all men, were pointedly ignoring her until she started to ask questions about heat loss gradients through the walls and the number of foot candles of light falling on work surfaces.

Personal Attractiveness

One thing we all discover early is that people treat us differently when they like us. They do nicer things for us. They are less likely to feel that we will be dishonest or attempt to coerce them (Tedeschi, Schlenker, and Bonoma, 1973). They are more likely to be influenced by us, to believe and trust us. Obviously, then, being nice and pleasant is a logical step to being more persuasive.

Sometimes we can carry "niceness" to its extreme by using ingratiation tactics. Ingratiation involves flattering or enhancing the other's self-image or reputation through our statements or actions, and thus, enhancing our own image in the same way. Ingratiation does not try to put the other person down, but to build him up. Handing out this flattery will presumably make others like us, and hence, others will be more prone to accept our persuasive arguments and point of view. The following tactics are frequently used as ways to enhance personal attractiveness or to make ingratiating strategies successful.

Pregiving.   In parts of Africa, particularly Nigeria, there is a custom of giving a small gift, called "dash," to a potential customer soon after they have walked into a shop—before there has been a chance for the customer to identify his or her needs. The shopkeeper will claim, legitimately, that it is a free gift, no strings, yours to keep even if you turn and walk out of the shop at this minute. However, knowing human nature, the shopkeeper does not really expect this to happen, and he is rarely disappointed. The shopkeeper knows that people like to receive gifts and will develop positive feelings toward those who give them. The shopkeeper also knows that there is an apparently universal norm of reciprocity that impells people to do nice things in return. Having preconditioned the customer, the shopkeeper can begin to discuss the customer's needs with a higher expectation of making a sale and at a better price than might otherwise have been obtained.

Similar opportunities exist in negotiating. A compliment, such as a reference to the other party's exemplary behavior in another negotiation, will make him/her feel good and set the scene for the other party to act in an exemplary manner toward us. Giving a quick concession on an issue that the other party wants will both please them and create the implicit obligation for them to do the same. Too often, negotiators begin by holding every advantage close to their chest and giving away things grudgingly, believing that this is the best way to succeed. Such rigid behavior is no more likely to lead to graceful and successful negotiation than it is to graceful and successful acting or public speaking. Flexibility and adaptability are necessary in all three.

Compliments.   Flattering another person by giving compliments is perhaps the most obvious form of ingratiation. Because it is obvious, it is often used and abused. Recognition for what we have done well, or for attributes we have, is pleasant even when we think those qualities are not too important. Compliments have great impact when our qualities or actions have been overlooked or unappreciated, but are now recognized and commented on favorably. But when people are complimented for attributes they do not have or actions they *know* they did not perform well, they are likely to become wary, wondering what the flatterer is after.

Compliments are a potent means of ingratiation, not only because people like to receive them, but because the norm of reciprocity leaves the other party with the obligation to return the compliment. Having paid us a compliment, the receiver faces some interesting pressures. Let us see why.

Human beings strive for cognitive consistency, that is, to have their various actions, opinions, attitudes, and statements about a topic be consistent or congruent with each other. We find it difficult to say nice things about people we dislike, not necessarily because we are mean or petty but because it does not seem consistent to us to recognize some quality we like about someone we dislike. In the same way, having said something positive about a person, we are likely to shape our impression of them to fit that prior statement.

At times we act, or are forced to act, in ways that are inconsistent with what we know about a person or situation. For example, people often object to giving money to "umbrella" charities like the United Way because they fear they will be contributing to some organization whose actions they disapprove. When we have beliefs, thoughts, or opinions that are inconsistent with our actions, we experience *cognitive dissonance* (Festinger, 1957). Cognitive dissonance is an uncomfortable condition; typically, people do one of several things to reduce dissonance. First, we can *forget* the thought, attitude, or action that is causing dissonance, e.g., we could forget that the offending charity is part of the United Way. Second, we can *change* one of our actions or opinions to make it more consistent with the other. For example, we might decide that the offending charity in the United Way is not too bad after all. Lastly, we can rationalize our *actions* or our way of looking at the situation to make the dissonance understandable. For example, we could tell ourselves that the offending charity gets such a small portion of our money that the impact is trivial compared to the importance of supporting the United Way as a whole.

The prospect of combining the norm of reciprocity with the effects of cognitive dissonance can make giving compliments, even to those who initially dislike us, a useful way of increasing our attractiveness. If they return the compliment, the resultant cognitive dissonance may lead them to alter their initial negative attitude toward us.

Helping the Other Party.   There are many ways one party can help the other in a negotiation, by doing them a favor, giving them time or information, or lending them a hand. We can help the other party avoid being caught by surprise. For example, an automobile salesperson may say, "In a moment I'm going to take you in to talk to the sales manager about the amount we are going to allow on your present car. You may hear me say some unfavorable things about your car. Don't let that bother you—we'll still get the figure you and I agreed on."

Frequently a negotiator is representing other people. Lawyers represent clients. Union leaders negotiate for their unions. Company executives negotiate for their firms. There are many ways one party can enhance the position of the other negotiator with his or her clients or organization. They can be respectfully listened to, and thereby appear to be respected. They can be allowed to demand (and receive) concessions from the other party, and thereby be seen by their organization as having influence. For example, company management might "agree" to hold contract negotiations in a neutral location rather than on company property. In another example, one of the authors of this book recently took on an administrative position in a university. In the first few days, he was confronted with a major problem concerning the shortage of office space for some new employees in one of his departments. He was able to get more space for this group without too much trouble, but was considered a "hero" by the department because they had been fighting for more space for years without success! The new administrator (naturally) felt a great sense of debt to the person who gave up that space so easily.

Finally, the other party can also be given information important to his organization which does not threaten the giver's position. For example, during negotiations on the sale of a large parcel of land to a major corporation, the seller privately told the company executive handling the negotiation about a forthcoming zoning change that would benefit the company. The executive got the credit for uncovering this "inside information."

Perceived Similarity.   When meeting someone new, people search for commonalities in experiences or characteristics. Perhaps they attended the same school, studied the same subjects, had the same type of job, traveled to the same places, or have friends in common. The possibilities are endless, and often, so is the search. The more similarities we find, the more bonds we establish, the better both parties feel, and most importantly, the more receptive they will be to each other's messages and efforts of persuasion. A useful negotiating tactic, therefore, is to search for experiences, characteristics, and opinions we hold in common with the other party. Pictures of a yacht on an office wall might suggest that we mention our own interest in sailing. The other party's February suntan might cue us to mention our own trips to the tropics. Does the other party have some special views on foreign policy? We might mention some of our own that are similar. The experiences, interests, and opinions that people may share are countless; thus, the opportunity to establish some common bonds almost always exists.

If it is to our advantage to find and explore commonalities in experience, attitude, and background with the other party, it is also to our disadvantage to highlight these areas where we differ or are in conflict but which are outside the realm of the dispute. Needless to say, differences about the substance of our negotiation will come out; resolving them is the purpose of our negotiation. However, there is no point to exploring the experiences one of us had in public high school if the other went to an elite prep school, or arguing about the merits of a politically controversial topic (for example, decriminalizing the personal use of marijuana) when this topic has no direct or important connection to the actual negotiations.

Balance Theory.   The principle of finding similar outlooks, experiences, shared likes and dislikes leads us to an important, but somewhat complicated theory of interpersonal influence. *Balance theory* was developed to analyze people's actions in a more fruitful way.

Balance theory is best applied to the following influence problem: one individual, P, talks with another individual, O, about some topic X. We are concerned with how P feels about O and how both of them feel about topic X.

Feelings may be positive (+) or negative (-). The situation is represented schematically in Figure 8–2. Part 2a shows a balanced situation; P has positive feelings toward O and both have positive feelings about X. Here P's positive feelings about O are not going to be disturbed by finding that O likes or is associated with X, since P also likes or is associated with X. In fact, information about O's feeling toward X is likely to make P's feelings about O even stronger. Parts 2b and 2c are also balanced situations. In 2b, both P and O have negative feelings about X which again could result in intensified feelings on P's part about X, O, or both. In 2c, P likes X while O does not like X; this is O.K. with P, since he or she does not like O—so there is no pressure on P to change his/her opinions. All three situations are "balanced," since from P's perspective, there is cognitive consistency. In general, when such "triangular relationships" have all positive elements, or two negative and one positive element, they are balanced and consistent.

The other three situations in Figure 8–2 are unbalanced. These are situations in which only one, or all three of the signs are negative. In 2d, P finds that O (whom he likes) dislikes X (which P likes). In 2e, P finds that someone he dislikes (O) likes something he likes (X). Finally, in 2f, P finds that O (whom he dislikes) shares his dislike of X. In these situations, P experiences cognitive dissonance; pressure is felt to change one or more of his or her opinions to restore balance in the situation. Any number of elements can be changed to bring the situation to all positive, or two negative and a positive; in general, people strive to change the *minimum* number of elements necessary to restore the situation to balance.

We can use this basic model to analyze three different situations faced in attitudes toward negotiation: when we, P, are unknown to O but O's feelings about X are known; when attitudes toward P are known but X are not; and where O has opinions about X that we do not like. Let us consider each one separately.

FIGURE 8–2

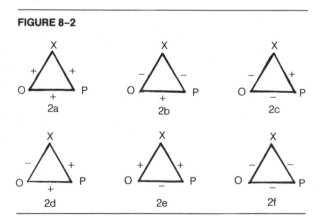

When we are meeting a person for the first time, and trying to develop a positive relationship with him, we can find something about his likes and dislikes and then choose our actions accordingly. For example, if he likes to go sailing (Figure 8–3a) and we indicate that we are interested in sailing (Figure 8–3b), we create a situation in which O will be inclined to develop positive feelings about us to preserve consistency (Figure 8–3c). In contrast, if we find, for example, that O dislikes Chinese food (Figure 8–3d), and we also dislike Chinese food (Figure 8–3e), we can expect that O (to preserve cognitive consistency) will develop positive feelings toward us (Figure 8–3f).

In a situation where the other party has positive feelings about us, but does not have any developed opinions about X, e.g., the concessions we may be offering as part of a negotiation (Figure 8–4a), we can, by declaring our interest and attraction to the item (Figure 8–4b), increase O's feelings about the item in a positive way (Figure 8–4c). We could also put pressure on O to form a negative opinion about an item or topic by declaring a negative opinion about the item (Figure 8–4d). When we are interacting with someone who likes us but dislikes something we are offering as part of a negotiation (Figure 8–4e), we are faced with a tricky situation. If we declare our liking for the item, we create an imbalanced condition (Figure 8–4f). We might have done this in the hope that the other person would resolve the imbalance by abandoning his or her prior negative feelings toward X (e.g., change the O–X relationship from negative to positive) (Figure 8–4g). But there is the risk that O will take this new information and conclude that anyone who could like X is not someone they want to associate with (Figure 8–4h). This is the risk a person takes when saying to someone they love, "Love me, love my dog." The lover may decide the dog is disliked more than the speaker is loved. In general, it is hard to predict whether O will change his decision toward X or P, but it is likely that the other person will change his or her opinion about the

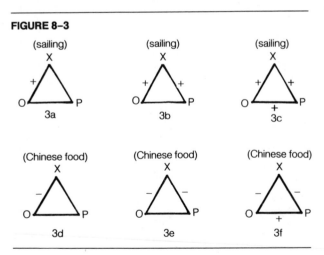

FIGURE 8–3

FIGURE 8–4

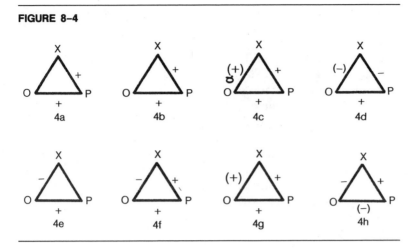

less highly valued thing. Hence, if O and P have been friends for a long time, O may decide that he would rather keep his friend and go along with P's opinion about X. On the other hand, if X is something that O values highly, like a religious belief, he is more likely to change his opinion about P. Given this risk, the better strategy, as noted earlier, is to avoid or minimize areas of strong differences of opinion. This action, called dissociation, occurs in long standing relationships where there is a disagreement about some important topic. Married couples, for example, often have topics on which they "agree to disagree," topics they avoid bringing up with each other. Another strategy, of course, is to diminish the importance of the "disagreeable topic" in the overall context of the relationship.

Summary.   Influencing how other people feel about us is a key element in persuasion. The more favorably inclined people feel toward us, the more likely they are to believe what we say, to interpret what we say in the most favorable light, and to support what we want. While there are many specific things we can do to influence another's feelings, they are all generally premised on the norm of reciprocity and principle of cognitive consistency, and all depend on making some assessment of the other person's initial attitudes and objectives.

TARGET FACTORS

Earlier, we examined ways to shape a message to influence the other party, and ways to manipulate images of the source of persuasion to influence the target's perception of the source. We now examine ways we can directly influence the target's views about himself or herself, his situation or his objectives. Before discussing these tactics, let us first examine the problem we face in attempting to alter the target's views about himself and his objective.

As mentioned in Chapter 1, when entering negotiation, many people assume a combative stance. They expect to defend themselves against the arguments of the other person, and to have a hard time getting the other party to listen and accept their points. Hence, while they often appear to be listening to the other party, they are often preparing counterarguments to refute the speaker, and planning the point they want to make. When speaking, they concentrate on what they want to say and often resist questions, comments, or anything that would distract them. Our objective in dealing with the other party is to defuse this defensive/combative stance and to make the other party feel that he has been heard, and understood.

Attending

We communicate not only with words and sentences, but also with gestures; the way we position our body, the tone of our voice, the movement of our head. Much of what we communicate to one another is through nonverbal body language. There are a number of nonverbal acts, called *attending behaviors*, that are very important in establishing contact with another person. These behaviors let the other know that we are listening to him, and prepare him to receive our own messages.

Eye Contact.   Dishonest people and cowards are not supposed to be able to look us in the eye. Poets claim that the eye is the lens that permits us to look into a person's soul. These and other maxims of conventional wisdom illustrate how important we believe eye contact to be. In general, making eye contact is one significant way we show others that we are paying attention, listening, and consider them important. If people do not look at us when we are speaking, we question whether they are listening. If someone is speaking and not looking at us, we wonder whether they are speaking to us or whether they consider us very important. Of course, we may listen very well even when we are not looking at the other person; the point is that we are not providing the other person with any cues that we are listening. Eye contact makes others feel that they are being listened to. In making eye contact, we generally do not keep our eyes fixed on the other person. In fact, if we did, we would be accused of staring, which usually leads to suspicion rather than trust. Instead, there are breaks when our eyes momentarily leave the other person. Generally, breaks are fewer and shorter when we are actively listening than when speaking. When we are speaking, more often than not we look away, perhaps as we search for a word or phrase or try to remember some detail. It is important to recognize that these patterns are characteristic of Western society. In other parts of the world, different patterns prevail. For example, in the Far East, to keep one's eyes down while another is speaking is a sign of respect (Ivey and Simek-Downing, 1980).

Body Position.   Parents frequently correct their children on how to stand and sit, particularly when they are in formal settings—school, church, or greeting older people. "Sit up" is often accompanied by, "pay attention." Here the parent is teaching the child another widely held belief: the way we hold our body indicates whether or not we are paying attention to the other party. We may be attentive while we slouch, but other people will have a hard time believing that. Hence, if we want to make sure others know we are attentive to them, we should hold our bodies erect, lean slightly forward and face the other person directly (Ivey and Simek-Downing, 1980).

Encouraging.   We can indicate our attention and interest in what another is saying by a variety of simple behaviors. A head nod, a simple hand gesture to "go on," or "uh huh" to indicate understanding, all tell the other person to continue, that we are listening. In fact, we can easily "condition" people to talk about almost any subject simply by nodding our heads when they talk about that subject.

Paraphrasing

Paraphrasing lets both the other party, and ourselves know that we have understood accurately. If we haven't, the other party has the opportunity to correct us. It is important to restate our understanding after being corrected, to make sure we have understood. We repeat *in our own words* what someone else has said. We do not literally repeat the other person's words; *we* repeat their *message* in our own words. It is best not to wait until the end of a long message, because the message may be forgotten. Instead, it is best to para- phrase what has been said after several paragraphs, or after each major point. "Let me see if I understand the point you just made . . . " We should repeat this correction process until the other person is satisfied with the way we paraphrase what he said.

Paraphrasing tells the other person not only that we have heard his words but that we have understood what they meant. It is here that the importance of repeating in our own words is most evident. We can repeat another person's words and not understand what was meant. To state the message in our own words means we had to comprehend the intended message. In addition, vocalizing the other person's ideas helps us remember them better than simply hearing them. Finally, when people have an impor- tant message to get across, they will talk vigorously and at length, often re-emphasizing the same point over and over. Once people know they have been understood, they usually stop; hence, paraphrasing can be very helpful in moving a discussion on to new topics.

When people find they are being listened to carefully, the feeling they may have had earlier—that they have to fight for attention and the opportunity to make their case—fades away. They not only present their points in a more reasonable way, but also become less defensive and more willing to listen. When we speak and actively listen, the norm of reciprocity encourages them to return the same sort of behavior.

We can also ask the other party to restate or paraphrase what we have said. We might say, "What I have said is very important to me, and I would appreciate it if you could restate what you understood to be my main points." This process accomplishes several things. First, it puts the other party in a position where they are being asked to listen closely, and recall what we have said. Second, it gives us the opportunity to check out the accuracy of their understanding. Third, it emphasizes the most important points of our presentation. If we have paraphrased some of the other party's statements earlier, it is not likely they will refuse or ignore our request.

Exploring the Other's Position

All too frequently, parties in negotiation want to give as little attention as possible to the other party's opinions and point of view. Actually, it is very much to our advantage to understand what the other party is really after, how things look to them, how they developed their position. We can explore their perspective with questions. In negotiation, questions are often used as a weapon of attack. "How in the world can you say that?" "What possible justification can you have for that position?" "Who in their right mind would believe that?" Questions asked this way are hardly likely to make the other party feel relaxed and willing to open up. On the other hand, questions like, "What would happen if you did not get everything you have asked for?", "How did you arrive at your current position?", "Have your needs changed since the last time we talked? How?", bring out more detailed information about the other party's position. Exploring the other person's outlook not only gives us more information, which can lead us to designing solutions to meet both sides' needs, but further increases the other party's feeling of being listened to and makes them more receptive to meeting our needs.

Reinforcing Points You Like in the Other's Proposals

Another common pattern that gets negotiators into trouble is for them to *respond* to what they *dislike* in the other party's statement or proposal, and to *ignore* things they *like*. To respond in this way, while very common, denies one of the most powerful means we have of shaping and guiding what another person is saying. A variety of behavioral science theories (e.g., exchange theory, learning and reinforcement theory, etc.) all essentially make the same point: *people are more likely to repeat behavior which is rewarded than behavior which is not rewarded* (Skinner, 1953; Homans, 1961). How can we reward people for what they say during a negotiation? The simplest way is by acknowledging a point that has been made. "That is an interesting point." "I had not heard that before." Give a simple "mm-hmm" or a nod of the head. Statements and actions like these separate the key statement from others the speaker has also made. Second, we can compliment the speaker on the points we want him to emphasize, and express our appreciation for things favorable to us that have been included in his statement. In a labor negotiation, for example, management might say to the union, "You raised an important point when you said that if we develop a history of bad labor relations, customers will be much less likely to give us long term contracts. We appreciate your being aware of some of our marketing and customer image problems." A third approach would be to separately identify particular parts of a statement we like from those parts we don't like, and to support and encourage the other party to go further. In negotiating a house sale, the buyer might say, "Let me focus on one of the points you made. I think making an adjustment in price for the necessary repairs is a good idea. Please go further and explain what type of repairs you have in mind, and how we might handle this adjustment." A fourth approach is to return favors. If the other party makes a concession and offers us something we want, we can reward this behavior by making a concession or offering a favor in return.

Public Commitment

One of the most effective ways of getting a person to stand firm on a position is to have him make a public commitment. Union leaders have said things to their rank and file like, "I will resign before I settle for a penny less than . . . " There are several pressures working on the union leader after making that statement. One is that he will lose face with the union members if he backs away from that position; he may be thrown out of office if he does not actually resign. A second pressure is that his credibility with management will be sharply reduced in the future if he does not follow through. Finally, he may have his own dissonance with which to deal, his failure to actually resign will be inconsistent with his earlier statement. Of course, the union leader knows this and he also knows that management knows it. Hence, he may make such a statement because he expects the other party to believe that he would not put himself in such a position unless he really meant what was said.

As negotiators, we can use the process of public commitment when trying to influence the other party. If we can get them to make a public statement that supports something we want, they will be very hard-pressed not to stand by their statement, even though they might later wish to abandon it. Sometimes negotiators make a statement such as, "I'm committed to finding an agreement that we can both benefit from," and then inviting the other party to make a similar statement. At other times the inviting statement may be more direct: "Are you interested in selling us this property or not?", or "Let's agree that we are going to work together, and then get down to work on the details of how to make it happen." Even better than eliciting statements of commitment is getting the other party to make a behavioral commitment. Retail merchants have used the idea of a downpayment or a lay-away plan to get a commitment when the total sale was not possible at that time.

Innoculating One's Self against Other's Arguments

One of the likely outcomes of listening carefully to the other, and of exploring and understanding the other party's point of view, is that we may have some of our own positions changed. This may lead us to give the other party what he or she wants. We may be able to come to a good agreement for both parties, particularly when we are engaged in integrative bargaining. However, at times we may not want to change our position, and therefore may want to "innoculate" ourselves against the other party's arguments in order not to be swayed by understanding of or empathy for his/her position.

If we are concerned with protecting ourselves or our associates against the arguments of opposing parties, how can we proceed? Three possible approaches have been studied. One is to prepare supporting arguments for our position. The second is to develop arguments against the reasons for supporting their position and then to develop counterarguments, to find ways for them to deny or deflect the attacks on their position. The third approach is a combination of the previous two: to develop arguments supportive of their original position, then to develop arguments against their position, and then to develop counterarguments to those. Which is best? Research (McGuire, 1964; Tannenbaum and Norris, 1966) reveals the following:

1. The latter, so-called "double defense" approach, is the best in innoculating people against being influenced by the other side.
2. The second approach, when people are asked to develop arguments against their position, and counterarguments as well, was the second best approach.
3. The least effective, by a large margin, was the first approach—to develop arguments only in support of one's position.
4. The best way to innoculate people against attacks on their position was to involve them in the process of developing a defense.
5. The larger the number of arguments in any defense, the more effective it becomes.

6. Asking people to make public statements supporting their original position increases their resistance to counterarguments.

Summary

There are a number of things we can do to decrease the other person's rigidity and defensiveness, and to make them more willing to listen and understand our statements and arguments. These tactics require us to show the other party that we are willing to listen to them and that we are working to understand, but not necessarily agree with, their position. We try to understand what they are after, how they are thinking, and also to decrease their defensiveness. These are powerful techniques, but there are also risks. In trying to understand their side, we may be persuaded by their arguments, be led to abandon some of our original positions, or be more willing to accept the other side's proposals. The other party's proposals may actually lead to a better agreement for all sides, particularly in integrative bargaining. However, there are times when we want to preserve our *own* position, and *not* be tempted or seduced by the other's arguments. At times like these, we need to take "innoculation" measures to permit us to hear the opponent, and enter into the other side's arguments, without the risk of being co-opted to their point of view.

SUMMARY

In this chapter, we discussed three major elements in the persuasion process: the semantic and logical structure of the message being sent, characteristics of the source sending the message, and characteristics of the receiver. Each of these elements will impact on the reception of the message and on its effectiveness in changing the receiver's viewpoint or attitude toward the issues.

With regard to the nature of the message, three major topics were covered: which facts or topics to consider in putting together a persuasive message, how to structure and arrange that information, and what style to use in presenting them. In general, information should be presented which highlights the attractive features it offers to the other, or appeals to the other's sense of what is fair, right, and principled. Messages which contain fear appeals and threats or try to distract the other may have limited effectiveness, and are only likely to work when used selectively. Messages should be structured so that the most important points are repeated, particularly at both the beginning and the end of the presentation. Either one-sided or two-sided messages may be used, depending upon the circumstances. The presenter should also find ways to break large demands or requests into smaller packages, and to help the receiver use the information presented to draw the conclusions that the speaker desires. Finally, messages are likely to be presented more effectively when the receiver takes an active role, when language intensity is frequently varied, when metaphor and graphic imagery is used, and when the receiver's expectations are occasionally violated so that his defenses are not allowed to build.

This chapter also proposed several factors that relate to the source presenting the message. One major source factor is credibility. Sources are more credible when they appear to be trustworthy, qualified to discuss their subject, of higher status, "professional" and well dressed, and when they appear to have high integrity. A second factor is the source's intent to persuade. Sources who are less forthright about their desire to change our minds, and use less of the "hard sell," are often more persuasive. Finally, sources are more persuasive when they treat us better. Use of compliments, pregiving, identification of similar personal characteristics or genuine offers to assist us lead us to like the source and hence to be more willing to accept his/her message. Models from balance theory were used to help describe this process.

Finally, this chapter examined factors which distinguish among the receivers of persuasive messages. Receivers can vary their attending behaviors—eye contact, body position, head nodding, etc.—to encourage or discourage a speaker. Receivers can also engage in a variety of behaviors to let the speaker know that the message was both received and understood: paraphrasing, asking questions, reinforcing desirable elements. Finally, receivers who want to resist having their position changed can engage in two tactics to help prevent this: making public commitments about their own position, or innoculating themselves against persuasive communications by developing counterarguments.

This chapter has only touched on some of the more important and well documented aspects of persuasive communication that can be used in bargaining. Negotiators usually spend a great deal of time devising ways to support and document their position; less time is devoted to considering how the information is presented, or how to use qualities of the source and receiver to increase the likelihood that persuasion will be successful. More careful attention to these factors is likely to have a very positive impact on negotiator effectiveness.

9

The Social Structure
of Negotiation

Probably one of the most influential factors in negotiations—and one which is the most poorly understood—is the social environment. The social environment includes all parties who are present in the negotiation, those affected by the outcome of negotiation (even though they are not actually negotiating), and observers of the negotiation. A bargainer who is only representing his own interests may behave very differently from someone who is negotiating as the representative of others. Moreover, bargaining is a process occurring at the interpersonal or inter-group level of interaction which means that negotiation processes are subject to the rules, customs, or practices governing interaction.

In this chapter, the impact of social structure on bargaining is described. As social settings become larger and more complex—from two individuals to two groups to multiple groups and organizations—negotiation becomes more complex as well. We also describe the strategy and tactics that are typically used to exert leverage on the opposition in various contexts.

An Example: Bolshoi Ballet Incident

On Wednesday, August 22, 1979, Aleksandr Godunov, a prominent member of the famed Russian Bolshoi Ballet Company which was on tour in the United States, walked into the New York office of the U.S. Naturalization and Immigration Service and announced that he wanted to defect. At the same time, Godunov informed U.S. officials that his wife, Lyudmila Vlasova, might also wish to defect. Before officials could question Vlasova, she was hustled to New York's Kennedy Airport and put on a Aeroflot Airlines flight bound for Moscow. Fearing that Vlasova was being taken out of the United States against her will, the U.S. government forbade the plane to take off. Thus began four days of tense negotiations between the United States and Soviet officials regarding the right to interview Vlasova and to determine her true intentions.

When immigration officials learned that Godunov wanted to defect and that Vlasova might be interested as well, they immediately contacted the Soviet Embassy in New York. Soviet officials were told that the United States would not permit Vlasova to leave until she was "interviewed" to determine if she were leaving of her own volition.[1] Contact was made with the Soviet officials three times during a period of 36 hours, and each time, Soviet officials agreed to comply with the request. However, U.S. officials then learned that Vlasova had been escorted to John F. Kennedy Airport by "eight Soviet officials," and that American customs officials also permitted her to board the Aeroflot jet. The plane, however, was not permitted to take off.

U.S. officials demanded that they be allowed to interview Vlasova under "noncoercive conditions," that is, not aboard a Soviet aircraft or accompanied by Soviet officials. Soviet officials demanded that the plane be cleared for takeoff immediately. They maintained that Vlasova had no interest in defection, and that if an interview were to occur, it would occur on the plane. In addition to Vlasova, 111 other passengers were on board the aircraft. Forty-four non-Soviet passengers were allowed to leave the aircraft early Saturday morning; but the remaining 67 Soviet passengers never left the aircraft throughout the three days of negotiation. Food service, sanitation, and external air cooling equipment for the plane were provided by Pan American Airways.

U.S. negotiations were being directed by acting Secretary of State Warren Christopher, and on-site deliberations were being conducted by Donald McHenry, U.S. Ambassador to the United Nations. Soviet negotiators were led by Yveny Nakayeu, a deputy Soviet representative at the United Nations, while McHenry negotiated for the United States. McHenry was often accompanied by Godunov and his American lawyer, Orville Schell, who attempted to make a "personal appeal" to Vlasova to defect. These negotiations occurred in a boarding lounge with two sets of chairs facing one another; Soviet negotiators would frequently huddle in the boarding ramp or in the aircraft, while U.S. negotiators used another airport waiting lounge as a meeting site. Numerous communiques were also

---

[1] U.S. Law provides that nonforeign nationals cannot be taken from the United States "under force."

exchanged between top United States and Soviet diplomatic officials during this period.

For the first 24 hours, there was no change in the negotiating positions of either side. Accusations and counteraccusations flew. Soviets charged that American officials had taken Vlasova's Soviet passport on Friday evening, and handed her an already-completed U.S. passport. U.S. officials admitted that they had taken Vlasova's passport for a period of time, but returned it to her undisturbed. Americans charged that Vlasova and other Soviet passengers were being "coerced" into suppressing their desire to defect or criticize the Soviet Union; Soviet officials denied the charge.

Late Saturday, in an apparent effort to break the deadlock, McHenry offered to interview Vlasova off the plane, and permit Soviet officials to be present. No response was received from the Soviets. Living conditions on the plane continued to deteriorate, but no passenger left the plane, except the flight crews that were regularly rotated in case the plane might be allowed to leave. Finally, at 11 A.M. Monday morning, 66 hours after the plane had been detained, a tentative agreement was struck to conduct the interview. It would be held in a New York Port Authority mobile lounge, (used to transport passengers from the terminal to planes parked away from the ramps). The actual meeting did not take place until approximately 3 P.M. due to a delay in deciding who would be allowed to be present.

The mobile lounge was docked into place against the aircraft, and the back steps of the lounge were lowered. McHenry and five other Americans, among them Orville Schell (Godunov's lawyer) and State Department interpreters, walked across the taxiway and entered by the stairs. Six Soviet officials entered from the aircraft with Vlasova. The delegations sat on opposite sides of the lounge, with Vlasova sitting across from McHenry. During the course of the meeting, the stairway door was left open, and presumably Vlasova could have left the lounge at any time, if she wished.

The meeting lasted for approximately 20 minutes, during which time U.S. officials apparently satisfied themselves that Vlasova was leaving the United States of her own volition. Near the end of the meeting, Schell and McHenry asked Vlasova if there were anyone she wanted to see or give a message to before leaving (an obvious reference to her husband); she replied, "nyet."

After determining that Vlasova was leaving of her own will, McHenry and the U.S. contingent left the lounge through the back stairs. The lounge was disconnected; and the aircraft was allowed to leave, 73 hours after its scheduled departure time. Vlasova later told a Soviet interviewer that the Americans had occupied the Soviet plane by force. "They got inside by force. . . .They had guns and handcuffs to guard me. . . . It was just madness." The Soviet press reported Godunov's defection as part of a Western conspiratorial plan. Vlasova, the martyr, was played up as the heroine.

The Structure of the Incident.   This incident provides an excellent illustration of the way that the negotiating objectives of one or two individuals can initiate a complex interchange between multiple groups at several levels of power and authority. The following individuals and groups were active parties in the resolution of the dispute between Aleksandr Godunov, his wife, and his country:

Godunov

Vlasova

Godunov-Vlasova as a married couple

Orville Schell, Godunov's American attorney

The Bolshoi Ballet Company and its management

The U.S. Immigration and Naturalization Service

The U.N. Ambassador Donald McHenry, and his staff

The U.S. State Department and its secretary, Warren Christopher

Soviet deputy to the United Nations, Nakayeu, and his staff

The Soviet embassy in New York

The Soviet government in Moscow

Pan American Airways and the New York Port Authority, manager of
     J. F. Kennedy Airport

The U.S. and Soviet passengers aboard the Aeroflot plane

The Soviet press

The international ballet community

"Public opinion" among various other groups around the world.

A representation of the relationship between these groups, and their interaction during the dispute, is shown in Figure 9–1. Initially Godunov's negotiation appears to be with the U.S. Immigration Service; he announces his intention to renounce his Soviet citizenship and become a U.S. citizen. However, his primary "constituent"—his wife—did not join him in this action. One can speculate on a variety of reasons why they failed to coordinate their actions; however, it is clear that by taking this action without synchronizing his efforts with his wife, Godunov created a significantly more complex negotiating event.

Godunov's meeting with immigration officials immediately led to the involvement of the governments of each country—the American State Department and U.N. delegation, the Soviet Embassy, and it's U.N. delegation. Once these groups became involved, Soviet officials agreed to comply with a request to let Vlasova be interviewed, but simultaneously refused access and attempted to hasten her out of the country. Had the pilot of the Aeroflot Airlines plane chosen to "defy" the tower at JFK airport, it would seem that no obstacle (short of a military threat on the plane) would remain to prevent Vlasova from returning to the Soviet Union without the interview.

FIGURE 9–1

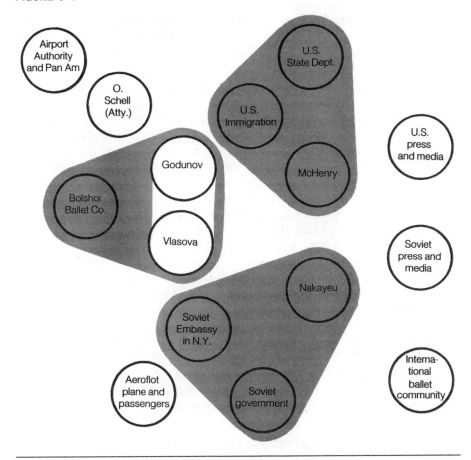

The next four days were spent in intensive deliberations at many levels: between Godunov and his attorney, Godunov and the U.S. Immigration Service, McHenry and Nakayeu and their staffs, U.S. and Soviet governments, Vlasova and her government, Vlasova and other Aeroflot passengers whose lives were greatly inconvenienced for four days, etc. Through the American and Soviet press, "public opinion" was shifted back and forth by the rhetoric in reporting the events. From the U.S. perspective, there were two major issues at stake: the right to interview Vlasova, and the place where the interview would take place. The Soviets wanted the plane to take off and would only permit the interview with Soviet officials present, while the United States wanted to interview her in a "noncoercive environment."

Concessions on both sides eventually allowed for the interview to occur on neutral turf—a mobile airport lounge. Godunov was not present; but his lawyer was, as were Vlasova and Soviet officials. The results were the defection of a famous Soviet citizen to the United States, a broken marriage, and the resolution of a tension-filled dramatic international incident.

The Bolshoi Incident: An Example of the Social Structure of Negotiation. The major theme of this chapter is that a thorough analysis of the social structure of a negotiation is essential to fully comprehend a negotiator's bargaining posture. Social structure may be represented in relatively "simple" structural situations—two individual negotiators, each with his own needs and desires—or relatively "complex" situations—multiple groups and organizations involved. The more individuals, groups, and organizations become involved in a negotiation or are affected by its outcomes, the more each group will exert direct and indirect pressures on the negotiators. It is therefore essential for a negotiator to understand how many other individuals, groups, or organizations may become involved in the negotiation, and what their position on the issues is likely to be. The negotiator will also need to design a strategy that will either utilize these resources on his own behalf or be prepared to defend against such tactics when they are used by others.
    Several levels of social structure may exist in negotiating; these include:

- *Negotiating Dyad*. The simplest is two isolated individuals negotiating for their own needs. Each is only accountable to himself and the other.

- *Negotiating Teams*. Negotiation can occur between parties rather than individuals. Teams exist when there are several people on either side who are working together and directly involved in negotiating with the other side.

- *Constituencies*. Often a negotiator (or team of negotiators) is acting not for him or herself, but for a constituency—others who are not physically at the table but whose interests are being represented.

- *Bystander*. A bystander may have a direct stake in a negotiation, have an indirect stake, or have no stake at all. The negotiators do not represent bystanders, but bystanders may be drawn into the negotiations, or be affected by the outcome.

- *Audience*. An audience is any individual or group of people who are not directly involved in a negotiation, but to whom a negotiator will direct messages in an effort to influence the outcome of negotiations. Bystanders and constituencies are audiences. So, too, are members of negotiating teams who are not actively engaged in dialogue with the other side.

The role and impact of each of these groups is as follows:

Two Individual Negotiators

In terms of the social structure, the "simplest" form of negotiation occurs when there are only two individuals. Each individual is responsible for representing only his own needs and interests in the negotiation (see Figure 9–2). For example, consider an individual who sets off to purchase a stereo system from another individual. The preferences of each party (the price, condition of the equipment, strength of the desire to buy or sell the particular article, etc.) will wholly be determined by the two individuals themselves. The price that they agree on, as well as any other terms and conditions of the purchase, will be affected solely by the give-and-take that occurs between them, and their willingness to meet the terms and conditions that are discussed.

FIGURE 9–2

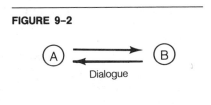

Dialogue

Audiences—Their Form and Type

As additional parties are added to the negotiating situation, the nature and complexity of the process changes significantly. The two negotiators are now aware that there are other individuals in the situation who are either observing the negotiating process, informed of its results, and/or affected by the outcomes. As a result, one or both negotiators will redirect their behavior in order to influence these additional parties as well as the opposing negotiator. The increased attention paid to these additional parties will be described as an "audience effect."

One form of "audience" is additional team members who are frequently active in the negotiation, but who may also serve as an audience. Negotiating team members may have multiple roles to perform: chief spokesman, expert on a particular issue, legal or financial counsel, statistician or cost analyst, recorder or observer. While a member of one team (chief spokesman) may appear to be talking directly to one member of the other team (the other chief spokesman), she in fact may be trying to influence the other team's legal expert on some point. This relationship is shown in Figure 9–3 (A and D are spokesmen; B, C, E, F are an "audience" as well as team members). Again, team members on one's own team or the opposing team may act as both negotiators and an audience to the conduct of the negotiating parties.

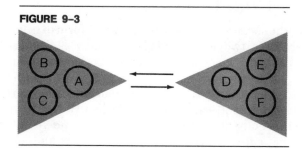

FIGURE 9-3

Another type of audience is a "constituency," a group whose interests, demands, or priorities the negotiator is representing. This is the group that delegates negotiating power and authority to the negotiators to represent their interests, and who expect to directly profit (or lose) as a result of the negotiator's effectiveness. The social structure of individuals or teams representing constituencies is depicted in Figure 9-4.

Finally, audiences may act as bystanders, and perform the role of indirect audiences. Bystanders may be directly or indirectly affected by the negotiating settlement, but are not directly represented at the negotiations, e.g., other unions whose own contract settlements will be affected by the outcome of the current negotiation, or the public who may be inconvenienced if a strike occurs, or vaguely defined audiences such as the public, the media, the community, or even the nation. Figure 9-5 represents the most complex social environment for a negotiator. When multiple audiences are available, a negotiator has several alternative ways to bring pressure and influence to bear indirectly on the other negotiator. We will examine some of the most common tactics later in this chapter.

There are a number of ways to describe the major characteristics of

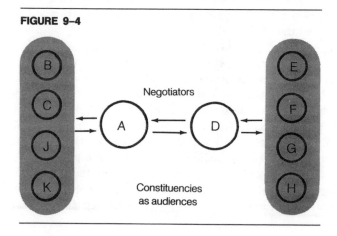

FIGURE 9-4

FIGURE 9-5

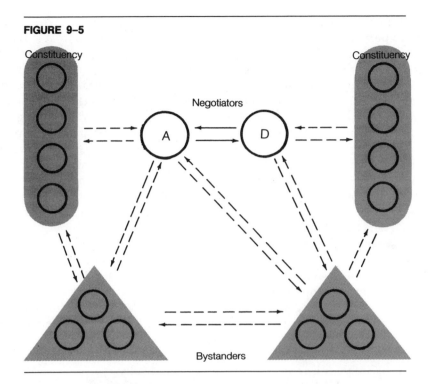

audiences. Perhaps the most comprehensive review may be found in Rubin and Brown (1975). Audiences vary according to whether they are physically *present* or *absent* from the negotiation itself. Some observers may actually be in the negotiating room and directly witness the events that occur; others may be physically removed, and only hear about what happens through reports from the negotiators themselves or from other observers.

Second, audiences can also be *dependent* or *nondependent* on the negotiators for outcomes. Audiences who are outcome-dependent will yield their gains as a direct result of the behavior of the negotiator; in a labor contract, the amount of salary increase for each union member will be a direct result of how the chief negotiator behaves in the negotiation. In contrast, a nondependent audience is one which can observe the negotiation, but will not be directly affected by the results. While the general public may be interested in the contract that union and management arrive at, it is unlikely that they will be directly affected by the settlement in any significant way.

A third major way that audiences affect negotiations is by their involvement in the process. Audiences may become *directly involved* in the negotiation; to the extent that they begin to take an active part in the deliberations, the interactions and social dynamics become increasingly complex. One example would be the intervention of the United States into the Israeli-

Egyptian negotiations that led to the Camp David accords. When more parties participate in the deliberation, they immediately create a situation that is more complex. Alternatively, audiences may become *indirectly involved* in the negotiation. Indirect involvement may occur when audiences make their own wishes and desires known in an effort to influence the course of negotiations, such as when consumers boycott the purchasing of raisins to support a grape pickers' strike. Audiences also give *feedback* to the negotiators, letting them know how well they are doing. Feedback may be in written or verbal form, such as notes, messages, letters or personal conversations and advice; or it may even be in nonverbal form, such as smiles and nods of approval or scowls and frowns of disapproval. Feedback may be directed toward the positions that a negotiator has taken, concessions he has made, agreements he has arrived at, or the manner in which he has conducted himself in the deliberations.

Audiences may vary in a number of other ways: (1) their identity (who they are and what they stand for); (2) their composition (the number of different points of view represented, amount of power, etc.); (3) size; (4) relationship to the bargainer (emotional ties, amount of power and control exercised over the negotiator); and (5) role in the negotiation situation (readiness to try to directly affect the negotiator's behavior, style and content of communication with the negotiator, etc.). In short, as soon as the negotiation setting is expanded to three or more parties, the nature and complexity of their interaction increases dramatically.

Before we review the types of audiences that are typically encountered by negotiators, and their role in negotiation, it is important to summarize the most significant ways that audiences influence the negotiator's choice of tactics.

Negotiators Seek a Favorable Audience Reaction. The mere presence of an audience motivates a negotiator to seek a favorable (positive) evaluation from the audience, and to avoid an unfavorable (negative) evaluation. The impact of a constituency who can exercise surveillance over a negotiator has been demonstrated in several research studies. First, merely being aware that they are under surveillance motivates negotiators to "act tough" (Benton and Druckman, 1974; Carnevale, Pruitt and Britton, 1979). For example, Carnevale, Pruitt, and Britton told some subjects in an experimental negotiating situation that they were being watched by their constituents through a one-way window, while others knew they were not being watched. Negotiators who believed they were under surveillance were significantly more likely to conduct their negotiations in a distributive bargaining mode, and significantly more likely to use threats, commitments and putdowns of their opponent in order to gain advantage. As a result, negotiators under surveillance were less likely to pursue integrative bargaining strategies, with the result that they obtained lower joint outcomes than negotiators not under surveillance. When questioned later about their behavior, negotiators under surveillance felt that it was more important to look tough and strong, and as a result were less likely to engage in the concession making that would facilitate mutual gain.

In addition to the mere presence of an audience, the presence of a "salient" audience—one whom the negotiator values for their opinions and evaluation—affects a negotiator even more dramatically. A classic study by Brown (1968) reveals the power of salient audiences. Using a competitive negotiating research scenario called the Acme-Bolt Trucking Game (Deutsch and Krauss, 1960), Brown set out to test the impact of an audience's feedback on a negotiator's subsequent behavior. The trucking game is a two-person bargaining problem in which each player is charged with maximizing his financial outcome. Two strategies are available for achieving this end: sharing a limited resource with his opponent (a one-lane highway), or avoiding his opponent entirely at the expense of losing money. In Brown's experiment, high school students were taught to play the trucking game. Each student first played the game with someone whom he thought was another student but in fact was an ally of the experimenter, playing a preprogrammed strategy. In all cases, the preprogrammed strategy was aggressive and exploitative of the student. Following this exposure to an exploitative opponent, the students received feedback from a group of their peers who had been watching them in the first round. Groups of students in the experiment were told one of two things: that they looked weak and foolish as a result of the way that they had been exploited in the first game, or that they looked good and strong as a result of the first round because they had "played fair." A third group received no feedback at all. All students then played a second round of the bargaining game. During this second round, they were given the choice of using a high retaliatory strategy (at great cost to themselves), or a low retaliatory strategy that may make them more money (but would require them to ignore the earlier events and the feedback that they had received). The nature of the experiment, therefore, pitted the incentive for monetary gain against the incentive for retaliation and restoring one's image with an important audience. As Brown summarized,

> The results were striking: Publicly humiliated subjects—those who received the derogatory feedback—were far more likely to retaliate, and with greater severity and self-sacrifice—than subjects who received the more favorable feedback. . . . Of special interest is the fact that when asked why they chose severe retaliation, 75 percent of the subjects who did so reported that they didn't want to look foolish and weak as a result of having been exploited, and that they retaliated in order to reassert their capability and strength (Rubin and Brown, 1975, p. 45).

There are several important implications to Brown's research. First, subjects in the study did not know the names or identity of the audience, only that they were from their school. Second, the feedback from the audience was not dependent on what the subject actually did. The subjects in the study were responding to what they were told by the audience, not to the actual outcomes. Hence, audiences who are never personally identified, never even *seen* by the negotiator, and who are only vaguely viewed as an important group to please, can nevertheless exert powerful influences over a negotiator's behavior when they perform an evaluative role.

Third, some retaliation occurred even when there was no audience present. While the retaliation in this experiment may have occurred because of the subject's need to "get even" with his opponent, it also suggests that *the opposing negotiator may act as an audience as well*. Negotiators who believe that the opposing negotiator has caused them to look foolish, or has evaluated their behavior as weak and ineffective, may behave in ways to regain a positive evaluation, even from an adversary. Anyone who has ever played a "friendly" game of tennis or golf will recognize that much of the banter and teasing which occurs is designed to undermine the opponent's self-confidence or to challenge him to play better in the future. In serious negotiations, one can imagine how a bargainer will respond when he is told in all seriousness by his opponent that he was "easy to beat."

Those people who received a favorable evaluation from the audience were considerably less retaliatory than those who received a negative evaluation or none at all. Hence, an audience can have strong impact on a bargainer's competitive or retaliatory behavior by helping him interpret how he has behaved. If bargainers who are humiliated are told that they look "o.k.," they will retaliate considerably less than if humiliated and told they looked "foolish."

Finally, there was an additional variation to Brown's study. In one condition, the experimental subjects were told that the audience was aware of the costs of retaliation—in other words, if they retaliated against the exploitative opponent, the audience would know how much personal cost the subject endured in order to retaliate. In a second variation, the audience did not know the costs. The results of these two variations demonstrated clearly that retaliation was greatest when the audience feedback had told the subject that he looked foolish *and* the audience did not know how much it cost the subject to retaliate. In this situation, Brown has created the classic case of "face-saving": a bargainer is most aggressive when he needs to regain a positive image with his audience, and no one knows how much it costs him to do it. Numerous examples come to mind from the history of international and labor relations. President Lyndon Johnson's characterization of the United States's role in Vietnam as a "pitiful, helpless giant" soon led to the massive military buildup in Southeast Asia, in order to "win" a war that continued to humiliate American military capability at home and abroad. Not only was this effort ultimately unsuccessful—thus sustaining the loss of face that Johnson and others had dreaded—but at phenomenal costs in dollars, military equipment, and human lives that were never fully disclosed to the American public.

Holding the Negotiator Accountable.   Audiences maintain control over a negotiator by holding him accountable for his performance, and by administering rewards or punishments based on his performance.   This "accountability" will occur under two dominant conditions: when a bargainer's performance is visible to his audience (so that the audience is able to judge how well the bargainer performs), and when the audience is dependent on the bargainer for their outcomes. An audience which is dependent upon a negotiator's performance for their outcomes will generally insist that he be tough, firm, demanding, and unyielding in his struggle to obtain the best possible outcome for his constituents. Failure to perform in this manner (in the eyes of the audience) may lead to public criticism of the negotiator, with the expectation that this criticism will "embarrass" him into performing in ways that guarantee a larger payoff for the constituency.

Continued accusations of the negotiator as weak, soft, or selling out may lead the negotiator to several forms of behavior. First, he may become increasingly rigid and inflexible in his negotiating behavior in order to demonstrate to his constituency that he is capable of defending their interests. Second, he may find himself forced to resign, judged by himself or others as incapable of representing the constituency's best interests. Over a long period of time, accountability generates strong pressures on a negotiator to be a loyal, committed, and dedicated advocate of the constituency's preferred outcomes and priorities.

There are many aspects of a negotiator's relationship with his/her constituency that can affect negotiation outcomes. Three that have received some research attention are the negotiator's *relative status* within the constituency, *relative power* over the constituency, and the amount of *accountability pressure* that the constituency exerts. The impact of relative status, for example, formally designated leaders doing the negotiating as opposed to randomly chosen group members, has not demonstrated strong impact. High status members do not appear to negotiate more quickly, achieve fewer deadlocks in the negotiating process, or attain better solutions (Klimoski and Ash, 1974; Kogan, Lamm, and Trommsdorff, 1972). In contrast, accountability pressures appear to have a more significant impact. Accountability has usually been manipulated in research simulations by having constituents watch the negotiation, having the negotiator formally report back to a constituency (and perhaps vote on the negotiated agreement) or play a role in determining how the negotiator would be compensated for negotiating effectiveness. In general, this accountability makes the negotiator feel more pressure to respond to the constituency's desires, act "tougher" in negotiations, and leads to longer, more time-consuming negotiations than when accountability pressures do not exist (Benton, 1972; Klimoski, 1972; Haccoun and Klimoski, 1975; Breaugh and Klimoski, 1977). Finally, power within a constituency can affect a negotiator's behavior. Jackson and King (1983) proposed that a negotiator who has a high level of power over his/her constituency would be more insulated from censure and accountability pressure than a lower power negotiator. The negotiator, therefore, should have more freedom to be flexible in the negotiation, and should be more effective in that negotiations should be completed in less time, with fewer deadlocks, with more resources exchanged during negotiation, and with greater feelings of satisfaction about the process and the outcome. Only the impact of time was firmly supported by their study, but the data on the other variables demonstrated nonsignificant trends in the predicted direction.

Tactical Implications of Social Structure Dynamics

The Negotiator's Dilemma.   The presence of an audience—particularly an outcome-dependent audience—creates a paradox for negotiators. The paradox is the result of two sets of pressures. One set comes from his constituency, who communicate expectations that he should be tough, firm, unyielding, and supportive of the constituency's demands. The second set comes from the opposing negotiator, and from the definition of negotiation itself: bargaining is a process of give-and-take, a meeting of 'the minds. Concession-making—particularly *mutual* concession making—is an integral part of negotiation. How, then, can a bargainer satisfy both his constituency's demand for firmness (and a settlement favorable to their interests), and his opponent's demand for concessions (and a settlement favorable to his opponent or to both sides)?

The answer: a negotiator must build relationships with both his constituency *and* his opponent. The relationship with the constituency must be cultivated on the basis of complete support for their demands, and willingness to advocate these demands in negotiation. The relationship with the opponent, on the other hand, must be developed by stressing the similarity and commonality of their fate together, and the desirability of establishing and maintaining that strong, productive working relationship. However, each of these relationships must be developed *privately, and without the visibility of the other group*. This privacy assures that a negotiator can conduct his negotiations without endangering accountability or face. Negotiators must first meet with their constituency to define their collective interests and objectives. Negotiations may then be held with opposing negotiators, so that objectives and demands may be stated clearly; however, privacy assures that the necessary concessions can be made without looking weak or foolish. Finally, a negotiator meets again with his constituency to "sell" the concessions to them, and persuade them that the settlement was the best achievable under the circumstances.

Successful negotiation requires that the negotiator have control over the visibility (or invisibility) of his negotiation behavior to his constituency and to audiences. A negotiator who cannot meet with the opposing negotiator, and be separated from his constituency, is going to be "on public display" all the time. Every statement, argument, concession, and mistake is going to be in full view of a critical audience to whom the negotiator is responsible and must attend. Similarly, a negotiator who cannot meet privately with his constituency is likely to have every element of strategy and tactics open for inspection to his opponent. These pressures are highly undesirable, and, as we have argued earlier, likely to lead to negotiator behavior that is more designed to appeal to the audience rather than to search for agreement.

Tactics That Manipulate Audience Visibility

When a negotiator can control both the visibility of his behavior to various groups and the communication that he has with these groups, he is able to use a wide repertoire of tactics to persuade and pressure the other party. Each tactic is designed to accomplish several objectives.

Limiting Concessions by Making Negotiations Visible to a Constituency, or by Having the Constituency Limit Authority To Make Concessions.   Negotiators who negotiate in full view of their constituency are less likely to make concessions than negotiators who deliberate in private. Thus, negotiators can use visibility to limit their own ability to make concessions and then convince the other party that certain options are not possible. They can also use visibility to show that they cannot make negotiating concessions without "permission" from their constituency.

Toughening a Negotiator's Stance.   Public negotiations are typically pursued by a negotiator when he wants to remain firm in his position. Since the negotiator knows that his constituency will approve of his behavior when he is tough and inflexible, bringing the constituency into the negotiations will accomplish this objective. The negotiator may insist on allowing his constituency to be present. Community groups who want to bring about change from public officials usually insist that the officials come to an open meeting of the community, in which community spokesmen confront the officials with their concerns or grievances. If the full constituency cannot be present, the negotiator may try to bring several representatives to the meeting. Frequently, these may be the constituency members who are the most demanding or militant, and who will be most likely to report back to the constituency on how the negotiator is behaving. The presence of militants also demonstrates to the opponent that the negotiator is dealing with a very tough, demanding constituency, and that the only way agreement is going to be reached (or disaster averted) is for the opponent to make concessions. Social observer and critic Tom Wolfe humorously describes this social ritual in his essay, *Mau-mauing the Flak Catchers*. In the late 1960s, the Kennedy and Johnson administrations' "War on Poverty" required that government funds be distributed to inner-city community groups for community development activities. According to Wolfe, since government bureaucrats had very poor ways of determining who were the relevant community groups and leaders, they simply set up offices in urban areas and waited for the community leaders to identify themselves. Groups of inner-city residents would coalesce and go to see the bureaucrats (the "flak catchers"). Since most of these groups had no way to prove that they had strong legitimate community support, they engaged in tactics designed to intimidate the bureaucrats into allocating some of the government funds ("mau-mauing"). The meanest and toughest community members armed themselves with "costumes:" knives, chains, guns, and other paraphernalia designed to communicate super-militancy, and then went to visit the flak-catchers. Their spokesman merely stated the group's demands, while the threatening presence of his constituents implied that if demands were not met, his constituency would be uncontrollable and disaster would befall the flak-catchers, their office, and the entire community.

While Wolfe's essay is entertaining satire, the success of these tactics *is* frequently visible in confrontations between negotiating groups, particularly when there are power differences between them. These tactics can have other benefits as well. Very militant constituency members (who publicly display their militancy in the negotiation session) may not only threaten and intimidate the opponent, but also allow the negotiator to demonstrate that he is a nice, pleasant, reasonable person compared to other members of his constituency. Opponents who prefer to deal with nice, pleasant negotiators rather than angry, militant ones are more likely to want to work with (and make concessions to) the negotiator, and even help the negotiator to work out his/her political problems, rather than see him/her replaced by one of the angry, militant constituents. This tactic is a variation of the classic "tough guy—nice guy" or "Mutt and Jeff" tactic to negotiation.

Limiting a Negotiator's Authority.   The third way a negotiator can use his constituency to limit concessions—and hence force concessions from his opponent—is by showing that the constituency has limited the negotiator's ability to make unauthorized concessions. This tactic may be used as a bluff or a genuine expression of limited authority. As a bluff, the negotiator actually has the authority to make concessions, but leads his opponent to believe that all concessions must be cleared with his constituency. As a genuine tactic, the negotiator's constituency has defined limits to his concession making, and required consultation or approval for all agreements which fall above this level. For example, a small businessman may approach the lending officer of his local bank to negotiate a business development loan. The businessman wants to borrow $50,000; the bank wants to make sure that if the loan is granted, it will be profitable to the bank (for example, high interest rates), and that if the businessman cannot make the payments, the bank will be protected (security, collateral, etc.). A new, young bank loan officer will probably have very limited lending authority on his own, and be required to constantly check with his constituency (senior bank officers). A senior bank official probably has very wide latitude in loan negotiations, and could make the loan on his own authority, but uses the constituency both for protection (to make sure that the loan is not granted foolishly) and to put pressure on the borrower to agree to the bank's terms.

Negotiators must be careful in the way that they reveal the amount of authority they have to make settlements without consulting with their constituency. On the one hand, it might seem that limiting one's own authority would be a distinct advantage. Every deviation from the originally stated position would have to be confirmed by the constituency. This tedious procedure puts pressure on the opposing negotiator to make concessions in order to "get things over with." On the other hand, the tactic may backfire. Not only is the process frustrating for the negotiator—who feels great limitations in the power and confidence placed in him by his constituency—but the tactic frustrates the opponent as well. Rather than leading to concessions to complete the negotiation, the opponent's frustration and anger may result in rigidity, stalemate, and demands that the negotiator send a representative who has the power to achieve a settlement. Moreover, if a negotiator is limited in the concessions he/she can make, the very idea of negotiation is undermined. When negotiation is understood as the process of making concessions toward mutual agreement, encountering an opponent who cannot make concessions violates expectations and creates anger. Negotiators with severely limited authority can be effectively embarrassed *by their opponents* when they don't have the authority to make agreements on their own.

Representatives Exceeding Authority.   The reverse side of this negotiating dilemma is that the negotiator who over-extends his authority, or the limits set by his constituency, may be unable to persuade his constituency that the achieved settlement is a good one. This happens frequently in union-management relations. A union negotiating team reaches a tentative settlement with management, only to have the union rank-and-file reject the proposed contract offer. The rejection vote is tantamount to a communication of "no confidence" in the negotiators. As a consequence, the negotiators are likely to become increasingly tough and militant. In the extreme, the negotiators may be willing to endure extremely high personal costs—a long strike, personal fines, jail sentences, and great outcries of negative public opinion—to restore their image with the constituency. The rejected negotiator will also have difficulty working with the opposing negotiator in the future, since there will be doubts that any future agreement will be ratified by the constituency.

A dramatic example of this process occurred in the Professional Air

Traffic Controllers Organization (PATCO) strike against the Federal Aviation Authority in 1981. The new leader of PATCO, Robert Poli, spent a number of months negotiating a new wage and benefits package with the Authority (FAA). When the package was finally presented to the local union for their ratification, almost 90 percent |of | the | membership rejected the tentative contract as inadequate in both salary and benefits. Poli returned to the FAA negotiators and insisted that they reopen contract talks; after two weeks of unsuccessful debate by both sides, PATCO called a strike. The strike (illegal under the terms of the government's contract with each union member) led the FAA and the Reagan administration to: (1) fire all of the striking controllers from their jobs, (2) obtain federal injunctions and impose fines of several million dollars per day against the union and its leadership, (3) jail some union members and officials, (4) impound the union's strike fund, and (5) ban all striking controllers from any further employment with the U.S. government, either as a controller or in any other federal job. Ninety percent of the union members supported Poli in the early days of this confrontation, confirming not only the "militancy" of the union but their expectations that Poli would either support the union's militant demands (and become a hero-martyr in defending them), or lose his right to maintain the job that he had fought for years to obtain. (Account based on a description of the events in the *New York Times*, August 3–11, 1981).

Increasing the Possibility of Concessions by Cutting Off Visibility to Audiences

If increased visibility to bystanders and constituencies increases the likelihood that negotiators will take tougher stands, be less flexible, and make fewer concessions, then a negotiator who wishes his or her opponent to be more flexible, less belligerent, and more conciliatory would want negotiations to be less visible. There are two approaches to accomplishing this objective:

Establish "Privacy" Prior to Beginning Negotiations. In Chapter 6, we discussed the importance of determining what negotiating ground rules should be established prior to the commencement of actual bargaining. One possible rule is that the negotiations will be conducted in private, that no interviews will be granted, and that contact with either party's constituency will be forbidden. To enhance the privacy of the negotiations, parties may select a remote location in neutral territory, where their comings and goings will not be too obvious and others will have great difficulty in making contact. When the time comes for announcements about negotiating progress or achievements, these announcements can be made jointly, with both parties present and able to coordinate their communications. Needless to say, if the other party wishes the negotiations to be held in a public environment—

where communication with constituencies is easy and they may actually have a direct view—setting the terms and conditions for the negotiation will be the first item for deliberations.

Screening Visibility during Negotiations.   If negotiators have not agreed beforehand to a location that is private and secure, there are other options for screening out unwanted observers. One of the simplest ways is to have discussions occur informally, during the course of some other event, or on a strictly "unofficial" basis. For example, negotiators sometimes schedule coffee breaks, or even exchange important information in a quick trip to the washroom. They may agree to meet for cocktails after a long day, or key officials may meet for breakfast before the day's formal deliberations begin. During such meetings, parties can speak more candidly, "off the record," or hint as to their bottom line position or their willingness to make certain concessions. "We've been sitting in that room for a long time, and you know, if your side were willing to name a proposal something like the following (insert specifics here), my people would probably be willing to go along with it."

Other kinds of information can also be privately exchanged. Negotiators can grumble and complain, brag about their constituency and it's support, or even let conversations with their own constituents be "overheard" by an opponent. All of these tactics give the other side information about what is really possible without saying it directly at the table. A union negotiator might say, "You know, Mike Moran is something else. He's been riding me about toughening up the work rules for the past six months. He's really after my job." The management negotiator may well decide to give a little more on work rules to keep the present union negotiator in his job, rather than to let the militant get elected and make work for himself.

Contacts can also be made at dinners, parties, speeches, luncheons, or even church services. Heads of state who negotiate major arms and trade agreements are frequently photographed at dinners, receptions, walks in the garden, etc. While there is a great deal that is public and ceremonial about such functions, "private time" is frequently arranged as well. At almost every funeral for a major political figure in Europe or the Middle East, there has been speculation *not* as to whether representatives of the United States and the Soviet Union will meet, but when and where they will meet and what will be discussed.

Communicate Indirectly with an Opponent by Communicating with His Constituency or with Audiences

A third technique that negotiators use by manipulating the social structure of negotiations is to communicate *indirectly*. *Indirect* communications are efforts by the negotiator to bring the opinion of others to bear on the opposing negotiator. While the opponent may believe he is well-defended against his adversary's arguments, he may not be able to defend himself against other people—his constituents, his friends, his superiors, or "public opinion"—when they appear to side with his opponent.

Communicating through superiors is one form of indirect communication. This technique is frequently used when negotiators are representatives of two hierarchically structured organizations, such as a company and a union, or two companies attempting to develop a contract, purchasing agreement, lease, etc. The technique is likely to be used when one or both negotiators are dissatisfied with the progress of negotiations or the behavior of the opponent. As a result, they may go to their own superiors (who are probably not directly involved) and ask the superiors to either attend a negotiating session, or, more commonly, to contact their counterpart in the opposing organization. The situation is represented in Figure 9–6.

Consider the following example from labor relations. A union negotiator has presented a set of wage demands to the management negotiator. Management has examined the demands, and is convinced that it will be financially impossible for the company to meet them. In spite of management's persistent argument and documentation, the union negotiator refuses to believe the accuracy and validity of the arguments. Therefore, the management negotiator goes to one of his superiors, e.g., the corporate treasurer, and asks him to contact the president of the local union. The corporate treasurer invites the union president to his office, and provides sufficient financial data to convince the president that the company simply cannot meet the union's demands. The union president is then asked to meet with the union negotiator, and to adjust the union's demands accordingly.

Several observations should be made about this process. First, the tactic depends upon a social structure in which the negotiator represents an organization or group with individuals who have more formal power and authority—and the opponent represents a similar organization. Most *formal* negotiations between organizational, political, and social groups fall into this

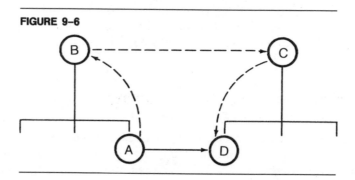

FIGURE 9–6

description. Second, the *negotiator is not the chief executive*. The reason the chief executive does not negotiate is *not* that he is too busy doing other things. The use of representatives allows a negotiating organization to limit its concessions by limiting the negotiator's power and authority to make decisions. Senior executives are only likely to become involved when negotiations are extremely delicate, critical, or essential to the entire well-being of the organization and its relationships with others. Observers of international relations will note, for example, that contacts between nations occur on a number of diplomatic levels, and that the Secretary of State or President of the United States become directly involved in only the most delicate, sensitive, or important international incidents.

The effectiveness of the tactic relies upon indirect communication originating from someone whom the opponent trusts more. Negotiators expect to have opponents try to change their positions, and hence defend themselves against it. When an individual expects that someone is going to attempt to change his opinion, he is likely to defend his own view more strongly (see Chapter 8). When the indirect communication comes from superiors it is even more effective since negotiators *expect* to acquiesce to their superiors. Similarly, in the previous illustration, the union president, confronted with valid information from the chief financial officer of the company (who is defined as a "non-negotiator"), is more likely to accept and believe the financial information than if the same information was presented at the bargaining table.

Communication through bystanders and constituency members is a second variation of indirect communication. This approach (see Figure 9–7) is frequently used when negotiators need to make "informal" contact with an opposing negotiator or constituency. Here the approach is made through any contact available.

Those selected to make the contact are usually chosen for some valid reason—personal experience in dealing with the opposing organization in a different context and time; personal friendships or relationships with mem-

FIGURE 9–7

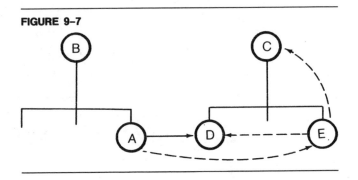

bers of the opposing organization that "transcend" the negotiation and the tension it has created; or a personal reputation for credibility, impartiality, and integrity. The tactic is most often used under several conditions: when a negotiator or his organization wants to "feel out" the opposing group to possibly gain "inside information," or when deliberations are deadlocked and need to be unfrozen. Consider the Acme Company, which manufactures thermostats. Acme wants to gain a contract with Kitchen Wonder, a major appliance manufacturer, to supply thermostats for all of Kitchen Wonder's electric ovens. Acme is aware that their vice president of manufacturing used to work in engineering at Kitchen Wonder, and hence the vice president is asked to contact some of his old friends at Kitchen Wonder. To feel out the opposing group, the vice president might be asked to find out "how Kitchen Wonder would respond" to a certain bid for the thermostat contract. He needs to find out what criteria Kitchen Wonder will be using to evaluate the bid, and how the Acme bid might compare to other bids that Kitchen Wonder has received. To gain inside information, the vice president might be asked to determine exactly what other bids Kitchen Wonder has received, so that Acme can set its bid to assure itself the contract. Finally when the two companies are actively engaged in deliberations but have not made significant progress, the vice president might be asked to unblock deadlocked negotiations. Neither side wishes to make a formal concession at the negotiating table. However, informal contacts might be used to determine "how Kitchen Wonder might respond to certain changes in our last offer." Similar to the tactic of communicating through superiors, the effectiveness of informal contact depends upon employing individuals who are not subject to the same accountability pressure that bind formal group representatives.

Communicating to opponent's constituency is a third form of indirect communication. In this approach, (see Figure 9–8) the negotiator seeks to bypass the opposing negotiator and communicate directly to his organization and it's members in order to persuade that group to change its instructions to its negotiator. This tactic may be initiated by the negotiator

FIGURE 9–8

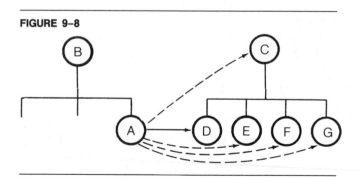

himself, or be initiated "by invitation" of the opposing negotiator. In the latter case, the opponent indicates that it might be useful for the negotiator to either communicate directly with the constituency, or to listen to their reactions to specific proposals. In the former case, the negotiator usually believes that the opponent may not be accurately transmitting information back to his constituency, or may be misrepresenting constituency interests, and that more open and direct communication is desirable. In a union-management situation, for example, management representatives frequently choose to speak to or write to the rank-and-file directly, rather than through the union leadership. The intent (and the impact) may not only be to insure that management's position is clearly heard and understood, but also to undermine the credibility and effectiveness of the union leadership. This is done by refusing to use them as the sole channel of communication and deliberation, or by implying to the constituency that their negotiator is not doing a satisfactory job of representing their interests. Obviously, direct communication with an opposing constituency—without the "permission" and sanction of the opposing negotiator—is usually an inflammatory tactic because it implies that the opposing negotiator is not communicating effectively with his own constituency, or representing their interests. Negotiators treated this way are likely to become defensive and more rigid in their bargaining posture. However, the impact on the negotiator's constituency is more complex. At times, they may perceive direct communication from the opponent as a tactic—that is, they are aware that management is trying to undercut the union leadership, and hence will rally around their leadership more strongly. At other times—particularly when an constituency may already have doubts about the effectiveness of it's own representation—direct, open, accurate communication from an opposing negotiator may be sufficient to undermine confidence in their representative even further.

Communicating through bystanders is the fourth form of indirect communication. Communication through bystanders can be witnessed when two individuals or small groups are in conflict, as well as in major disputes between large groups and organizations. In all cases, the negotiator's intent is to manipulate the opinion of bystanders (other than constituencies), either toward one's own position or away from the opponent's position (see Figure 9–9). Communication through bystanders may occur: (1) as an explicit and conscious tactic to exert indirect influence on the opponent; (2) as an effort to build alliances and support for one's own position; or (3) as a result of the natural tendency for conflict to proliferate and envelop innocent bystanders. In all cases, negotiators are very public about their own (or their organization's) demands. They will tell anyone who will listen how fair, legitimate, and just their own side's position is, and how unfair, unjust, and illegitimate the opponent's position is. As a result, negotiators hope that third parties will openly side with them (hence lending strength and credence to their argu-

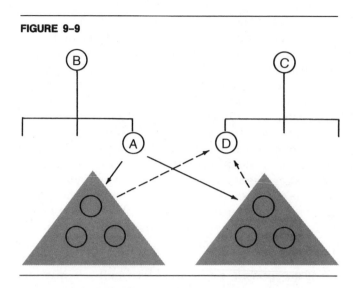

FIGURE 9-9

ments), and/or that the third party will communicate their dissatisfaction and displeasure to the opponent, (thus undermining the strength and credence of the opponent's arguments).

Communication through audiences is extremely common in major interorganizational negotiations—intergovernmental, international, or labor-management relations. Most of these deliberations are well known for having a "public phase" to them, in which the negotiators primarily address their arguments to audiences rather than to one another. In this phase, the media—radio, television, and newspaper—play an integral role by providing ready access to communication channels. Media relations and "image management" often become ends in themselves, since the better the performance before radio microphones or television cameras, the more likely a negotiator will be to win "public opinion" to his side.

Communication through the media is usually designed to reach *one's own constituency* or *interested audiences*. The quickest and most efficient way of letting one's own constituency know their negotiating posture is to represent that position in the media. This approach is more likely to be used when one wants to communicate firmness and toughness in a position. It is less likely to be used when one wants to communicate concession-making or defeat. Communication may also be designed to *"activate" and win over interested audiences* who will communicate directly with the opponent. In public sector labor relations, such as a community's negotiations with school teachers, policemen, firemen, sanitation workers, etc., it is not uncommon for the mayor or school board president to appear on television, state the union's salary demands, depict those demands as exorbitant, and "point out" how much those demands are likely to cost the taxpayers. The expectation is that the taxpayers will communicate their dissatisfaction to the union leadership, hence bringing strong social pressure on the union to modify its demands. Obviously, union leadership engages in similar tactics, attempting to win community support by stressing the wide variety of services they provide for minimal compensation, and portraying the dire consequences that might occur if these services were not available. Taxpayers are urged to call their local government representatives immediately and urge complete capitulation to the union's "fair and legitimate" requests.

The effectiveness of communicating through audiences to build alliances for one's own side or to undermine the opposition's strength, is dependent on several factors. First it depends upon the degree to which an audience's outcomes are directly dependent on the negotiator's behavior, and how severe the consequences are likely to be. *Degree of effect* can vary from outcomes directly affecting the audience to those only minimally and indirectly affecting the audience. If I live on the East Coast, a strike by farm workers in California will probably not affect me very strongly, particularly if I can purchase fruit and vegetables grown locally. On the other hand, a strike by the drivers of milk trucks in my local area is likely to affect me and my family very strongly. *Severity of effect* can vary from a small to a great degree. The California workers' strike would not affect me if I did not eat many fruits and vegetables. Similarly, I would be greatly affected by the milk strike if I had three small children.

The second factor in the effectiveness of communicating through audiences is the degree to which the audience is "organized" as a coherent unit. An audience may be directly and severely affected by the results of a particular negotiation, but unable to exert leverage on either negotiator because they have no means for communicating and making decisions among themselves, no means for polling opinions and determining their collective sentiments, and no way of presenting their group's interest. Community members who may be greatly inconvenienced by a transportation strike have no way to *collectively* express their dissatisfaction to strikers or management. Few people will actually call or write to these officials, and the only way that community sentiment may be determined is from a few letters to the local newspaper or several "man on the street" interviews by local radio and television. Even when a very large group of people may be negatively affected, they are *unlikely to have significant impact on the negotiations if the reaction cannot be brought to bear on the negotiators themselves*.

The reverse is also true: *well-organized audiences can have significant effect on the outcome of negotiations even if their total number is small*. The effectiveness of particular political lobbies in State and Federal government is testimony to the positive effect of strong organization. For example, numerous public opinion polls in recent years have demonstrated strong popular support for limiting the sale of handguns. In spite of apparent widespread public support for this legislation, several national lobbies have effectively "killed" most anti-handgun legislation in Congress and state legislatures. Their success is based upon their ability to identify and contact audience members who support their position, to "mobilize" these members toward a common purpose, and to bring pressure on all legislators who might support a gun-control bill. Such pressure usually takes the form of massive letter writing and telephoning campaigns, promises of financial contributions to the legislator's campaign if he votes "the right way," etc. This last tactic suggests that an audience will be effective in persuading a negotiator to the extent not only that it is "organized," but also that it can exert direct pressure (e.g., financial support) on the opponent rather than just "indirect pressure" (e.g., insisting that he listen to them and change his mind).

Finally, appeals to audiences will be effective to the degree that the negotiator is sophisticated in his/her use of media relations. To the individual who may be naive in dealing with and using the media as an effective indirect negotiating tool, media relations may be no more than appearing before a camera or microphone and reading a prepared statement. Unfortunately, as has been pointed out, the content of one's message, particularly on television, is considerably less important than the visual presentation and the "performance." Portraying an image of confidence, control, and steadfast determination is essential. The negotiator needs to be well dressed, well spoken, and in control of the situation. He needs to be able to respond to hostile and loaded questions effectively. Finally, he may wish to be surrounded by his constituency—the rank-and-file, his supporters, his closest advisors—who will openly demonstrate their solidarity and support for their negotiator.

Building Relationships with Opponents

Finally, rather than undermine an opponent's support, negotiators frequently try to develop personal relationships with the opponent. The negotiator's underlying assumption is that it is easier (and definitely more pleasant) to work with and persuade a friendly opponent than an unfriendly one. These assumptions parallel much of the research on the impact of "source factors" in attitude change (see Chapter 8). Individuals who see themselves as similar to one another, or who are attracted to one another, or who are likely to experience a common fate, are more likely to change their attitudes toward one another. Since negotiation may easily be viewed as a mutual effort by both parties to change the others' attitudes (i.e., objectives, opening demands), the same principles apply.

Negotiators use a variety of techniques to make this tactic work. Some negotiators meet informally, to get to know the other party outside of the context of negotiations. Cocktails, a meal, or even a coffee break are well-known opportunities for promoting friendliness, easy conversation and cordiality. The agenda for both sides is usually *not* to conduct formal deliberations, but to build a relationship that will make the tension and conflict of formal negotiations more palatable, and less likely to end in deadlock or an angry walkout. Hence, they need to drop their negotiator roles and meet as individual people. Conversation is usually light and informal, designed to be nonthreatening and pleasant. Strong mutual interests and concerns—are essential to creating bases of similarity, commonality, and liking for one another.

In addition to developing a relationship based on commonality of personal interests, or genuine liking for one another, negotiators frequently stress their "common fate" in the negotiations. If both negotiators feel pressured by their constituencies, or if the nature of the negotiation will result in a long-term relationship between the parties, they are likely to stress their common fate as a way to build the relationship. "You and I are in this together," "we both have our constituencies to deal with," "we want to achieve the best for all of us," or "we want to develop an agreement that is based on mutual respect, and which we can live with successfully in the future," are all phrases that typify the opening stages of negotiation. Many experienced negotiators refer to these expressions of common fate as "the harmony and light speech;" they believe that such expressions are merely a tactical ploy to soften them up before the opposing negotiator presents tough demands. While that may be true, the "harmony and light speech" plays a critical role in negotiation. Even if the speech is ritualistic, it *does* communicate that the opposing negotiator is interested in building a personal relationship. Moreover, the absence of the speech may indicate that the parties are so adamant in their positions, or angry at one another, that they cannot bring themselves to make the speech. This may be a clear sign that the negotiations will be tense and likely to be deadlocked.

A further purpose of these informal meetings is to permit each party to gather a sense of each other's objectives. In many union-management negotiations, for example, it is not uncommon for a major company official to invite the president of the union to lunch prior to the first meeting. The purpose of this meeting is usually twofold: to sense what the other side's major demands will be, and also to develop a relationship and an "open channel of communication" that can be used regardless of how tense and conflictful the negotiations become. Such meetings are usually held without publicity, since publicizing the event might lead other management or union members to view the meeting as "collusion." However, some negotiators may choose to publicize the event in order to demonstrate a "spirit of cooperation." When the President of the United States appears before the television cameras in the White House Rose Garden with some visiting foreign dignitary, the two are usually shown smiling, shaking hands, embracing, and demonstrating to their constituencies and audiences that they have developed a harmonious relationship which will hopefully lead to mutual agreement on substantive problems. The discussion between them, however, is private and we rarely know what was actually said.

SUMMARY

Sometimes negotiation is a private affair between two parties. Up until now we have talked about negotiation in a private context. Often, however, there are audiences to a negotiation, and the presence of an audience has both a subtle and a direct impact on negotiations.

Three types of audiences may be encountered. First, when negotiations are between teams of people (rather than individuals), much of the actual dialogue is conducted between chief negotiators. While these two usually talk directly to one another, they also use their own and opposing team members as an audience. Messages will often be sent to other members of the opposing team who the negotiator believes will be more receptive to the idea and also be able to influence the other chief negotiator.

A second type of audience is the constituency whom the negotiator represents. This may be a husband representing a family in the negotiations for a new house, diplomats negotiating for their countries, or division heads on a company-wide budget committee negotiating over their share of capital resources for the coming year. These audiences have a stake in the outcome of the negotiation and benefit or suffer according to the skills of their representatives. The third type of audience is bystanders. Bystanders see or hear about the negotiations and, while they have little or no stake in the outcome, form opinions (favorable or unfavorable) of the settlement and the parties involved.

Audiences influence negotiators through two different routes. One way is that negotiators desire positive evaluations from those who are in a position to observe what they have done. The other is that audiences can (and do) hold negotiators responsible for the outcomes of negotiations. They can reward negotiators by publicly praising them, and punish negotiators by firing those who represent them. They can intrude and change the course of negotiations—as when the public requires mandatory arbitration or fact-finding in some disputes. They can find ways of making their preferences known, e.g., talking to the press, thereby putting pressure on one or both negotiators.

Audiences can have both favorable and unfavorable impacts on negotiations. Sometimes a negotiator tries to use an audience to his advantage, as when he thinks it will help pressure his opponent into a more flexible or desirable position; he may also try to prevent an audience from having influence effect when he thinks it might be undesirable for his position. While there are many different ways of manipulating an audience, they all involve controlling the visibility of or the communication with that audience. In this chapter, we suggested four basic strategies to manipulate the effect an audience can have:

1. Limit concessions by making one's actions visible to one's constituency, thereby putting oneself in a position which the opponent will recognize as difficult to change.

2. Increase the possibility of concessions by cutting off the visibility of negotiations to the audience.

3. Communicate indirectly with the other negotiator by communicating with his or her audiences.

4. Facilitate the building of a relationship with the other negotiator by reducing visibility and communication with both parties' audiences.

When negotiations move from a private to a public context, negotiations become more complex and more formal. In setting strategy, a negotiator needs to consider whether negotiations should be held privately or involve audiences in various ways. To ignore this social context is to ignore a very potent factor in determining negotiation outcomes.

10

The Role of Power

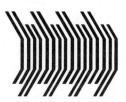

Power is a word that has multiple, often overlapping, or even contradictory meanings. It is often used interchangeably with leadership, influence, and even negotiation. Power is an important factor in negotiations; and, before going further, we need to clarify what we mean by the term and how it is going to be used in this book.

A DEFINITION OF POWER

In a broad sense, people have power when they have "the ability to bring about outcomes they desire," or " . . . the ability to get things done the way one wants them to be done," (Salancik and Pfeffer, 1977). However, the same people could also be described as having influence, being persuasive, or being leaders. We need some way of separating power from other influence processes that are used in interpersonal relations.

One way of defining power builds on the observation that with power one party can get another to do what the latter normally would not do (Dahl, 1957; Kotter, 1979). Often, this is interpreted to mean that the other person is doing something he or she does not want to do, hence, that some sort of force is being used. When we mention force, it is common to think of *physical* force such as killing, beating, restraint in handcuffs, holding people in custody such as jail—the sort of things we associate with police power or military power. These are not particularly useful forms of power to consider in negotiations. However, there are many other ways people can end up doing something they would not ordinarily do, or might not want to do, as a result of some form of force other than physical. Let us consider several examples:

1. In recent years, union officials have been negotiating new labor contracts which *reduce* the wage package, hardly something union officials want to do. They have usually done so because the company officials have stated that unless wages go down, the firm will go bankrupt, will move away, will drop this line of business, or some similar action. The union officials can be seen as making a rational or calculated decision to do something they ordinarily would not do.

2. Many individuals promoted "from the ranks" into managerial positions find they have to direct and control people who were (or still are) peers and, perhaps, close friends. Even though they may not want to direct and control these people because of a fear of losing their friendship, their role as a manager requires that he/she must exercise some control. Here, they are doing something which, while not liked, is seen as required and proper.[1]

3. The role a person fills not only leads to changes in the behavior of those who occupy it, but also in those who interact with the role occupant. An individual worker who approaches his or her superior with a list of grievances about the job may receive little or no attention. However, if the same individual has just been elected spokesperson for the office staff, the boss is far more likely to listen and to take action on the grievances.

In these three illustrations, we confront the same problem: the individual who is responding to power—the target person—sees the options open to him being changed. The union leader agrees to reduced wages because the alternative option, a closed plant, is even less desirable (in fact, it may not be seen as an option at all). The newly appointed supervisor recognizes that, as part of the new job, he/she must direct or control others. The boss, who now talks with a worker he/she would earlier have ignored, is not doing so because he/she likes that person's company, but because that person now speaks for others, and they cannot be ignored.

Fredrick Douglass, born a slave in Maryland, describes in his autobiography (1856) how he was regularly beaten by a slave breaker to force him to be more obedient. After one particularly severe beating, he decided that he would never be beaten again, even though he might be killed. The next time the slave breaker attempted to beat him, he fought back, not defeating the

---

[1] In fact, some of the most intriguing writing and discussion have focused on the question of whether (to quote the old adage), "power corrupts." In other words, does the acquisition of power—by stepping into power roles, or acquiring control over instrumental resources-lead otherwise low-power-impulse people? Some of the more interesting questions in this regard will be mentioned later in this chapter, and in our discussion of values and ethics in Chapter 13.

other man but also not letting him win. The draw established the point; Douglass was not beaten again. What changed were the options Douglass saw that he had. Earlier, as would be true for most of us threatened with severe physical abuse, Douglass saw the situation as one of submitting or being killed–and chose submission. Douglass changed this perspective and included being killed as an option—in fact as an acceptable option—and that removed the power of the other person.

In this book we will define power as the ability to get another party to do something they ordinarily would not do by controlling the options they perceive open to them. In the remainder of this chapter, as we consider the different sources and uses of power, we shall essentially be looking at how options available to the target person are changed. We shall particularly be looking at how the perceptions the target person has of his/her options are influenced.

SOURCES OF POWER

Understanding the different ways that power can be exercised is best accomplished by a description of the various sources (or bases) of power and the ways that these are typically exercised. Five different bases of power were identified by French and Raven (1959): reward power, coercive power, legitimate power, expert power, and referent power. To this we shall add a sixth base, the power of information itself. We will first discuss how to evaluate the effectiveness of various sources of power on negotiating behavior, and then discuss each source of power in detail.

Criteria for Effective Power Use

In discussing power, we will need some criteria for assessing the effectiveness of a particular power source. A variety of ways has been suggested to evaluate power sources (e.g., French and Raven, 1959; Raven and Kruglanski, 1970; Kipnis, 1976; Cuming, 1981). For our purposes the following criteria will be used:

1. What are the *advantages* of this source of power?

2. What are the *disadvantages* of this source of power?

3. Will this source of power change another's *overt behavior* and/or *private attitudes* (what they "really believe")? Some forms of power are likely to change both behavior and attitudes; other forms are likely to change only overt behavior.

4. Does the power from this source require *surveillance* for long-run compliance? Surveillance takes the agent's time, money and resources to monitor the target's behavior, and hence is likely to be less preferable than power approaches which do not require surveillance.

TABLE 10–1

Type of Power	Advantages	Disadvantages	Target of Change	Surveillance	Impact on Relationship
Informational	Based on "facts" and information, leads to internalized motivation, does not require outlay of resource to implement	Time consuming; requires others' receptivity	Negotiator's attitude and behavior	No	No likely impact
Reward	Direct control over negotiator's behavior; rapid action	Rewards may lose potency; may be seen as illegitimate; "minimum level" compliance may be obtained	Negotiator's behavior—specific focus	Frequently, requires some surveillance—target likely to help in surveillance	Positive impact on target; liking for agent; may engender continued dependence by the target
Coercive	Direct control over negotiator's behavior; compliance, rapid action cathartic for power-holder	Costs of surveillance high over time; potential for retaliation; coercion may lose potency as fear decreases	Negotiator's behavior—specific focus	Definitely yes; requires close and continued surveillance	Negative, particularly over long run
Legitimate	Power based on "office," not the person—can be depersonalized; wide-ranging impact if target acknowledges officeholder	May lose impact if legitimacy questioned; may require supplementary power bases (reward and coercive) to be effective	Negotiator's attitude and behavior	Unlikely, unless target sees officeholder or request as "illegitimate"	Neutral, may be negative if office is abused by agent
Expert	No outlay of resources required; quick; tied to facts and "correctness"; builds commitment to ideas	Likely to fail if request is outside the area of expertise, or seen as illegitimate; must work to maintain expertise	Attitude and behavior within the range of expertise	Unlikely	Positive or no impact
Referent	No outlay of resources required; quick; creates a positive climate and disposition in target person	Likely to fail if request is outside the scope of identification with powerholder, or seen as illegitimate; may lead to rejection	Attitudes and behavior within range of identification	Unlikely	Positive and supportive

5. How will the exercise of power affect the *relationship between the negotiating parties*? Some forms of power are likely to engender and promote strong, positive relationships between the power agent and the target; others are likely to contribute to its deterioration and decline.

Each of these criteria will be evaluated in our discussion of power from various sources. In addition, the power types and the various criteria are summarized in Table 10–1.

TYPES OF POWER

Reward Power: *The Golden Rule or Whoever Has the Gold Makes the Rules*.[2]

Reward power is an effort by the powerholder to use rewards in order to gain the other's compliance. The use of reward power assumes several key factors: that the target is dependent on the powerholder in some ways (a condition already established by virtue of their negotiating relationship), that the target person believes the powerholder controls some form of resources which are desired by the target person, and that the rewards can be administered in a manner that will insure the target person's compliance.

While rewards are often illustrated by referring to money or other tangible items, they need not take this form. Research has shown that verbal approval, encouragement, and praise are frequently acceptable substitutes for tangible rewards. Experiments on the use of positive reinforcement and behavior modification in classroom and work settings have clearly shown that praise and positive approval may produce strong and durable behavior change.

The use of reward power in negotiation is an effort to exert more direct control over the opposing negotiator than may be achieved by simple presentation of information. Baldwin (1971), in his research on international relations and diplomacy, proposes that "rewards are most likely to be used when the powerholder has low expectations that simple persuasion will overcome a target person's resistance." Research reviewed by Kipnis (1976) generally supports this view. Rewards tend to be used when the powerholder expects resistance from the target, when the target is perceived as dissimilar to the powerholder, and when rewards (primarily money) are most likely to be used to prevent the occurrence of resistance in the future rather than to eliminate the present resistance. Unfortunately, most of the research that Kipnis reviews was done in contexts other than negotiation; therefore, we do not have clear-cut evidence that negotiators will use rewards or reward-

---

[2]Quotes taken from Murphy's Laws (Bloch, 1982).

based power only when persuasion efforts fail or are believed likely to fail. We do know that the potency of reward power is traceable to simple principles of reinforcement as a mechanism for shaping and changing behavior. A number of comprehensive reviews of this research and its application to managerial settings are available (e.g., Hamner, 1977). Impressive results have been obtained by psychologists who have advocated the use of reinforcement and behavior modification programs in industrial settings, creating rewards and positive incentives for the desired changes in behavior.

There are a number of advantages and disadvantages to using reward power. However, it is first necessary to understand coercive or punishment power as well. Since reward and coercive power are sometimes used together and often subject to semantic confusion about their distinctions, we shall describe coercive power before comparing and evaluating it with reward power.

Coercive Power: *A Smith and Wesson Beats 4 Aces.*

Coercive power is the opposite of reward power; it is the ability of the powerholder to take something away from the target person or to punish the target for noncompliance with a request. Like reward power, coercive power is also a frequently observed phenomenon. A sales manager cuts his salesman's pay for failing to make sales target projections during the previous month. An executive fires his secretary for failing to improve her typing skills. A father denies his son television privileges for a week because he didn't help clean out the garage. A supplier puts a "late charge" on an overdue bill to a customer. And, like reward power, coercive or punishment power can be as effective in "verbal" form as the withdrawal or denial of "tangible" resources. If the sales manager berates his salesman for failing to make target sales quotas rather than cutting his pay, or if the father yells at his son rather than denying him television privileges, the impact may be just as great.

The conditions for the use of coercive power are similar to those described in the use of reward power: the target is dependent on the powerholder in some way, the powerholder controls some form of resources which can be denied or taken away from the target, and the punishment can be administered in a manner that will insure the target person's compliance. The decision to use coercive power is most likely related to the powerholder's perception of the willingness of the target to comply. Kipnis (1976), following on Baldwin's earlier statements about reward power, states that *"sanctions, whether positive or negative, are most likely to be involved when expectations of successful influence are lowest*. Positive sanctions appear to be preferred when the powerholder wishes to retain the good will of the target person, or when the powerholder anticipates that compliance is likely to drop off in the future. Negative sanctions appear to be preferred when the good will of the target is less involved, and the influence attempts are directed at changing some behavior rather than maintaining it" (p. 104, emphasis his).

Kipnis proposes that there are a number of reasons why a powerholder may decide to use coercive power. Coercive power may be used as a way to *express anger*, to gain retribution, or "get even" for something the target person has done. In a negotiation extending over a series of meetings, one party, who has been very flexible on meeting times or locations previously, may insist that the only times possible for future meetings are those known to be inconvenient to the other party as a way of showing anger or of using coercive power. Research by Goodstadt and Hjelle (1973) has shown that the use of coercive power is likely to be greatest when the "target's resistance or influence is attributed to motivational causes (I refuse) rather than to a lack of ability (I can't)" (Kipnis, p. 105). Thus, if the son had said, "I can't clean the garage; I've got to go to basketball practice this morning," the father would be much more likely to accept the excuse as reasonable and less likely to resort to coercive influence. In this instance, the objective is to get the target person to want to avoid angering the powerholder, since this is known to cause difficulties.

Also, Kipnis suggests that coercive power may be used as an expression of *role behavior*—that is, because the job (or role) requires it. For example: a banker forecloses on a loan "because bank rules mandate it," or a Dean terminates a poorly performing student because "she didn't meet minimum standards." Such activities demonstrate to the other party that the negotiator is not just an individual but someone acting in a role; he is doing it because the job requires it.

As Kipnis points out, all institutional roles have certain job specifications and requirements that may require the use of coercive power in order to exercise the duties of the job. The banker has an obligation, as a lending officer, to follow the bank's rules with regard to delinquent loans. The Dean has an obligation, as an academic administrator, to terminate students who do not meet minimum standards of academic performance. However, the existence of such role requirements frequently leads to abuse. Many times, the powerholder will "extend" the use of coercive power beyond the scope and boundaries for which it was meant. Such behavior is not defined by the role, but abused by the powerholder in the role.

No direct empirical research documents the reasons for the use of coercive power in negotiation. Coercive power is likely to be used as an instrument for material gain—to coerce a particular concession or settlement out of the opponent—and also as a retaliatory expression of anger for failure to behave in anticipated or expected ways. The use of coercion as "role behavior" may occur more frequently when a negotiator has more power than his opponent, when he is acting in an "official capacity" or when the powerholder chooses to use the power of the office (rather than the power of information and persuasion) to extract concessions. This process will be explored in more detail in the discussion of legitimate power.

Comparing Reward Power and Coercive Power

At times, clear and clean distinctions between the use of power as reward or punishment are difficult to draw. One frequent source of confusion is semantics. Is withholding reward really a form of coercion? Is withholding punishment a form of reward? How would we classify an "unspecified" contingency statement, i.e., "Your annual raise will depend upon how you perform in the next three months"? Is this the use of reward or coercive power? both? neither? Yet many negotiators will prefer this kind of statement. Ambiguity is often preferred by the powerholder, who presumably has the power to reward or punish the target dependent on the target's performance. Let us look at the effects produced by the use of reward and coercive power.

There is a greater likelihood that the person using reward power will engender feelings of positive liking and attraction toward himself, while the person using coercive power will engender greater dislike and other negative feelings (Rubin and Lewicki, 1973; Rubin, Lewicki, and Dunn, 1973). Liking and positive regard by the target are desirable for negotiations, since positive feelings will enhance the effectiveness of other forms of power used by the powerholder (as we shall note later in this chapter). In addition, positive feelings will preserve the relationship between the negotiators. This may be desirable if the two parties expect to negotiate again in the future.

When coercive power is used, the target is likely to try to leave the situation; when reward power is used, the target is likely to remain in the environment, particularly if further rewards are anticipated. The use of coercive power is, therefore, likely to be disruptive to negotiation, since the target may wish to leave before a settlement can be reached or before a negotiated agreement can be fully implemented.

While both reward power and coercive power require surveillance, surveillance is likely to be easier with reward power. Since the target has to comply in order to receive the reward he is likely to let the powerholder know if the desired behavior has gone unrewarded. The son who is promised $5.00 for cleaning the garage is likely to notify his father when the job is done; the son who is threatened with punishment may still try to escape the responsibility, or do the task with minimal effort, but certainly not tell his father.

Surveillance itself is likely to be damaging to the relationship between the parties (Strickland, 1958). The more a powerholder must monitor a target to insure compliance, the more likely the powerholder will attribute good task performance to the threat of coercion *and* the very presence of the surveillance itself, rather than to the target's actions. Moreover, the powerholder would then assume that continued surveillance would be required to get the target to perform again in the future. The use of coercive power and the use of surveillance can, therefore, create a rather vicious set of self-fulfilling prophecies that justify their continued use, while at the same time greatly endangering the relationship between the parties.

As we review these points, it seems clear that reward power is far more likely to produce desired consequences, with less surveillance, than coercive power. Yet, efforts at coercive power are a common occurrence in negotiation. When simple persuasion fails, when tempers flare, when self-esteem is threatened, or when the vision of material gain overshadows the understanding of the potential cost of its use, the escalation of threats, hostile language, and efforts at coercion are likely to increase. It is at these times that the emotional expression of anger, or feelings of frustration and impotence may overwhelm the rational understanding of the effectiveness of reward strategies.

Legitimate Power: *Boren's Laws, or When in Doubt, Mumble. When in Trouble, Delegate. When in Charge, Ponder.*

We previously examined the use of role behavior as a form of coercive power. In that instance, the powerholder (the role occupant) was doing something to force a change in the target person's behavior. When the target person complied, it was not because the target person was directly following the powerholder's orders, but rather that he/she was responding to the threatened use of coercive action by the powerholder.

There are times, however, when people respond to directions from another, even directions they do not like, because they feel it is proper (legitimate) for the other to tell them and proper (obligatory) for them to obey, even though they do not like what they are being directed to do. This type of power is legitimate power.

Legitimate power comes about in several ways. In most societies, elderly people are listened to and obeyed by the young. People listen to those who occupy high offices and certain occupations, like the clergy. They do what these people say because, "It is proper to do so." At times, these same powerholders also have some reward and coercive power, but these forms of power are infrequently utilized. Clergy, college presidents, and many others have precious little they can actually give as rewards or use as coercive punishments; yet they have considerable legitimate power. Sometimes people have great authority, not because of the position they occupy but because of the personal relationship they have with others, or their past reputations. Ghandi and Martin Luther King were people who had great personal authority, whom others would obey because of who they were.

It can be shown quite convincingly, that legitimate power is at the foundation of most of our social structure. When individuals and groups seek to organize themselves into any form of a social system—a family, a combat unit, a union, a work group, a sports team, a school, etc.—they will almost immediately form a social system. A "leader" will be elected or appointed; informal rules will evolve on how decisions will be made, work divided, responsibilities allocated, and conflicts managed. Without this social ordering, chaos would prevail. Group coordination would take forever. All of us have been part of a group in which the absence of effective leadership led to long and tedious meetings, destructive conflict of personalities, and great feelings of frustration. Even in informal groups which have no formal roles defined, members may press for this type of definition in order to facilitate group functioning.

The need for social ordering and social structure, then, creates the basis for legitimate power. People are willing to vest rights, responsibilities and power in an office, title, or role. By their very acceptance of the same social system that gives the powerholder his power base, they are *obligated* to obey his directives and follow his influence.

There are several ways to acquire legitimate power. First, it may be acquired by birth; Elizabeth as Queen of England has little actual power in the form of rewards, coercion, or legal power but a great deal of legitimate power. Second, it may be acquired by election; the President of the United States has substantial legal and some reward and coercive power and very substantial legitimate power. Legitimate power can also be created from other sources of power, such as reward, coercive, or expert. Military officers have known this for a long time. All military establishments drill and march their personnel. At one time, when armies had to move large numbers of people with speed and precision during combat, this practice had an obvious, useful place. From ancient Greece to the early 1800s, wars were fought by moving densely packed groups of soldiers around a battlefield. This military strategy began to change with the advent of cannons, and disappeared when machine guns were introduced; but we still find that all armies spend vast amounts of time in close-order drill. There are several reasons for this: it is easy to give instructions, closely monitor large numbers of people, and quickly punish or reward performance. It gets large numbers of people used to accepting, without question, orders from a specific person or class of persons. After a while, the need to use rewards and punishments drops off; and it seems natural, "legitimate," to accept orders from an officer without asking why or inquiring about the consequences.

Another way the ability to control rewards, punishments and resources can be converted into legitimate power is by creating obligations. In his studies of the use of power in organizations, Kotter (1979) emphasizes that a manager must recognize, create, and cultivate dependence among those around him—subordinates, peers, and even superiors—and to convert these dependencies into obligations.

Obligations may be created in several ways. The legitimate power conveyed by a title itself may create obligations—the target accepts the legitimacy of the office of the President and believes that he "owes" the President a certain amount of loyalty and compliance. Doing favors for people, recognizing and praising them for their accomplishments, helping people out, paying them individual attention when the job demands do not "require" it or people do not "expect" it, dispensing "extra" funds for special projects in a tight budget year are but a few examples of the way that resources can be controlled and measured to help people do their jobs better and to generate liking for the powerholder. In his study of power use in organizations, Kotter reports the following interview.

> Most of the people here would walk over hot coals on their bare feet if my boss asked them to. He has an incredible capacity to do little things that mean a lot to people. Today, for example, in his junk mail he came across an advertisement for something that one of my subordinates had in passing once mentioned that he was shopping for. So my boss routed it to him. That probably took 15 seconds of his time, and yet my subordinate really appreci-ated it. To give you another example, two weeks ago, he somehow learned that the purchasing manager's mother had died. On his way home that night, he stopped off at the funeral parlor. Our purchasing manager was, of course, there at the time. I bet he'll remember that brief visit for quite a while (p. 130).

Similarly, Pfeffer and Salancik (1974) stress that one of the major sources of power in organizations is the ability to control and dispense desired re-sources. The powerholder's ability to accumulate "slack resources" and to allocate these resources in exchange for reciprocal favors, obedience or compliance, is central to cultivating a power base.

Negotiation, as we have shown earlier in Chapter 9, occurs in a social structure. That structure may be simply two people, it may be two teams, or it may be individuals, teams, constituencies and even bystanders. In a negotia-tion, there are obligations to respond in an appropriate way to the other party. Some negotiators may attempt to deny the other party some of their legitimate power by denying them an opportunity to talk, by refusing to make reciprocal offers while insisting the other party continue to make conces-sions, by ignoring prior agreements on how to proceed, etc. In such situations a negotiator finds it necessary to establish some minimal legitimate author-ity before proceeding, and may in fact be advised to refuse to proceed until the other party shows by his or her behavior that that authority is in place.

Once a small, secure base of legitimate authority is established, a negoti-ator can, like a drill sergeant, extend it. As noted earlier, all negotiators have the ability to reward and punish the other negotiator; they can also do favors for the other negotiator, thereby creating positive feelings and obligations. All of these tactics can be used to extend legitimate authority.

Informational Power: *Katz's Law or Men and Nations Will Act Rationally When All Other Possibilities Have Been Exhausted.*

Within the context of negotiation, informational power is perhaps the most common form of power in use. Informational power refers to the persuasive, influential nature of the information itself.

Informational power refers to the accumulation and presentation of information that will change the other's point of view or position on an issue. Informational power will vary according to any or all of the following:

1. The amount of information accumulated.

2. The number of different sources used as references.

3. The prima face persuasiveness of the information itself.

It will also vary according to the way that information is presented: which parts of the information are highlighted; the order in which they are presented; whether charts, graphs or other visual aids are employed; how numerical data such as statistics are treated and presented, etc. Finally, informational power will vary according to the credibility and trustworthiness of the source of information, and the variety of persuasive techniques used by the presenter in communicating.

Within the context of negotiation, informational power is at the heart of the process. In even the simplest negotiation, the parties take a position, and then present facts, arguments, viewpoints, and data to support that position. I want to sell a used bicycle for $100; you say it is only worth $50. I proceed to tell you how much I paid for it, point out what good condition it is in, what the attractive features are, and why it is worth $100. You point out the fact that it is 5 years old, emphasize the paint chips and rust spots, comment that the tires are worn and really should be replaced. You also tell me that you can't afford to spend $100. After 20 minutes of discussion about the bicycle, we have exchanged extensive information about the original cost and age of the bicycle, its depreciation and current condition, the benefits and drawbacks of this particular style and model, your financial situation and my need to raise cash, and settled on a price of $80.

The exchange of information in negotiation is also at the heart of the concession-making process. Through the information presented by each side, a "common definition" of the situation emerges. We are likely to derive a realistic picture of the current condition of the bicycle, the ability of the buyer to pay, etc. This information need *not* be 100 percent true—bluffs, (overstatements, exaggerations), omissions and distortions of information occur all the time. I may tell you I paid $200 for the bicycle, when I only paid $150; I may not tell you that the rear brake falls apart easily and really needs to be replaced. You may not tell me that you can pay $100, but simply don't want to spend that much. Nevertheless, the information exchanged, and the "common definition" of the situation that emerges, serve as a rationale for each side to modify their positions and eventually, to accept a settlement. Both of us arrive at a price we feel satisfied with; those feelings of satisfaction are derived in part from the price itself, and in part because the price is "justified" to us in terms of our revised view of the bicycle and of the other party in the negotiation. Thus, information exchange in negotiation serves as the primary medium for justifying our own and the other's position, and eventually for making concessions.

Communication and information are used in a number of different ways in negotiation. When used to create power over another, information is manipulated to control the options open to the other party. We may direct and manipulate the other's choice behavior by sending them positive information about an option we want them to choose, or by concealing information about an option we don't want them to choose. Since we have already discussed these processes in the chapters on Planning, Communication, and Persuasion, we shall not give informational power further attention in this chapter.

Expert Power: *Weinburg's Corollary or An Expert Is a Person Who Avoids the Small Errors While Sweeping on to the Grand Fallacy.*

Expert power is a special form of informational power. Informational power can be used by anyone who has studied and prepared his position for negotiation. Expert power is accorded to those who are seen as having mastered and organized a great wealth of information.

There are a number of ways of establishing oneself as an expert. One is to show some credentials: a university degree, a license, holding a position that comes from having expert qualifications, etc. Hence, physicians hang degrees and license certificates on their walls, accountants use the letters CPA after their name, health inspectors refer to their title, etc. All of these are ways people can show that an outside party has examined their qualifications and found them to be qualified experts.

A second method is to demonstrate expert knowledge by citing facts and figures, referring to important, but not commonly known features and facts, discussing a point from several perspectives. The danger in doing this is that a person can seem to be pontificating, or a "name dropper" and thereby reduce some of the desired effect. Sometimes the desired effect can be achieved by introducing a significant piece of information at an appropriate time, or even by asking a question that could only be asked if one knew a lot about the subject at hand.

A third method is by having evidence that other people have found a person to be an expert. We commonly provide references for previous work or experience. Some individuals weave into their discussions references to significant work they have performed or the names of others with whom they have worked to indicate the caliber of things they have done.

Still another method is to have publications that can be cited. An article or a book on a topic suggests expert knowledge. Being referred to or quoted in an article or interview again suggests expert status.

All these are methods a negotiator can use to establish him or herself as an expert in the eyes of the other party. If credentials can be hung on the wall, why not have the negotiation in your office? If you have had a recent article published or have been quoted by someone else, why not send a copy to the other party? The action may be seen as a little gauche, but the point is established. There are many points during negotiation when references can be made or facts cited to convey the image of expert knowledge. The intent of all of this is to establish that the negotiator is an expert, and is better able than others to determine which options are possible and which are not. In a real estate negotiation, if the seller is able to establish that he or she is an expert in the zoning laws of a particular area, he or she can more readily show the other party that some options are open (or closed as the case may be) to make their position more acceptable. In addition to mentioning the zoning law, the negotiator could reinforce his position by citing the particular section or specific ruling in the law that validates his point, or by showing a copy of the zoning law itself.

Expert power, and also legitimate power, can be seriously undermined when a person is seen as using his power for personal gain (Hovland and Weiss, 1951). For example, surgeons have considerable expert power, but it can be sharply eroded if it appears that operations are proposed more to provide income for the surgeon than to cure the patient. Obviously, the expert who is also negotiating is hardly going to be seen as disinterested and therefore needs to take extra steps to counter the suspicions that will understandably arise.

Expert power is used for more than convincing the other party of the soundness of one's statements in negotiation. People are less likely to argue with a perceived expert in the area of his expertise. To really take on the challenge, the nonexpert would probably have to consult with another expert, which is costly, time consuming, and somewhat risky. Hence, when facing an expert in their area of expertise, the nonexpert often takes a less expansive, less aggressive posture and hence gives the expert a considerable advantage.

Referent Power: *Peter's Placebo or An Ounce of Image Is Worth a Pound of Performance.*

Referent power is derived from the personal qualities of the powerholder and the personal relationship created with the target. It is based on the target's attraction to the powerholder—liking, perceived similarity, admiration, desire to be close to or friendly with the agent. This attraction may be based on physical attractiveness, dress, mannerisms or lifestyle; but the qualities of attractiveness are more likely to include friendliness, gregariousness and congeniality, honesty and candor, integrity, etc. It is difficult to specify all of the "qualities" of referent power because the base of referent power is frequently "in the eyes of the beholder"—that is, determined by what the target finds attractive, rather than what the powerholder *thinks* is attractive. The more recipients are attracted to a powerholder because of his attractive qualities—physical or personal—the broader will be the base of referent power. Handsome men and beautiful women generally don't have much trouble making friends and influencing people. Truly "charismatic" people—those who have some unique blend of physical characteristics, speech, mannerisms and self-confidence—are able to influence very large groups of people by their action.

The effectiveness of referent power can be derived from two sources. First, to the degree that the powerholder has qualities which others desire or value, i.e., poise, confidence, wealth, or other forms of power—*identification* may occur. The target person seeks to imitate or "be like" the powerholder, occasionally without the powerholder's knowledge that he is being imitated. A child will wear his father's hat or coat, or sit in his chair, or mimic his mannerisms, to "be like Dad." Teenagers will spend lots of time imitating their "idols"—basketball players, rock singers, television personalities. Adults will follow the latest "trends" and "fads" in clothing, food and lifestyle—Gucci shoes, Polo shirts, Scarsdale diets, Prince tennis rackets and Perrier cocktails. Of course, imitation and identification can be much more subtle. The more the target "admires" or "identifies with" an individual, the more referent influence the powerholder has, and the more control the powerholder can exert because of his identification.

Referent power through identification is an uncertain tool in negotiation. As mentioned earlier, identification is in the eye of the beholder. The likelihood that a negotiator will be able to know what the other party will identify with and then be able to utilize that information is problematic. If identification does not occur, then other routes to power are available.

Referent power is also obtained from establishing and maintaining a relationship with the target person. Since there are strong psychological relationships between the perceived similarity, liking and attraction for another person, a powerholder may work to establish referent power by building a relationship. Relationships can be started by finding out what things the parties have in common—attending the same college, knowing the same friends, sharing common interests in sports or hobbies, identifying common attitudes and values. The parties may also have the same jobs, work for the same organizations, enjoy the same type of vacations, like the same television programs, or have experienced the same illnesses and tragedies. All of these events create the basis for gaining a deeper knowledge of the other, increasing the self disclosure for one's own personal feelings and thoughts, and enhancing the trust between the parties. This process may be greatly speeded up when the relationship develops under conditions of stress or external threat. We may ride the same elevator or bus daily with people whom we recognize, but never get to know them until the elevator or bus stalls one day and we are stranded. Two top managers in the same company may think they have little in common, and talk to one another infrequently, until they are required to travel together on company business to a foreign country. Negotiation brings people together in a stressful situation, too, and while the competitive nature of the situation can impede the exchange of personal information, the nature of their interdependence and shared fate may also provide a basis for information exchange. Hence, skilled negotiators often make reference to this interdependence and common fate in order to start a more cooperative exchange, thus getting the opposing negotiator to the point where he is more likely to say "yes" and less likely to say "no."

Whether through identification and imitation or through the cultivation of commonality and friendships, referent power serves to develop a relationship between the powerholder and the target. These relationships usually are predicated on expectations of trust, openness, honesty and cooperation, and that expectation is the motivating force for preserving the relationship. The target is attracted to the powerholder because of the referent power, and trusts that the powerholder will not "abuse" the power and endanger the relationship. As we have emphasized before, the establishment and maintenance of the referent power bases and the relationship between the parties is essential to long-term negotiating arrangements. Neither side can afford to abuse the trust and openness that may be developed between parties at the expense of short-run gain, unless one is prepared to terminate the relationship or live with the consequences of this betrayal.

Indirect Power or *Many People Know My Face, but Not My Name, and That's Why I Carry the American Express Card.*

The previous discussion has focused on *direct* ways a powerholder can influence a target. All forms of power can also be used indirectly. In the use of indirect power, power must be used by the powerholder to influence the intermediary, and by the intermediary to influence the target. Any form of power may be used in both steps of the process. In the examples below, we will assume that the powerholder always "persuades" the intermediary, while the intermediary uses various forms of power to influence the target.

Reward power may be exercised by the intermediary on the target. A management negotiator complains to the press about the tough, inflexible position assumed by the union negotiator, knowing the union membership will be pleased by their representatives' stance, and therefore support and trust this representative.

Coercive power may be exercised by the intermediary on the target. The same management negotiator could remark to the press that the union representative was "cooperative, understanding and extremely flexible." The union membership is likely to interpret this as a "sell-out" by their representative, and therefore pressure him to "get tough or get fired."

Informational power is used when intermediaries provide persuasive facts and information to a target person. Two men are negotiating over the cost of an item. The target person does not believe some of the cost projections that the powerholder has presented. The powerholder tells the target to talk to the cost analyst who prepared the data and who will be able to supply complete records and documentation on the way that the cost projections were determined.

Expert power may be used indirectly when a key expert person or source is selected as the intermediary. In attempting to persuade the target of the credibility of certain information, the powerholder is likely to cite an authoritative source or bring in an expert to verify information and directly persuade the target. A teacher's union is attempting to establish that its salaries are the lowest in the country. To do so, the union might invite an economist from the State University or an expert from the State Department of Education to present "expert testimony" on its claim.

Legitimate power is used indirectly when the powerholder seeks out someone with "authority" to persuade the target. Two managers negotiating difficulties in the working relationship between their department may call on a superior to establish "ground rules" or clarify policies for making decisions. Needless to say, the negotiator who seeks out this "legitimate authority" usually believes that the authority's statements and rulings will be in his favor.

Finally, *referent power* is used indirectly when the powerholder enlists an intermediary who is well liked, respected or trusted by the target person. Product endorsement by celebrities or famous people in advertising is a well-known use of indirect referent power.

Associative Power: *Rule of the Great or When Somebody You Greatly Admire and Respect Appears To Be Thinking Deep Thoughts, They Probably Are Thinking about Lunch.*

Finally, indirect power may be used "in reverse"—that is, the powerholder's *own* power may be enhanced because of his publicized relationship with others who are perceived as powerful. Associative power occurs when a powerholder seeks to enhance his power by "who he knows"—those who are respected, admired or well-known. The clearest example of associative power is "name dropping," a technique used by many to enhance their esteem in their own eyes and the eyes of the target. Example:

> We (the authors) were really pleased when Henry Kissinger returned the manuscript of this book and said it was the best thing on negotiating he had ever read.

> We (the authors) could never have published this book had it not been for the support and financial assistance that we received from the Rockefeller family every step of the way.

> We had a really nice vacation in Washington this year. One especially memorable part was the night that the President had us over for dinner.

Associative power can also be communicated nonverbally. Offices filled with pictures of the powerholder's meeting with influential politicians or celebrities, or gifts from famous people, communicate that the powerholder "knows the right people" or associates with those who are highly influential; therefore, he has "power."

Associative power, like other forms of indirect power, depends upon a two step process: the powerholder's relations with the intermediary need to be established and documented, and the intermediary needs to be seen by the target person as "powerful." Associative power is more likely to work if used sparingly and carefully, and much less likely to have impact if it is overused or abused.

SUMMARY

While a great deal has been written on power and its use, these analyses have not shed a great deal of light and understanding on helping negotiators to use power effectively. In order to make our knowledge of power more useful in negotiations, we have tried to show that power can be defined in a variety of ways, and that any working definition of power must take into consideration several key criteria:

1. the *advantages* and *disadvantages* of using any particular form of power;
2. the impact that any form of power use is likely to have on the target's *overt behavior* and/or *private attitudes*;
3. the degree to which the form of power requires *surveillance* over the target in order to insure compliance;
4. the impact of power use on the *quality of relationship* with the target.

With these criteria in mind, we then evaluated the use of six major forms of power: informational power, reward and coercive power, legitimate power, referent power and expert power. It was shown how each of these forms of power could be developed and implemented in negotiation. In addition, it was shown how these various forms of power could be exercised indirectly, (that is, through third parties) in order to have comparable influence.

Negotiators must be careful in deciding what forms of power they would like to exert, and what the consequences of that power use might be on their ability to change the opponent's attitudes or behavior, and on the long-run relationship between the parties. While short-run tactics may lead a negotiator to accomplish his/her immediate goal, long-term relationships and real attitude change have often been sacrificed as a consequence. Negotiators must use power with care and caution in order to ensure that their goals are obtained and that long-term relationships are preserved for future interactions. While power use may be effective in the short-run, it may also ruin any long-run relationship. It is a strong but often problematic tool.

11

The Role of a Negotiator's Personality

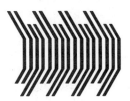

One of the controversial areas of research in the negotiation field centers around the nature of a bargainer's individual personality and its impact on negotiation outcomes. The first part of the chapter discusses the research taking place on this subject. Later parts of the chapter focus on specific personality dimensions that define individual differences in negotiating behavior and explore how such differences impinge on negotiation strategies and outcomes.

EARLY RESEARCH EFFORTS

Research efforts to define the impact of background, demographic and personality factors in negotiations began in the late 1950s. Jeffrey Rubin and Bert Brown, in their book *The Social Psychology of Bargaining and Negotiation* (1975), reviewed 200 empirical studies of background, demographic, and personality factors that might contribute to differences in bargaining outcomes. Later studies examined the impact of differences in age, sex, race, cultural and national heritage, and socioeconomic status on negotiation outcomes. Studies concerned with the effect of personality variables have also examined risk-taking propensity, perceived locus of control, level of cognitive complexity or tolerance for ambiguity, level of self-concept, nature and strength of social motives (such as needs for achievement, power and/or affiliation), attitudes (interpersonal trust, cooperativeness, authoritarianism, etc.), and normal or abnormal personality structure, to name some of the more prominent variables.

The research findings are widely disparate, inconclusive, and sometimes directly contradictory. For example, Rubin and Brown review over 100 studies on sex differences and their impact on bargaining behavior. Of the 100 studies, approximately 30 studies report no difference between men and women; 20 studies report that males bargain more cooperatively than females; and a large number of others reported that females bargain more cooperatively than males. Similar contradictory results can be noted for many of the other personality variables mentioned previously. Explaining and coping with the reasons for these patterns of contradictory and/or nonsignificant findings has become a major research problem in this field. At least four different explanations have been proposed to account for the current state of research:

1. Differences in negotiation style and approach are too "subtle" and elusive to be picked up and confirmed with current research methodologies and scenarios. In effect, our measuring instruments are too primitive to really detect the differences that probably exist.

2. A great deal of the inconclusive and contradictory findings are due to failures in research methodologies. The variables examined, and the methods by which they were examined, consistently differed from one study to the next. Studies were designed and conducted in a disorganized and unsystematic manner. As a result, contradictory findings can be traced to the use of different research designs, methods, and experimental bargaining problems.

3. The inconclusive findings could reveal a great deal if they were properly reconceptualized. In effect, these critics argue that we have been defining the key personality factors in the wrong way.

4. Finally, a negotiator's background and personality *do* affect his/her approach to negotiation (and the outcomes obtained), but new and different variables must be uncovered to discover the true relationship. These "new" variables are then proposed, and occasionally research data is reported.

These four perspectives are not necessarily mutually exclusive, nor contradictory. Each opens a different line of inquiry that throws light on a complex subject. We'll examine each of the four.

Differences in Negotiation Style and Approach.   The first perspective is that the impact of personal differences is too subtle and elusive to be revealed by contemporary research strategies and methodologies. Hamner (1980), in his review of the impact of individual differences on bargaining outcomes, noted that research has failed to find significant relationships between personality variables and negotiation outcomes (e.g., Terhune, 1968, 1970; Druckman, 1971; Hermann and Kogan, 1977). He suggests several reasons for this repeated failure.

First, the impact of "structural" variables in negotiation may override or "swamp" the effects of personality variables. While individual differences may predispose bargainers to particular behavior in the early rounds of negotiation, key "structure" factors such as the nature of the bargaining problem, the relative power between negotiators, pressures from constituencies, or simply the behavior of the other negotiator may quickly override the effect of whatever individual differences may exist. Moreover, these same "structural" variables may inhibit opportunities for individual differences to emerge and actually have an impact. For example, much of the early research on demographic and personality differences employed a simple, two-choice conflict game called Prisoner's Dilemma (refer to Chapter 2 for explanation of this game). Prisoner's Dilemma, and other similar games, are traditionally "played" by experimental subjects who cannot see one another, do not talk to one another, and whose "negotiating" consists of making simple choices between more cooperative and more competitive decision options. Limited and constrained interaction of this form is hardly comparable to the complex verbal and nonverbal messages and persuasion efforts that occur in face to face negotiation. Hence, the scenarios and settings must be rich enough to allow the impact of personality variables to emerge, but not so dominated by major structural relationships that when personality factors do emerge, they are quickly obscured. Similarly, personality factors should not be obscured by specific interaction patterns that develop between negotiators.

Second, personality variables may also *interact* with structural variables in complex and (perhaps) unpredictable ways. Not only do the structural variables—win-win vs. win-lose, relative power, time pressure, accountability—dominate the prediction of the likely outcomes, but if personality does have an impact, its impact is *in combination* with structural elements. For example, Christie and Geis (1970), in their research on a personality variable called Machiavellianism, specifically conclude that individuals who measure high on Machiavellianism scales also require specific types of situations to be effective. If these specific situational factors are not present, or if the situation does not allow a Machiavellian individual to behave in the way that he would prefer, the impact is quickly nullified. This specific line of research will be reviewed in more detail later in this chapter.

Finally, the impact of a particular personality predisposition may go undiscovered because previous research efforts have been limited to a unique and/or homogeneous population of research subjects who did not possess that predisposition. Most experimental negotiating studies have been conducted on "volunteer" college populations, usually freshmen and sophomores enrolled in psychology courses. This particular population may be so homogeneous with respect to age, demographic background, and other personality characteristics that "true" differences in negotiation style may not be readily noted. One possible research strategy for avoiding this problem while studying bargaining behavior would be to concentrate only on those who actually negotiate full-time in their occupation.

"Definitive" Tests of the Relationship between Personality Predispositons and Negotiation Outcomes. In an effort to remedy the deficiencies of earlier research in this field, several groups of researchers have attempted more "definitive" and better-controlled experimental studies. For example, Hermann and Kogan (1977), building on earlier research, proposed eight personality factors that should differentially affect negotiation outcomes: level of manifest anxiety, authoritarianism, cognitive complexity, tendency to be conciliatory, dogmatism, propensity toward risk taking, level of self-esteem, and predisposition toward suspiciousness. Each of the factors was predicted to affect (1) a bargainer's predispositions toward the negotiating situation, affecting the individual's own behavioral intentions and expectations of the other negotiator's behavior; (2) actual behavior of the negotiator in negotiations, regardless of the conduct of his opponent, and (3) actual behavior of the negotiator in negotiations, *given* that the opponent's personality dispositions were similar to, or the opposite of the negotiator's. After administering a battery of personality instruments to 108 Princeton undergraduates, pairs of these students were then asked to play a number of rounds of a Prisoner's Dilemma game.

While the results are complex due to the number of variables studied and their impact on the negotiator's predispositions and actual behavior, they can be summarized as follows:

1. Only four of the eight personality variables—level of anxiety, level of cognitive complexity, tendency to be concilliatory and level of self-esteem—predicted a student's predisposed strategy toward his opponent, and only two of the four (cognitive complexity and self-esteem) predicted at a statistically significant level.

2. Only two of the eight personality variables—authoritarianism and self-esteem—differentiated the ways that students described their own actual strategy in the game.

3. Only three out of 32 analyses between personality variables and actual game-playing strategy reached acceptable levels of statistical significance.

4. Certain personality variables, such as cognitive complexity, conciliatory tendency, dogmatism, risk-avoidance and suspiciousness, did emerge as important when bargainers were matched with pairmates who scored similarly on the particular variable. Hence, the pairing of negotiators with similar styles allowed for the interactive effect of personality and behavior to emerge.

Thus, while selected results did emerge, they reveal no consistent pattern with regard to the clear impact of any one personality element across all three outcome measures. Many of the predicted results were nonsignificant or inconclusive. Moreover, the concerns raised by Hamner can be clearly applied to this research. First, we do not know the demographic characteristics of Princeton undergraduates, nor whether this sample of students represents a "reasonable approximation of the general population." Second, the constrained choices of the Prisoner's Dilemma game may well minimize the subtlety and strength that these variables could have on more complex negotiating behavior. Finally, the authors themselves note that once the gaming interaction has begun, personality elements were considerably less successful at predicting negotiating behavior. This supports the assertion that in the long run, structural and interactive factors may be likely to dominate initial personality differences.

Efforts to Reconceptualize the Inconclusive Nature of Previous Findings. The third way that efforts have been made to deal with much of the inconclusive nature of personality variables is to propose that the results can be explained more productively by different, "underlying" variables that have not yet been identified. Probably the most significant effort in this regard is by Rubin and Brown(1975). In an effort to explain and organize the diverse and often contradictory findings that were revealed by their review, Rubin and Brown propose a single dimension of personal style—Interpersonal Orientation (IO)—to explain the results.

Individuals may be classified as either high or low in their interpersonal orientation. A high-IO is "responsive to the interpersonal aspects of his relationship with the other. He is both interested in, and reactive to, variations in the other's behavior" (Rubin and Brown, p. 158). High IOs determine their own behavior in a conflict setting by "tuning in" to the other's behavior—the other's cooperativeness or competitiveness, relative amount of power and use of power, and adherence to certain bargaining norms such as equity, exchange, and reciprocity.

High IOs use this information in one of two ways, depending upon whether they are cooperatively or competitively disposed. A Cooperative high IO attends to other's behavior for the purpose of maximizing cooperation. He is likely to search for behavioral cues that the other can be trusted; he will act trustworthily himself, and maximize the exchange and flow of information to enhance a cooperative, mutually satisfactory outcome. Faced with an opponent who is competitive or exploitative, however, a Cooperative high IO will change his strategy in order to defend himself against exploitation, and retaliate against the other for treating him in an exploitative, hostile, perhaps even "unethical" manner.

In contrast, a Competitive high IO attends to the behavior of the other person for the purpose of using this information to gain strategic advantage. Competitive high IOs are suspicious of others' motives and intentions (expecting to be exploited), and untrustworthy themselves (either to gain advantage or as a "defense" against the expected exploitation). Information flow is either unilateral (to gain information about the other without divulging one's own intentions, or minimized in order to beat the other). If the other actually behaves cooperatively, his behavior is discounted ("he is a fool" or "he's just trying to set me up so that he can take advantage of me"). If the other behaves competitively, the Competitive high IO will see the other as similar ("we are both cut-throat competitors"), but will behave competitively in order to defend himself against the other and keep him from gaining advantage.

In contrast to the high IO, a low IO is characterized by "a nonresponsiveness to the interpersonal aspects of his relationship with the other. His interest is neither in cooperating nor competing with the other, but rather in maximizing his own gain—pretty much regardless of how the other fares." (Rubin and Brown, 1975, p. 159). Low IOs determine their behavior in conflict situations on the basis of their own goals and preferred outcomes, and an evaluation of the situation they are in. They are likely to attribute the other's behavior to variations in these same factors, and therefore to attend more to the nature of the situation and their own goals rather than to variations in the other's behavior. In short, in order to achieve his goals and preferred outcomes, a low IO is less concerned with the behavior of the other—either cooperative or competitive—than with the situational variations and complexities that might yield this outcome.

The major value of the IO construct, and the IO continuum, is that it provides a single uniform dimension for organizing and explaining many of the discrepant, conflicting findings of earlier research. Rubin and Brown (1975) demonstrated that much of the conflicting research could be successfully explained if IO were considered to be the major element of differentiation between groups. (See Table 11–1.)

More recently, Swap and Rubin (1983) have constructed a self-report measure of IO, and conducted two experiments to test the utility of the IO construct. The first experiment was designed to test for the effect of sex differences vs. differences in IO on one person's liking for another—a component of negotiation we examined in Chapter 8. Earlier research had previously revealed contradictory findings. The results of the Swap and Rubin study indicated clearly that IO was a better predictor of liking for another person than were differences in sex.

A second experiment was conducted to test for the effect of sex vs. IO on a preference for equity vs. equality in the distribution of outcomes. It has frequently been proposed that men demonstrate a greater preference for *equity* in outcomes (each party in the relationship gets what he earns or deserves), while women demonstrate a greater preference for *equality* in distribution (each party gets the same amount). In the Swap and Rubin experiment, IO and sex differences were systematically controlled in a re-

---

TABLE 11–1
Summary of Individual Differences in Background and Personality That Appear to Lie at Opposite Ends of the "Sensitivity to the Opponent" Continuum

High Sensitivity to Opponent	*Low Sensitivity to Opponent*
Older children and college students	Young children
Blacks	Whites
Females	Males
Low risk-takers	High risk-takers
Externals	Internals
Abstract thinkers	Concrete thinkers
Persons high in need for affiliation and power	Persons low in need for achievement
Cooperators	Competitors
Persons low in authoritarianism	Persons high in authoritarianism
Persons high in internationalism	Persons low in internationalism
Persons high in machiavellianism	Persons low in machiavellianism
Normal personalities (e.g., nonparanoids)	Abnormal personalities (e.g., paranoids)

---

source-distribution task. The results indicate that males and low IOs tended to allocate rewards according to equity standards, while females and high IOs seemed more concerned with equality of outcomes.

As a measure of personal style, IO seems to offer more promise than other previously mentioned dimensions as a prediction of predispositions toward negotiation.

Recent Research on Personality Differences and Their Relationship to Negotiating Behavior.   Finally, much of the earlier research on personality effects can also be faulted for selecting personality variables more on the basis of convenience than on a strongly reasoned relationship between the variable and the negotiation process. For example, many of the earlier personality variables which were chosen for study seem to have been selected because well-established scales had already been developed for measuring the variable, rather than because of a clearly logical presumed difference in negotiating approach. While this rationale may make sense for research reasons—having a basis for confidence in the reliability and validity of measurement—the dimensions themselves may make less difference in negotiation settings than other, more meaningful personality distinctions. In this final section, several approaches will be reviewed that have more promise as predictors of personal differences in approach to negotiation.

CONFLICT MANAGEMENT STYLE

Dealing with conflict is a central part of the negotiating process. In Chapter 5, we identified five modes of behavior which are commonly used to deal with conflict: competing, collaborating, avoiding, and accommodating. We also examined the effect on outcomes that would be created by choosing one style over another; what we did not examine were the *reasons* that one style is commonly chosen over another. A negotiator may make this choice based on rational criteria, i.e., selecting that style which is assumed to most likely lead to the desired outcomes. However, everyday experience (and systematic research) indicates that the choice may also be an expression of a negotiator's personality. It is that personality predisposition that we shall discuss here.

Underlying the four conflict management styles are two levels of concern. One is the degree of concern a conflicting party shows for his own outcomes, and the second is the degree of concern shown for the other's outcomes. Thomas (1976) has proposed that two personality dimensions best represent these two levels of concern: the degree of *assertiveness* that a conflicting party maintains for his own preferred solutions or outcomes, and the degree of *cooperativeness* a party shows toward working with the other party to achieve goals for both of them. Analogous to the approaches we described in Chapter 5, Thomas' research identified five major conflict management styles (see Figure 11-1):

- A *competing* style, high on assertiveness and low on cooperativeness;
- An *accommodating* style, low on assertiveness and high on cooperativeness;
- An *avoiding* style, low on both assertiveness and cooperativeness;
- A *collaborative* style, high on both assertiveness and cooperativeness;
- A *compromising* style, moderate on both assertiveness and cooperativeness.

Research by Thomas and his colleagues (Thomas, 1976, 1977; Killman and Thomas, 1977) has supported the premise that individual conflict man-

FIGURE 11–1
Killman–Thomas Conflict Orientations

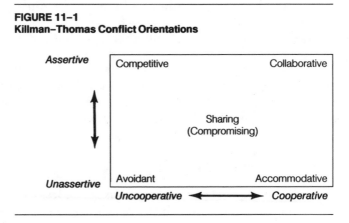

agement styles vary according to two factors: the nature of the situation (i.e., that negotiators make "rational" choices about which strategy to use), and individual "biases" to use certain styles regardless of the situation. In addition, individual differences in conflict management style have been correlated with other measures of personality. Using the Myers-Briggs measure of personality styles, Thomas (1976) reports a significant relationship between preference for: (1) "integrative styles" (a win-win perspective on conflict) and extraversion; (2) "distributive styles" a (win-lose perspective on conflict) and introversion ; and (3) styles of conflict management and "thinking" vs. "feeling" individuals. A relationship between high scores on Machiavellianism (Christie and Geis, 1970) and a preference for a compromising style is also reported. Thomas (1976) suggests that individuals high in a competitive style would be lower in risk taking, more internally controlled, higher on needs for power and control, and lower on needs for affiliation. Similarly, individuals strong in collaboration would be more likely to be task oriented, creative, and capable of dealing with complexity. Each of these relationships is derived through inference, however, and not a result of direct research with the Killman-Thomas instrument. Similar inferences are drawn between individuals with particular conflict orientations and their actual behavior in conflict situations. If the stakes for winning are high, and outcomes are derived through individual effort, then individuals with strong competing modes should dominate the situation; if outcomes are derived from joint efforts, then individuals with a strong collaborative mode should dominate. In contrast, if the stakes are low for an individual, then he should be more likely to ignore the conflict (avoiding mode), or allow the other to reap what little resources are available (accommodating mode).

The Killman-Thomas model (and subsequent research on conflict management styles), represent a simpler and far more coherent model for viewing the impact of personality variables on bargaining and conflict management behavior. The development of the measuring instruments, identification of common "styles," and the relationship of these styles to situational conflict behavior has received considerably greater verification than between variables in previously cited lines of research.

Christie and Geis—Studies of Machiavellianism

A second stream of systematic research relating a personality predisposition to conflict and bargaining behavior is by Christie, Geis, and their associates. After extensive study of the historical writings of Machiavelli and similar political philosophies, Christie and Geis (1970) developed an attitude scale based on Machiavelli's writings. Three groups of items were initially created, each with positively and negatively directed statements. The first group was concerned with interpersonal tactics, or preferred ways of dealing with people (e.g., "The best way to handle people is to tell them what they want to hear."). The second group's views of human nature represented perspectives on the human condition (e.g., "It is hard to get ahead without cutting corners here and there."). The third group represented different perspectives on morality (e.g., "All in all, it is better to be humble and honest than important and dishonest."). The scales were developed to control for measurement biases resulting from social desirability (people wanting to represent themselves in a socially acceptable way) and from respondent efforts to "fake" scale responses. Several versions were created to measure predispositions toward agreement with Machiavelli's philosophy and his espoused political strategy.

Extensive follow-up research was conducted on the relationship of Machiavellianism to other personality variables. No significant relationships were discovered between Machiavellianism and measures of intelligence or political party preference. Christie reports a trend for a strong negative correlation between scores on the Mach scale and the California F scale, (a measure of authoritarian attitudes) particularly with college-age populations. No significant relationships were reported between Machiavellianism and various forms of psychopathology. Those scoring high in Machiavellianism (high Machs) tend to have a cynical view of people. As a result, they are much more candid about feelings of hostility and mistrust, and much less likely to think or act in ways that others judge as socially desirable. Strong relationships were also obtained between Machiavellianism and a Philosophies of Human Nature scale developed by Wrightsman (1964). Individuals scoring high in Machiavellianism tend to be low in standards of conventional morality, honesty, and reliability, to behave unaltruistically, selfishly, and unsympathetically toward others, to be unwilling to change their convictions under social pressure, and to disagree that people have strong will power.

Christie and Geis conducted a number of specific research studies on the relationship between Machiavellian orientation and behavior in specific situations. Several of these experiments will be described here because of their applicability to interpersonal negotiation:

1. One experiment was designed to test differences in individual moral conduct (implication in a cheating situation, and subsequent coverup of that behavior). No differences were reported between high and low Machs in their willingness to resist becoming involved in a cheating situation. The structure of the situation created opportunities for subjects to dissuade another subject (an experimental confederate) from cheating, "expose" the confederate to the experimenter, refrain from using unethically obtained information, confess the behavior to the experimenter (either at the first opportunity, or after direct accusation by the experimenter), and lie with varying degrees of plausability about his behavior. High Machs initially tried harder to persuade the confederate not to cheat, and initially resisted using the confederate's unethically

obtained information in the experimental task. But high Machs were no different from low Machs in the infrequency or plausability of lying before being directly accused by the experimenter; however, once accused, high Machs maintained their ability to lie with far greater credibility. They confessed less, and were able to maintain more direct, convincing eye contact with the experimenter while lying than low Machs.

2. A second experiment explored the willingness of experimental subjects to engage in manipulative behavior when they were in a high power position. After experimentally creating the legitimacy for subjects to deceive and manipulate other subjects in a test-taking situation, subjects were placed in a role that allowed the manipulative behavior to occur. High Machs attempted significantly more manipulative behaviors than low Machs, both in the total number and variety of behaviors. They told bigger lies, were more verbally distracting in their behavior, and far more innovative in the manipulative techniques employed. Finally, high Machs enjoyed being in the high power role far more, and in being manipulative.

3. A third experiment reported on behavior in an experimental Con Game. A parchesi-like board game was created, and game rules were structured to allow players to enter into coalitions in order to win at the game. Coalitions could be formed or broken at will. In addition, players differed in the amount of "power" they contributed to the coalition (point values that were assigned to their position); these power differences were either public knowledge to all players, or privately known only to the player himself. The results indicate that high Machs won significantly more points than low Machs, regardless of game variation; that they also won significantly more when the amount of their power (point value contribution) was ambiguous (private). However, high Machs did not necessarily increase their winnings more than low Machs when given more formal power.

Follow-up research explored the game tactics most commonly used by high Machs. First, they were far more "proactive" in their game playing strategies, particularly in testing the limits of the rules. Second, they displayed a more "opportunistic" sense of timing with regard to making or breaking a coalition. Third, high Machs more clearly controlled the initiation of bids, and the structure of the coalition negotiations—they initiated more offers, decisively dissolved coalitions when they were unadvantageous, and were constantly sought after by others to be in coalitions. As a result, compared to low Machs, they were usually a member of the winning coalition, and seldom lost the game or were shut out of points. Fourth, as reported earlier, they thrived more when their power was ambiguous, not publicly known to others in the game; this allowed them to manipulate the structure of the negotiation. Finally, high Machs were less responsive to the personal or ethical concerns of others in the situation. They tended to treat both the game and other players with emotional detachment, rather than become personally excited or involved with other people or outcomes. When there were differences in power, low Machs were more concerned with disclosure of their power and with determining the most appropriate ethical behavior consistent with their power. Such concerns did not trouble the high Mach, who showed a depersonalized, consistent manner of play regardless of his relative power or whether his power was publicly known.

4. When a variation of the Con Game was played for real money stakes ($10), high Machs out-performed themselves. Every high Mach who played the game became a member of a winning coalition.

5. An experiment similar to Prisoner's Dilemma (see Chapter 2) was conducted with high Machs, to discover both their behavior in this situation and to investigate the effect of real money (as opposed to imaginary points) on behavior. Playing against a variety of preprogrammed strategies, high Machs did not perform significantly better, although they tended to become more exploitative over time. When real money was introduced into a game that had been previously played for points, high Machs became more *cooperative*, presumably because this behavior was more rational and would assure them a positive financial outcome. High Machs are therefore not always exploitative, but only when the outcomes in a situation warrant it.

Interpersonal Trust

As we observed in Chapter 1, one of the fundamental dilemmas in negotiation is the degree to which negotiators can trust their opponent. Negotiators must gather information and determine how much the opponent is likely to be deceptive or deceitful—misrepresenting his true position, distorting relevant facts, or introducing spurious information and positions. In addition, the trustworthiness of an opponent may change over time, depending upon whether negotiations are beginning or near the end, and depending upon whether the negotiation has proceeded cooperatively or competitively. Negotiators expect to bluff and distort more in the early stages of a negotiation, in order to "leave themselves some room" for concession making. In addition, competitive negotiations are characterized by a great deal of bluffing and distortion; all means and tactics available are used to win. In contrast, cooperative negotiations are characterized by higher levels of trust and trustworthiness to maximally share information and achieve the best possible solution (Chapter 5).

Since bluffing, distortion, and information sharing all vary as a function of the type of negotiation, the differences in individual motives and the stage of the negotiation, we might assume that individuals would rationally calculate the appropriate level of trust at any given moment. However, Rotter (1967, 1971, 1980) has proposed that interpersonal trust can also function as a personality variable. According to Rotter's research, individuals differ in their level of interpersonal trust—defined as "a generalized expectancy held by an individual that the word, promise, oral, or written statement of another individual or group can be relied upon" (1980, p.1). Unlike a broad-based belief in the "goodness of others and the benign nature of the world," Rotter argues that interpersonal trust is determined by the experiences individuals have in dealing with others. The development of interpersonal trust is largely shaped by an individual's history of interactions with others in trust-related situations. If individuals have had experiences when they have trusted others, and this trust has been "rewarded" by reciprocal trust and productive relationships, then generalized interpersonal trust should be high. In contrast, if individuals have had their trust "punished" by others through exploitation, deception, and dishonesty, then interpersonal trust is likely to be low.

Rotter and his colleagues developed a test for diagnosing the level of interpersonal trust, and used the scores to measure levels of interpersonal trustworthiness. First, individuals who act more trusting, or say that they are willing to act more trustingly, are also less likely to lie or cheat. When placed in situations where the cost of being caught for cheating was perceived as low, individuals high in interpersonal trust are clearly less likely to resort to cheating than those low in interpersonal trust. High trusters believe that others will be trustworthy, and that they need to be trustworthy themselves; hence they are more likely to impose high moral standards on themselves and behave ethically. In contrast, low trusters believe that others cannot be trusted to observe the rules, and therefore feel less pressure themselves to tell the truth. As a result, they believe that lying, cheating, and similar behaviors are necessary as a defensive reaction—to protect themselves against others.

Second, high trusters are liked more by their peers. When individuals were asked to describe an individual who scored high on the trust scale— either male or female—they tended to see the individual in a positive light. Everyone liked the high truster more. He/she is seen as being happier, more ethical, more attractive to the opposite sex, having a happier childhood, and more desirable as a close friend than the low truster. In contrast, the low truster is seen as having more common sense, perhaps a cynical view of what the world is really all about, and as having more interesting, varied and unusual experiences than the high trust individual.

Third—and surprisingly, to some people—high trusters were no more gullible than low trusters. It might be assumed that high trusters would be more likely to believe communications from other people without questioning their validity, and therefore would be more likely to be "taken in." High levels of trust would be equated with naivete—a failure to assess whether or not the other party deserved to be trusted. The studies summarized by Rotter (1980) indicate that the high trust individual is *not* more prone to gullibility than the low trust individual. As Rotter states,

> . . . it seems that high trusters can read the cues as well or as poorly as low trusters. They differ, however, in their willingness to trust the stranger when there are no clear-cut data about previous behavior. The high truster says to himself or herself, "I will trust the person until I have clear evidence that he or she can't be trusted." The low truster says, "I will not trust the person until there is clear evidence that he or she can be trusted" (p. 6).

In addition, it should be noted that both orientations are prone to self-fulfilling prophecies. An individual with high interpersonal trust is likely to approach the other person, in attitude and style, in a way that communicates trust. Should the other be searching for cues as to appropriate behavior in this situation, he/she may respond with similarly high levels of trusting behavior. The other's behavior is thus likely to reward and reinforce the initial orientation of the high trust individual, and lead to a high trust (cooperative) relationship between the parties. In contrast, a low trust individual is likely to approach the other, in attitude and style, in a way that communicates suspicion and mistrust of the other's motives and intentions. If the other is searching for cues as to the appropriate behavior, he/she may respond with low self-disclosure, dishonesty, and mistrust of the party. This behavior will thus "reward" and reinforce the initial low trust orientation, and lead to a low trust (competitive) relationship between the parties. In this way, levels of interpersonal trust can dramatically affect the cycle of trust and cooperation/mistrust and competition between negotiating parties, particularly if they have not had any significant prior interaction with one another. When there *has* been prior interaction, the parties would most likely pay more attention to the nature of the prior relationship to determine their initial orientation. In situations in which a high trust individual is matched with a low trust individual, we would again expect that each would be searching for cues as to the way that the other will behave, and to adjust their behavior as a result of what the other does. Since the high truster's behavior may provide cues for the low truster to be exploitative, while the low truster's behavior will put the high truster on his guard, we would expect a competitive, low trust relationship to evolve over time. Thus, over the long term, low trust and competition "drive out" high trust and cooperation.

Managerial/Organizational "Style"

Behavioral scientists have made numerous attempts to classify and describe different styles of leadership and management in organizations. Studies of leadership style (e.g., McGregor, 1960; Blake and Mouton, 1978;

Hersey and Blanchard, 1977) have primarily focused on the relationship between a manager and his subordinates. These studies have examined two major dimensions of leader behavior: the degree to which the manager concentrates on the task or goals to be accomplished by the group, and the quality of the relationship between manager and subordinates.

In contrast to this rather limited approach to managerial style, Maccoby (1976) undertook a more systematic and broad-based examination of executives and their broad orientations to life, career, and organizational goals. Long, unstructured interviews were conducted with a number of highly successful senior corporate executives in major leadership positions. Extensive biographical information was also collected, and each executive agreed to complete a battery of psychological tests. Based on this data, Maccoby proposed that the corporate executives could be aggregated into one of four dominant "styles": Craftsman, Company Man, Jungle Fighter, and Gamesman. The following descriptions of each style are derived from Maccoby's work, and from a scale developed by Lewicki (1982) to measure Maccoby's styles in abbreviated format.

The *Craftsman* style is predominantly interested in the process of creating something of value for himself, his organization, and the society at large. He is strongly committed to the work ethic, and to skillfully and creatively accomplishing goals. Building things and solving problems "turns him on." The challenge of work itself or the creation of a quality product is a primary source of motivation. He prefers to miss a deadline rather than to do something that is inadequate or half-baked. His sense of self-worth is largely based on the assessment of his skills, abilities, self-discipline, and self-reliance. He tends to see himself as quiet, sincere, modest, and practical. In his relationships with others, he tends to enjoy groups of people who have similar commitments to quality and doing a job well. His most successful and productive relationships are formed when working in small groups on a similar task with people who share his commitment to a quality product. He does not find himself competing against others, but rather searching for ways to use others to inspire his effort toward goal accomplishment. On the other hand, he knows that some other people *do* share this commitment to the best possible output, and that he has to protect himself against exploitation from more aggressive people or from those who want to compromise quality for quantity. In short, the Craftsman is most concerned with setting goals, accomplishing them, and taking pride in creating a quality product. Chief executives whose careers had started as scientists and engineers were most typical of the Craftsman style.

The *Company Man* is fundamentally similar to the "Organization Man" characterized years earlier by William Foote Whyte (1956) in his description of the typical corporate executive. The Company Man is primarily oriented toward organizational loyalty and commitment, in exchange for guaranteed employment and a gradual rise up the corporate ladder. He derives a sense of security from organizational membership, from the day-to-day activities of the corporation, and from establishing and maintaining high quality relationships with others. His motto is usually something like "service above self," and he is committed to working hard in order to enhance the organization's status (and hence his own). Company Men typically see themselves as trustworthy, responsible, "nice guys" who can get along with almost everyone. They want to make a good impression. Company Men also work hard to develop an organizational climate in which cooperation, commitment, and integrity are highly valued. They are most upset with aggressive, manipulative individualists who exploit others in order to advance their own careers.

The *Jungle Fighter* style is concerned with the acquisition and maintenance of power. Jungle Fighters tend to view their careers and lives in the organization in terms of power—who has it, who doesn't, and how it may be acquired to advance their own position or status. The world is dog-eat-dog, and it is either "eat or be eaten" on the road to personal and professional success through prestige, wealth, and power. Jungle Fighters use a wide variety of tactics to accomplish these ends. They tend to be bold, innovative, entrepreneurial, and willing to take large risks if they think that the payoff is power and financial success. This boldness and innovation is frequently accompanied by a willingness to manipulate and exploit others. People are treated like objects in the service of their larger goals; Jungle Fighters prefer to have others working *for* them rather than *with* them. In short, the Jungle Fighter is out to accumulate power, by whatever means possible, in the service of greater financial wealth and positions of power.

Finally, Maccoby proposes the fourth type—the *Gamesman*. According to Maccoby, the Gamesman has always been present in organizations, but the leadership demands of modern corporate America have made the conditions for the Gamesman more "ripe" now than at other times in history. These demands include the need to confront strong national and international competition, to continually innovate and create new products in order to maintain competitive advantage, to work interdependently with specialists who define, manufacture and market the product, and to be sufficiently flexible to adapt to the changes that arise in this competitive and dynamic marketplace. The Gamesman therefore has some qualities of the Craftsman, Company Man, and Jungle Fighter, but adds some new elements of his own. He tends to see his life and work as though it were all one big game, and his dominant objective is to be a winner at this game. His primary motivation is to play the game, to take calculated risks, and to savor the exhilaration that comes from playing the game. Pushing oneself to play to the limits, and savoring the victories, is the spice of life. Competition is the essence of interaction with others. The goal is not to beat them into humiliation, or to gain power over them, but merely to win the game and have them come back to renew the challenge. Fairness and adherence

TABLE 11–2
Roots of Competition

Character Type	Craftsman	Jungle Fighter	Company Man	Gamesman
Typical meaning of Competition.	Drive to build the best. Competition vs. self and the materials.	Kill or be killed. Dominate or be dominated.	Climb or fall. Competition as price for secure position.	Win or lose. Triumph or humiliation.
Source of Psychic Energy for Competitive Drive.	Interest in work, goal of perfection, pleasure in building something better.	Lust for power and pleasure in crushing opponent, fear of annihilation. Wish to be the only winner.	Fear of failure, desire for approval by authority.	The contest, new plays, new options, pleasure in controlling the play.
Negotiating Style.	Achieve goals and standards for a high quality agreement.	Use power and manipulation to dominate the other; "win" at any cost.	Maximally, problem-solving or minimally, accommodation to preserve relationship with other side; fairness, equity concerns.	"Winning" through competitive style. Process and outcome receive equal importance.

to rules are an integral part of the game. If the Gamesman has a negative side, it is that he tends to view *all* parts of his life as a game, and categorizes others as either winners or losers. However, he also values teamwork in the organization, and contributing to the betterment of the team is as strongly valued as winning. Therefore, "losers" may be those who refuse to invest the effort, or who seek to coast along despite their weaknesses, rather than to develop their strengths. The Gamesman works hard to get the best effort out of both himself and others.

Maccoby's styles are potentially very relevant to understanding different approaches to negotiation. In Table 11–2, we have represented Maccoby's description of the four styles in terms of the way each style approaches competition, and the primary source of psychological energy for the competitive drive. We have also added our own interpretation of the typical approach each style would take in a negotiation setting. Thus, the Craftsman's primary source of energy is directed toward building, creating and attaining a standard of excellence; the drive is to build the best, to surpass the quality of what others have done before. As a result, we suggest that a Craftsman would be most likely to focus on the overall quality and integrity of the negotiated agreement. He would set detailed objectives for negotiation, strive to accomplish these objectives in the negotiation process, and focus on a high quality solution (one that would probably meet the needs of both parties). The

Jungle Fighter, in contrast, would be most concerned with domination, acquiring power, and conquering the opponent. As a result, the Jungle Fighter's negotiation style would most likely be deceptive, manipulative, or even oppressive in his effort to beat the opponent and "win" at any cost. The Company Man is primarily oriented toward achieving security, making gradual progress up the organizational ladder with a minimum of visibility, and preserving relationships that have been built with others. Fear of failure and the desire for approval are dominant sources of motivation. Hence, a negotiating style for the Company Man may be mutual accommodation (or even appeasement) to insure that his own position is not endangered, and that others are pleased with the agreement. Cooperation and problem solving may be hoped for, but appeasement as the price of security and an intact relationship with the other party is not uncommon. Finally, the Gamesman is primarily concerned with winning and losing, and is motivated to "play the game" within the defined rules. As a negotiator, a Gamesman wants to win, appreciates a "good fight" by his opponent, and probably derives a large part of his satisfaction from the *process* of negotiating as well as from the actual outcome. A Gamesman would be delighted with a negotiation in which he had a worthy opponent, in which each put in his best effort, in which the "negotiating game" is well played and the results close, and in which one or both of them can declare themselves "winners" at the end of the contest—and look forward to the next match. Personal experience with professional full-time negotiators in labor relations, purchasing, merger, and acquisition, etc. suggests that they do, in fact view much of their negotiating in these terms. This definition of the negotiation process provides them with a constant source of energy and excitement.

Conclusion

From what is known now, it does not appear that there is any single personality type or characteristic that is directly and clearly linked to success in negotiation. There are plenty of indications, however, both from everyday experience and research, that personality does play a role in negotiation processes and outcomes. Two explanations have been offered for this frustrating inability to discover clear relationships:

1. We have not identified the "right" characteristic, since we do not know enough either about the negotiation process or the complexities of personality to know how the two interact. Hence, the personality variables previously studied—sex differences, intelligence, etc.—may have no significant connection with negotiation. These characteristics may have been chosen because of the convenience of measuring them rather than for their closely reasoned relationship to negotiating behavior.
2. We may be looking at negotiation from the wrong perspective. Most negotiation research has been done on college sophomores and juniors,

with simple games often identified as "negotiations," and using outcome measures specified by the investigator. What the investigator defines as "success" in negotiation may be vastly different from what the negotiators themselves believe to be success. Who is really to say what is success? It seems somewhat arrogant for a person who believes they have succeeded in negotiation to be called unsuccessful by an outsider. It seems obvious that we need to study negotiating in situations in which the parties themselves define the success criteria.

The research to date shows that more complex models of personalities and negotiation are needed. The structure of issues in the negotiation, the social context of the negotiation, and the nature of the outcomes all substantially temper the relationship between the two. More "contingency-type" models are necessary to replace the simple cause-effect models used so frequently in the past. We need models that connect personality variables with particular components and/or stages of negotiation. Thus, sensitivity to other people's characteristics may be found important in selecting strategy and tactics for negotiation, while insensitivity to other people's characteristics may be more useful when the other party is bluffing, threatening, etc. At this point, it seems fair to say that personality has an effect on negotiations, but that the effect is complex and not at all obvious. Studies of several personality predispositions (conflict management style, Machiavellianism, interpersonal trust, and Maccoby's managerial/organizational types) show promising results. However, the structural dimensions of negotiation—the goals of the parties, the nature of the issues, and the interactive dialogue between the parties—still have the most dominant impact on negotiation outcomes.

The conclusion of this chapter suggests that those who believe they are "not the negotiating type" may be significantly misjudging the impact of their personality on attaining the desired outcomes. Instead, the research shows that most of the factors which affect outcomes are behaviors which are under the negotiator's control. Negotiation may well be more of a "learned" set of skills and behaviors than attributes of qualities individuals are "born with"; hence, individuals can practice and develop these skills and behaviors to improve their effectiveness.

SUMMARY

In this chapter, we have reviewed the current state of affairs on a controversial question: what impact, if any, does a negotiator's personality make on his/her success in negotiating, and on negotiating outcomes. We have tried to show that this is a very difficult question to answer based on controlled, systematic research. A wealth of research has shown that clear and simple effects do not exist. In many cases, the research methods have been inadequate to allow personality differences to emerge; in other cases, personality differences were obscured by major "structural" differences in the bargaining situation (the nature of the bargaining problem, relative power of negotiators, constituency pressures, etc.), or personality and structure "interact" together in complex ways. Even definitive experiments which were designed to overcome many of these methodological problems have yielded inconclusive results.

Nevertheless, the search for strong and clear-cut "personality" variables goes on. In this chapter, we proposed several approaches to describing personalities that may have some promise for characterizing differences among negotiators. These include Interpersonal Orientation, Conflict Management style, Machiavellianism, Interpersonal Trust, and styles proposed by Maccoby's research on organizational character and leadership. Each of these approaches appear to have good *prima face* reasons for being directly related to individual differences in trusting other people, handling conflictful relationships, and working competitively or collaboratively with others. Future research will need to explore the impact of these approaches in detail, as well as to determine how various situational variables "interact with" differences in individual style.

It should be noted again in closing that many researchers have come to believe that differences in a negotiator's personality play a far less important role in affecting negotiating outcomes than many of the other key elements we have reviewed earlier in this book. Thus, if a negotiator has a good understanding of the issues at stake, understands the dynamics of distributive and integrative bargaining, knows the role that likely will be played by differences in power and constituency pressures, has prepared for negotiation and worked out a plan to use effective persuasion, it is highly likely that he/she will succeed. The negotiator's personality may do no more than give this negotiation a particular "flavor" or "tone," while the remaining elements will likely have the major impact on the results obtained. If this is true, then negotiators need to worry far more about their planning and preparation for negotiation than how to change or manipulate their "personality" and "style" in order to achieve the desired results.

12

Converting Win/Lose to Win/Win: The Tactics of Conflict Resolution

As discussed in Chapter 5, integrative bargaining, leading to a win/win outcome, is a very attractive process. For each party, it holds out the prospect of a larger, more satisfactory gain than might be realized through distributive bargaining. Further, by establishing a cooperative rather than a competitive relationship, integrative bargaining supports many societal expectations and values. In Chapter 5, we discussed the strategies and tactics of integrative bargaining that may be used once commitment to the process is established. In this chapter, we address ways to convert a win/lose relationship into a win/win relationship; that is, getting out of distributive bargaining and into integrative bargaining.

Let us begin by reviewing the structure of distributive and integrative bargaining (Table 12–1). The difference between the two processes is substantial. The primary concern is how to convert distributive bargaining into integrative given this difference. Distributive bargaining begins with a fundamental conflict over the allocation of limited resources; the accompanying tension, hostility, defensiveness and distrust perpetuates and magnifies the conflict even further. For productive negotiating to occur, this conflict must be handled in a way that arrests the escalation, reduces conflict, opens lines of communication, and increases trust and cooperativeness.

Put simply, in order to successfully convert a win/lose to a win/win situation, we must effectively deal with the dynamics of escalating, polarizing conflict. In this chapter, we will explore a variety of approaches and techniques that can be used to put derailed negotiations back on the track.

TABLE 12-1

	Distributive Bargaining	Integrative Bargaining
Pay-off structure	Fixed amount of resources to be divided.	Variable amount of resources to be divided.
Primary motivation	Gains of one will be the sacrifices of the other.	Parties concerned about maximizing joint outcomes.
Interests	Diametrically opposed.	Convergent or congruent.
Relationships	Short term relationship; people do not need to work together in the future	Long term relationship; parties expect to work together in the future.

Many of these techniques are applicable to a broader range of conflict settings than negotiation. Some of the approaches are predominantly directed at reducing the level of emotional tension and hostility; others are designed to enhance accurate communication between the parties, and still others help to create new alternatives for agreement on the substantive issues. Initially, we will discuss all of these techniques as actions that the parties themselves can take to move from unproductive polarization to productive deliberation. However, as we shall also point out, it is often difficult for negotiators to initiate these actions "in the heat of battle." Under conditions of high mistrust and suspicion, overtures of cooperation and conflict reduction are frequently seen as strategic ploys, tricks to lure the other party into a false sense of trust and vulnerability. As a result, intervention by neutral third parties is often necessary. At the end of the chapter, we will examine the approaches that third parties traditionally take in breaking negotiation deadlocks.

CONFLICT MANAGEMENT BY THE PARTIES THEMSELVES

In this section, five major types of conflict reduction strategy will be reviewed:

- Reducing tension and synchronizing de-escalation of hostility.
- Controlling the number and size of issues at stake.
- Enhancing communication, particularly in understanding the other party.
- Establishing "common ground" on which the parties can find a basis for agreement.
- Enhancing the desirability of the options and alternatives that each side presents to the other side.

Each of these approaches will be described in some detail. Several general comments about the various approaches are helpful. First, there is nothing firm or rigid about the number of different techniques for resolving disputes. Research on the nature of conflict and its resolution (e.g., Deutsch, 1973; Brown, 1983) and the activities of third parties (e.g., Walton, 1969; Wall 1981; Sheppard, 1982) has suggested a wide array of different dispute resolution techniques that can be aggregated in several different ways. Second, these approaches to conflict de-escalation and control are based on the premise that a highly polarized, unproductive conflict is characterized by the following dynamics:

1. The atmosphere is charged with anger, frustration, resentment, and perhaps futility. Mistrust and hostility are directed at the opposing negotiator.

2. Channels of communication, previously used to exchange information and supporting arguments for each side's position, are now closed. Each side attempts to use communication channels to criticize and blame the opponent, while simultaneously attempting to close off the same type of communication from his opponent.

3. The original issues at stake have become blurred and ill-defined, and perhaps new issues have been added. Negotiators have become identified with positions on issues, and the conflict has become personalized. Even if a negotiator were ready to make a concession to the other side, he would not make it due to his strong dislike for his opponent.

4. The parties tend to perceive great differences in their respective positions. Conflict heightens the magnitude of perceived differences between the two parties, and minimizes areas of perceived commonality and agreement. The parties see themselves as farther apart than they may actually be, and do not recognize areas where they may be in agreement.

5. As anger and tension increase, the parties become more locked into their initial negotiating positions. Rather than searching for ways to make concessions and move toward agreement, the parties become firmer in stating their initial demands, and in resorting to threats, lies and distortions to force the other party to comply with those demands. These threats are usually met with counterthreats and retaliation by the opponent.

6. If there is more than one person on a side, those on the same side tend to view each other more favorably. They see the best qualities in the people on their side, and minimize whatever differences exist; yet they also demand more conformity from their team members and will accept a more militant, autocratic form of leadership. If there is dissention in the group, it is hidden from the opposing party; an attempt is always made to present a united front to opponents. (Blake and Mouton, 1961a, 1961b, 1961c; Corwin, 1969; Harvey, 1953).

The techniques for conflict reduction and resolution presented in this chapter are designed to respond to each of these dynamics. Moreover, we suggest that the most productive procedure for resolving a highly polarized dispute is to approach it in the order that we present these tactics. We suggest that the first step should be some effort at reducing tension, followed by efforts to improve the accuracy of communication and to control the proliferation of issues. Finally, the parties should engage in techniques for establishing commonalities and enhancing the attractiveness of each other's preferred alternatives. This procedure is by no means firm and inflexible; many disputes have been successfully resolved by invoking the steps in a somewhat different order. However, the order in which we present these procedures is the one frequently used by third parties in resolving disputes, and hence we believe it will be most effective if employed by the negotiators themselves.

REDUCING TENSION AND SYNCHRONIZING DE-ESCALATION

Unproductive deliberations usually become highly emotional. Parties are frustrated, angry, and upset. They are heavily committed to their viewpoints and have argued strenuously for their preferred alternatives. The other side, by behaving the same way, is seen as stubborn, bull-headed, inflexible and unreasonable. The longer they debate, the more likely emotions will overrule reason; name-calling and verbal assaults on the opponent replace logic and reason. When the dispute becomes personalized, turning into a win-lose feud between individuals, negotiation loses all hope of productivity.

Several approaches for controlling conflict are specifically directed at defusing volatile emotions, will now be discussed.

Tension Release

Tension is a natural by-product of negotiations. Consequently, negotiators should be aware that it is bound to increase, and know how to act to correct or diminish it. Some negotiators who are sensitive to increases in tension know how to make a witty remark or crack a joke that causes laughter and releases tension. Others know that it is sometimes appropriate to let the opponent become angry, and to let him ventilate his anger and frustration, without having to respond in kind. Skilled negotiators also know that by listening to the other person and allowing him to express his feelings, a "cathartic release" will occur that vents emotion and returns negotiations to a calmer pace.

Acknowledgment of Other's Feelings— Active Listening

When one party states his views and the other openly disagrees, the disagreement is often heard by the first negotiator as more than just a disagreement. It may be heard as a put-down, an assertion that the position is wrong or not acceptable, or an accusation that he is lying or distorting the facts. While this might not be the message that is intended, it is frequently the one received. Understandably, such misinterpretations escalate conflict.

There is a difference between accurately *hearing* what an opponent has said, and *agreeing* with his statements. When conflict escalates, accurate listening frequently becomes confused with agreeing and accepting. Every negotiator has been in the position of knowing how another person thinks and feels about an issue, even though the parties may differ on all points. Situations like this may be effectively handled by simply letting the other person know that their message has been heard and understood, both in its content and emotional strength. This technique is called *active listening*, (Rogers, 1961), and is frequently used in interviews and therapy settings as a way of encouraging a person to speak more freely. Rather than challenging and confronting an opposing negotiator's position by bolstering one's own position, the negotiator may respond with statements such as "You see the facts this way," "You feel very strongly about this point," or "I can see that if you saw things this way, you would feel threatened and upset by what I have said." These statements do *not* indicate agreement by the first negotiator; rather, they communicate only that the other person has been accurately heard and understood.

Separation of the Parties

The most common approach to letting tempers cool down is to break off face-to-face relations. Declare a recess or call a caucus. Agree to adjourn and come back together later, when the parties have had a chance to unwind. It is best for the parties to explicitly acknowledge that the purpose of the caucus is to allow tempers to cool and for the dialogue to become less emotional. Each also agrees to return with a renewed effort to make deliberations more productive. This recess will allow each negotiator to regain a more placid composure, and to change the pace to more productive dialogue.

Separation of the parties may occur for short periods of time such as several hours, or may be planned to last for several days or weeks. Variations in the time period are related to level of hostility, as well as unique situational circumstances. Parties may use the time to check with their constituencies, gather new information, and reassess their position and commitments. When third parties intervene in disputes, they frequently call for "cooling off periods" to permit negotiators to gain composure.

Synchronized De-escalation—GRIT

Conflict situations are dynamic; they are constantly changing. Occasionally, there is a reduction in tension and emotion; more commonly, however, tension increases. The escalation process is rooted in the reciprocal nature of dialogue during conflict. Party A says or does something; Party B responds, perhaps going just a bit further, (in intensity or discomfort), thereby escalating the conflict. There are several reasons for this escalation. B may be trying to punish A for what A said or did. B may have been hurt and seeks revenge. B may be attempting to appear strong by showing that A's actions will not be tolerated. Even if B attempts to match A's behavior, it is likely that A will see B's action as more punishing than B intended (a "magnification factor"). This occurs because B, not understanding the tension and anxiety experienced by A, or the degree of A's negative feelings, will underestimate the magnitude of A's reaction. In any event, A experiences B's response as hostile, punishing, negative, and threatening, and replies in kind, thereby repeating the cycle and increasing the level of tension and hostility. Clearly, the parties must find some way to de-escalate this conflict cycle.

Charles Osgood (1962), in writing about the cold war and disarmament, suggested a unilateral strategy for conflict de-escalation called GRIT (Graduated Reciprocation and Tension Reduction). The party who desires to de-escalate a conflict initiates the action. He/she decides on some small concession that each side could make which would be a signal of both sides' good faith and desire to de-escalate. The concession should be large enough so that it can be read as an unambiguous signal of a desire to change the relationship, but not so large that if only one side followed through, it would make itself weak or vulnerable. The unilateral action should then be publicly announced to the other side, stating

1. exactly what the concession is;
2. that the concession is part of a deliberate strategic policy to reduce tension;
3. that the other side is explicitly invited to reciprocate in some specified form;
4. that the concession will be executed on some stated time schedule; and
5. that each party commits to execute the concession without knowing whether the other will reciprocate.

The concession is then executed. The specific concession should be something that is obvious, unambiguous, and subject to easy verification. Making it public and symbolic will help.

If the opposing party does *not* respond, then the initiator goes through with the action and repeats the sequence again, selecting a simple, low-risk concession in an effort to attract the opponent into synchronized de-escalation. If the opponent *does* respond, then the initiator proposes a second action, slightly riskier than the first, and once again initiates the sequence. As the synchronized de-escalation takes hold, the parties can both propose larger and riskier concessions that will bring them back into a productive negotiating relationship.

GRIT strategies can be observed in simple situations such as a married couple "making up" after a fight, or complex conflicts such as nuclear disarmament. A good example is provided by two groups in a company planning a major expansion in production capacity. Hostility and conflict had developed between the engineering group designing the new plant and the manufacturing group that was going to operate it. The issue of the way that each handled reports and information generated by the other had grown to major proportions. Each looked for flaws, errors and weaknesses in the other's reports, and, once discovered, loudly proclaimed that these flaws were evidence of the other side's incompetence and untrustworthiness. As a result, neither side was willing to reveal any data to the other, and work came to a complete standstill. Recognizing what was happening, the head of the manufacturing group announced his diagnosis of the problem and said that at the next meeting, his group would take some appropriate action. At that meeting, he stated that in order to encourage information exchange, his group was going to release a newly prepared report to representatives of the engineering department. The choice of this particular action was strategically planned. The information was badly needed, and the report had been prepared by an outside consulting group, making the information less subject to bias and criticism. The next day, the engineering representatives reciprocated by handing over data that manufacturing had requested a long time ago. Manufacturing then responded by releasing some additional data to the engineers, explicitly stating that this release was a "reward" for the cooperation shown by the engineers. This process resulted in a significant improvement in communication and data sharing between the two departments.

GRIT strategies are efforts to change the nature of relationships—from hostile and mistrusting, with each side attempting to "punish" the other—to more open and trusting, in which one side initiates a trusting gesture, and each side "rewards" the other's gestures with more cooperative efforts. This "mutual reward" syndrome will help to de-escalate conflict and often leads to a positive, productive climate for negotiation.

IMPROVING THE ACCURACY OF COMMUNICATION

The second step in conflict reduction is to insure that the parties accurately understand the other's position. As stated earlier, when conflict becomes more heated, communication efforts concentrate on managing emotions and directing the next assault at the opponent. Effective listening declines. We think we know what they are going to say, and do not care to listen to it anymore. In intense conflict, listening becomes so diminished that the parties are frequently unaware that their positions may have much in common. Rapoport (1964) has termed this syndrome the "blindness of involvement." This syndrome inhibits the development of trust and the problem solving process.

Outsiders to a conflict usually have a perspective on conflict that is not shared by the parties themselves. For example, they often notice that the two conflicting parties see the same event differently; moreover, outsiders often understand that each side's viewpoint, while admittedly limited and incomplete, nevertheless is justifiable and "makes sense." As an outsider, we can understand how one party's actions, which is to them rational and justifiable, may appear to the other to be misleading, threatening or just wrong. We also usually recognize that if each party could understand how the other side sees the conflict, the other side's position would be more comprehensible and less threatening. This insight would increase the likelihood of a mutually acceptable solution.

While it is easy for outsiders to see conflicts in this way, recognizing these options when we are personally involved in a conflict is another matter. Role reversal is one way of helping each side see things from the other's perspective. One party attempts to put himself or herself in the other's shoes, looking at the issue from the other's perspective. Hence, a member of management can put him or herself in the position of a union negotiator; a salesman can take the position of a customer, a purchasing agent that of a salesman. This can be done simply by playing out scenarios in one's imagination, or more effectively, by both parties mutually agreeing to swap roles in a mock negotiating session. While role reversal will not tell a negotiator exactly how the opponent thinks and feels about the issues, the process can provide useful and surprising insights as to the way the opponent in that situation might see, feel and think about things.

During negotiations, efforts are often made to encourage an opponent to see issues from the other's perspective. The plea is made: "look at this from my perspective. What you're saying (or doing) puts me in this position, and you can't expect . . . " A variant on this occurs when one party tells the other, "If I were in your shoes, I would . . . " If engaging in the process conveys to the negotiator an accurate understanding of the other's position, that his/her previous view was incorrect, it gives the other party a chance to correct specific misperceptions. This corrected understanding gives the negotiator a broader, more integrated view of the possible options. Role reversal also gives the negotiator an opportunity to find out how some planned action may affect the relationship. Hence, a member of management taking labor's role may discover that some of their arguments or tactics may have an ineffective or undesirable impact, permitting management to drop the tactics before they cause problems (Johnson and Dustin, 1970).

Another variation on role reversal, called *bilateral focus*, can also be used during negotiation. Here one party (A) takes a statement of the other's (B) and tries to understand the way things must look and/or feel to B for B to make that statement. A then describes that view or feeling to B. The purpose here is for A to make a statement that B will agree is, in fact, the way he or she sees things. If B does not accept the statement as accurately describing B's position or feelings, A asks for feedback to correct the statement, and tries again. The process is repeated until B acknowledges that A has described his/her position accurately. The dialogue might go as follows:

> *A:* "You must feel really angry if you are actually threatening to walk out of these negotiations."
>
> *B:* "Yes, I'm angry, but also I really feel betrayed by the lack of good faith you have shown in the negotiating thus far."
>
> *A:* "You really feel betrayed because you think I have shown bad faith?"
>
> *B:* "Yes. I think you have been putting a lot of new issues on the table that you didn't talk about when we started."
>
> *A:* You think I have shown bad faith because I have been bringing up issues that I didn't discuss back when we started these negotiations."
>
> *B:* "Yes, that's correct."
>
> *A:* "O.K. I think I understand what's going on now. Let me tell you why I raised those additional issues ... "

By this process, A has been able to articulate, and therefore accurately understand, how B sees things, and B is in a position of knowing that he/she has been understood (Rapoport, 1964). The process continues with A asking B to repeat the procedure. (In this example, B would question A to make sure B understands why A has raised additional issues as the negotiation has proceeded.)

A number of research studies have been performed to examine the impact of the bilateral focus perspective (role reversal) vs. self-representation in simulated debates. The results are not as clearcut as might be anticipated. Bilateral focus did enhance objective understanding of the other's position over self-representation; however, bilateral presentation per se did *not* lead to more frequent attainment of agreement over self presentation. Moreover, role reversal only tended to lead to greater understanding of the other's position under the following circumstances:

1. The role reversers performed well, that is, they were skillful and effective role reversers.

2. The positions they were advocating were *actually* compatible. Bilateral focus did not increase agreements when the negotiator's positions were actually *incompatible*. When positions are incompatible, bilateral focus may serve to sharpen the areas of incompatibility and inhibit progress rather than promote it.

3. One party actively proposed compromises to reconcile any incompatibilities that may be recognized. (See Walcott, Hopmann, and King, 1977, for a complete review.)

Thus, bilateral focus is clearly more effective in enhancing an understanding of the other side's position, and the perspective from which he views issues. In negotiation, the purpose of role reversal is to highlight areas of commonality and overlap between positions; however, this purpose cannot be achieved unless such compatibilities actually exist, and at least one party acts to move toward areas of commonality by proposing compromises. When *no* actual compatibility exists, role reversal may simply sharpen the differences between actual positions. While some negotiators would find this to be undesirable information, since it inhibits the search for common ground, others would prefer to be aware of this lack of compatibility in order to switch their efforts toward other means to resolve the dispute. In attempting to create a win-win situation, where integrative bargaining is possible, both parties need accurate knowledge of the other's goals. Only this type of information will permit a productive effort to satisfy each party's objectives. If the use of bilateral focus reveals that the parties' goals are actually incompatible, integrative bargaining is impossible, and the sooner that is discovered, the better. We showed earlier that the existence of a negative settlement range had severe consequences for the distributive bargaining process. Similarly, efforts at integrative bargaining will be a waste of everyone's time and energy if some compatibility does not exist among the parties' goals. Thus, bilateral focus is a powerful tool for uncovering the goals of both parties. Many times it can reveal the opportunities for a win-win settlement, but other times it may reveal that the parties are truly incompatible in their objectives.

Imaging

Like role reversal, imaging is also a method for gaining insight into the other party's perspective. In imaging, parties in conflict are asked separately:

1. To describe how they see themselves.
2. To describe how the other party appears to them.
3. To state how they think the other party would describe them.
4. To state how they think the other party sees themselves.

This information is then exchanged. Parties first comparing how they described themselves, how they would describe the other, and then comparing how they think the other party would describe them, and lastly, how they think the other would describe themselves. The differences between the two sets of statements are frequently surprising and even shocking to the parties in the dissimilarities and inconsistencies revealed. Step 4, describing how the other party sees themselves, however, often helps prepare participants for what will emerge. There is usually lots of animated discussion as the parties clarify and substantiate what they have said or heard. A common result is that many apparent differences and areas of conflict are recognized as not real, while those which *are* real become more understandable. As an example of this process, in a merger between two organizations, top executives met to work out the new organization structure for the combined firm. Executives from both sides were deeply concerned that they would be outmaneuvered by the other and would "lose" as a result of the merger. A consultant suggested having an imaging meeting prior to actual negotiations. This meeting sharply altered the perceptions of both parties, and successful integrative bargaining became possible (Alderfer, 1977).

Mirroring

Mirroring is similar to imaging but not as structured, and involves less risk taking. It begins with a third party, someone not directly involved with the conflict, interviewing both parties to determine what they see as their difficulty in working together. At a meeting with both parties, the findings from these interviews are presented. One party is given the opportunity to discuss and explore this report, identifying what parts they think are accurate and what issues it raises; the other side listens but does not comment. Then, the second party is given a chance to discuss the report, as well as respond to the first group's comments; the first listens, takes notes, but also does not comment (Fordyce and Weil, 1971).

When this round of discussion is completed, several things have usually been accomplished. Misconceptions or misinterpretations have been clarified and corrected. Needs, goals, and priorities as well as limitations are surfaced to be used in the problem-solving process. Parties gain an understanding of the other party's true needs. Perhaps even more importantly, the process sets a positive climate. Parties find that they can make their needs and concerns heard, and not be interrupted. This reduces defensiveness and encourages people to listen. Most people begin the process with a rather clear idea of what they need from the other party; in this phase, they learn more about the other's needs. Joint problem-solving moves from being an unattainable ideal to an achievable process.

Needless to say, techniques such as Mirroring and Imaging require considerable effort and time; however, when the time and effort are allocated, the results can be very valuable. For example, one firm was an almost exclusive supplier of raw materials for another. Hostilities had become so intense that they were often failing to settle elementary purchasing agreements, and both firms were losing business as a result. One of the authors, functioning as a consultant, conducted interviews with both parties in a mirroring project. As a result, both parties heard for the first time how vulnerable each felt in regard to the other. As one said, "It was like learning that the town bully was as terrified of you as you were of him, and really only wanted peace and quiet." Mirroring calmed the hostile feelings, and the parties began a process of real negotiation, first on relatively simple matters where agreement was easy and immediately necessary for both, and then moving on to more difficult and long-term issues.

CONTROLLING ISSUES

As noted earlier, a third major difficulty that inhibits parties from resolving conflict is that as conflict intensifies, the size and number of the issues expand. As conflict escalates, it snowballs; bits and pieces of other issues are accumulated in a large, unmanageable mass. While smaller conflicts can be managed one at a time, each in a way satisfactory to the details of the incident, larger conflicts become unwieldy and less amenable to any easy resolution. The problem for negotiators in escalated disputes, therefore, is to develop strategies to contain issue proliferation, and reduce the dispute to manageable proportions.

Roger Fisher (1964; Fisher and Ury, 1981) has been a major advocate of strategies of issue control in negotiation, particularly in international affairs. In a well-known article on *fractionating conflict,* Fisher suggests six major approaches for reducing a large conflict into smaller parts:

1. Reduce the Number of Parties on Each Side.   When conflict escalates, each side seeks to build alliances for strength, or to bring their constituencies into the dispute; either they increase the number of parties at the negotiation or they bring more clout to the table. Additional parties, such as lawyers, expert witnesses, etc. are often brought into negotiations for the information they can provide. Rather than having them present their testimony and leave, however, experts often remain on the scene to provide additional input. Since the sheer number of parties at the table can make negotiations considerably more complex (more parties = more perspectives on the issues, more time needed to hear each side, more opportunities for disagreement, etc.), groundrules are needed for ways to limit the number of parties. One way to control conflict size is to return the dispute to the original negotiating parties. The fewer the actors present, or the more the conflict can be limited to two individuals, the more likely the parties will be to reach a favorable settlement.

2. Control the Number of Physical Issues Involved.   A second way to control the size of a conflict is to keep the number of issues small enough to manage. When conflict escalates, the size and number of issues proliferate. Some conflicts escalate to the point where there are too many issues to constructively manage. At the same time, keeping negotiations limited to a very few issues also raises problems. Single issue conflicts are frequently harder to manage because they quickly lead to win-lose polarization over the issue. Achieving a win-win solution requires a negotiating situation where all parties can win. In such circumstances, it is often desirable to expand the

number of issues, in order to permit each side to view itself as having gained. This can be done by a) defining the issue more broadly so that resolution can benefit both sides, or b) coupling the issue with another issue so that two issues are involved, and each party can receive a preferred settlement on one of the issues. Small packages of two or three issues are frequently easier to resolve because multiple issues facilitate packaging and trading off on concessions.

3. State Issues in Concrete Terms Rather Than as Principles. A third way that conflict issues become difficult to control is when events or issues are treated as matters of "principle." Small conflicts can rapidly become intractable disputes when their resolution is *not* treated as an isolated event, but instead must be consistent with a broader "policy" or "principle." Since any deviation from policy is viewed as a threat to that policy, and since broad policy is far more difficult to change than a concession on a single issue negotiations are immediately problematic. For example, a union may request binding arbitration of grievances in a labor dispute; management not only does not want to grant the request, but states that the request is inconsistent with management's rights to handle discipline cases. "It's a matter of principle," they assert. Resorting to arguments of "principles" and "policies" is often a strategic defense by high power parties against any change from the status quo; the more arguments are conducted at that level alone, the less likely those disputes can be successfully resolved.

There are, of course, times when a single event is properly seen as an indicator of new principles or policy. That being the case, the negotiations should be arranged to specifically address the policy or principle. Many times, people are reluctant to do this, because they know negotiations over principles are difficult and lengthy. However, to attempt to negotiate a concrete issue when the negotiation is really on the "hidden agenda" of a major principle only results in frustration. If this is occurring, it is wise to face the issue and raise it directly. There are at least two strategies:

• Question whether the issue needs to be addressed at the principle or policy level. Ask with which established policy or principle the issue is closely connected. If none exists, and one party wants to look at the matter from a policy or principle level, suggest that the immediate concrete issue be handled and discussed separate from the underlying principle or policy. If need be, the parties can agree that the concrete issue can be settled in this instance, with no expectation as to how the policy will later be established.

• Point out that exceptions can be made to all policies, and that principles and policies can be maintained even if minor deviations are permitted to exist. For example, while "honesty is the best policy," there are often times when we know that deviations from the truth may be necessary. The parties may be willing to agree that this might be one of those times.

4. Restrict the Precedents Involved—Both Procedural and Substantive. The final type of issue magnification is that the parties treat concessions on a single issue as violations of some substantive or procedural precedent. When a substantive precedent is at stake, one party will imply that to concede on this issue at this time will render him vulnerable to conceding on the same issue, or a similar issue, in the future. "If we give one inch on a cost-of-living clause this year," management argues, "you will be back wanting a foot next year." In contrast, procedural precedents are at stake when parties agree to follow a process they haven't followed before. For example, a procedural precedent may be set when the parties agree to negotiate in a relationship that previously has not been characterized by negotiation, and/or one has more power than the other. Parents are confronted by their children, who no longer wish to "obey orders;" teachers find their authority challenged by students. Belief in the domino theory is strong. The high power party, who supports the precedent, believes that if he/she negotiates now, rather than "quelling the rebellion," there will be no end to the number and types of demands in the future.

Issues of precedent are usually as thorny to control as issues of principle. Once again, a negotiator trying to move a conflict toward de-escalation and resolution should try to keep single issues from becoming translated into major questions of precedent. Focus the dialogue on the key issue, and persist in arguments that concessions on *this* issue at *this* time do not necessarily dictate any precedents—substantive or procedural—for the future.

5. Search for Ways to "Fractionate" the Big Issues. Fisher (1964) calls these "salami tactics"—ways to slice a large issue into smaller pieces. Issues that can be expressed in quantitative terms are easy to slice—wage demands, for example, can be cut down to pennies per hour increment, or lease rates can be sliced down to pennies per square foot. When trying to fractionate issues of principle or precedent, use time horizons (when the principle goes into effect or how long it lasts) and the number of different applications of the principle as ways to slice the issues. Thus, a cost-of-living escalator may seem like an all-or-nothing issue. However, a cost-of-living escalator can be "sliced" according to *when* it is introduced, or to the *number of different worker classifications* to which it applies.

6. Issues Are Resolved Quickly When They Are "Depersonalized,"—Separated from the Parties Who Are Advocating Them (Fisher and Ury, 1981). The most common approach to negotiation—positional bargaining—tends to create conflict over both the issues and the relationship between negotiators. People become identified with positions on issues, and vice versa.

Effective negotiation requires separating the issues from the parties, not only by working to establish a productive relationship between the parties (leaving only the issue conflict at stake), but by trying to resolve the issues without regard to the people.

ESTABLISH COMMONALITIES

As we noted earlier, escalated conflict tends to magnify (in the parties' eyes) their perceived differences and to minimize their perceived similarities. The parties tend to see themselves as farther apart and having less in common than may be true. Therefore, a fourth major action that parties can take to de-escalate conflict is to establish commonalities or focus on common objectives. Several approaches are possible.

Superordinate Goals

Superordinate goals are common goals; they are desired by both parties and require the cooperation of both parties to achieve. In a corporation, for example, people do different jobs (e.g., marketing, manufacturing) which have different objectives, yet they must work together in some basic ways (for example, to get the product to the customer) or the corporation will not survive. A local city council and community members may disagree as to the ways to spend limited funds for community development; however, they may be able to agree if it is possible for them to write a joint grant proposal that will provide enough money to meet all objectives. Two negotiators may be in a heated conflict over how to resolve an issue, but if they share the common objective of completing negotiations by a certain deadline, then the deadline will increase the likelihood of concession making.

In order to have significant impact on negotiations, superordinate goals must be jointly desired by both sides, and must not be seen as benefiting one side more than the other. In a research study, Johnson and Lewicki (1969) showed that superordinate goals which were closely related to the issues of the conflict, and which were introduced by one party in the dispute, often became caught up in the conflict dynamics and lost their effectiveness. Random events (under neither party's control) or events created by neutral third parties, are frequently better superordinate goals than those which are searched for and planned by the parties. For example, natural disasters such as floods, storms, blackouts, fires, etc. bring divisive people and communities together in a common purpose of survival; the same impact can be seen in negotiations.

Common Enemies

A common enemy is a negative form of superordinate goal. The parties find new motivation to resolve their differences in order to avoid intervention by a third party, or to pool resources to defeat a common enemy. Political leaders of all persuasions have often provoked outside enemies to attack in order to bring their own constituencies together. Managers who are in conflict are sometimes told by their superiors that if they do not reach agreement, someone else will make the decision for them. Labor and management may behave more collaboratively when threatened with binding arbitration or government intervention in their dispute.

Agreement on the Rules and Procedures

A third way parties can establish commonalities is by mutual agreement on the rules by which negotiations will be conducted. Escalated conflict tends to exceed its bounds; as parties become more upset, they may be more likely to resort to any and all tactics to defeat their opponents. Efforts at effective conflict de-escalation and control may require that the parties rededicate themselves to basic ground rules for how they will manage their dispute. These include:

- Determining a site for a meeting. Changing the site or finding "neutral turf" may be helpful to get things moving again.
- Setting a formal agenda as to what may be discussed, what may *not* be discussed, and agreeing to abide by that agenda.
- Determining who may attend the meetings. Changing key negotiators or representatives may be a "signal" of intention to change negotiation approach or tactics.
- Setting time limits for the individual meeting, and for the overall negotiation session. As we have pointed out, progress in negotiation is paced according to the time available; therefore, setting limits is likely to create more progress than if no limits are set.
- Setting procedural roles—who may speak, how long they may speak, how issues will be approached, what facts may be introduced, how records or "minutes" will be kept, how agreements will be affirmed, what clerical or support services are required, etc.

Finally—and perhaps a very radical step for some negotiators—the parties may agree to set aside a short period of time during negotiations for the expressed purpose of critiquing *how they are doing*. This mechanism effectively designates a selected time for the parties to critically evaluate their own progress in negotiation, and to suggest a time when groundrules may be reevaluated, procedural mechanisms changed, or perhaps even changing negotiator behavior. This "process orientation" (e.g., Walton, 1969) may provide the opportunity for the parties to self-correct the procedural mechanisms that will allow them to make greater progress on their substantive disagreements.

Integrative Frameworks

Superordinate goals, common enemies and mutual commitment to rules are factors *outside* the boundaries of the dispute; they transcend the specific issues and bring the parties together in unified action. However, superordinate goals and common enemies do not establish the foundation for long-term cooperation; when the common goal or common enemy is removed, the parties may find that they have no greater basis for resolving their dispute than they did before. Hence, other mechanisms must be pursued to establishing a common ground for deliberation.

There are two primary vehicles for developing commonalities in disputes: first, by focusing on similarities between the parties rather than on differences; and second, by searching for cognitive ways to redefine the dispute such that all parties' interests may be accommodated.

Maximizing similarities is simply a process of refocusing the parties' attention on what they have in common, rather than where they disagree. As noted earlier, conflict processes tend to highlight perceived differences and magnify the importance of these differences. The longer the parties are in dispute, the more they quibble about the differences, and the more they recognize other differences that are then drawn into the dispute. One way to control this escalation is to re-emphasize what the parties have in common—objectives, purposes, overall philosophies and viewpoints, long-range goals, styles of operation, etc. Another is to review what they have accomplished together. Re-emphasizing the commonalities tends to put the differences back into their proper perspective, and de-emphasizes their importance. This process either defuses the emotionality tied to the differences, or creates a positive emotional bond based on similarities that will allow differences to be bridged.

Integrative frameworks are ways of redefining the issues to create a common perspective from which initial positions appear more compatible (Eiseman, 1978; Fisher and Ury, 1981). Eiseman (1978) refers to this process as creating an integrative conceptual framework, while Fisher and Ury (1981) state that successful negotiators focus on *interests,* not positions. By defining negotiated issues in terms of positions—my position on this issue is X—parties tend to treat complex phenomena by simplisticly defining a single point, and then refusing to move from it. In order to create movement, parties must establish ways of redefining the conflict so that they can explore compatible interests. Fisher and Ury use the simple example of two women quarreling in a library. One wants the window open and the other wants it closed. They bicker back and forth about how much to leave it open: a crack, halfway, three quarters of the way. No solution satisfies them.

Enter the librarian. She asks one why she wants the window open: "To get some fresh air." She asks the other why she wants it closed: "To avoid the draft." After thinking a minute, she opens a window in the next room, bringing in fresh air without a draft (p. 41).

Eiseman notes that there are several ways to create integrative frameworks out of polarized positions:

1. Dimensionalize the Problem. Instead of treating the conflict as distinctly different categorical viewpoints, treat it as points along a continuum. In the above example, the parties were in dispute about whether the window would be open or closed. In fact, there are almost an infinite number of degrees that the window can be open, from very slightly to a great deal. Once the parties redefine the issue as the amount it will be open, they can then "negotiate" more easily over the size of the opening.

2. Increase the Number of Dimensions. The successful intervention of the librarian in the above example is predicated on her imaginative solution, that fresh air and no draft can be accommodated if one does not restrict the solution to opening a window in the same room. Multiple dimensions allow one party to "win" on one dimension and the other to "win" on the second. Increasing dimensions allows for the possibility that an additional dimension can be identified on which the parties can more easily reconcile their differences. It may also provide an entirely new way of looking at the problem, so that both sides can now recognize degrees, shades, and variations that may satisfy all parties.

3. Construct an "Ideal Case." Sometimes parties are in dispute because each is proposing a solution which meets only his/her own needs but not those of the other side. One way to break this deadlock is to construct an ideal case that would meet the needs of both sides. In the above example, the librarian did this by saying to herself, "Ideally, how can one party get fresh air while the other avoids a draft?" Negotiating parties can construct ideal solutions by creatively devising ways that both parties could ideally have their needs met, and then determining how that ideal scenario might be attained.

4. Search for Semantic Resolutions. Particularly in cognitive conflicts, where parties are negotiating over contract language, setting policy or establishing memoranda of agreement, conflict frequently intensifies over key words, phrases and expressions. Sometimes this conflict can be reduced to irrelevant hairsplitting, yet to the parties the wording has significance in its meaning and intent. Discovering how parties attach different meanings to some words, or exploring language that can accommodate both sides, is another alternative for achieving an integrative framework.

MAKE PREFERRED OPTIONS MORE DESIRABLE TO THE OPPONENT

A final alternative method that parties can use to increase the likelihood of agreement is to make their desires and preferences more palatable to their opponent. We have noted that as conflict escalates, the parties become more locked into defining their *own* position on an issue. Moreover, as this position is formulated over time, negotiators try to remain consistent with the original position—that is, to establish clearcut "policy" which applies in all circumstances. Because these policies are designed to apply to a variety of circumstances, of necessity they become broader rather than more specific. If the other does not readily comply with a negotiator's position or policy, the negotiator's tendency is to escalate and rigidify his demands, or increase the magnitude of the threat for noncompliance. These actions heighten conflict.

Roger Fisher (1969, Fisher and Ury, 1981) suggest that most influence situations can be characterized by a "demand" (what we want), and offers and threats that state or imply the consequences of meeting or not meeting the demand. The basic dynamics of this process are depicted in Table 12–2.

Fisher suggests that this emphasis is greatly misplaced and self-destructive. Rather than focusing on their own positions, demands, and threats, negotiators should direct their effort to the following question: how can we get them (our opponents) to make a choice which is best for us, given that our interests diverge? This approach is largely a matter of perspective-taking—focusing on the other's interests rather than one's own. Like role-reversal, it requires negotiators to focus less on their own position, and more on a clear understanding of opponent's needs. Moreover, once those needs are under-

TABLE 12–2

	Demand	*Offer*	*Threat*
	The decision desired by us	The consequences of making the decision	The consequences of not making the decision
Who?	Who is to make the decision?	Who benefits if the decision is made?	Who gets hurt if the decision is not made?
What?	Exactly what decision is desired?	If the decision is made, what benefits can be expected? —what costs?	If the decision is not made, —what risks? —what potential benefits?
When?	By what time does the decision have to be made?	When, if ever, will the benefits of making the decision occur?	How soon will the consequences of not making the decision be felt?
Why?	What makes this a right, proper, and lawful decision?	What makes these consequences fair and legitimate?	What makes these consequences fair and legitimate?

Every feature of an influence problem can be located somewhere on this schematic map. The nature of a given problem can be discovered through estimating how the presumed adversary would answer the above questions.
© 1969 by Roger Fisher. Reprinted by permission of Harper & Row, Publishers, Inc.

stood, parties should invest their efforts *not* in the tactics of getting the opponent to come to us, but in the ways we can move toward them. Several alternatives can be pursued to accomplish this objective (Fisher, 1969):

1.   Give Them a Yesable Proposal.   Rather than increasing the emphasis on *our* position, a negotiator's efforts should be directed at creating a position that *opponents* will find acceptable. Rather than stating our position and letting *them* suggest alternatives which we may approve or overrule, a negotiator should give attention to understanding *their* needs and devising a proposal which will meet those needs. Fisher terms this a "yesable" proposal—one to which their only answer can be, "yes, it is acceptable." To succeed, however, this approach requires a negotiator to begin to think about what the other party would want or would agree with, rather than exclusively considering his own goals and needs.

2.   Ask for a Different Decision.   Rather than making demands more general, to fit with our "position" or "policy," negotiators should endeavor to make demands more specific. Negotiators must determine what specific elements of the demands are most palatable or offensive to the opponent, then use this information to *refine the demand.* "Ask for a different decision," asserts Fisher. Reformulate, repackage, reorganize, rephrase. Fractionate, split, divide, make more specific. Making demands more specific is not making them more rigid; they *would* be rigid if it were the *only* demand to be made. Rather, specific demands which can be reformulated are easier to recast to meet the other's needs.

Fisher and Ury (1981) describe an analogous procedure in their recommendation that successful negotiators be skilled at inventing options for mutual gain. This principle has already been discussed several times in our review of integrative bargaining. By inventing and refining ways that both parties can succeed, and by providing a variety of these options to the opponent, the likelihood that both parties can select a desirable option is greatly enhanced.

3.   Sweeten the Offer Rather Than Intensifying the Threat.   Negotiators can also make options more palatable by enhancing the attractiveness of accepting them. Again, this is a matter of placing the emphasis on the positive rather than the negative; in the traditional "carrot and stick" tactics of managerial motivation, it is making the carrot more attractive rather than enlarging the stick. Promises and offers can be made more attractive in a variety of ways: maximizing their attractive qualities and minimizing their negative ones, showing how they meet the opponent's needs, reducing the disadvantages to them of accepting an offer, making offers more credible (i.e., that it will actually be given if they accept), or setting deadlines on offers so that they expire if not accepted quickly. Many would argue that these are

common "sales tricks" akin to rebates, "two for the price of one" offers, "today only" sales, "extra added attraction" elements, etc. They are. The same techniques that salesmen use to move their products can and should be used by negotiators to get their position accepted by an adversary. Many of these techniques were described in the chapter on persuasion.

4.   Use Legitimacy or Objective Criteria to Evaluate Solutions.   Finally, negotiators may insist that alternative solutions and settlements be evaluated by "objective" criteria that meet the test of fairness and legitimacy. Each side should be able to demonstrate that its "demands" are based on sound facts, calculations and information, and that preferred solutions are consistent with those facts and information. This procedure will frequently require disclosing and sharing facts, rather than disguising and distorting them. "Here's how we arrived at our proposal. Here are the facts we used, the cost data we estimated, the calculations we made. You can verify these by the following procedures." The more this data is open to public verification, and demonstrated to be within the bounds of fairness and legitimacy, the more convincing will be the position "independent" of the negotiator who advocates it, and the more persuasive it will be in achieving a settlement.

CONFLICT MANAGEMENT BY THIRD PARTIES

The preceding section reviewed a number of techniques that are available to the negotiators themselves in order to break deadlocks, reduce unproductive tension and hostility, and return negotiations to a productive pace. However, as we stated at the beginning of this chapter, there are frequently circumstances when the parties cannot effectively implement these techniques by themselves. When the "heat of battle" overwhelms negotiators, when mistrust and suspicion are high, or when the parties cannot take actions toward conflict de-escalation without those actions being misinterpreted and mistrusted by others, third parties become necessary. This section will describe the typical roles that third parties play, and how those roles contribute to conflict resolution.

Third parties work to manage disputes in a wide variety of different styles and techniques. Often third parties need to do no more than to implement some of the dispute resolution techniques we reviewed in the first part of this chapter—aiding in the reduction of tension, controlling the number of issues, enhancing communication, establishing a common ground, and highlighting certain decision options such that they are more attractive to the parties. As we will point out, some of these techniques are more specific to certain styles of third party behavior than others. In this section, we shall describe three major styles of third party behavior: arbitration, mediation and process consultation. The objectives, style and impact of each approach will be reviewed, and their impact on negotiation outcomes will also be described. As with many of the other areas of research that we have reviewed, the literature on third party intervention in dispute resolution is large and growing rapidly. As a result, we can only hope to extract the most basic concepts and applications of each third party style. The reader who is interested in exploring the research in greater detail, or achieving a richer understanding of how to apply certain third party models, should refer to the references that we will provide.

Arbitration

Arbitration is probably the most common and well known form of third party dispute resolution. The process of arbitration is fairly clearcut: parties in dispute, after having reached a deadlock or a time deadline without successful resolution of their differences, present their positions to a third party. The third party listens to both sides, and then makes a ruling with regard to the outcome of the dispute (Prasow and Peters, 1983).

There are several common variations in arbitration procedures. First, arbitrators (arbiters) may hear and rule on a *single issue* that is under dispute, or they may rule on *multiple issues* in a total settlement package. (Feigenbaum, 1975). Second, arbitration may be *voluntary* or *binding*. Under *voluntary* arbitration, the parties may submit their arguments to an arbiter, but they are not required to comply with the arbiter's decision; only the arbiter's professional stature and reputation, or the impact of announcing (his) decision to others, might bring pressure on the parties to accept his ruling. In contrast, *binding* arbitration requires the parties to comply with the decision, either by law or by their own previous commitment. A third variation in approaches to arbitration is between the *conventional* and *final offer* methods. Under conventional arbitration, the arbitrator is free to offer and recommend any settlement that he/she believes to be appropriate. The arbiter may simply decide in favor of the arguments being made by either side; this outcome occurs most commonly when grievances and contract violations are being heard. However, arbiters may also select a middle ground between the positions of the two parties, or even propose a solution different from that suggested by the disputants. In contrast, final offer arbitration requires the arbiter to choose between *one* of the final proposals made by the parties; "new" solutions cannot be invented by the arbiter in this case. The pros and cons of these variations will become evident as we critique arbitration.

Arbitration is most commonly used as a dispute resolution mechanism in labor relations. New contracts which cannot be achieved through negotiation are frequently submitted for arbitration, and grievance disputes on existing contracts are traditionally resolved by arbitration. Our civil and criminal justice systems are also basically conducted by an arbitration model; the judge (and jury) listens to evidence from both sides and then make a ruling on the case. A form of non-binding arbitration known as the mini-trial is receiving increased acceptance in the resolution of corporate and regulatory disputes. Disputing companies or governmental groups may invest thousands and thousands of dollars in legal fees, wait several years before having their cases heard by a judge in court, and then spend a great deal more in time and money to present that case. This burdensome cost on the plaintiff, defense and court system has led groups to experiment with mini-trials—a quasi-legal forum in which both sides condense their arguments into several hours and present the evidence to an arbitrator or retired judge. The arbitrator then offers a non-binding "interpretation" of a fair settlement that may help the parties determine what would result if the case actually went to trial, and/or create the basis for a negotiated compromise to the dispute. Mini-trials and other similar proceedings (hearings, forums, moot courts, etc.) offer great promise in the future for resolution of disputes in a manner dramatically more efficient and less costly than the formal courts (Green, 1980).

Arbitration has come under increasing scrutiny and criticism as a dispute resolution mechanism, even in the labor relations area. Arbitration initially appears to have two distinct advantages as a resolution procedure: a clearcut resolution to the dispute is proposed (and perhaps imposed), and relatedly, the costs of prolonged, unresolved disputes can be avoided. However, as noted by Kochan (1980) and others, arbitration appears to have several negative consequences as well:

1.   The Chilling Effect.   Under conventional arbitration procedures, the arbiter may select the recommendation of one of the two disputing parties, or invent a new solution. Moreover, the arbiter may have the power to bind the parties to his decision. If the parties in negotiation anticipate that their own failure to agree will lead to an arbiter's intervention, it may cool their incentive to seriously work for a negotiated settlement. This chilling effect occurs as "the parties avoid making compromises they might be otherwise willing to make, because they fear that the factfinder or arbitrator will split the difference between their stated positions" (Kochan, p. 291). If it is anticipated that the arbitrator will split the difference, then it is in the parties' best interest to maintain an extreme, hard-line position, since "difference splitting" is more likely to result in the hard-liner's favor. Recent research (Long and Fueille, 1974; Starke and Notz, 1981) supports this claim, and suggests final offer arbitration as a solution to this problem. Under final offer arbitration, it is not in the negotiator's best interest to take a hard line, but instead to concede enough to be close to the arbitrator's likely judgment of a fair settlement. Since the arbitrator can only pick one of the two offers, it is anticipated that he is most likely to select the "fairest" offer, that is, one closest to his own judgment of the middle ground.

2.   The Narcotic Effect.   When arbitration is anticipated as a result of the failure of parties to agree, negotiators may also lose interest in the process of negotiating. Since hard-bargaining is costly in time and effort, since there is no guarantee that agreement will be reached, and since an imposed settlement is a guarantee under arbitration, negotiators may take the easy way out. Negotiator passivity, loss of initiative and dependence on the third party are common results of recurring dispute arbitration. These results are even more likely when negotiators are accountable to constituencies, since negotiators can take tough, unyielding stands on issues and blame compromise settlements on the arbitrator rather than on their own concessions. Although there is no known laboratory research on the narcotic effect, commonplace examples are available. Many parents have experienced the consequences of frequent arbitration of their children's disputes: increased demands on the parental arbitrator for further decisions, frequently coupled with escalated conflict and more outrageous charges and counter-charges in order to shape and bias the parent's decision.

3.   The Half-Life Effect.   Using the same example of a parent's resolution of children's disputes, parents are also aware that as the demand for arbitration increases, the sheer number of decisions required also increases, and with it comes the likelihood that a decision will not please one or both sides. This is known as the half-life effect. For example, as one of the authors worked at home one Sunday afternoon, he was frequently subject to the demands of his children to adjudicate disputes in sharing a home video game. After a series of decisions involving both his own children and half of the surrounding neighborhood, said arbitrator was informed by his own child that his decisions were generally viewed as capricious, unfair, and without appropriate compassion for his own sons, and that his services were no longer desired. As the frequency of arbitration increases, disenchantment with the adequacy and fairness of the process develops (Anderson and Kochan, 1977), and the parties may resort to other means to resolve their disputes.

4.   The Biasing Effect.   Arbiters must be careful that their decisions do not systematically favor one side or the other, and that they maintain an image of fairness and impartiality. Even if each decision, taken separately, appears to be a fair settlement of the current conflict issue, perceived patterns of partiality toward one side may jeopardize the arbiter's acceptability. The more biased an arbitrator is believed to be, the less effective (he) is.

5.   The Decision-Acceptance Effect.   Finally, arbitrated disputes may engender less commitment to the settlement than alternative forms of dispute resolution. Research in the dynamics of group decision-making (Vroom, 1973) has continually demonstrated that commitment to problem solutions,

and willingness to implement these solutions, is significantly greater when group members participate in developing that solution than when it is imposed by a single member. While no experimental research in arbitration has directly confirmed this finding, the very distinction of binding vs. voluntary arbitration suggests that voluntary arbitration frequently may not lead to solution acceptance and implementation.

Mediation

In contrast to arbitration—and as a way to alleviate some of the problems with the arbitration style that we just discussed—mediation has developed increasing support (Kochan and Jick, 1978; Kochan, 1980). While the ultimate objective of mediation is the same as arbitration—to resolve the dispute—the major difference is that mediation seeks to achieve the objective by having the parties themselves develop and endorse the agreement. Mediators have no formal power, and cannot resolve the dispute on their own or impose a solution. Instead, their effectiveness comes from their ability to meet with the parties individually, secure an understanding of the issues in dispute, identify areas of potential compromise in the positions of each side, and encourage the parties to make concessions toward agreement.

Mediation generally proceeds in several stages (Kressel, 1972; Kochan, 1980; Wall, 1981). In the early stages of a dispute, a mediator will assume a reasonably passive role; he/she is most concerned with securing acceptance by the parties, and with understanding the nature of the dispute. Strategies may include separating the parties, questioning them about the issues, and actively listening to each side. The mediator must be able to separate rhetoric from true position, and to identify each side's priorities. Once this has been accomplished, the mediator will then begin exchanging proposals and counterproposals, testing each side for areas where concessions may be possible.

As mediation progresses, the third party assumes a more active and aggressive role. He may bring the parties together for face-to-face deliberations, or may keep them separate. He may press one or both sides to make concessions that are judged essential for the opponent. Many of the tactics we described earlier in this chapter are used at this stage. He may invent proposals and solutions that he thinks will be acceptable, testing them with each side or even announcing them publicly. The mediator will try to get the parties to mutually agree in private. If the mediation effort has been successful, the mediator will ultimately bring the parties together to endorse a final agreement, or to publicly announce their settlement. As noted by Rubin (1980), mediators primarily "facilitate concession-making without loss of face by the parties, and thereby promote more rapid and effective conflict resolution than would otherwise occur" (p. 380).

There are several elements to the mediation process that are integral to its success. The first is the timing of his efforts, based on the readiness of the parties. Since mediation is a voluntary process—the parties are not bound to enter into mediation except by their willingness to do so—mediation cannot be effective if the parties do not choose to cooperate. If they believe that they have more to gain by holding out or protracting the dispute, then mediation cannot work. Mediators who judge that the parties are not ready for their intervention frequently tell them "call me when you're ready," and leave until the parties have softened their positions.

Second, mediators must be acceptable to the parties. In contrast to an arbitrator, who may be an appointed official with formal and legal power, the mediator is frequently a neutral individual whom the parties recognize as impartial, experienced and potentially helpful. "Certification" by an organization of third parties, such as the Federal Mediation and Conciliation Service, adds to this credibility. But not just any mediator will do; a variety of highly desirable qualities such as integrity, impartiality, experience in comparable disputes, etc. may be required to be viewed as acceptable by both sides.

Like arbitration, mediation has most commonly been practiced in the field of labor relations, as a preliminary step to arbitration in contractual negotiations and some grievances. But mediation is also experiencing a dramatic rise in popularity as an alternative to the courts—particularly when the parties desire solutions that are low-cost and largely shaped by the parties themselves. The Ford Foundation, in a 1978 report, documented many of the areas in which mediated settlements are now occurring: malpractice suits, tort cases, small claims, pretrial diversions of alcohol and drug cases to treatment centers rather than criminal proceedings, consumer complaints, liability claims, etc. Mediation has become an extremely popular alternative in divorce proceedings, since the parties must be willing to abide by the terms of the settlement, and therefore should have the most influence in shaping its terms (Kressel, Jaffe, Tuchman, Watson and Deutsch, 1977; Coogler, 1978). Mediation has also become a more common form of resolution for civil and community disputes (Kessler, 1978); community mediation centers, staffed by trained volunteers, are springing up around the country. Mediation has also received increased use as a way of avoiding costly litigation in the resolution of business-government disputes, particularly in the area of environmental regulation (Drayton, 1981; Reich, 1981). Finally, mediation is being suggested more frequently as a mechanism for the resolution of international disputes. Roger Fisher (1978) has prepared an extensive manual which offers an insightful array of analytical tools and action techniques for international mediation, and Jeffrey Rubin (1981) has documented the success of Henry Kissenger as an extremely skilled international mediator.

Several studies have shown that mediation is only effective in certain kinds of disputes. Kochan and Jick (1978), for example, in their review of mediation in the public sector, report that mediation was most successful in conflicts that involved a breakdown in negotiations, where bargainers were inexperienced or became overcommitted to their positions. In contrast, mediation was less effective when there was internal conflict within one or both of the negotiating parties—for example, major differences between the demands of a union's rank and file and their chief negotiator's belief about what was attainable at the negotiating table. Mediation was also less effective as a strategy when the parties differed on major economic issues, or had very strong differences in their expectations for a settlement. In negotiating terms, if there is a nonoverlap in the resistance points of both sides (Stevens, 1963), then mediators had to exert greater direct and indirect pressure on the negotiators to create a "positive contract zone," an overlap of resistance points. Direct pressure occurs if the mediator uses tactics to encourage the parties to soften their positions; indirect pressure typically comes through the passage of time, increasing the cost of holding out. Finally, it also appears that mediation is less effective in more "intense" conflicts (Rubin, 1980)—when the conflict is large, when there are many issues at stake, or when the parties disagree on major priorities. Again, under such conditions, mediation tactics may be insufficient to "rock" the parties toward mutual agreement.

It should be clear from this review that both mediation and arbitration have their liabilities. The liabilities of arbitration result from the negotiator's anticipation that a third party will make a binding decision, and the consequences that this has on their negotiating behavior. Thus, arbitration is problematic because it removes control over outcomes from the negotiators, and puts it in the hands of a third party. Moreover, solutions from an arbitrator may be less acceptable to the parties and lead to difficulties in implementation. In contrast, the liabilities of mediation occur because the settlement is *not* imposed on the parties, and the mediator does *not* remove control from them; thus, disputes are perpetuated. Several researchers have proposed that by combining mediation and arbitration into a two-stage dispute resolution model, the liabilities of each may be minimized (Starke and Notz, 1981; Grigsby, 1981; Grigsby and Bigoness, 1981). Starke and Notz proposed that mediation, as a preliminary step to arbitration, should have a complimentary and facilitating effect, but only when the arbitration is of the "final offer" format. Under conventional arbitration, the parties expect a compromise ruling by the arbitrator; since mediation also promises a compromise, the parties choose to wait for the arbitration ruling rather than make concessions during mediation. In contrast, under the expectation of final offer arbitration, mediation provides the parties with an incentive to evaluate the reasonableness of their current positions. As a result, they may be more willing to modify their positions prior to expected arbitration, in order to improve their chances that the arbitrator will rule in favor of their side. Efforts to test these assertions have gained inconclusive results (Grigsby, 1981; Grigsby and Bigoness, 1981). Further research is necessary to explore the combined effects of mediation and type of arbitration on variables such as the speed of dispute resolution, satisfaction with the settlement, willingness to live by and implement the solution, etc.

Process Consultation

A third approach to the resolution of disputes is process consultation (Walton, 1967, 1969). The objective of process consultation is to defuse the emotional basis of conflict and improve communication between the parties. The difference between mediation and process consultation is that mediators focus on both the outcome of conflict (the issue under dispute) as well as the process (the procedures that the parties use to achieve a settlement). Process consultants, in contrast, focus only on procedures; they assume that if they are able to teach the parties how to manage conflict more productively and effectively, these improved procedures will lead to productive outcomes. The purpose of the third party's intervention is to create the foundation for more productive dialogue over substantive issues, and to teach the parties how to prevent conflicts from destructively escalating in the future.

Process consultants usually employ a variety of tactics. Their first step is to separate the parties, and interview them individually. Each side is interviewed to determine its view of the other side, its own position, and a history of the relationship and its conflicts. Following this diagnostic phase, the consultant uses this information to structure a series of dialogues or confrontations between the parties (Beckhard, 1967). These meetings are specifically designed to address the causes of past conflicts, and each side's perceptions of the other. Meetings are held on neutral turf, and planned to determine who should attend and what issues should be discussed. The purpose of the third party is to encourage the parties to confront their differences and the reasons for these differences. He is referee, timekeeper, and gatekeeper of the process, and he works to keep the parties on track while also insuring that the conflict does not escalate. Finally, the third party directs all sides toward some type of problem solving and integration. His assumption is that by confronting and airing their differences, the parties can create a format for working on their substantive differences in the future, and can pursue this agenda without a reoccurence of unproductive escalation. Thus, changing the climate for conflict management, promoting constructive dialogue around differences of opinion, and creating the capacity for other people to act as their own third parties, are major parts of the process consultant's agenda.

The description of successful process consultation suggests that the consultant should possess many of the same attributes that we have ascribed to other third parties. He should be perceived as an expert in the technique, knowledgeable about conflict and its dynamics, able to be emotionally supportive and yet confronting of the parties, and able to diagnose the dispute. Second, he should be perceived as clearly neutral, without bias to one side or the other. Third, he should be authoritative—that is, able to establish power over the *process* that the conflicting parties are pursuing, so he can intervene and control it. While he does not attempt to impose a particular solution or outcome, he must be able to shape the manner in which the parties interact, separating them or bringing them together, and control the agenda that they follow when interaction occurs. Without such control, the parties will resort to their earlier pattern of destructive hostility.

It should be apparent from this discussion of process consultation that the primary focus is not to resolve the substantive differences between the parties, but to teach them how to resolve those differences themselves. Thus, process consultation goes the farthest in putting the issues under dispute back in the hands of the disputing parties. In order to make process consultation work, however, the parties must put aside these substantive differences—something that is hard for them to do.

Process consultation has been most commonly used to improve long-standing relationships. Marital and family therapy are forms of process consultation, as are organizational development and team building between work groups. Process consultation has also been tried in labor-management relationships, and in international conflict between ethnic, political and cultural groups such as Protestants and Catholics in Northern Ireland or Arabs and Israelis in the Middle East. Many of the early efforts at process consultation in these environments were less than 100 percent successful (Lewicki and Alderfer, 1973; Brown, 1977; Boehringer, Zeruolis, Bayley and Boehringer, 1974; Cohen, Kelman, Miller, and Smith, 1977; Benjamin and Levi, 1979; Hill, 1982). However, these research studies have contributed to a better understanding of process consultation, in the following ways:

1. Process consultation is less likely to work as an intervention technique when the parties are deeply locked in a dispute over major unresolved issue(s). Since process consultation seeks to change the nature of the working relationship between the parties, it may only work before the parties confront conflict, or in between major outbreaks of hostility (Walton, 1969).

2. Process consultation may be an ineffective technique in short-term relationships. There is probably little need to teach parties to resolve disputes effectively when they will not be working together in the future.

3. Process consultation may be ineffective when the substantive issues in dispute are zero-sum. The objectives of process consultation are to create both the relationship and the skills for integrative bargaining. If the nature of their dispute or constituency pressures on the bargainers do not encourage and support the integrative process, then process

consultation will not work. Efforts at process consultation will constantly be undermined by the divisive issues in the dispute.

4. Process consultation may be ineffective when the level of conflict is so high that the parties are more intent on revenge or retribution than reconciliation. In effect, process consultation may only work when sustained conflict has worn the parties out, making them want resolution more than continued warfare. If there is not sufficient incentive for the parties to want to work together, efforts at process consultation will be undermined. Trust, cooperation and honesty will be exploited by one side, and the dispute will quickly deteriorate.

Other Third Party Styles

In this section, we have reviewed several major approaches used by third parties to resolve disputes. These approaches—arbitration, mediation and process consultation—represent "textbook" approaches to the resolution of disputes, and are the three most commonly described in the research on third party behavior. However, there are a variety of other third party approaches possible, and many of them have only recently been investigated in research. Sheppard (1984) has proposed a generic classification of third party intervention procedures that spans a wide variety of different conflict environments. Sheppard's model describes how managers actually intervene in conflict, rather than prescribing how they should intervene. His model was developed from an earlier model proposed by Thibaut and Walker (1975) to describe the psychological aspects of procedural justice systems (e.g., courts, tribunals, etc.). Thibaut and Walker conceived of dispute resolution as involving two stages: a procedural or process stage, in which evidence and arguments are gathered and presented, and an outcome or decision stage, in which the evidence is evaluated to determine which party has the weight of evidence in his/her favor. They then distinguished among major conflict intervention styles based on the amount of process control and/or decision control used by the third party. These two approaches to control may be thought of as independent dimensions of conflict intervention, and a third party may exert varying amounts of each in handling a dispute. For our current purposes, we shall simply refer to situations where a third party exerts "high" or "low" amounts of process or decision control, and represent the possibilities in matrix form (Figure 12–1). Sheppard (1983) asked practicing managers to describe the last time they intervened in a dispute between their subordinates, and then coded their responses according to the amount of process and decision control used by the third party. He concluded that managers use one of three dominant styles when they intervened in a subordinate conflict:

FIGURE 12–1
A Taxonomy of Conflict Intervention Styles

		Process Control	
		High	Low
Outcome Control	High	Inquisitorial Intervention	Adversarial Intervention
	Low	Mediation	Providing Impetus

1. **Inquisitorial Intervention.**   This was the most common style. A manager who uses this style exerts high control over both the process and the decision. He/she tells both sides to present their cases, asks lots of questions to probe into each side's position, and frequently controls who is allowed to speak and what they say. He/she then invents a solution that he thinks will meet both parties' needs, and usually enforces that solution on both parties. Inquisitorial intervention is a judicial style of handling conflicts that is found most commonly in European courtrooms.

2. **Adversarial Intervention.**   Managers who use this style exert high control over the decision, but not the process. The manager does not control the process in that he does not ask questions, try to "get the whole story," or control the destructive aspects of the conflict between the parties. Instead, he passively listens to what each side chooses to tell him, and then makes a decision (tells the parties how to solve the conflict) based exclusively on the presentations. This style is most similar to the style used by most American courtroom judges.

3. **Providing Impetus.**   Managers who use this style typically do not exert control over the decision, and only a small amount of control over the process. The manager typically tries to make a quick diagnosis of what the conflict is about, and then tells the parties that if they don't find a solution, he will impose one on them. In short, the manager first says, "what's going on here?" When he finds out what's going on, he says, "you'd better get this problem solved, or else I'll solve it for you, and neither of you will like the solution!"

Sheppard's research indicates that managers spontaneously tend to use styles which resemble acting like an arbitrator, acting like one of several forms of judges, or provide a "common enemy" by threatening to settle the dispute for the parties in an undesirable way if they can't settle it themselves. Note that the remaining cell in Figure 12–1, which we have labeled "Mediation," is NOT a style that is commonly observed among managers. While subsequent research has shown that managers clearly prefer mediation as a third party style (Lewicki and Sheppard, 1985), it is not clear that managers really understand how to mediate. When handling a conflict, managers seem to be very prone to want to assume responsibility for having a major impact on the outcome of the conflict, that is, the specific decision or outcome arrived at by the disputing parties. Therefore, managers may be very uncomfortable using a mediation strategy, which, by Sheppard's definition, requires that they control the process of conflict but leave the solution in the hands of the disputants. Further research is necessary to determine how managers can learn to mediate more effectively, and whether these findings are true for third parties in other conflict situations.

SUMMARY

Through any number of different avenues—breakdowns in communication, escalation of anger and mistrust, polarization of positions and refusal to compromise, or simply the inability to invent options that are satisfactory to both sides—negotiations often break down. Productive dialogue stops. The parties may continue talking, but the communication is usually characterized by trying to sell or force one's own position, and/or talking about the other's unreasonable position and uncooperative behavior. When these breakdowns occur, the parties may simply agree to recess, "cool off," and come back tomorrow. More commonly, however, the parties fail to agree, walk away angry and upset, and while privately wishing there was some way to get back together, don't know how to arrange a reconciliation.

This chapter reviewed actions that the parties can take to return to a productive dialogue. Two major groups of tactics were described: those that parties can try without assistance, and tactics used by third parties who may intervene in the dispute. When left to their own devices, the parties themselves might try to:

- Reduce tension through separating themselves from one another by imposing cooling-off periods, talking about emotions and feelings, and attempting to synchronize de-escalation of their conflict.

- Improve the accuracy of communication through mirroring of the other's statements, and role reversal.

- Keep the number of issues under control so that new issues do not get added, and large issues get divided into smaller ones.

- Search for commonalities in positions, ways to define the issues so that both parties can achieve objectives (integrative frameworks), and super-ordinate goals that will unite parties toward a common objective.

- Make each one's own preferred options more desirable and palatable to the opponent by the way they state, propose and package their proposals.

If the parties themselves are unable to engage in these activities, third parties can do all of this and more. We tend to think of third party efforts at conflict resolution in terms of the style typically used by the third party. In this chapter, we reviewed three prototypical styles of third party intervention: arbitration, mediation, and process consultation. Each of these styles has its strengths and weaknesses as a third party approach. The styles differ in the degree to which the party controls the outcome of the dispute, and the degree to which the third party controls the process by which the parties interact during dispute resolution. Arbitrators typically specify a very formal process by which the parties can present their "case" to the third party. They also tell the parties how to resolve the dispute (the outcome). Mediators exert a great deal of control over how the parties interact by separating them and managing the communication between them; they sometimes point the parties toward particular solutions by suggestions and guidance, but rarely make the decision for the parties. Finally, process consultants are heavily involved in helping to re-establish a productive communication process between the parties, and exert almost no pressure on outcomes. As we pointed out, each of these styles has its assets and liabilities, and therefore may be more or less preferable in particular kinds of disputes. In addition, recent research has shown that there may be other third party styles in common use which have not been systematically studied to determine their impact. A great deal is left to be done in this area, both in determining the appropriateness of particular third party styles and techniques for various types of conflict, as well as achieving a better understanding of the kinds of conflicts that negotiating parties can effectively manage themselves.

13

Ethics in Negotiation

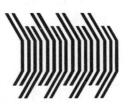

In this final chapter, we shall explore a subject not often addressed: the ethical and value questions that arise in negotiations. Little has been published on this topic. It is our belief that fundamental questions of ethical conduct arise whenever we negotiate. The effective negotiator must recognize when the questions are relevant, and what factors must be considered to answer them.

WHY DO NEGOTIATORS NEED TO KNOW ABOUT ETHICS?

Consider the following situations:

1. You are a manager badly in need of more clerical assistance for your office. While work is getting done, there are unnecessary delays, and some of your staff are complaining that things could be considerably more efficient if another clerk were added. However, you also know that your boss is not sympathetic; she thinks that the problem could be eliminated if all of the current clerks simply worked harder. Moreover, the company's budget is tight, and a strong need for more help will have to be demonstrated if a new position is to be approved. You see the following options open to you:

   a. Document the amount of work that each of your clerks is doing, and make a complete report to your boss.

b. Give each of your clerks a lot of extra jobs to do now that could really be deferred for a few months, thus creating a false overload in their required work.

c. Talk to your boss about the office down the hall (which you think is overstaffed) and ask to have one of these clerks transferred to your department.

d. Have your clerks stage an "artificial slowdown" so that work is delayed, and argue that the only way to get work back to a reasonable pace is to hire another clerk.

Question: Are some of these approaches more ethical than others? Which ones? Which ones would you try?

2. You are an entrepreneur interested in acquiring a business currently owned by a competitor. The competitor, however, has not shown any interest in either selling his company or merging with your business. In order to gain some advantage over your competitor and to pressure him to sell, you instructed one of your own executives to determine if there were any "seriously dissatisfied" people in the competitor's firm who might provide inside information about the firm's financial position.

Question: Is this ethical? Would you be likely to do it if you were the entrepreneur?

3. You are a vice president of personnel, negotiating with a union representative for a new labor contract. The union has insisted that it will not sign a new contract until the company agrees to raise the number of paid holidays from four to six. Management has calculated that it will cost approximately $75,000 for each paid holiday, and has argued to the union that the company cannot afford to meet the demand. However, you know that in reality, money is not the issue—rather, the company simply doesn't think the union's demand is justified. In order to convince the union that they should withdraw their demand, you have been considering the following alternatives:

a. Telling the union that their request is unacceptable to you because their demand isn't justified.

b. Telling the union that the company simply can't afford it.

c. Preparing some erroneous financial statements that show it will cost about $150,000 per paid holiday, and that the company can afford to give only one (if any).

d. Preparing some erroneous financial statements that show that the company is in dire financial straits, and cannot afford to make any major financial concessions for the new contract.

Question: Do any of the strategies raise ethical concerns? Which ones? Why?

The scenarios described are hypothetical; however, the problems they present are real ones for negotiators to consider. Managers are frequently confronted with important decisions about the strategy and tactics that they will use to accomplish important objectives, particularly when a variety of influence options are open to them. In this chapter, we will turn our attention to major ethical questions that arise in negotiation. Three major questions will be considered:

1. What factors motivate ethically marginal behavior?
2. What major types of ethical and unethical conduct are likely to occur in negotiation?
3. In what ways are ethical issues and criteria likely to affect a manager's decisions about which strategy and tactics to use?

Laying the Groundwork

First, it is not our intention to advocate a specific ethical position for all negotiators or for the conduct of all negotiations. Many recent publications take a strongly prescriptive or "normative" position, and obscure the central ethical questions. Instead, we propose to identify the major dimensions of ethics that are relevant to the conduct of negotiation, and to suggest how those dimensions affect a negotiator's choice of strategy and tactics. We will provide negotiators with a framework for assessing negotiating situations, and making more informed decisions about the strategy and tactics they select. In doing so, we will be working in an area in which there has been little systematic research—or even a clear statement of the major questions. Therefore, we will draw heavily from some philosophical writings on the nature of ethics, and from some psychological research on the way that people make complex decisions.

We also wish to distinguish among several different standards for judging a manager's actions that are frequently grouped together under the umbrella term "ethics." Missner (1980) states that when evaluating various business strategies and tactics, it is important to understand the differences among judgment processes based on standards of ethics, and those based on prudence and practicality. Judgments based on ethics are judgments as to what is right and wrong according to some *standards* of moral behavior. Judgments based on prudence are judgments as to what is beneficial or harmful for people who perform those actions. Finally, judgments based on practicality are judgments about what is the best, easiest, or most effective way of undertaking some action in order to achieve an objective. For example, a salesperson preparing a presentation on a new product might be concerned with all three standards in determining her strategy. The ethical salesperson would ask, "What is right? What is the truth about this new product? How can I present this product fairly compared to its competitors on the market?" The prudent salesperson would ask, "How can I best present this product? What can I say about it that will make it attractive? What information should I present and what should I withhold? Can I tell lies about it and get away with them?" Finally, the practical salesperson will ask, "How should we lay out the advertisements? Should I come up with a slogan for this product? What famous endorsements should I get?" Discussions of business ethics frequently confuse the ethical, prudent, and practical criteria for judging conduct. In earlier chapters, we have extensively evaluated negotiation strategy and tactics by prudence and practicality criteria; we will now judge them by ethical criteria of rightness and wrongness.

Finally, we believe judgments about what is "ethical" or "unethical" are subjective, defined in shades and degrees rather than in absolutes. Reasonable people will disagree as to where they "draw the line" between ethical and unethical acts, and whether a given tactic falls on one side of the line or the other (Lewicki, 1982; Raiffa, 1982). While this makes the scientific study of ethical and unethical conduct somewhat elusive (since individuals will differ in their judgments), it does not make ethics themselves elusive. The fact that research in ethics has been more limited than in other fields of negotiation in no way diminishes the importance of confronting the important questions and encouraging negotiators to examine their own ethical decision making processes. In addition, sharpening these questions may create the opportunity for further research that can examine the psychological complexity of these judgments in much more detail.

Having made these precautionary statements, we now turn to a consideration of how negotiators view strategy and tactics that may have ethical overtones.

WHAT MOTIVATES UNETHICAL CONDUCT?

There are several major dimensions of human conduct, and the business system that motivate unethical conduct. Missner (1980) suggests four: profit, competition, justice, and generating wants (advertising). While the strategies and tactics of negotiating have little to do with advertising strategies in the conventional sense, questions and issues of profit, justice and competition are common to the evaluation of negotiating behavior. What are some of the major concerns about each dimension?

Profit. The pursuit of profit is fundamental to the business system, whether it be the company president who is striving to maximize the earnings of the corporation, the stockholders who are looking for bigger dividends, or the salaried clerk who is pushing for a raise. In this context, we define profit as the desire to get "more," rather than in strict accounting terms.

Profit is clearly a motive in negotiating. By its very nature, negotiating is a process by which individuals strive to maximize their outcomes. Individuals trying to maximize their profit frequently use negotiating strategies and tactics because they are recognized as techniques for enhancing profit.

Businessmen frequently defend profit and the profit motive as ethically neutral, not inherently bad or good. In contrast, however, many ethical philosophers and political theorists have argued that profit is a "dirty six-letter word." At the root of this debate between businessmen and their critics are some fundamental questions: What are the standards that should be used to judge the ethical integrity of an economic system? Is the motive for profit "innate" or is it determined by the culture in which we grow up? Is the motive to maximize one's own outcome inherently unethical, or does it inherently lead to unethical behavior to accomplish that end? These are the questions that become relevant for judging the profit motive and the consequences it has for profit-maximizing (and negotiating) behavior.

Competition.   The pursuit of profit is a fundamental principle of both our economic system and individual economic behavior. This behavior occurs in a social context in which the total amount of resources available is insufficient to satisfy everyone's desires; therefore, competition occurs. As Missner points out, "as one embarks on one's journey to become a millionaire, one must face a salient, and perhaps disturbing fact: Others also want to become millionaires, and in the resulting competition, not everyone will be successful" (p. 69).

In the business system, there are several different types of competition. The fundamental differences between these types are whether competitors know that they are competing, whether they know the identity of their competitors, and whether they attain their goal by simply "getting there first" or by blocking their opponent in his pursuit of the goal. An example of the first type is someone trying to set a record for pizza-eating to win recognition in the Guiness Book of World Records; an individual is trying to surpass a previous record without knowing whether anyone else is trying to do so as well. The second case, knowing that others are competing but not knowing who the competitors are, is exemplified by many scientists simultaneously searching for a cure for cancer. These scientists know that they are in a competition, but generally don't know where each one stands in the race. An example of the third case might be two scientists, each of whom knows the other well, and each racing to gain recognition for solving a specific scientific problem. While both may ultimately achieve their goal, only one will get the recognition. An example of the fourth case would be two athletic teams competing in a track meet. In most events, team members know who their competitors are, and know that they have to beat their opponent in their individual events. The key distinguishing aspect of this fourth type is that the competitor can only achieve his objective by defeating the opponent. If there were only one team in the track meet—and none of the team members was good enough to set world records—then the fundamental nature of the competition would be lost. We shall call the first three types *incidental* competition, and this last type *essential* competition.

Much of the competition that occurs in the economic marketplace is incidental, but what occurs in negotiation is largely essential (except in a few types of auction or bidding situations). Bargainers are motivated to gain a favorable outcome, and they are seldom motivated to directly defeat their opponent. In contrast, when labor and management sit down to negotiate, each knows that they need the other side (management cannot exist without labor, and vice versa) but both are also motivated to achieve the best deal they can.

These distinctions between various forms of incidental and essential competition raise some fascinating questions about the impact of competition on a negotiator's predisposition toward unethical action. On the one hand, it can be argued that the closer a negotiator comes to a situation of essential competition, where a specific adversary has to be defeated in order to achieve a goal, the more a party is predisposed to use tactics that are ethically questionable. In most competitions, there are rules that limit what people can and cannot do. It can be argued that when the goal is to defeat an opponent, there may be considerably greater pressures to violate the rules in order to make sure that "defeat" occurs. In contrast, however, it can also be argued that the greatest pressures to violate ethical standards may not arise from essential competition, but from various forms of incidental competition. In these environments, the rules may not be as clearcut, monitoring of the rules may be far less formal and rigid, and the opportunities for unnoticed rule violation may be greater. Do more "rule violations" (instances of unethical conduct) occur when individuals compete in an international track meet or when scientists compete to win the Nobel Prize for chemistry? Obviously, the question is not easily answered, and may be subject to controlled research investigation. In either case, however, it is clear that competition motivates parties to behave unethically.

Justice.   The third major dimension of human conduct that motivates parties toward unethical action is the search for justice. In Chapter 6, we reviewed the ways negotiators judge fairness. These same fairness questions also lead negotiators to question which standards are operating at any given time, and what standards will be necessary to insure that justice is preserved.

As we pointed out in Chapter 6, questions of justice are largely based on differing standards of outcome distribution: what parties actually receive (in economic or social benefits) compared to what they believe they deserve. Conflict arises when parties disagree as to how well they have actually performed, and how much they deserve for their performance. As an example of the first case—determining how well they have performed—suppose one person becomes a millionaire through inheritance while the other person has had to work 60 hours a week for 20 years to attain the same status. In the second case—determining what they deserve for their performance—a justice question may arise over whether an athletic star is worth his new $5 million dollar contract, or whether a labor union deserves an across-the-board increase of 25 cents/hour. Moreover, justice questions arise when parties disagree about whether the rules were followed in attaining a particular end. As we noted in Chapter 6, these are fundamentally questions of distributive justice. The more parties fundamentally disagree about the nature of the rules that apply in a given situation, or the manner in which the rules were (or were not) observed, the more likely these disagreements will lead to an ethical controversy about which fairness standards are "right" and "wrong."

Summary

We have identified three major dimensions of human conduct and the business system which may lead to unethical conduct: the pursuit of profit, the nature of competition, and the appropriate standards for assuring justice. Each of these three dimensions is central to the evaluation of ethical issues in negotiations. When parties seek to maximize their profits, they are more likely to use ethically questionable tactics than when they are not strongly profit-oriented. Similarly, when negotiators are strongly competitive, they are more likely to violate ethical standards in order to defeat their opponent and/or secure their goal. Finally, when parties disagree about what outcomes are deserved, or whether the outcomes were fairly obtained, they are more likely to violate ethical standards to gain what they feel they deserve, or to block others from benefiting unfairly. We shall now consider the various ways that these ethical violations are likely to occur.

HOW DO WE CLASSIFY THE MAJOR ETHICAL QUESTIONS?

Based on a review of the literature in philosophy and ethics, we propose that there are three major dimensions of ethical conduct which account for most of the ethical questions that arise in negotiations: means/ends, relativism/absolutism, and truth-telling.

Means/Ends.   Many of the ethically questionable incidents in business that upset the public are instances where people have argued that the ends justify the means. How much and what kinds of influence can a corporation use to push for an important piece of legislation that will benefit it? What practices can a pharmaceutical company use in order to rush a new "miracle" drug through testing and onto the market? Even when a negotiator has a very noble objective to attain for his constituency, can he use whatever strategy and tactics he wants to obtain his goal? What is the best way to approach and answer these questions?

Questions of means vs. ends are best evaluated by understanding a theory of ethics known as *utilitarianism*. Utilitarianism holds that the moral value and worth of a particular action is judged on the basis of the consequences it produces. Since morality is measured by the quality of consequences, utilitarians believe that the way to maximize virtue is by maximizing the best consequences. Debate then centers on several key questions about how this virtue is attained. First, how do we define (and who defines) what is "good," and how do we measure it? Second, should utilitarian acts be judged primarily on the virtues of the acts themselves (those acts that lead to the greatest good for the greatest number) or by complying with some specific set of correct and virtuous rules of conduct which will lead to good outcomes. The *act utilitarian* will argue that the best standard of moral conduct is to maximize the greatest good for the greatest number. The *rule utilitarian* will argue that this kind of decision is not always clearcut, and could get a decision-maker into trouble; instead, they argue that the best way to achieve the greatest good is to closely follow a set of rules and principles. For example, let us suppose that a militant subgroup within a union has called a wildcat strike over what it feels are critical questions of worker safety. Some other rank and file members support the strike because they think the questions are very important. The group has made a series of demands to management; if these demands are met, they have agreed to end the strike. Management agrees to meet the demands, and the strike is ended. Management then immediately dismisses all of the wildcatters for participating in the illegal strike, and takes no action on the safety issues. The union leadership accuses management of "unethical negotiating."

In this situation, act utilitarians would argue that management's tactic of agreeing to meet the worker's demands was necessary to end an illegal strike. However, it is management's job (not the workers') to determine conditions of worker safety, and these overriding responsibilities justify the tactic of falsely agreeing to meet the wildcatter's demands (and then punishing the strikers as well). In contrast, rule utilitarians might argue that management has a responsibility to adhere to standards of credibility and integrity in conducting its negotiations, because that behavior produces the best results and the best union-management relations. By lying to the strikers, management has compromised its integrity and will have to suffer the consequences.

This scenario, and many others like it, constitute the "grist" by which act and rule utilitarians debate the virtues of their respective cases. These different approaches to utilitarianism are closely related to the motivation for profit that we discussed earlier in this chapter. Since we defined profit broadly—as the desire to get "more"—maximizing profit can be viewed as an end in itself, or as an objective that can only be legitimately attained by following some accepted rules and practices. These different views of maximizing profit are central to many debates about individual and societal economic values. For example, the continued debate between the "free market" economists vs. the "regulatory" social economists reflects two different sets of values about how utilitarianism should be pursued in economic policy. Similarly, when business students argue about the competing objectives of profit vs. social responsibility, they are debating utilitarian questions that usually have important means vs. ends issues attached to them.

When addressing means vs. ends questions in competition and negotiation, we usually focus the most attention on the question of what strategy and tactics may be used to achieve certain ends. Are exploitative, manipulative, or devious tactics ever justifiable? Under what circumstances? Even when such tactics are within the law, they may still be judged as unethical by two other standards: the ethical systems of the negotiators themselves, and the ethical norms of the environment in which they operate. We will address these standards more completely later in this chapter.

Relativism/Absolutism.   The second major ethical dimension is relativism vs. absolutism. Individuals who are absolutists are committed to the view that there are some ethical standards which hold in every situation. Whether individuals hold these views as a result of serious philosophical study, religious teachings or other forms of moral education, absolutists believe that there are some fundamental, uncompromisable "rules" in the world. For example, an absolutist who believes in the commandment "thou shalt not kill" would argue that the commandment is the same, regardless of whether we are talking about a case of murder, the death penalty, abortion, or euthanasia (mercy killing of terminally ill or suffering patients). Similarly, an absolutist committed to the Golden Rule ("Do unto others as you would have them do unto you.") believes in kindness and generosity toward others even in the face of violence, abuse, and exploitation.

A pure relativist, in contrast, would argue that we cannot determine what is good ethics in any absolute sense because "everything is relative." Ethics are determined by an individual's personal values. Ethical judgments must be made by each individual. There are no absolutes. Everyone must determine for himself/herself what is right and appropriate to do, and no one should impose his/her standards on others. An ethical relativist would believe it right to make up his/her own mind about whether the death penalty is different from euthanasia, and many would find it acceptable to condemn death-producing actions in the first case and condone them in the second. Similarly, relativists would argue that the "Golden Rule" is no rule at all, and that each individual should make up his/her own mind about how to respond to others who are hurting or harming you.

The distinctions we have just drawn are extremes. In reality, there are probably few pure absolutists or pure relativists in the world. Most people's views are probably within some middle range, varying slightly toward the relativistic vs. absolute sides of the scale. The mild absolutists generally adhere to a philosophy that one should always try to "do good" whenever possible, and usually believe that "doing good" is not hard to define. Similarly, the mild relativists are usually highly educated and believe, based on their own values, that in general they know what's right for themselves. Moreover, these relativists are likely to believe that while individuals must determine for themselves what conduct is appropriate, factors in the situation and the culture will play an important role. Finally, as in the questions of means vs. ends, debates between relativists and absolutists emphasize different standards of conduct in business situations. Relativists will argue "when in Rome, do as the Romans do;" in other words, it is necessary to know something about your opponent, and the cultural and social environment in which you are negotiating, in order to know what tactics are most suitable and appropriate. One does not bargain with thieves the same way one bargains with principled men. In contrast, absolutists will argue that one must adhere to certain fundamental principles (integrity, trustworthiness, honor), or negotiating will quickly deteriorate into a free-for-all argument or even into the use of force. This relativism vs. absolutism debate raises an intriguing question: are there some basic and fundamental "absolutes" of principled (ethical) negotiation? We will directly address this question later in this chapter.

Truth-Telling. While we judge the "proper" orientation toward profit maximization and competition by standards of utilitarianism, standards of truth-telling help to define what communication is ethical or unethical. Most people would agree that they would value a reputation for being truthful; however, it is not always as easy to define what this means. While the ethical questions about truth-telling are quite straightforward, once again the answers are not so clear. First, how does one define "truth?" Second, how does one define and classify various deviations from the truth? Are they all "lies?" Finally, we can add a relativistic dimension to these questions: should a person tell the truth all the time, or are there times when not telling the truth is an acceptable (or even necessary) form of conduct? These are the questions that concern negotiators in deciding what they can and cannot say.

A number of articles in business journals have addressed the ethical question of truth-telling. For example, Carr (1968) argued in the *Harvard Business Review* that strategy in business is analogous to strategy in a game of poker. He advocated that, short of outright cheating (the equivalent of marking cards or hiding an ace up your sleeve), business ought to play its game as poker players do.

> Most executives from time to time are almost compelled, in the interests of their companies or themselves, to practice some form of deception when negotiating with customers, dealers, labor unions, government officials, or even other departments of their companies. By conscious misstatements, concealment of pertinent facts, or exaggeration—in short, by bluffing—they seek to persuade others to agree with them. I think it is fair to say that if the individual executive refuses to bluff from time to time—if he feels obligated to tell the truth, the whole truth and nothing but the truth—he is ignoring opportunities permitted under the rules and is at a heavy disadvantage in his business dealings (p. 144).

In making this assertion, Carr advocates a modified ethical relativism for the standards of truth-telling, i.e. that bluffing, exaggeration, and concealment or manipulation of information are legitimate ways for both individuals and corporations to maximize their self-interest. By advocating this approach, an executive might condone "pleading poverty" and try to convince the opponent that he has no more money, in order to minimize the settlement in a contract negotiation. However, at the same time he might also condone the marketing and sale of a product known to be defective or hazardous. As the reader can well imagine, Carr's position sparked lively debate among *Harvard Business Review* readers. A number of critics argued that individual businessmen and corporations should be held to higher standards of ethical conduct, and took Carr to task for the position he advocated.

Questions and debate regarding the ethical standards for truth-telling are central and fundamental in the negotiating process. As we pointed out when we discussed interdependence (Chapter 2), negotiation is based on "information dependence" (Kelley and Thibaut, 1969)—the exchange of information in order to learn the true preferences and priorities of the other negotiator. The more a party has accurate information about his own preferences and priorities, and those of the opponent, the more likely he can achieve a more effective, precise negotiating position. At the same time, the negotiator wants to disclose as little of his own position as possible. As Kelley (1966) has pointed out, this results in two fundamental negotiation dilemmas:

First, negotiators must resolve the dilemma of trust—that is, they must infer the other's true intentions or preferences while knowing that the other is attempting to inflate, magnify or justify those preferences. As Kelley writes, "to believe everything the other says is to place one's faith in his hands, and to jeopardize the full satisfaction of one's own interests. On the other hand, to believe nothing the other says is to eliminate the possibility of accepting any arrangement with him" (p. 60). Similarly, negotiators must also resolve their own dilemma of honesty and openness, that is, how frank and candid one should be about one's own true preferences and priorities. If one is completely honest and candid, he/she may be vulnerable to exploitation by his opponent, commit himself to a position that allows no further concessions, or sacrifice gains that might have been successfully derived through less candid approaches. As Rubin and Brown (1975) note, "to sustain the bargaining relationship, each party must select a middle course between the extremes of complete openness toward, and deception of, the other. Each must be able to convince the other of his integrity while not at the same time endangering his bargaining position" (p. 15).

Deception and disguise may take several forms in negotiation (Lewicki, 1983):

1. Misrepresentation of one's position to an opponent. By misrepresentation, the negotiator lies about her preferred settlement point or resistance point. She tells the opponent that she wants to settle for more than she really expects, or threatens to walk away from a deal when she actually would be prepared to make further concessions. Misrepresentation is the most common form of deceit in negotiation.

2. Bluffing. Bluffing is also a very common deceptive tactic. The negotiator falsely states his intentions to commit some action, making false threats or promises. A false threat might be a negotiator's statement that he will walk out if his terms and conditions are not met; a false promise might be a negotiator's commitment to perform some personal favor for the opposing negotiator later on, when in fact he has no intention of ever performing that favor.

3. Falsification. Falsification is the introduction of factually erroneous information into a negotiation. Falsified financial information, false statements of what other parties are doing, will do, or have done before, are common examples.

4. Deception. The negotiator constructs a collection of true and/or untrue arguments in order to lead his opponent to the wrong conclusion. For example, a negotiator may describe in detail what actions he took in a similar circumstance in the past, and lead the opponent to believe he intends to take the same actions again in the future.

5. Selective disclosure or misrepresentation to constituencies. The negotiator does not accurately tell his constituency what has transpired in negotiation, and/or does not tell his opponent the true wishes, desires or position of his constituency. Each side (the constituency and the opponent) may therefore be played off against the other while the negotiator tries to engineer the agreement he wants most.

This is not meant to be an exhaustive list of the way lying and deceit can enter into negotiation; nor is it meant to create further confusion by trying to split semantic hairs over the different ways people can lie. It is meant, however, to show that various forms of lying and deceit are an integral part of effective negotiation. Distinguishing the difference between "ethical" and "unethical" lying, or even between "necessary" and "unnecessary" lying in negotiation, is therefore not as easy as one might think.

Summary

Three major ethical questions confront negotiators in evaluating strategy and tactics: means-ends, relativism, and truth-telling. Means-ends questions arise when a negotiator must consider whether to use ethically marginal tactics in order to accomplish objectives. In other words, does the end justify the means? Such choices are more likely to be made when negotiators are strongly profit-oriented, are heavily competing with others, or perhaps are attempting to redress situations of inequity and injustice. Truth-telling questions arise when a negotiator must consider whether to deviate from telling the truth, the whole truth, and nothing but the truth (in order to achieve his objectives). Deviations from the truth—through bluffs, misrepresentations, distortions or even outright falsification of facts—give a negotiator temporary tactical advantage, but at the expense of his ethical integrity and perhaps his reputation. Finally, questions of relativism arise when negotiators must determine the appropriate criteria for dictating ethical standards. The more a negotiator leans toward ethical relativism, the more he will look to aspects of the specific situation or his personal values to dictate how he should behave, or what is appropriate to do. In contrast, the more he is prone toward an absolutist perspective, the more he will turn to established moral and ethical codes to direct his behavior. We shall now explore some of the factors that tend to influence and dictate how negotiators are disposed to deal with these ethical questions.

A SIMPLE MODEL OF ETHICAL DECISION MAKING

Why do people choose unethical behavior? The first answer that normally occurs to us is that people are corrupt, degenerate, or immoral. In fact, these answers are too simplistic; moreover, they do not help us understand and control our own behavior, or successfully influence and predict the behavior of others in a bargaining environment. Building in part on the material we have already covered in this chapter, we have developed a relatively simple model of decision making to help us understand the decision to behave unethically. There are three major components to this decision: the motivation to behave unethically, the functions served by this unethical conduct, and the consequences resulting from this decision.

The Motivation to Behave Unethically

Earlier in this chapter, we identified three primary motivations that may lead to unethical conduct: profit, competition, and the restoration of justice. While many ethical philosophers have questioned the ethical aspects of these objectives per se, we will accept them as ethically legitimate objectives for negotiators to pursue. We propose, however, that the more a negotiator desires these objectives, the more pressure he will feel to behave unethically. Thus, the stronger the desire to achieve a profit, compete with an opponent, or restore some standard of justice (or punish injustice), the more predisposed a negotiator is to select an unethical tactic.

The Function of Unethical Conduct

Tactics can be primarily grouped into two categories: truth-telling tactics and means-ends tactics. These categories reflect two of the major ethical dimensions we described earlier. (The third dimension, relativism, will be introduced later as important to judging the situations in which a given tactic can be used.) The purpose of using either of these groups of tactics is to increase the negotiator's power in the bargaining environment.

Let us first examine unethical truth-telling tactics. As we have proposed several times, information is one of the major bases of power in negotiation. Violations of the truth (lies) manipulate information in favor of the holder of that information. Thus, a lie enhances the power of the liar by changing the balance of "accurate" information in the negotiating relationship. Through the tactics we described earlier—bluffing, falsification, misrepresentation, deception, and selective disclosure—the liar gains "advantage" by appearing to have more valid or accurate information. This information is then used to change the opponent's preferences or priorities toward the negotiator's own objectives.

Means-ends tactics constitute a second class of unethical behavior. Means-ends tactics also give the negotiator additional power, but, unlike truth-telling, more than one basis of power may be manipulated: the negotiator's perceived expertise, ability to reward or punish the opponent, or even perceived legitimacy and reputation. The following tactics often raise serious ethical concerns in the means they employ, but nevertheless are used by negotiators to gain advantage:

- Using gifts, entertainment or even "bribes" to get an opponent to soften his position.
- Using networks or "spies" to try to learn about an opponent's confidential information and resistance point.
- Undermining an opponent in the eyes of his constituency by persuading or even bribing that constituency.
- Using electronic surveillance to "bug" an opponent's office or constituency meetings.
- Theft of an opponent's private files or confidential information.
- Trying to demean or humiliate an opponent by making public charges or accusations (either publicly or privately).
- Misrepresenting one's own office, credentials, status, or reputation in order to fool the opponent.

- In a competitive bidding environment, deliberately underpricing an offer in order to "steal" the business from an opponent.

In summary, both lies and means/ends tactics are used to gain power in a negotiating environment. Power is derived either by giving the negotiator "better information" (through a lie), gaining some form of tactical advantage over a competitor, or undermining his opponent's negotiating position. Using these tactics frequently leads to consequences for the negotiator, the opponent, and observers.

The Consequences of Unethical Conduct

As a result of employing an unethical tactic, the negotiator will experience positive or negative consequences for that action. These consequences will occur depending on whether the tactic "worked" or not, and the overall strategy of influence. Moreover, since other people will evaluate unethical tactics as "proper" or "improper" to use in negotiating, the result is that the tactic will evoke strong emotional reactions—from the negotiator himself, from the "victim," and from any observers that are present.

A simple model of the decision to use an unethical tactic and its consequences is presented in Figure 13–1. Let us first consider how an unethical tactic is evaluated by the "victim." People who discover that they have been deceived or exploited are typically angry. They usually feel manipulated, both because they may have lost the negotiation as a result of a deceptive tactic, and because they feel foolish for having let themselves be deceived by a clever ploy. As a result of both, the actual loss they may have suffered in negotiations, and the embarrassment they feel from having been deceived, most "victims" are likely to seek retaliation and revenge. Thus, while the use of unethical tactics may lead to short-term success for the negotiator, it may also lead to revenge by the victim because he is either upset about his loss or discovers the way that he has been taken. Moreover, the experience of having been exploited is likely to have a strong effect on the victim's view of negotiations in the future. Not only will he not trust this opponent again, and be extremely wary of his tactics, but the experience will frequently generalize to his negotiations with others. He will be less likely to trust others, and be more wary of being exploited again.

From the negotiator's perspective, as we stated earlier, the primary motivation to use an unethical tactic is to increase power and control. The decision to use such a tactic may have been made casually and quickly, or after careful evaluation of several options and their likely consequences. Because we believe that most negotiators are not inherently dishonest or pathological, *but are* generally aware of their social and moral responsibilities, we propose that when a negotiator decides to use an unethical tactic, he/she searches for "reasons" to justify his behavior. The primary purpose of this justification is to "excuse" the behavior—there is some good, reasonable,

FIGURE 13–1

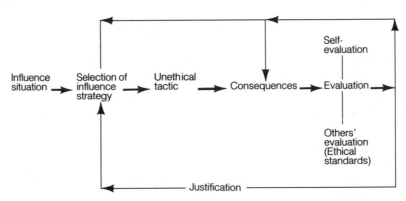

legitimate reason why this tactic was necessary. Some of the most frequent justifications used by those who employ unethical tactics are as follows (adapted from Bok, 1978, and her studies of lying):

- The tactic was unavoidable. The negotiator was not in full control of his actions, and hence should not be held responsible. Perhaps he never intended to hurt anyone, or his words were misinterpreted, or he was pressured into using the tactic by someone else.

- The tactic was harmless. What the negotiator did was really trivial and not very significant. Several authors have pointed out that we tell "white lies" all the time. For example, we greet our neighbor with a cheery "good morning, nice to see you"; in fact, it may not be a good morning and we really aren't pleased to see our neighbor at all. Exaggerations, bluffs, or peeking at our opponent's private notes during negotiations can all be easily explained away as "harmless" actions.

- The tactic will help to avoid negative consequences. When using this justification, we are arguing that the end justifies the means. In this case, the justification is that the tactic helped to avoid greater harm. In a holdup, it is okay to lie to a gunman about where you hide your money, because the consequences of telling the truth are that you will get robbed. Similarly, lying (or other similar means/ends tactics) may be seen as justifiable in negotiation if it protects the negotiator against undesirable consequences should the truth be known—e.g., the negotiator agrees to pay us a sum of money but really has no money in his bank account.

- The tactic will produce good consequences. Again, the end justifies the means, but in a positive sense. As we stated earlier, a negotiator who judges a tactic on the basis of its consequences is making judgments according to rules of utilitarianism—that the quality of any given action is judged by its consequences. A strong act utilitarian usually doesn't get involved in the complex questions of ethics because he judges actions based on the consequences they produce, rather than on some absolute standard of right and wrong. As a result, utilitarians will argue that certain kinds of lies or means/ends tactics are appropriate because they may provide for the larger good—"Robin Hood-type" tactics. However, most negotiators use these tactics for their own advantage, not for the general good. In this case, their actions are likely to be viewed by others as less excusable than tactics which avoid negative consequences.

- The tactic is "fair" or "appropriate" to the situation. Finally, negotiators frequently justify their actions by claiming that the situation made it necessary for them to act the way they did. Most social situations, including negotiations, are governed by a set of generally well-understood rules of proper conduct and behavior. These rules are sometimes suspended for two reasons: because it is believed that others have already violated the rules (therefore legitimizing the negotiator's right to violate them as well), and because it is anticipated that someone else will violate the rules (and therefore the other's actions should be pre-empted). The first case is an example of using unethical tactics in a tit-for-tat manner, to restore balance, to give others their due. Justifications such as "an eye for an eye," or "he started it and I'm going to finish it!" are commonly heard as a defense for resorting to unethical tactics in these cases. Anticipatory justification, the second case, usually occurs as a result of how one perceives one's opponent, and usually leads to its own self-fulfilling prophecy. For example, a negotiator uses an unethical tactic because he believes his opponent is likely to use one; the opponent retaliates with an unethical tactic of his own (because the first negotiator used one), which only goes to justify to the first negotiator that his opponent was likely to behave unethically anyway.

Justifications, therefore, are self-serving rationalizations for one's own conduct. They allow the negotiator to convince himself, and perhaps others, that conduct which would ordinarily be "wrong" is, in this situation, okay. We propose that the more frequently a negotiator engages in this self-serving justification process, the more his judgments about ethical standards and values will become biased, leading to a lessened ability to make accurate judgments about the truth. Moreover, while the tactics were initially used to gain power in a negotiation, we propose that the negotiator who uses these tactics frequently will experience a loss of power over the long run. The negotiator is less likely to be trusted, seen as having less credibility and integrity, and treated as someone who will act exploitatively if the opportunity arises. Negotiators with these characteristics are probably less successful in the long run unless they are skillful at continually staying ahead of the negative reputation generated by their conduct.

FIGURE 13-2

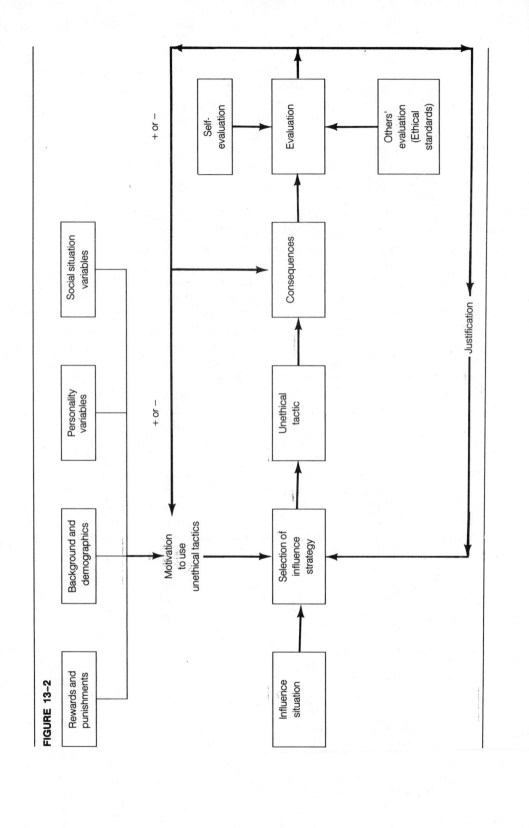

In summary, we propose that the successful use of unethical tactics, and their successful justification, will be self-serving toward the negotiator's short term goals, but they are also likely to distort the negotiator's perception of what is fair, necessary, and appropriate. Negotiator who use these tactics are likely to use them again in the future, but in using them, they will damage both their reputation and the long-term relationship with their opponent.

FACTORS CREATING A PREDISPOSITION TO CHOOSE UNETHICAL TACTICS

In addition to the motivations described earlier, the predisposition to use unethical tactics may also be influenced by four other factors:

- The background and demographic characteristics of the negotiators.
- The personality characteristics and value system of the negotiators.
- The contingent rewards and punishments associated with using a particular tactic.
- The normative nature of the social environment or culture that encourages or discourage unethical conduct.

In this final section, we suggest how each of these factors can have some influence on a negotiator's willingness to use ethically questionable tactics. Figure 13–2 illustrates how these factors affect the negotiator's decision-making process.

Personality, Background, and Demographic Influences

A number of authors have suggested that differences in ethical choices may be traced to fundamental differences in value systems and moral development. Allport, Vernon and Lindzey (1960), England (1967), and Rokeach (1973), have all proposed major classifications and descriptions of human values and value systems. While these classifications are useful for broadly describing the differences between individuals with different value orientations, they do not appear to be very effective for predicting how individuals will behave in any particular situation.

Somewhat more promising research on the impact of moral development may be derived from the work of Kohlberg (1969). Kohlberg proposed that an individual's moral and ethical judgments are a consequence of his achieving a particular level, or "stage" of moral growth during his/her development. The more "complex" an individual's moral reasoning, the higher a stage he/she has achieved. A number of studies have confirmed this stage model. For example, Leming (1978) administered a paper-and-pencil test of moral development to a group of college undergraduates, and then observed their behavior on a second self-scoring test that permitted "cheating." Students who had reached higher levels of moral development cheated less on the second test.

Finally, Forsyth (1980) has also proposed a taxonomy of ethical ideologies, and developed a paper-and-pencil test to measure differences in ethical orientation. Forsyth proposed that individuals differ along two dimensions of ethical ideology: their level of idealism (a belief that desirable consequences can always be obtained if one does the "right thing") and their level of relativism (as we described earlier in this chapter, the commitment to universal moral rules vs. situational determination of those rules). Categorizing individuals as either high or low on each of these two dimensions leads to the groupings shown in Figure 13–3. While we might predict that Situationalists and Subjectivists would be more likely to behave more unethically than Absolutists and Exceptionists, Forsyth's data indicate that a more thorough understanding of each type is needed in order to make accurate behavioral predictions.

Other Personality Variables. Other researchers have sought to identify additional personality dimensions that would successfully predict the predisposition to behave unethically. We will mention two of these here.

1. *Machiavellianism*. In Chapter 11, we noted that differences in Machiavellian orientation appeared to have a significant impact on negotiating behavior. Machiavellians adhere to a very pragmatic and expedient view of human nature—"the best way to handle people is to tell them what they want to hear" or "it is hard to get ahead without cutting corners here and there." A number of research studies have shown that individuals

FIGURE 13–3
Taxonomy of Ethical Ideologies

| | Relativism | |
	High	Low
Idealism	*Situationalists*	*Absolutists*
High	Rejects moral rules; advocates an individual analysis of each act in each situation to determine what is right; relativistic.	Assumes that the best possible outcome can always be achieved by following universal moral rules.
	Subjectivists	*Exceptionists*
Low	Appraises the situation based on own personal values and perspectives rather than universal moral principles; relativistic.	Moral absolutes guide personal judgments but pragmatically open to exceptions to these standards; utilitarian.

who are strongly Machiavellian are more willing and able con artists, more likely to lie when they need to, better able to tell bigger lies without feeling anxious about it, and more persuasive and effective in their lies (Christie and Geis, 1970; Exline, Thibaut, Hickey, and Gumpert, 1970; Braginsky, 1970; Geis and Moon, 1981). Machiavellianism thus appears to be a very important predictor of ethical conduct.

2. *Internal-External Control.*   We also mentioned in Chapter 11 that individuals differ in the degree to which they are internally or externally controlled, that is, the degree to which they believe that the outcomes they obtain are largely a result of their own ability and effort (internal control) vs. fate or chance (external control). Research on the impact of this orientation shows that differences in internal vs. external control, by themselves, are not good predictors of cheating behavior. However, when situational variables are taken into account, more predictive accuracy is achieved. Faced with a situation in which it is not clear whether skill or luck will determine the outcome, internally controlled individuals are more likely to cheat when they believe that skill will determine the outcome, and externally controlled individuals are more likely to cheat when they believe that luck will determine the outcome (and they aren't lucky enough to be successful at the task) (Hegarty and Sims, 1978).

Demographic Factors.   Several survey-oriented research studies on ethical behavior have attempted to relate ethical conduct to differences in individual background, religious orientation, age, sex, nationality, education, etc. For example, Hassett (1981, 1982) reported in the magazine *Psychology Today* that individuals who were older, and/or who had a stronger commitment to some religious philosophy, would be less likely to behave unethically. Others have shown that more ethical conduct was evident among individuals who have been educated in parochial schools, or among those who claim a stronger personal and moral code (Absolutists, in Forsyth's scheme) (Maier and Lavrakas, 1976). Finally, in judging the behavior of others, certain occupational groups (such as politicans) are trusted less and expected to behave more unethically. A number of recent social critics have noted the decreased trust and confidence placed in political leaders and despaired about the consequences of this decreased confidence for the integrity of the democratic political system.

History of Reward and Punishment

In addition to the effects that personality and background differences may have on the decision to use unethical tactics, we propose that the rewards or punishments associated with ethical or unethical behavior will also have an impact. More specifically, we suggest that if ethical conduct is seen as leading to reward and unethical conduct is believed to lead to punishment, then the frequency of ethical conduct should increase (and unethical conduct decrease). Conversely, if unethical conduct is not punished by others, and/or leads a negotiator to attaining rewarding outcomes that would be unavailable to him if he behaved ethically, we would expect the frequency of unethical conduct to increase when the negotiator believed he could "get away with it."

Reward and punishment factors should not only motivate a negotiator's present behavior, but also affect the negotiator's predisposition to use similar strategies in similar circumstances in the future. Obtaining "success" or "failure" in an influence strategy involving ethical criteria should also affect the predisposition to behave ethically or unethically again. Research by Hegarty and Sims (1978) appears to support both of these assertions. In their study, when research participants expected to be "rewarded" for making an unethical decision, e.g., participating in a kickback scheme, they not only participated, but also were willing to participate again when a second opportunity arose. Moreover, when there were also strong pressures on the research subjects to compete with others—by announcing how well each person had done on the task, and giving one a prize for the highest score—the frequency of unethical conduct increased.

Situational Influences on Unethical Conduct

The last set of factors which should have an impact on a negotiator's willingness to act unethically are situational factors. We will briefly examine three elements from this group: the negotiator's relationship with the opponent, differences in power and status between the two negotiators, and the social or cultural norms that govern the negotiation process.

Relationship between the Negotiator and the Opponent.   There are two aspects of the negotiator-opponent relationship that will affect the disposition to use certain tactics: what the relationship has been like in the past, and what they would like it to be in the future. The negotiator's past relationship will affect current behavior if the parties have been previously competitive or cooperative, are friends or enemies, feel indebted to one another or hold grudges toward one another. For example, research by Gruder (1971) showed that negotiators were more likely to make more deceptive arguments, negotiate for a longer period of time, and make fewer concessions to an opponent they previously experienced as "exploitative" compared to one who had been cooperative. Similar behavior would be likely to occur if one expected an opponent to behave exploitatively, even if that behavior had not yet been experienced. By describing the opponent as one to be viewed with suspicion—exploitative, competitive, dishonest—negotiators can then justify a relativistic approach to their strategy and claim that anticipatory self-defense legitimizes their actions. This form of rationalization may be very prone to distortion as a result of fear and suspicion, and creates its own self-fulfilling prophecy. All a negotiator needs to justify his own pursuit of an unethical tactic is to experience some mildly competitive or exploitative bit of behavior in an opponent, or even imagine that it is going to occur. Naturally, this will motivate the opponent to seek revenge and act in exactly the ways that the negotiator anticipated.

Relative Power between the Negotiator and His Opponent.   A second situational factor is relative power—how much power one negotiator has relative to his opponent. In general, negotiators with more power are more likely to abuse that power by using less ethical tactics. For example, in one research study, negotiators with more power bluffed more often and communicated less with their opponent than those with less power (Crott, Kayser, and Lamm, 1980). This result will seem paradoxical to some people. Why should negotiators with more power, who can presumably get what they want by using their power legitimately, use unethical tactics which increase their power even more? The results seem to support the "intoxication" theories of power. These theories hold that power corrupts the thinking of the powerful; results confirming the theory have been consistently observed in both laboratory research, and in the power dynamics between "haves" and "have nots" in our society. A balance of power should lead to more stable, ethical conduct than an imbalance.

Group and Organizational Norms.   Finally, many negotiators look to the social norms of the particular situation to decide how to behave. Norms are the informal social rules—"dos and don'ts"—that govern social behavior. In negotiation, the rules are defined in two ways: by what people believe is appropriate in negotiation, and by what other people say is appropriate in that situation. As an example of the first case, some negotiators may define negotiation as a "game," and thus feel that "gaming rules" apply to negotiation. For example, if negotiating is a game like poker, then it is very appropriate to bluff, fake, or bet in order to try to drive others out of the game. Is it appropriate to do these things in negotiation? Do all people agree? (See McDonald, 1963; Carr, 1968.) What happens when some people believe these tactics are appropriate, and proceed to use bluffing tactics, while others don't believe they are appropriate (but neither side discusses the issue until someone behaves in a questionable manner)? The answer is that the process is seriously disrupted because the negotiators failed to agree upon (or even discuss) the rules they assumed they were playing by. If negotiators are working in a new environment—where they have never negotiated before and are not sure how each views the implicit rules—then one or both parties should take the initiative to discuss those rules before they are unintentionally violated.

In addition to adhering to "implicit" rules of negotiating that legitimize certain kinds of unethical conduct, negotiators also look to their peers or knowledgeable advisors to determine what is appropriate. For example, a recent survey of American managers revealed that 80 percent of the sample believe that their organizations are guided by highly ethical principles. However, when asked what factors actually influence ethical or unethical behavior in their organization, "formal organization policy" was rated as *least* important. In contrast, the actual behavior of one's boss or peers was rated most important, regardless of the age, gender, education level or organizational level of those answering the questionnaire. Therefore, what is judged as ethical or unethical is very much influenced by the norms and group culture created within various subgroups of the organization. These findings suggest again that many managers are relativistic in their orientation, looking not to moral absolutes but to the environment around them to determine what is appropriate or inappropriate to do. Many recent exposés of unethical conduct in business and politics—from Watergate on down—have shown that the guilty parties truly believed that this type of behavior was condoned or even necessary in their particular environment in order to accomplish their objectives.

SUMMARY

In this chapter, we have discussed some of the primary factors that affect how a negotiator evaluates and decides to use unethical tactics. We began by suggesting that there were three primary motivational factors which lead negotiators to consider using unethical tactics: the pursuit of profit, the desire to beat an opponent in a competitive environment, and the need to insure or restore some standard of justice that has been violated. Any of these motives may be sufficient to prompt a negotiator to move toward the use of marginally ethical and questionable behavior in order to accomplish his objectives.

Three major categories of ethical conduct were used to describe the broad range of questionable negotiating strategies and tactics: means/ends, truth-telling, and relativism. Means–ends tactics are judged according to the philosophical tenets of utilitarianism—that one can achieve the greatest good by pursuing certain ends, or by abiding by certain rules and procedures which will lead to those ends. The more one is committed to attain certain ends, the more one may be prone to believe that it is occasionally necessary to deviate from "the rules" to attain those ends. In contrast, the more one is committed to abide by certain rules and procedures, the more one believes that following the rules will eventually lead to the desired ends. The second group of tactics, relativistic vs. absolute, forces us to deal with questions of whether there are truly absolute rules and principles of right and wrong, or whether questions of ethics must be answered by each individual in his own personalized, subjective view of the world. A negotiator who looks only to himself or to the dynamics of the immediate situation, rather than to broad principles of what is right and proper, would be more likely to espouse relativism as a standard for making his decisions. Lastly, truth-telling standards determine whether it is appropriate (or even necessary) to deviate from the truth in order to effectively negotiate. Many authors have suggested that bluffing, misrepresentation or factual distortion is sometimes necessary in order to effectively negotiate; such behavior, however, may well be seen by others as unethical and inappropriate.

We have included this chapter because we believe that the negotiation process raises a host of ethical issues, more so than most other interpersonal transactions. Much of what has been written on negotiating behavior has been strongly normative about ethics, and prescribed "dos and don'ts." We do not believe that this approach facilitates the understanding of how negotiators actually decide to act unethically. In contrast, we believe this process can best be understood by a simple decision-making model. We proposed that an negotiator who chooses to use an unethical tactic usually decides to do so in order to increase his negotiating power. Power is gained by manipulating the perceived base of accurate information (lying), getting better information about an opponent's plan, or undermining an opponent's ability to achieve his objectives. Using these tactics leads to two kinds of consequences: first, actual attainment or nonattainment of the goals he was seeking; and second, evaluation and criticism of the tactics by the negotiator himself, by his opponent and by observers. As a result of the consequences and the evaluation, negotiators usually feel compelled to justify their actions—i.e., they know they have done something "wrong" and need to establish a "good reason." The purpose of this justification is to rationalize the action to themselves and to others. In addition, if the tactic produced successful consequences, the negotiator will be likely to try it again in the future. Finally, we suggested that the decision to use ethical or unethical tactics may be influenced in varying degrees by differences in individual backgrounds, personality, rewards or punishments associated with ethical or unethical actions, and the social and cultural norms that dictate what is appropriate or inappropriate in a given environment.

In proposing this model, we have made a number of assumptions about ways to judge and evaluate human conduct in the realm of ethics. We have intentionally avoided taking a strong normative stance, and have *not* tried to emphasize our own biases about what kinds of conduct are ethical or unethical. Instead, we have proposed several conclusions that can be drawn from research, experience and common sense:

1. Individuals will often disagree as to what kinds of negotiating tactics are "ethical" and "unethical," and in which situations it is appropriate or inappropriate to use them.

2. The decision to use an unethical tactic can probably best be understood as a quasirational decision making process in which a variety of personality and situational variables are likely to affect that decision.

3. In deciding to use an unethical tactic, a negotiator is likely to be most heavily influenced by what he believes the consequences will be for his choice: will it help him accomplish his objectives, and what kind of feedback is he likely to receive from others?

4. Negotiators who have used unethical tactics in the past, or might be considering their use in the future, should strongly consider three possible consequences of using unethical tactics:

    (a)   will they really help achieve objectives?

    (b)   how will they affect the quality of the relationship with this opponent in the future?

    (c)   how will they affect their reputation?

Negotiators frequently overlook the fact that while unethical or expedient tactics may get them what they want in the short run, these same tactics typically lead to long-term problems and to diminished effectiveness.

Bibliography

Adams, J. S. (1965). Inequity in social exchange. In L. Berkowitz, (Ed.), *Advances in experimental social psychology, 2,* New York: Academic Press.

Alderfer, C. P. (1977). Group and intergroup relations. In J. R. Hackman & J. L. Suttle, (Eds.), *Improving life at work: Behavioral science approaches to organizational change.* Santa Monica, CA: Goodyear.

Allport, W. W., Vernon, P. E., & Lindzey, G. (1960). *The study of values.* (3rd ed.). Boston: Houghton Mifflin.

Anderson. J. C., & Kochan, T. (1977). Impasse procedures in the Canadian Federal Service. *Industrial and Labor Relations Review, 30,* 283–301.

Athos, A. G., & Gabarro, J. J. (1978). *Interpersonal behavior: Communication and understanding in relationships.* Englewood Cliffs, NJ: Prentice Hall.

Baldwin, D. A. (1971). The power of positive sanctions. *World Politics, 24,* 19–38.

Baldwin, D. A. (1971). The costs of power. *Journal of Conflict Resolution, 15,* 145–155.

Bales, R. F. (1950). *Interaction process analysis: A method for the study of small groups.* Cambridge, MA: Addison-Wesley.

Baranowski, T. A., & Summers, D. A. (1972). Perceptions of response alternatives in a prisoner's dilemma game. *Journal of Personality and Social Psychology, 21,* 35–40.

Bazerman, M. H., & Lewicki, R. J. (1983). *Negotiating in organizations.* Beverly Hills, CA: Sage Publications.

Beckhard, R. (1967). The confrontation meeting. *Harvard Business Review, 45*(2), 149–155.

Benjamin, A. J., & Levi, A. M. (1979). Process minefields in intergroup conflict resolution: The Sdot Yam workshop. *Journal of Applied Behavioral Science, 15,* 507–519.

Benton, A. A. (1972). Accountability and negotiations between representatives. *Proceedings, 80th Annual Convention, American Psychological Association,* Hawaii, 227–228.

Benton, A. A., & Druckman, D. (1973). Salient solutions and the bargaining behavior of representatives and nonrepresentatives. *International Journal of Group Tensions, 3,* 28–29.

Benton, A. A., & Druckman, D. (1974). Constituent's bargaining orientation and intergroup negotiations. *Journal of Applied Social Psychology, 4* (2), 141–150.

Berlo, D. K., Lemert, J., & Mertz, R. (1966). *Dimensions for evaluating the acceptability of message sources.* East Lansing, MI: Michigan State University.

Bettinghaus. E. P. (1966). *Message preparation: The nature of proof.* Indianapolis: Bobbs-Merrill.

Bettinghaus E. P. (1966). *Persuasive communication.* New York: Holt, Rinehart and Winston.

Bettinghaus, E. P. (1980). *Persuasive communication* (2nd ed.). New York: Holt, Rinehart and Winston.

Blake, R. R. & Mouton, J. S. (1961a). *Group dynamics: Key to decision making.* Houston: Gulf Publications.

Blake, R. R. & Mouton, J. S. (1961b). Comprehension of own and outgroup positions under intergroup competition. *Journal of Conflict Resolution, 5,* 304–310.

Blake, R. R. & Mouton, J. S. (1961c). Loyalty of representatives to ingroup positions during intergroup competition. *Sociometry, 24,* 177–183.

Blake, R. R. & Mouton, J. S. (1964). *The managerial grid.* Houston: Gulf Publications.

Blake, R. R., & Mouton, J. S. (1978). *The new managerial grid.* Houston: Gulf Publications.

Blau, P. M. (1964). *Exchange and power in social life.* New York: John Wiley.

Bloch, A. (1982). *Murphy's law.* Los Angeles: Price/Stern/Sloan.

Boehringer, G. H., Zeruolis, V., Bayley, J., & Boehringer, K. (1974). Stirling: The destructive application of group techniques to a conflict. *Journal of Conflict Resolution, 18,* 257–275.

Bok, S. (1978). *Lying: Moral choice in public and private life.* New York: Pantheon.

Bonoma, T., Horai, J., Lindskold, S., Gahagan, J. P., & Tedeschi, J. T. (1969). Compliance to contingent threats. *Proceedings of the 77th Annual Convention of the American Psychological Association, 4,* 395–396.

Bowers, J. W. (1964). Some correlates of language intensity. *Quarterly Journal of Speech, 50,* 415–420.

Bowers, J. W. & Osborn, M. M. (1966). Attitudinal effects of selected types of concluding metaphors in persuasive speeches. *Speech Monographs, 33,* 147–155.

Braginsky, D. D. (1970). Machiavellianism and manipulative interpersonal behavior in children. *Journal of Experimental Social Psychology, 6,* 77–99.

Breaugh, J. A., & Klimoski, R. J. (1977). Choice of group spokesman in bargaining—member or outsider. *Organizational Behavior and Human Performance, 19,* 325–336.

Brock, T. C. (1963). Effects of prior dishonesty on post-decision dissonance. *Journal of Abnormal and Social Psychology, 66,* 325–331.

Brown, B. R. (1968). The effects of need to maintain face on interpersonal bargaining. *Journal of Experimental Social Psychology, 4,* 107–122.

Brown, L. D. (1977). Can "haves" and "have-nots" cooperate? Two efforts to bridge a social gap. *Journal of Applied Behavioral Science, 13,* 211–224.

Brown, L. D. (1983). *Managing conflict at organizational interfaces.* Reading, MA: Addison-Wesley, 97–98.

Brown, R. (1983, September). *Group identification and intergroup differentiation.* Paper presented at the Social Psychology Section, Annual conference, British Psychological Society, University of Sheffield, U.K.

Bruner, J. S. & Tagiuri, R. (1954). The perception of people. In G. Lindzey (ed.), *The handbook of social psychology, 2,* Cambridge, MA: Addison-Wesley.

Burgoon, M., & Bettinghaus, E. P. (1980). Persuasive message strategies. In M. Roloff & G. R. Miller (Eds.), *Persuasion: New directions in theory and research,* Beverly Hills: Sage.

Burgoon, M., & King, L. B. (1974). The mediation of resistance to persuasion strategies by language variables and active-passive participation. *Human communication research, 1,* 30–41.

Burgoon, M., & Stewart, D. (1975). Empirical investigations of language: 1. The effects of sex of source, receiver, and language intensity on attitude change. *Human communication research, 1,* 244–248.

Calero, H. H., & Oskam, B. (1983). *Negotiate the deal you want.* New York: Dodd, Mead & Company.

Carnevale, P. J. D., Pruitt, D. G., & Britton, S. D. (1979). Looking tough: The negotiator under constituent surveillance. *Personality and Social Psychology Bulletin, 5,* 118–121.

Carr, A. Z. (1968). Is business bluffing ethical? *Harvard Business Review,* January–February, 143–153.

Chertkoff, J. M., & Baird, S. L. (1971). Applicability of the big lie and technique and the last clear chance doctrine to bargaining. *Journal of Personality and Social Psychology, 20,* 298–303.

Chertkoff, J. M., & Conley, M. (1967). Opening offer and frequency of concessions as bargaining strategies. *Journal of Personality and Social Psychology, 7,* 181–185.

Christie, R., & Geis, F. L. (Eds.) (1970). *Studies in Machiavellianism.* New York, NY: Academic Press.

Cohen, H. (1980). *You can negotiate anything.* Secaucus, NJ: Lyle Stuart.

Cohen, S. P., Kelman, H. C., Miller, F. D., & Smith, B. L. (1977). Evolving intergroup techniques for conflict resolution: An Israeli-Palestinian pilot workshop. *Journal of Social Issues, 33,* 165–189.

Coogler, O. J. (1978). *Structural mediation in divorce settlement: A handbook for marital mediators.* Lexington, MA: Lexington Books.

Corwin, R. G. (1969). Patterns of organizational conflict. *Administrative Science Quarterly, 14,* 504–520

Crott, H., Kayser, E., & Lamm, H. (1980). The effects of information exchange and communication in an asymmetrical negotiation situation. *European Journal of Social Psychology, 10,* 149–163..

Crumbaugh, C. M., & Evans, G. W. (1967). Presentation format, other persons strategies and cooperative behavior in the prisoner's dilemma. *Psychological Reports, 20,* 895–902.

Cuming, P. (1981). *The power handbook.* Boston, MA: CBI Publishing.

Dahl, R. A. (1957). The concept of power. *Behavioral Science, 2,* 201–215.

Delbecq, A., Van de Ven, A., & Gustafson, D. (1975). *Group techniques: A guide to nominal and delphi processes.* Glenview, IL: Scott, Foresman.

Deutsch, M. (1958). Trust and suspicion. *Journal of Conflict Resolution, 2,* 265–279.

Deutsch, M. (1960). Trust, trustworthiness, and the F scale. *Journal of Abnormal and Social Psychology, 61,* 138–140.

Deutsch, M. (1962). *Cooperation and trust: Some theoretical notes.* In M. R. Jones, (Ed.), Nebraska symposium on motivation, Lincoln Nebraska: University of Nebraska Press, 275–318.

Deutsch, M. (1973). *The resolution of conflict.* New Haven: Yale University Press.

Deutsch, M. (1975). Equity, equality and need: What determines which value will be used as the basis for distributive justice? *Journal of Social Issues, 31,* 137–149.

Deutsch, M., & Krauss, R. M. (1960). The effect of threat upon interpersonal bargaining. *Journal of Abnormal and Social Psychology, 61,* 181–189.

Deutsch, M., & Krauss, R. M. (1962). Studies of interpersonal bargaining. *Journal of Conflict Resolution, 6,* 52–76.

Deutsch, M., & Lewicki, R. J. (1970). "Locking-in" effects during a game of chicken. *Journal of Conflict Resolution, 14,* 367–378.

Douglas, A. (1962). *Industrial peacemaking.* New York: Columbia University Press.

Douglass, F. (1856). *My bondage and my freedom.* New York: Miller, Orton and Milligan.

Drayton, W. (1981). Getting smarter about regulation. *Harvard Business Review, 59*(4), 38–52..

Druckman D. (1967). Dogmatism, prenegotiation experience, and simulated group representation as determinants of dyadic behavior in a bargaining situation. *Journal of Personality and Social Psychology, 6,* 279–290.

Druckman, D. (1971). The influence of the situation in interparty conflict. *Journal of Conflict Resolution, 15,* 523–554.

Eiseman, J. W. (1978). Reconciling incompatible positions. *Journal of Applied Behavioral Science, 14,* 133–150.

Emerson, R. M. (1962). Power-dependence relations. *American Sociological Review, 27.*

England, G. (1967). Personal value systems of American managers. *Academy of Management Journal, 10,* 53–68.

Etizioni, A. (1969). Social psychological aspects of international relations. In G. Lindzey & E. Aronson (Eds.), *Handbook of social psychology, 5,* 538–601, New York: Addison-Wesley.

Exline, R., Thibaut, J., Hickey, C., & Gumpert, P. (1970). Visual interaction in relation to Machiavellianism and an unethical act. In R. Christie & F. Geis (Eds.), *Studies in Machiavellianism.* New York: Academic Press.

Farance, R. M., Monge, P. R., & Russell, H. M. (1977). *Communicating and organizing.* Reading, MA: Addison Wesley.

Feigenbaum, C. (1975). Final-offer arbitration: Better theory than practice. *Industrial Relations, 14,* 311–317.

Festinger, L. A. (1957). *A theory of cognitive dissonance.* Stanford, CA: Stanford University Press.

Festinger, L. A., Hoffman, P. J., & Lawrence, D. H. (1954). Tendencies toward group comparability in competitive bargaining. *Human Relations, 7,* 141–160.

Festinger, L. A., & Maccoby, N. (1964). On resistance to persuasive communication. *Journal of Abnormal and Social Psychology, 68,* 359–366.

Filley, A. C. (1975). *Interpersonal conflict resolution,* Glenview, IL: Scott, Foresman.

Fischer, C. (1970). The effects of threats in an incomplete information game. *Sociometry, 32,* 301–314.

Fisher, R. (1964). Fractionating conflict. In R. Fisher (Ed.), *International conflict and behavioral science: The Craigville papers.* New York: Basic Books.

Fisher, R. (1969). *International conflict for beginners.* New York: Harper and Row.

Fisher, R. (1978). *International mediation: A working guide.* New York: International Peace Academy.

Fisher, R., & Ury, W. (1981). *Getting to yes: Negotiating agreements without giving in.* Boston: Houghton-Mifflin.

Ford Foundation. (1978). *New approaches to conflict resolution.* New York: Ford Foundation.

Fordyce, J. D., & Weil, R. (1971). *Managing with people: A manager's handbook of organization development methods.* Reading, MA: Addison-Wesley.

Forsyth, D. (1980). A taxonomy of ethical ideologies. *Journal of Personality and Social Psychology, 39,* 175–184.

Freedman, J. L., & Fraser, S. C. (1966). Compliance without pressure: The foot in the door technique. *Journal of Personality and Social Psychology, 4,* 195–202.

French, J. R. P., & Raven, B. (1959). The bases of social power. In D. Cartwright (Ed.), *Studies in social power.* Ann Arbor, MI: Institute for Social Research.

Froman, L. A., & Cohen, M. D. (1970). Compromise and logrolling: Comparing the efficiency of two bargaining processes. *Behavioral Sciences, 15,* 180–183.

Fry, W. R., Firestone, I. J., & Williams, D. (1979). *Bargaining process in mixed-singles dyads: Loving and losing.* Paper presented at the Eastern Psychological Association meetings.

Gahagan, J. P., Long, H., & Horai, J. (1969). Race of experimenter and reactions to Black preadolescents. *Proceedings of the 77th Annual Meeting of the American Psychological Association, 4,* 397–398.

Gallo, P. S. Jr. (1966, April). Prisoners of our own dilemma. Paper presented at the meeting of the Western Psychological Association, San Diego, California.

Geis, F. L., & Moon, T. H. (1981). Machiavellianism and deception. *Journal of Personality and Social Psychology, 41,* 766–775.

Gibb, J. (1961). Defensive communication. *Journal of Communication, 3,* 141–148.

Gladwin, T. N., & Walter, I. (1980). *Multinationals under fire: Lessons in the management of conflict.* New York: Wiley.

Godunov defection stories. (1979, August). *New York Times.*

Goffman, E. (1969). *Strategic interaction.* Philadelphia: University of Pennsylvania Press.

Goodstadt, B. E., & Hjelle, L. A. (1973). Power to the powerless: Locus of control and the use of power. *Journal of Personality and Social Psychology, 27,* 190–196.

Gordon, T. (1977). *Leader effectiveness training.* New York: Wyden Books.

Green, E. D. (1980). *The minitrial approach to complex litigation.* Dispute Management. New York: Center for Public Resources.

Greenberg, B. S., & Miller, G. R. (1966). The effects of low-credible sources on message acceptance. *Speech Monographs, 33,* 135–136.

Grigsby, D. W. (1980). *The effects of mediation and alternative forms of arbitration on pre-intervention bargaining.* Doctoral dissertation, University of North Carolina, Chapel Hill, NC.

Grigsby, D. W. (1981). *The effects of intermediate mediation step on bargaining behavior under various forms of compulsory arbitration.* Paper presented to the Annual Meeting of the American Institute for Decision Sciences.

Grigsby, D. W., & Bigoness, W. J. (1981). *The effects of mediation and alternate forms of arbitration on bargaining behavior.* Chapel Hill: University of North Carolina.

Grigsby, D. W., & Bigoness, W. J. (1982). Effects of mediation and alternative forms of arbitration on bargaining behavior—a laboratory study. *Journal of Applied Psychology, 67,* 549–554.

Gruder, C. L. (1971). Relationships with opponent and partner in mixed-motive bargaining. *Journal of Conflict Resolution, 15,* 403–416.

Gruder, C. L., & Duslak, R. J. (1973). Elicitation of cooperation by retaliatory and nonretaliatory strategies in a mixed motive game. *Journal of Conflict Resolution, 17,* 162–174.

Haccoun, R. R., & Klimoski, R. J. (1975). Negotiator status and accountability source: A study of negotiation behavior. *Organizational Behavior and Human Performance, 14,* 342–359.

Haire, M. (1955). Role perceptions in labor-management relations: an experimental approach. *Industrial and Labor Relations Review, 8,* 204–216.

Hamner, W. C. (1977). Reinforcement theory. In H. L. Tosi & W. C. Hamner (Eds.),

Organizational behavior and management: A contingency approach. Chicago, IL: St. Clair Press.

Hamner, W. C. (1980). The influence of structural, individual and strategic differences. In D. L. Harnett & L. L. Cummings (Eds.), *Bargaining behavior.* Houston, TX: Dame Publications.

Harsanyi, J. C. (1966). A bargaining model for social status in informal groups and formal organizations. *Behavioral Science, 9,* 357–369.

Harvey, O. J. (1953). An experimental approach to the study of status relations in informal groups. *Sociometry, 18,* 357–367.

Hassett, J. (1981, June). Is it right? An inquiry into everyday ethics. *Psychology Today,* 49–53.

Hassett, J. (1981, November). But that would be wrong. . . . *Psychology Today,* 34–53.

Hassett, J. (1982, August). *Correlates of moral values and behavior.* Paper presented at a symposium, "Current empirical perspectives in business ethics and values," Academy of Management Meetings.

Hegarty, W., & Sims, H. P. (1978). Some determinants of unethical decision behavior: An experiment. *Journal of Applied Psychology, 63,* 451–457.

Heller, J. R. (1967). The effects of racial prejudice, feedback, strategy, and race on cooperative-competitive behavior. *Dissertation Abstracts International, 27,* 2507–2508-b.

Hermann, M. G., & Kogan, N. (1977). Effects of negotiators' personalities on negotiating behavior. In D. Druckman (Ed.), *Negotiations: Social-psychological perspectives.* Beverly Hills: Sage Publications.

Hersey, P., & Blanchard, K. H. (1977). *Management of organizational behavior: Utilizing human resources* (3rd ed.). Englewood Cliffs, NJ: Prentice Hall.

Hill, B. J. (1982). An analysis of conflict resolution techniques: From problem solving workshops to theory. *Journal of Conflict Resolution, 26,* 109–138.

Hinton, B. L., Hamner, W. C., & Pohlan, N. F. (1974). Influence and award of magnitude, opening bid and concession rate on profit earned in a managerial negotiating game. *Behavioral Science, 19,* 197–203.

Homans, G. C. (1961). *Social behavior: Its elementary forms,* New York: Harcourt, Brace and World Company.

Hovland, C. I., Janis, I. L., & Kelley, H. H. (1953). *Communication and persuasion.* New Haven, CT: Yale University Press.

Hovland, C. I., & Mandell, W. (1952). An experimental comparison of conclusion-drawing by the communicator and by the audience. *Journal of Abnormal and Social Psychology, 47,* 581–588.

Hovland, C. I., & Weiss, W. (1951). The influence of source credibility on communication effectiveness. *Public Opinion Quarterly, 15,* 635–650.

Ikle, F. C. (1964). *How nations negotiate.* New York: Harper & Row.

Ivey, A. E., & Simek-Downing, L. (1980). *Counselling and psychotherapy,* Englewood Cliffs: Prentice Hall.

Jackson, C. N., & King, D. C. (1983). The effects of representatives' power within their own organizations on the outcome of a negotiation. *Academy of Management Journal, 26,* 178–185.

Jacobs, A. T. (1951). *Some significant factors influencing the range of indeterminateness in collective bargaining negotiations.* Unpublished doctoral thesis, Ann Arbor, Michigan, University of Michigán.

Johnson, D. W. (1971). Role reversal: A summary and review of the research. *International Journal of Group Tensions, 1,* 318–334.

Johnson, D. W., & Dustin, R. (1970). The initiation of cooperation through role reversal. *Journal of Social Psychology, 82,* 193–203.

Johnson, D. W., & Lewicki, R. J. (1969). The initiation of superordinate goals. *Journal of Applied Behavioral Science, 5,* 9–24.

Jones, S. B., & Burgoon, M. (1975). Empirical investigations of language intensity: 2. The effects of irrelevant fear and language intensity on attitude change. *Human Communication Research, 1,* 248–251.

Karrass, C. (1974). *Give and take.* New York: Thomas Y. Crowell.

Kelley, H. H. (1966). A classroom study of the dilemmas of interpersonal negotiations. In K. Archibald (Ed.), *Strategic interaction and conflict* (49–73). Berkeley: University of California Press.

Kelley, H. H., Beckman, L. L., & Fisher, C. S. (1967). Negotiating the division of an award under incomplete information. *Journal of Experimental and Social Psychology, 3,* 361–398.

Kelley, H. H., & Schenitzki, D. P. (1972). Bargaining. In C. G. McClintock (Ed.), *Experimental social psychology* (pp. 298–337). New York: Holt Rinehart and Winston.

Kelley, H. H., & Thibaut, J. (1969). Group problem solving. In G. Lindzey & E. Aronson (Eds.), *Handbook of social psychology* (2nd ed.), Vol. IV. Reading, MA: Addison Wesley.

Kessler, S. (1977). *Creative conflict resolution: Participant's guide.* Atlanta: National Institute for Professional Training (NIPT).

Kessler, S. (1978). *Creative conflict resolution: Mediation.* Atlanta: NIPT.

Kilmann, R. H., & Thomas, K. W. (1977). Developing a forced-choice measure of conflict-handling behavior: The MODE instrument. *Educational and Psychological Measurement, 37,* 309–325.

Kimmel, M. J., Pruitt, D. G., Magenau, J. M., Konar-Goldband, E., & Carnevale, P. J. D. (1980). Effects of trust aspiration and gender on negotiation tactics. *Journal of Personality and Social Psychology, 38,* 9–23.

Kipnis, D. (1976). *The powerholders.* Chicago, IL: University of Chicago Press.

Kleinke, C. L., & Pohlan, P. D. (1971). Effective and emotional responses as a function of other person's gaze and cooperativeness in two person games. *Journal of Personality and Social Psychology, 17,* 308–313.

Klimoski, R. J. (1972). The effects of intragroup forces on intergroup conflict resolution. *Organizational Behavior and Human Performance, 8,* 363–383.

Klimoski, R. J., & Ash, R. A. (1974). Accountability and negotiator behavior. *Organizational Behavior and Human Performance, 11,* 409–425.

Klimoski, R. J., & Breaugh, J. A. (1977). When performance doesn't count: A constituency looks at its spokesman. *Organizational Behavior and Human Performance, 20,* 301–311.

Kochan, T. A. (1980). *Collective bargaining and industrial relations.* Homewood, IL: Irwin.

Kochan, T. A., & Jick, T. (1978). The public sector mediation process: A theory and empirical examination. *Journal of Conflict Resolution, 22,* 209–240.

Kogan, N., Lamm, H., & Trommsdorf, G. (1972). Negotiation constraints in the risk-taking domain: Effects of being observed by partners of higher or lower status. *Journal of Personality and Social Psychology, 23,* 143–156.

Kohlberg, L. (1969). Stage and sequence: The cognitive-development approach to socialization. In D. Goslin (Ed.), *Handbook of socialization theory and research* (347–380). Chicago: Rand McNally.

Komorita, S. S., & Brenner, A. R. (1968). Bargaining and concessions under bilateral monopoly. *Journal of Personality and Social Psychology, 9,* 15–20.

Komorita, S. S. & Kravitz, D. A. (1979). The effects of alternatives in bargaining. *Journal of Experimental Social Psychology, 15,* 147–157.

Kormorita, S. S., & Mechling, J. (1967). Betrayal and reconciliation in a two person game. *Journal of Personality and Social Psychology, 6,* 349–353.

Korda, M. (1975). *Power!: How to get it, how to use it.* New York: Random House.

Kotter, J. (1979). *Power in management.* New York: AMACOM Books.

Krauss, R. M., & Deutsch, M. (1966). Communication in interpersonal bargaining. *Journal of Personality and Social Psychology, 4,* 572–577.

Kressel, K. (1972). *Labor mediation: An exploratory survey.* Albany, NY: Association of Labor Mediation Agencies.

Kressel, K., Jaffe, N., Tuchman, M., Watson, C., & Deutsch, M. (1977). Mediated negotiations in divorce and labor disputes: A comparison. *Conciliation courts review, 15,* 9–12.

Lawrence, P. R., & Lorsch, J. W. (1967). New management job: The integrator. *Harvard Business Review, 45,* 142–151.

Leaventhal, H. (1970). Findings and theory in the study of fear communications. In L. Berkowitz (Ed.), *Advances in experimental social psychology,* New York: Academic Press.

Leming, J. S. (1978). Cheating behavior, situational influence and moral development. *Journal of Educational Research, 71,* 214–217.

Leventhal, G. S. (1976). Fairness in social relationships. In J. W. Thibaut, J. T. Spence, & R. C. Carson (Eds.), *Contemporary topics in social psychology.* Morristown, NJ: General Learning Press.

Lewicki, R. J. (1970). The effects of cooperative and exploitative relationships on subsequent interpersonal relations. *Dissertation Abstracts International, 30,* 4550–A.

Lewicki, R. J. (1980). *Bad loan psychology: Entrapment in financial lending.* Paper presented at a symposium, Escalation Processes in Organizations, Academy of Management Meetings.

Lewicki, R. J. (1982). Career style inventory: An assessment exercise. In D. T. Hall, D. D. Bowen, R. J. Lewicki, and F. S. Hall (Eds.), *Experiences in Management and Organizational Behavior,* New York: John Wiley & Sons.

Lewicki, R. J. (1982). Ethical concerns in conflict management. In G. B. J. Bomers & R. B. Peterson (Eds.), *Conflict management and industrial relations.* Boston, MA: Kluwer Nijhoff Publishing.

Lewicki, R. J. (1983). Lying and deception: A behavioral model. In M. H. Bazerman & R. J. Lewicki *Negotiating in Organizations.* Beverly Hills: Sage Publications.

Lewicki, R. J., & Alderfer, C. P. (1973). The tensions between research and intervention in intergroup conflict. *Journal of Applied Behavioral Science, 9,* 424–468.

Lewicki, R. J., & Sheppard, B. (in press). Choosing how to intervene: Factors affecting the use of process and outcome control in third party dispute resolution. *Journal of Occupational Behavior.*

Lindskold, S., & Tedeschi, J. T. (1971). Self esteem and sex as factors affecting influenceability. *British Journal of Social and Clinical Psychology, 10,* 114–122.

Long, G., & Feuille, P. (1974). Final offer arbitration: Sudden death in Eugene. *Industrial and Labor Relations Review, 27,* 186–203.

Longley, J., & Pruitt, D. D. (1980). A critique of Jain's theory of groupthink. In L. Wheeler (Ed.), *Review of personality and social psychology, 1,* Beverly-Hills, CA: Sage.

Loomis, J. L. (1959). Communication, the development of trust and cooperative behavior. *Human Relations, 12,* 305–315.

Luce, D., & Raiffa, H. (1957). *Games and decisions.* New York: John Wiley and Sons.

Maccoby, M. (1976). *The gamesman.* New York: Simon & Schuster.

Maier, R. A., & Lavrakas, P. J. (1976). Lying behavior and the evaluation of lies. *Perceptual and Motor Skills, 42,* 575–581.

Marecki, S. (1974). *Elements of competitive decision making: Non-zero sum games.* Cambridge, MA: President and Fellows of Harvard College.

Martindale, D. A. (1971). Territorial dominance behavior in dyadic verbal interactions. *Proceedings of the 79th Annual Convention of the American Psychological Association, 6,* 305–306.

Maslow, A. H. (1954). *Motivation and personality.* New York: Harper and Row.

McClelland, D. (1975). *Power: The inner experience.* New York: Irvington Publishers.

McCroskey, J. C., Jensen, T., & Valencia, C. (1980). Measurement of the credibility of mass media sources. In M. E. Rolf & G. R. Miller (Eds.), *Persuasion: New directions in theory and research.* Beverly Hills, CA: Sage Publications.

McDonald, J. (1963). *Strategy in business, poker and war.* New York: W. W. Norton Company.

McGregor, D. (1960). *The human side of enterprise.* New York: McGraw-Hill.

McGuire, W. J. (1962). Resistance against persuasion. *Journal of Abnormal and Social Psychology, 63.*

McGuire, W. J. (1964). Inducing resistance to persuasion: Some contemporary approaches. In L. Berkowitz (Ed.), *Advances in Experimental Social Psychology, 1,* New York: Academic Press.

McGuire, W. J. (1973). Persuasion, resistance and attitude change. In I. S. Poole, F. W. Frey, W. Schramm, N. Maccoby, and E. B. Parker (Eds.), *Handbook of Communication* (pp. 216–252). Skokie, IL: Rand McNally.

Meeker, R. J., & Shure, G. H. (1969). Pacifist bargaining tactics: Some 'outsider' influences. *Journal of Conflict Resolution, 13,* 487–493.

Messe, L. A. (1971). Equity in bilateral bargaining. *Journal of Personality and Social Psychology, 17,* 287–291.

Michelini, R. L. (1971). Effects of prior interaction, contact, strategy, and expectation of meeting on gain behavior and sentiment. *Journal of Conflict Resolution, 15,* 97–103.

Michener, H. A., Vaske, J. J., Schleifer, S. L., Plazewski, J. G., & Chapman, L. J. (1975). Factors affecting concession rate and threat usage in bilateral conflict. *Sociometry, 38,* 62–80.

Michener, S. K., & Suchner, R. W. (1971). The tactical use of social power. In J. T. Tedeschi (Ed.), *The social influence process.* Chicago: AVC.

Miller, M., & Burgoon, M. (1979). The relationship between violations of expectations and the induction of the resistance to persuasion. *Human communications research, 5,* 301–313.

Mintzberg, H. (1973). *The nature of managerial work.* New York: Harper & Row.

Missner, M. (1980). *Ethics of the business system.* Sherman Oaks, CA: Alfred Publishing Company.

Morgan, W. R., & Sawyer, J. (1967). Bargaining expectations and the preference for equality over equity. *Journal of Personality and Social Psychology, 6,* 139–149.

Morley, I., & Stephenson, G. (1977). *The social psychology of bargaining.* London: Allen and Unwin.

Nash, J. F. (1950). The bargaining problem. *Econometrica, 18,* 155–162.

Nicholson, M. (1970). *Conflict analysis.* London: English University Press.

Nierenberg, G. (1973). *Fundamentals of negotiating.* New York: Hawthorn Books.

Northrup, H. R. (1964). *Boulwarism.* Ann Arbor: Bureau of Industrial Relations, University of Michigan.

Osgood, C. E. (1962). *An alternative to war or surrender.* Urbana, IL: University of Illinois Press.

Oskamp, S. (1970). Effects of programmed initial strategies in a prisoner's dilemma game. *Psychometrics, 19,* 195–196.

PATCO stories. (1981, August). *New York Times.*

Petty, R., Wells, G., & Brock, T. (1976). Distraction can enhance or reduce yielding to propaganda: Thought disruption versus effort justification. *Journal of Personality and Social Psychology, 34,* 874–884.

Pfeffer, J., & Salancik, G. R. (1974). Organizational decision making as a political process: The case of a university budget. *Administrative Science Quarterly, 19,* 135–151.

Pilisuk, N., & Skolnick, P. (1978). Inducing trust: A test of the Osgood proposal. *Journal of Personality and Social Psychology, 8,* 121–133.

Prasow, P., & Peters, E. (1983). *Arbitration and collective bargaining: Conflict resolution in labor relations* (2nd ed.). New York: McGraw-Hill.

Pruitt, D. G. (1972). Methods for resolving differences of interest: A theoretical analysis. *Journal of Social Issues, 28,* 133–154.

Pruitt, D. G. (1981). *Negotiation behavior.* New York: Academic Press.

Pruitt, D. G. (1983). Strategic choice in negotiation. *American Behavioral Scientist, 27*(2), 167–194.

Pruitt, D. G., & Carnevale, P. J. D. (1982). The development of integrative agreements. In V. J. Derlega & J. Grezlak (Eds.). *Cooperation and helping behavior.* New York: Academic Press.

Pruitt, D. G., & Drews, J. L. (1969). The effect of time pressure, time elapsed, and the opponent's concession rate on behavior in negotiation. *Journal of Experimental Social Psychology, 553–60.*

Pruitt, D. G., & Lewis, S. A. (1975). Development of integrative solutions in bilateral negotiation. *Journal of Personality and Social Psychology, 31,* 621–633.

Pruitt, D. G., & Lewis, S. A. (1977). The psychology of integrative agreements. In D. Druckman (Ed.), *Negotiations: Social psychological perspectives.* Beverly Hills, CA: Sage Publications.

Rahim, M. A. (1983). A measure of styles of handling interpersonal conflict. *Academy of Management Journal, 26,* 368–376.

Raiffa, H. (1982). *The art and science of negotiation.* Cambridge: Bellknap Press of Harvard University Press.

Rapoport, A. (1960). *Fights, games and debates.* Ann Arbor, MI: University of Michigan Press.

Rapoport, A. (1963). Formal games as probing tools for investigating behavior motivated by trust and suspicion. *Journal of Conflict Resolution, 7,* 570–579.

Rapoport, A. (1964). *Strategy and conscience.* New York: Harper & Row.

Rapoport, A. (1966). *Two-person game theory.* Ann Arbor, MI: University of Michigan Press.

Raven, B. H., & Kruglanski, A. W. (1970). Conflict and power. In P. Swingle (Ed.), *The structure of conflict.* New York: Academic Press.

Raven, B. H., & Rubin, J. Z. (1973). *Social psychology: People in groups.* New York: John Wiley.

Ravich, R. A. (1969). The use of the interpersonal game-test in conjoint marital psychotherapy. *American Journal of Psychotherapy, 23,* 217–229.

Reardon, K. K. (1981). *Persuasion theory and context.* Beverly Hills, CA: Sage Publications.

Reich, R. B. (1981). Regulation by confrontation or negotiation. *Harvard Business Review, 59*(3), 82–93.

Richardson, R. C. (1977). *Collective bargaining by objectives.* Englewood Cliffs, NJ: Prentice Hall.

Rogers, C. (1961). *On becoming a person: A therapist's view of psychotherapy.* Boston: Houghton-Mifflin.

Rogers, C. (1965). *Client centered therapy.* Boston: Houghton-Mifflin.

Rokeach, M. (1973). *The nature of human values.* New York: Free Press.

Rosnow, R. L., & Robinson, E. J. (1967). *Experiments in persuasion.* New York: Academic Press.

Rotter, J. B. (1967). A new scale for the measurement of interpersonal trust. *Journal of Personality, 35,* 651–665.

Rotter, J. B. (1971). Generalized expectancies for interpersonal trust. *American Psychologist, 26,* 443–452.

Rotter, J. B. (1980). Interpersonal trust, trustworthiness, and gullibility. *American Psychologist, 35,* 1–7.

Rubin, J. Z. (1980). Experimental research on third party intervention in conflict: Toward some generalizations. *Psychological Bulletin, 87,* 379–391.

Rubin, J. Z. (Ed.) (1981). *Dynamics of third party intervention: Kissinger in the Middle East.* New York: Praeger.

Rubin, J. Z., & Brown, B. R. (1975). *The social psychology of bargaining and negotiation.* New York: Academic Press.

Rubin, J. Z., & Lewicki, R. J. (1973). A three-factor experimental analysis of promises and threats. *Journal of Applied Social Psychology, 3,* 240–257.

Rubin, J. Z., Lewicki, R. J., & Dunn, L. (1973). Perceptions of promisors and threateners. *Proceedings of the 81st Annual Convention of the American Psychological Association, 8,* 141–142.

Salancik, G. R., & Pfeffer, J. (1974). The bases and uses of power in organizational decision making: The case of a university. *Administrative Science Quarterly, 19,* 453–473.

Salancik, G. R., & Pfeffer, J. (1977). Who gets power—and how they hold on to it: A strategic-contingency model of power. *Organizational Dynamics, 5,* 3–21.

Sampson, E. E. (1969). Studies in status congruence. In L. Berkowitz (Ed.), *Advances in experimental social psychology, 4,* New York: Academic Press.

Schein, E. H. (1954). The effect of reward on adult imitative behavior. *Journal of Abnormal and Social Psychology, 49,* 389–395.

Schelling, T. C. (1960). *The strategy of conflict.* Cambridge, MA: Harvard University Press.

Schlenker, B. R., & Riess, M. (1979). Self-presentation of attitudes following commitment to proattitudinal behavior. *Journal of Human Communication Research, 5,* 325–334.

Scodel, A., Minas, J. S., Ratoosh, P. & Lipetz, M. (1959). Some descriptive aspects of two-person, non-zero-sum games. *Journal of Conflict Resolution, 3,* 114–119.

Seigel, S., & Fouraker, L. E. (1960). *Bargaining and group decision making: Experiments in bilateral monopoly.* New York: McGraw-Hill.

Selekman, B. M., Fuller, S. H., Kennedy, T., & Baitsel, J. M. (1964). *Problems in labor relations*. New York: McGraw-Hill.

Selekman, B. M., Selekman, S. K., & Fuller, S. H. (1958). *Problems in labor relations*. New York: McGraw Hill.

Seligman, C., Bush, M., & Kirsch, K. (1976). Relationship between compliance missing the foot in the door paradigm and size of first request. *Journal of Personality and Social Psychology, 33*, 517–520.

Sen, A. K. (1970). *Collective choice and individual values*. San Francisco: Holden-Day.

Sermat, V. (1967). The effects of an initial cooperative or competitive treatment on a subject's response to conditional operation. *Behavioral Science, 12*, 301–313.

Sermat, V., & Gregovich, R. P. (1966). The effect of experimental manipulation on cooperative behavior in a checkers game. *Psychometric Science, 4*, 435–436.

Shannon, C., & Weaver, W. (1948). *The mathematical theory of communication*. Urbana: University of Illinois Press.

Shea, G. F. (1983). *Creative Negotiating*. Boston: CBI Publishing Co.

Shelling, T. C. (1966). *Arms and influence*. New Haven, CT: Yale University Press.

Sheppard, B. H. (1982). Toward a comprehensive model of dispute intervention procedures. In T. Tyler (Chair), *New Directions in Procedural Justice Research*. Symposium presented at Annual Meeting of the American Psychological Association, Toronto.

Sheppard, B. H. (1983). Managers as inquisitors: Some lessons from the law. In M. Bazerman & R. J. Lewicki (Eds.), *Negotiating in Organizations*. Beverly Hills: Sage Publications.

Sheppard, B. H. (1984). Third party conflict intervention: A procedural framework. In B. M. Staw & L. L. Cummings (Eds.), *Research in Organizational Behavior, 6*, Greenwich, CT: JAI Press.

Sherif, M. (1979). *Intergroup conflict and cooperation: The Robbers Cave experiment*. Norman, OK: University Book Exchange.

Skinner, B. F. (1953). *Science and human behavior*. New York: Macmillian.

Solomon, L. (1960). The influence of some types of power relationships and game strategies upon the development of interpersonal trust. *Journal of Abnormal and Social Psychology. 61*, 223–230.

Sommer, R. (1965). Further studies of small group ecology. *Sociometry, 28*, 337–348.

Starke, F. A., & Notz, W. W. (1981). Pre- and postintervention effects of conventional vs. final-offer arbitration. *Academy of Management Journal, 24*, 832–850.

Steers, R. M. (1984). *Introduction to organizational behavior* (2nd ed.). Glenview, IL: Scott Foresman and Company.

Stevens, C. M. (1963). *Strategy and collective bargaining negotiations*. New York: McGraw-Hill.

Strickland, L. H. (1958). Surveillance and trust. *Journal of Personality, 26*, 200-215.

Swap, W. L., & Rubin, J. Z. (1983). Measurement of interpersonal orientation. *Journal of Personality and Social Psychology, 44*, 208–219.

Swinth, R. L. (1967). The establishment of the trust relationship. *Journal of Conflict Resolution, 11,* 335–344.

Swinth, R. L. (1967). Review of R. E. Walton and R. D. McKersie: A behavioral theory of labor negotiations. *Contemporary Psychology, 12,* 183–184.

Szilagyi, A. D., Jr., & Wallace, M. J., Jr. (1983). *Organizational behavior and performance* (3rd ed.). Glenview, IL: Scott, Foresman and Company.

Tannebaum, D., & Norris, E. (1966). Effects of combining congruity principle strategies for the reduction of persuasion. *Journal of Personality and Social Psychology, 3,* 233–238.

Tedeschi, J. T., Bonoma, T., & Brown, R. C. (1971). A paradigm for the study of coercive power. *Journal of Conflict Resolution, 15,* 197–223.

Tedeschi, J. T., Schlenker, B. R., & Bonoma, T. V. (1973). *Conflict, power and games: The experimental study of interpersonal relations.* Chicago: AVC.

Teger, A. I. (1970). The effect of early cooperation on the escalation of conflict. *Journal of Experimental Social Psychology, 6,* 187–204.

Teger, A. (1980). *Too much invested to quit.* New York: Pergamon Press.

Terhune, K. W. (1968). Motives, situation and interpersonal conflict within prisoner's dilemma. *Journal of Personality and Social Psychology, Monograph supplement, 8,* 1–24.

Terhune, K. W. (1970). The effects of personality in cooperation and conflict. In P. Swingle (Ed.), *The structure of conflict.* New York: Academic Press.

Thibaut, J., & Kelley, H. H. (1959). *The social psychology of groups.* New York: John Wiley.

Thibaut, J., & Walker, L. (1975). *Procedural justice: A psychological analysis.* Hillsdale, NJ: Lawrence Erlbaum Associates.

Thomas, K. W. (1976). Conflict and conflict management. In M. D. Dunnette (Ed.), *Handbook of industrial and organizational psychology,* Chicago: Rand McNally.

Thomas, K. W. (1977). Toward multidimensional values in teaching: The example of conflict behavior. *Academy of Management Review, 2,* 484–490.

Thomas, K. W. (1979). Conflict. In S. Kerr (Ed.), *Organizational behavior,* Colombus OH: Grid Publications.

Thomas, K. W., & Kilmann, R. H. (1975). *The Thomas-Kilmann conflict mode survey.* Tuxedo, NY: Xicom.

Vroom, V. H. (1973). A new look at managerial decision making. *Organizational Dynamics, 4* (1), 66–80.

Vroom, V. H., & Yetton P. (1973). *Leadership and decision making.* Pittsburgh: University of Pittsburgh Press.

Walcott, C., Hopmann, P. T., & King, T. D. (1977). The role of debate in negotiation. In D. Druckman (Ed.), *Negotiations: Social-Psychological Perspectives.* Beverly Hills, CA: Sage.

Wall, J. A. (1977). Intergroup bargaining: Effects of opposing constituent's stance, opposing representative's bargaining, and representative's locus of control. *Journal of Conflict Resolution, 21,* 459–474.

Wall, J. A. (1981). Mediation: An analysis, review and proposed research. *Journal of Conflict Resolution, 25,* 157–180.

Walster, E. H., Walster, G. W., & Berscheid, E. (1978). *Equity: Theory and research.* Boston: Allyn & Bacon.

Walton, R. E. (1967). Third party roles in interdepartmental conflict. *Industrial Relations, 7,* 29–43.

Walton, R. E. (1969). *Interpersonal peacemaking: Confrontation and third party consultation.* Reading, MA: Addison-Wesley.

Walton, R. E., & McKersie, R. B. (1965). *A behavioral theory of labor negotiations: An analysis of a social interaction system.* New York: McGraw-Hill.

Whyte, W. F., Jr. (1956). *The organization man.* New York: Simon & Schuster.

Wolfe, T. (1970). *Radical chic and mau-mauing the flak catchers.* New York: Farrar, Straus & Giroux.

Wrightsman, L. S., Jr. (1964). Measurement of philosophies of human nature. *Psychological Reports, 14,* 743–751.

Zimbardo, P. G., Ebbesen, E. B., & Maslach, C. (1977). *Influencing attitudes and changing behavior.* Reading, MA: Addison-Wesley.

Author Index

Subject Index

Credits and Acknowledgments

Figure 1-1	From *The Wall Street Journal,* with permission of Cartoon Features Syndicate.
Figure 2-2 (a,b)	From J. Thibaut and H. H. Kelley, *The Social Psychology of Groups.* John Wiley & Sons, Inc., 1959. Reprinted with permission of John Thibaut.
Quote, Page 35 and Figure 2-4	Reprinted from *Games and Decisions: Introduction and Critical Survey* by D. Luce and H. Raiffa, © 1957. Reprinted by permission of John Wiley & Sons, Inc.
Figure 2-8	Adapted from S. Marecki, *Elements of Competitive Decision-Making: Non-Zero-Sum Games.* Copyright 1974, Presidents Fellowship Harvard College.
Figure 6-1	Reprinted from *Bargaining and Group Decision Making: Experiments in Bilateral Monopoly* by S. Seigel and L. E. Fouraker, © 1960. Reprinted by permission of McGraw-Hill.
Figure 6-2	Reprinted by permission from the book *The Successful Meeting Master Guide* by Barbara C. Palmer and Kenneth R. Palmer, © 1983 by Prentice-Hall, Inc.
Figure 7-1	Reprinted from *The Mathematical Theory of Communication* by C. Shannon and W. Weaver, © 1948. Reprinted by permission of the University of Illinois Press.
Figure 7-2	Reprinted from *Organizational Behavior and Performance* by A. D. Szilagyi, Jr. and M. J. Wallace, Jr., Copyright © 1983 by Scott, Foresman and Company. Reprinted by permission.
Quote, Page 170	From R. M. Farance, P. R. Monge, and H. M. Russell, *Communicating and Organizing.* Copyright © 1977 by Random House, Inc. Used with permission

Table 7-1	From J. R. Gibb, "Defensive Communication," *Journal of Communication,* vol. 11, no. 3, 1961, published by the International Communication Association. Used with permission.
Table 7-2	From Gerard Nierenberg, *Fundamentals of Negotiating,* Hawthorn Books, 1973, pp. 125-26. Used with permission of the author.
Quotes, Pages 243-55	Taken from *Murphy's Laws,* by Bloch, 1982.
Quote, Page 249	From J. Kotter, *Power in Management.* Published by AMACOM, a division of American Management Associations, 1979.
Table 10-1	Adapted from Raven and Kruglanski, 1970; Kotter, 1979; and Cuming, 1981.
Table 11-1	From J. Z. Rubin and B. R. Brown, *The Social Psychology of Bargaining and Negotiation.* Published by Academic Press, 1975. Used with permission.
Table 12-2	From R. Fisher, *International Conflict for Beginners.* Copyright © 1969 by Roger Fisher, Reprinted by permission of Harper & Row, Publishers, Inc.
Quote, Page 323	Reprinted by permission of the *Harvard Business Review.* Excerpt from "Is Business Bluffing Ethical?" by Albert Z. Carr (January-February 1968). Copyright © 1968 by the President and Fellows of Harvard College, all rights reserved.
Quote, Page 323-24	Reprinted from H. H. Kelley, "A Classroom Study of the Dilemmas of Interpersonal Negotiations" in K. Archibald, *Strategic Interaction and Conflict.* University of California Press, 1966. Used with permission.
Figure 13-1, 13-2	Reprinted from R. Lewicki, "Lying and Deception: A Behavioral Model," in Bazerman, M. and Lewicki, R., *Negotiating in Organizations.* Published by Sage Publications, 1983. Used with permission.
Figure 13-3	From D. Forsyth, "A Taxonomy by Ethical Ideologies," *Journal of Personality and Social Psychology* 39, 1980. Copyright © 1980 by the American Psychological Association. Reprinted by permission of the author.